Marx and *Le Capital*

Over the past few years, Marx's *Capital* has received renewed academic and popular attention. This volume is dedicated to the history of the making, the theoretical evaluation and the analysis of the dissemination and reception of an almost unknown version of *Capital*: the French translation, published between 1872 and 1875, to which Marx participated directly.

In revising this version, Marx decided to introduce some additions and modifications, not hesitating to describe in the postscript *Le Capital* as 'a scientific value independent of the original'. To mark the 150th anniversary of the French translation of *Capital* (1872–2022), 15 authors have helped to shed light on its history and main features, as well as analysing its later fortunes in France and in the rest of the world. They also provide a more exhaustive account of the ideas of the 'late' Marx. The book also includes a previously unpublished selection of 31 letters from correspondence of Karl Marx, Maurice Lachâtre, Just Vernouillet and Friedrich Engels related to the making of *Le Capital*. Ten of these letters by Marx were only recently rediscovered and are translated here for the first time in English.

This book is an indispensable source for academic communities who are increasingly interested in rediscovering Marx beyond 20th-century Marxism. Moreover, it will be of appeal to graduate students, as well as established scholars, interested in French socialism and the history of the labour movement.

Marcello Musto is Professor of Sociology at York University, Canada.

Routledge Frontiers of Political Economy

Marx and *Le Capital*

Evaluation, History, Reception

Edited by Marcello Musto

 Routledge
Taylor & Francis Group

LONDON AND NEW YORK

First published 2022
by Routledge
4 Park Square, Milton Park, Abingdon, Oxon OX14 4RN

and by Routledge
605 Third Avenue, New York, NY 10158

Routledge is an imprint of the Taylor & Francis Group, an informa business

© 2022 selection and editorial matter, Marcello Musto; individual chapters, the contributors

British Library Cataloguing-in-Publication Data
A catalogue record for this book is available from the British Library

ISBN: 978-1-032-37307-2 (hbk)
ISBN: 978-1-032-37310-2 (pbk)
ISBN: 978-1-003-33636-5 (ebk)

DOI: 10.4324/9781003336365

Typeset in Bembo
by Newgen Publishing UK

Contents

About the Editor

Marcello Musto is Professor of Sociology at York University (Toronto – Canada). He is the author of: *Ripensare Marx e i marxismi. Studi e saggi* (Carocci, 2011); *Another Marx: Early Manuscripts to the International* (Bloomsbury, 2018); *Karl Marx. Biografia intellettuale e politica 1857–1883* (Einaudi, 2018); and *The Last Years of Karl Marx: An Intellectual Biography* (Stanford University Press, 2020). Among his edited volumes there are: *Karl Marx's Grundrisse: Foundations of the Critique of Political Economy 150 Years Later* (Routledge, 2008); *Marx for Today* (Routledge, 2012); *Workers Unite! The International 150 Years Later* (Bloomsbury, 2014); *The International After 150 Years: Labour Versus Capital, Then and Now* (with George Comninel and Victor Wallis, Routledge, 2015); *Marx's Capital after 150 Years: Critique and Alternative to Capitalism* (Routledge, 2019); *Karl Marx's Life, Ideas, Influences: A Critical Examination on the Bicentenary* (with Shaibal Gupta and Babak Amini, Palgrave Macmillan, 2019); *The Marx Revival: Key Concepts and New Interpretations* (Cambridge University Press, 2020); *Karl Marx's Writings on Alienation* (Palgrave Macmillan, 2021); *Rethinking Alternatives with Marx: Economy, Ecology and Migration* (Palgrave Macmillan, 2021); and *The Routledge Handbook of Marx's 'Capital': A Global History of Translation, Dissemination and Reception* (with Babak Amini, Routledge, forthcoming, 2023). His articles appeared in many journals, including the *International Review of Social History*, *Contemporary Sociology*, *Science & Society*, *Critical Sociology*, and *Labor History*. His writings – available at www.marcellomusto.org – have been published worldwide in more than 25 languages. He is also the co-editor of the book series *Marx, Engels, Marxisms* (Palgrave Macmillan, with Terrell Carver); and *Critique and Alternatives to Capitalism* (Routledge).

Contributors

About the Editor

Babak Amini is a visiting research fellow in sociology at the London School of Economics, UK. He is the author of *The Making of Council Democracy* (Routledge, forthcoming, 2023). He is the editor of *The Radical Left in Europe in the Age of Austerity* (Routledge, 2016), *Karl Marx's Life, Ideas, and Influences: A Critical Examination on the Bicentenary* (with Shaibal Gupta and Marcello Musto, Palgrave, 2019) and *Routledge Handbook of Marx's Capital: A Global History of Translation, Dissemination and Reception* (with Marcello Musto, Routledge, forthcoming 2023).

Kevin B. Anderson is Distinguished Professor of Sociology at the University of California, Santa Barbara, with courtesy appointments in feminist studies, global studies and political science. Among his authored books there is *Marx at the Margins: On Nationalism, Ethnicity, and Non-Western Societies* (University of Chicago Press, 2010). He is the editor of *Rosa Luxemburg Reader* (with Peter Hudis, Monthly Review, 2004), the *Dunayevskaya-Marcuse-Fromm Correspondence* (with Russell Rockwell, Lexington, 2012) and *Raya Dunayevskaya's Intersectional Marxism* (with Kieran Durkin and Heather Brown, Palgrave, 2021).

Alix Bouffard is a researcher at the Department of Philosophy of Strasbourg University, France. She is the co-author of *Ce qu'est le Capital de Marx?* [What is Marx's *Capital*?] (with Alexandre Feron and Guillaume Fondu, Editions sociales, 2017). She is currently translating a new version of Volumes II and III of *Capital* into French (with Alexandre Feron and Guillaume Fondu, Éditions sociales, forthcoming, 2023 and 2024).

Patrick Camiller is a translator and a former member of the editorial board of the *New Left Review*.

Terrell Carver is Professor of Political Theory at the University of Bristol, UK. His latest authored books include *Marx* (Polity, 2018), *Engels Before Marx* (Palgrave, 2020) and *The Life and Thought of Friedrich Engels* (Palgrave, 2020; 30th-anniversary edition). He is also the editor (with Smail Rapic) of *Friedrich Engels for the 21st Century: Reflections and Revaluations* (Palgrave, 2022).

Jean-Numa Ducange is Professor of Contemporary History at the Rouen-Normandie University, France, and a member of Institut Universitaire de France. He is the author of *Jules Guesde: The Birth of Socialism and Marxism in France* (Palgrave, 2020). Among his latest edited books there are: *The End of the Democratic State: Nicos Poulantzas, A Marxism for the 21st Century* (with Razmig Keucheyan, Palgrave, 2018) and *Selected Writings of Jean Jaurès: On Socialism, Pacifism and Marxism* (with Elisa Marcobelli, Palgrave, 2021).

Alexandre Feron is an FNRS postdoctoral researcher at the Université de Liège, Belgium. He is the author of *Le Moment marxiste de la phénoménologie française: Sartre, Merleau-Ponty, Tran Duc Thao* [*The Marxist Moment in French Phenomenology: Sartre, Merleau-Ponty, Tran Duc Thao*] (Springer, 2021).

Guillaume Fondu is a postdoctoral researcher at EHESS, France. He is currently collaborating on the French translation of *Capital*, Volume II (with Alix Bouffard and Alexandre Feron).

Kenneth Hemmerechts is a postdoctoral researcher at the Department of Political Sciences of the Vrije Universiteit Brussel, Belgium.

Michael R. Krätke is Emeritus Professor of Sociology at Lancaster University, UK. He is the author of *Kritik der Politischen Ökonomie heute. Zeitgenosse Marx* [*Critique of Political Economy Today: Contemporary Marx*] (VSA, 2017).

Marcello Musto is Professor of Sociology at York University, Canada. He is the author of *Another Marx: Early Manuscripts to the International* (Bloomsbury, 2018); and *The Last Years of Karl Marx: An Intellectual Biography* (Stanford University Press, 2020).

Jean Quétier is a postdoctoral researcher at the Faculty of Philosophy of the University of Strasbourg, France. He is the author of *Découvrir Marx* [Discovering Marx] (with Florian Gulli, Éditions sociales, 2016).

Paul Reitter is Professor of German at Ohio State University, USA. His authored books include *Permanent Crisis: The Humanities in a Disenchanted Age* (University of Chicago Press, 2021). He is working on a new English translation of *Capital*, Volume I (with Paul North, Princeton University Press, forthcoming, 2023).

David Norman Smith is Professor of Sociology at the University of Kansas, USA. He is the author of *Marx's Capital Illustrated* (Haymarket, 2014) and *George Orwell Illustrated* (Haymarket, 2018). Among his edited books there are *Authority, Culture, and Communication: The Sociology of Ernest Manheim* (with Frank Baron and Charles Reitz, Synchron, 2015) and *Marx's World: Global Society and Capital Accumulation in Marx's Late Manuscripts* (Yale University Press, forthcoming 2023).

Nohemi Jocabeth Echeverria Vicente is a postdoctoral researcher at the Department of Political Sciences of the Vrije Universiteit Brussel, Belgium.

Note on the Text

Marx's writings have been generally quoted from the 50-volume *Marx Engels Collected Works* (MECW), Moscow/London/New York: Progress Publishers/Lawrence and Wishart/International Publishers, 1975–2005, but sometimes the reader is referred to single works translated into English not included in MECW.

Texts that have not yet been translated into English are often referenced to the *Marx-Engels-Gesamtausgabe* (MEGA²), Berlin: Dietz/Akademie/De Gruyter, 1975–..., of which 68 of the originally planned 114 volumes have so far appeared in print.

As regards the secondary literature, quotations from books and articles not published in English have been translated for the present volume.

Preface

This book is the final part of a trilogy on the making of Marx's *Capital*. The first volume appeared in 2008, with the title *Karl Marx's Grundrisse: Foundations of the Critique of Political Economy 150 Years Later*, in a hardback edition that quickly sold out and was reprinted in 2009, with a paperback edition the next year. The first translations followed soon afterwards: a Farsi edition came out in 2010 at the Nika Publishing House in Tehran, Iran; and a Chinese one in 2011 at the prestigious China Renmin University Press of Beijing, with a print run of 5,000 and a reprint with the same number of copies in 2016. In 2013, Manohar in New Delhi, part of the Routledge – Taylor & Francis Group, brought out a much lower-priced English edition for the Indian and South-East Asian market, which would be reprinted in 2020. The turn of Italian came in 2015, with a print run of 1,000 copies published by Edizioni ETS and reprinted in a further thousand in 2021. Finally, in 2018 the Fondo de Cultura Económica brought out a Spanish translation that would be distributed in 4,000 copies throughout Hispanic America. In less than 15 years since the original edition appeared, and despite its character as a collective work, this book has been a significant international success, coming close in sales and number of translations to the best-known texts in the critical literature on the *Grundrisse*: Roman Rosdolsky's *Genesis and Structure of Marx's "Capital"* (1968) and Toni Negri's *Marx beyond Marx* (1979).

The second volume saw the light of day in 2019: *Marx's Capital after 150 Years: Critique and Alternative to Capitalism*. It was based on the proceedings of the largest international conference anywhere on this occasion – held at York University, Toronto, from 24 to 26 May 2017, to celebrate the 150th anniversary of the publication of *Capital*. This work too has been translated into other languages; the Italian version is currently being printed for Edizioni Alegre, and a Chinese edition is in preparation.

This third volume brings the project to completion and, like the first two, is being published in the Routledge Frontiers of Political Economy series. To mark another anniversary – 150 years since the completed printing of the French translation of *Capital* – 15 authors have helped to shed light on its history and main features, as well as analysing its later fortunes in France and the rest of the world. A final section contains an interesting selection of letters – between Karl

Marx, Maurice Lachâtre, Just Vernouillet and Friedrich Engels – on the making of *Le Capital*, including ten letters by Marx that were only recently rediscovered and published in French in 2019.

Last but not least, next year Routledge will publish a 400,000-word volume, titled *The Routledge Handbook of Marx's 'Capital': A Global History of Translation, Dissemination and Reception*, that I am editing with Babak Amini.

Marcello Musto
Toronto, June 2022

Acknowledgements

The editor and publisher would like to thank the Faculty of Liberal Arts & Professional Studies, York University, Toronto, Canada, for the financial support it provided to this work.

This research benefited from a Partnership Development Grant (Project No. 890-2020-0091) 'The Global History of Karl Marx's *Capital*' of the Social Sciences and Humanities Research Council of Canada (SSHRC).

1 Introduction

The Making and the Dissemination of *Le Capital*

Marcello Musto

Capital: An unfinished masterpiece

In February 1867, after several years of hard work, Marx was finally able to give Engels the long-awaited news that *Volume I* of his masterpiece was finished. Marx went to Hamburg to deliver the manuscript and, in agreement with his editor Otto Meissner, it was decided that *Capital* would appear in three volumes. The first of them – 'The Process of Production of Capital' – was put on sale on 14 September. A few months before that date, Marx had written to his friend Johann Philipp Becker that the publication of his book was, 'without question, the most terrible missile that has yet been hurled at the heads of the bourgeoisie (landowners included)' (Marx to Becker, 17 April 1867, Marx and Engels 1987: 358).

Following the final modifications, the table of contents was as follows:

Preface
1. Commodity and money
2. The transformation of money into capital
3. The production of absolute surplus value
4. The production of relative surplus value
5. Further research on the production of absolute and relative surplus value
6. The process of accumulation of capital
Appendix to Part 1, 1: The form of value.

(Marx 1983: 9–10)

Despite the long labour of composition before 1867, the structure of *Capital* would be considerably expanded over the coming years, and various further modifications would be made to the text. *Volume I* therefore continued to absorb significant energies on Marx's part even after its publication.

In October 1867, Marx returned to *Capital, Volume II*. But this brought a recurrence of his health issues: liver pains, insomnia and carbuncles (see Musto 2018). The new year began much as the old one had ended and at times he was even unable to attend to his correspondence. As soon as he could return to

DOI: 10.4324/9781003336365-1

work, he took a great interest in questions of history, agriculture and ecology, compiling notebooks of extracts from works by various authors. Particularly important for him were the *Introduction to the Constitutive History of the German Mark, Farm, Village, Town and Public Authority* (1854), by the political theorist and legal historian Georg Ludwig von Maurer, and three German works by Karl Fraas: *Climate and the Vegetable World throughout the Ages, A History of Both* (1847), *A History of Agriculture* (1852) and *The Nature of Agriculture* (1857).

While affording Marx a little energy for these new scientific studies, the state of his health continued its ups and downs. Anyway, he was able to put together a group of preparatory manuscripts on the relationship between surplus value and rate of profit, the law of the tendency of the rate of profit to decline and the metamorphoses of capital – which occupied him until the end of 1868 (see Musto 2019: 26–7).

The next year, however, the carbuncles flared up with exhausting regularity and his liver took another turn for the worse. Despite his plan to finish *Volume II* by September 1869, which had once seemed realistic, his continuing misfortunes over the following years prevented him from ever completing the second part of his magnum opus.

There were, of course, also theoretical reasons for the delay. From Autumn 1868 to Spring 1869, determined to get on top of the latest developments in capitalism, Marx compiled copious excerpts from texts on the finance and money markets that appeared in *The Money Market Review, The Economist* and similar publications.[1] His ever-growing interest in developments on the other side of the Atlantic drove him to seek out the most up-to-date information. He wrote to his friend Sigfrid Meyer that 'it would be of great value [...] if [he] could dig up some anti-bourgeois material about landownership and agrarian relations in the United States'. He explained that 'since [he would] be dealing with rent in [his] 2nd volume, material against H. Carey's "harmonies" would be especially welcome' (Marx to Meyer, 4 July 1868, Marx and Engels 1988: 61). Moreover, in Autumn 1869, having become aware of recent literature on socio-economic changes in Russia, he decided to learn Russian so that he could study it for himself. He pursued this new interest with his usual rigour.[2]

The search for the definitive version of *Volume I* and *Le Capital*

After many more interruptions and a period of intense political activity for the International Working Men's Association, following the birth of the Paris Commune, Marx turned to work on a new edition of *Capital, Volume I*. Dissatisfied with the way in which he had expounded the theory of value, he spent December 1871 and January 1872 rewriting the 1867 appendix (see Musto 2018: 167–8). This led him to address again the first chapter itself, resulting in the manuscript known as 'Additions and Changes to *Capital, Volume I*' (Marx 1983: 1–55). During the revision of the 1867 edition, Marx inserted a number of additions and clarifications and also refined the structure of the entire book.[3] Some of these changes concerned surplus value, the difference between constant capital and variable capital and the use of machinery and technology. He also expanded the new edition from six chapters to seven books containing 25 chapters, themselves subdivided into more detailed sections. The new edition came out in 1872, with a print run of 3,000 copies.

The year 1872 was a year of fundamental importance for the dissemination of *Capital*, since April saw the appearance of the Russian translation – the first in a long series (Musto and Amini, forthcoming 2023). Begun by German Lopatin and completed by the economist Nikolai Danielson, it was regarded by Marx as 'masterly' (Marx to Davidson, 28 May 1872, Marx and Engels 1989: 385).

In this year, too, the publication of the French edition of *Capital* got under way. Entrusted to Joseph Roy, who had previously translated some of Ludwig Feuerbach's texts, it was scheduled to appear in batches with the French publisher Maurice Lachâtre, between 1872 and 1875. Marx agreed that it would be good to bring out a 'cheap popular edition' (Marx to Lafargue, 18 December 1871, Marx and Engels 1989: 283). 'I applaud your idea of publishing the translation […] in periodic instalments', he wrote. 'In this form the work will be more accessible to the working class and for me that consideration outweighs any other'. Aware, however, that there was a 'reverse side' of the coin, he anticipated that the 'method of analysis' he had used would 'make for somewhat arduous reading in the early chapters' and that readers might 'be put off' when they were 'unable to press straight on in the first place'. He did not feel he could do anything about this 'disadvantage', 'other than alert and forewarn readers concerned with the truth. There is no royal road to learning and the only ones with any chance of reaching its sunlit peaks are those who do not fear exhaustion as they climb the steep upward paths' (Letter 4 in Part IV of this volume; also Marx to Lachâtre, 18 March 1872, Marx and Engels 1989: 344).

In the end, Marx had to spend much more time on the translation than he had planned for the proof correction. As he wrote to Danielson, Roy had 'often translated too literally' and forced him to 'rewrite whole passages in French, to make them more palatable to the French public' (Marx to Danielson, 28 May 1872, Marx and Engels 1989: 385). His daughter Jenny had told Ludwig Kugelmann that her father was 'obliged to make numberless corrections', rewriting 'not only whole sentences but entire pages' (Jenny Marx to Kugelmann, 3 May 1872, Marx and Engels 1989: 578) – and a month later she added that the translation was so 'imperfect' that he had been 'obliged to rewrite the greater part of the first chapter' (Jenny Marx to Kugelmann, 27 June 1872, Marx and Engels 1989: 582). Subsequently, Engels wrote in a similar vein to Kugelmann that the French translation had proved a 'real slog' for Marx and that he had 'more or less to rewrite the whole thing from the beginning' (Engels to Kugelmann, 1 July 1873, Marx and Engels 1989: 515).

In revising the translation, moreover, Marx decided to introduce some additions and modifications. These mostly concerned the section on the process of capital accumulation, but also some specific points such as the distinction between 'concentration' and 'centralization' of capital. In the postscript to

Le Capital, he did not hesitate to attach to it 'a scientific value independent of the original' and to state that the new version 'should be consulted even by readers familiar with German' (Marx 1996: 24). It was no accident that in 1877, when an English edition already seemed a possibility, Marx wrote to Sorge that a translator 'must without fail [...] compare the 2nd German edition with the French edition, in which [he had] included a good deal of new matter and greatly improved [his] presentation of much else' (Marx to Sorge, 27 September 1877, Marx and Engels 1991: 276). In a letter of November 1878, in which he weighed the positive and negative sides of the French edition, he wrote to Danielson that it contained 'many important changes and additions' but that he had 'also sometimes been obliged – principally in the first chapter – to simplify [*aplatir*] the matter' (Marx to Danielson, 15 November 1878, Marx and Engels 1991: 343). For this reason, he felt it necessary to clarify later in the month that the chapters 'Commodities and Money' and 'The Transformation of Money into Capital' should be 'translated exclusively from the German text' (Marx to Danielson, 28 November 1878, Marx and Engels 1991: 346).[4]

The drafts of *Capital, Volume II*, which were left in anything but a definitive state, present a number of theoretical problems. The manuscripts of *Capital, Volume III* have a highly fragmentary character, and Marx never managed to update them in a way that reflected the progress of his research.[5] It should also be borne in mind that he was unable to complete a revision of *Capital, Volume I* that included the changes and additions he intended to improve his book.[6] In fact, neither the French edition of 1872–75 nor the German edition of 1881 can be considered the definitive version that Marx would have liked it to be.

Marx through *Le Capital*

Following its original appearance in German in 1867, *Capital* was published in its entirety in only three more editions during Marx's lifetime.[7] All of them came out, at least in part, in 1872: the Russian translation in the month of March, the revised second German edition – in nine parts – between Spring of that year and January 1873 and the series of 44 instalments of the French translation, from September 1872 to May 1875.

The appearance of *Le Capital*, translated by Joseph Roy and revised by Marx himself, had considerable importance for the diffusion of his work around the world. It was used for the translation of many extracts into various languages – the first in English and Spanish, for example – as well as for compendia such as the one put together in 1879 by the Italian anarchist Carlo Cafiero (1879), which received Marx's approval and achieved a wide circulation. More generally, *Le Capital* represented the first gateway to Marx's work for readers in various countries. The first Italian translation – published in instalments between 1882 and 1884 and then as a book in 1886 – was made directly from the French edition. In the case of Spanish, *Le Capital* made it possible to bring out some partial editions and two complete translations: one in Madrid, in 1967, and one in Buenos Aires, in 1973. Since French was more widely known than German, it was thanks to this version that Marx's critique of political economy was able to reach many countries in Latin America more rapidly. Much the same was true for Portuguese-speaking countries. In Portugal itself, *Capital* circulated only through the small number of copies available in French, until an abridged version appeared in Portuguese shortly before the fall of the Salazar dictatorship. In general, political activists and researchers in both Portugal and Brazil found it easier to approach Marx's work via the French translation than in the original. The few copies that found their way into Portuguese-speaking African countries were also in that language.

Colonialism also partly shaped the mechanisms whereby *Capital* became available in the Arab world. While in Egypt and Iraq it was English that featured most in the spread of European culture, the French edition played a more prominent role elsewhere, especially in Algeria, which in the 1960s was a significant centre for the circulation of Marxist ideas in the Maghreb, as well as in the Levant, where two full Arabic translations of *Capital* appeared in Syria and Lebanon, in 1956 and 1970, respectively. Moreover, between 1966 and 1970, a serialised Farsi edition was produced in exile, in the German Democratic Republic.

The great significance of *Le Capital* stretched to Asia. The first Vietnamese translation of *Volume I*, published between 1959 and 1960, was based on the Roy edition. The highly rigorous studies of Marx in Japan in the second half of the twentieth century enabled a Japanese translation of *Le Capital* to appear there in 1979, preceded by two anastatic reprints of the French edition in 1967 and 1976. As to China, a Mandarin translation first came out in 1983 – in a series of publications to commemorate the hundredth anniversary of Marx's death.

Thus, as well as being often consulted by translators around the world and checked against the fourth German edition – published by Engels in 1890 – *Le Capital* has until now served as the basis for complete translations into languages, to which we should add numerous partial editions in various countries (Marcello Musto and Babak Amini, forthcoming 2023). One hundred and fifty years since its first publication, it continues to be a source of stimulating debate among people interested in Marx's work.

In a letter to Friedrich Adolph Sorge, the last general secretary of the International Working Men's Association, Marx himself remarked that with *Le Capital* he had 'consumed so much of [his] time that [he would] not again collaborate in any way on a translation' (Marx to Sorge, 27 September 1877, Marx and Engels 1991: 276). The toil and trouble that he put into producing the best possible French version were remarkable indeed. But we can certainly say they were well rewarded.

Notes

1 Still unpublished, these notes are included in the IISH notebooks, Marx-Engels Papers, B 108, B 109, B 113 and B 114.

2 In early 1870 Marx's wife told Engels that 'instead of looking after himself, [he had begun] to study Russian hammer and tongs, went out seldom, ate infrequently, and only showed a carbuncle under his arm when it was already very swollen and had hardened' (Jenny Marx to Engels, 17 January 1870, Marx and Engels 1988: 551). Engels hastened to write to his friend, trying to persuade him that 'in the interests of the Volume II' he needed 'a change of life-style'; otherwise, if there was 'constant repetition of such suspensions', he would never finish the book (Engels to Marx, 19 January 1870, Marx and Engels 1988: 408). The prediction was spot on.
3 In 1867 Marx had divided *Capital, Volume I*, into chapters. In 1872 these became sections, each with much more detailed subdivisions.
4 For a list of the additions and modifications in the French translation that were not included in the third and fourth German editions, see Marx (1983: 732–83).
5 The editorial work that Engels undertook after his friend's death to prepare the unfinished parts of Capital for publication was extremely complex. The various manuscripts, drafts and fragments of Volumes II and III, written between 1864 and 1881, correspond to approximately 2,350 pages of the MEGA². Engels successfully published *Volume II*, in 1885, and *Volume III*, in 1894. However, it must be borne in mind that these two volumes emerged from the reconstruction of incomplete texts, often consisting of heterogeneous material. They were written in more than one period in time and thus include different, and sometimes contradictory, versions of Marx's ideas.
6 See, for example, Marx to Danielson, 13 December 1881:

> In the first instance I must first be restored to health, and in the second I want to finish off the 2nd vol. [...] as soon as possible. [...] I will arrange with my editor that I shall make for the 3d edition only the fewest possible alterations and additions. [...] When these 1,000 copies forming the 3d edition are sold, then I may change the book in the way I should have done at present under different circumstances.
>
> (Marx and Engels 1993: 161)

7 See the section 'The Early Dissemination of *Capital* in Europe' in Musto (2020: 77–85).

References

Cafiero, Carlo (1879) *Il Capitale di Carlo Marx brevemente compendiato da Carlo Cafiero*, Milan: Bignami.

Marx, Karl (1983 [1867]) *Das Kapital. Kritik der Politischen Ökonomie. Erster Band, Hamburg 1867 Marx Engels Gesamtausgabe* (MEGA²), vol. II/5, Berlin: Dietz Verlag.

Marx, Karl (1996 [1875]) 'Afterword to the French Edition', in *Marx Engels Collected Works*, vol. 35: *Karl Marx, Capital, Volume I*, Moscow: Progress Publishers, p. 24.

Marx, Karl, IISH, Marx-Engels Papers, B 108, B 109, B 113 and B 114.

Marx, Karl and Engels, Friedrich (1987) *Marx Engels Collected Works*, vol. 42: *Letters, 1864–68*, Moscow: Progress Publishers.

Marx, Karl and Engels, Friedrich (1988) *Marx Engels Collected Works*, vol. 43: *Letters 1868–70*, Moscow: Progress Publishers.

Marx, Karl and Engels, Friedrich (1989) *Marx Engels Collected Works*, vol. 44: *Letters 1870–73*, Moscow: Progress Publishers.

Marx, Karl and Engels, Friedrich (1991) *Marx Engels Collected Works*, vol. 45: *Letters 1874–79,* Moscow: Progress Publishers.

Marx, Karl and Engels, Friedrich (1993) *Marx Engels Collected Works*, vol. 46: *Letters 1880–83,* Moscow: Progress Publishers.

Musto, Marcello (2018) *Another Marx: Early Manuscripts to the International*, London; New York: Bloomsbury.

Musto, Marcello (2019) 'Introduction: The Unfinished Critique of *Capital*', in Marcello Musto (Ed.), *Marx's Capital after 150 Years: Critique and Alternative to Capitalism*, London–New York: Routledge, pp. 1–35.

Musto, Marcello (2020) *The Last Years of Karl Marx: An Intellectual Biography*, Stanford: Stanford University Press.

Musto, Marcello and Amini, Babak Eds. (2023 forthcoming) *The Routledge Handbook of Marx's 'Capital': A Global History of Translation, Dissemination and Reception*, London; New York: Routledge.

Part I
The Value of *Le Capital*

2 Marx's *Capital* after the Paris Commune

The Falling Rate of Employment and the Fate of the Working Class

David Norman Smith

Introduction

We owe serious engagement with Marx's writings – *Capital* above all – to the heightened and ultimately tragic class conflicts of the period after World War 1. Until then Marx had been an effectively spectral figure among socialists, honoured but unread. Robert Wilbrandt, writing on the centenary of Marx's birth, offered a critical guide to the rapidly expanding but still superficial exegetic literature, reaching this conclusion: 'One desperately needs a commentary to facilitate the study of Marx [...] In German scholarship there is neither a Marx biography [nor] a Marx study that covers the whole of his work'. He saw Karl Kautsky's 'people's edition' of *Capital, Volume I*, the famous *Volksausgabe* (Marx 1914), as a step in the right direction, and he held out hope for Franz Mehring's impending 'major biography' – which, so far, had appeared only serially, as magazine articles – but he stressed the need for much more (Wilbrandt 1918: 4–5).

Mehring's biography, which appeared soon after, showed just how much more was needed. Mehring was a representative figure in German Social Democracy, which had long revered both Marx and Ferdinand Lassalle, despite their defining differences over unions, strikes, and democracy from below, which Marx supported and Lassalle opposed.[1] In 1877, as Wilbrandt observed, Mehring had lionised Lassalle and saw in Marx only abstraction personified, only 'the serpent's cold, sparkling eye' (Mehring 1877: 55). A quarter century later, when he edited the first volumes drawn from Marx's *Nachlass*, Mehring paired them with Lassalle's letters (1902, Vol. 4). In *Karl Marx*, while he no longer attacked Marx, he said only that it would be 'greatly exaggerated' to call Marx's final decade – when he twice revised *Capital, Volume I*, and wrote the 1877–78 manuscripts on global accumulation that form the heart of *Capital, Volume II* – a 'slow death' (Mehring 1918: 507).[2]

Wilbrandt's call for greater scholarly depth was soon answered, not least by his proteges Karl Korsch and Felix Weil. Wilbrandt, in 1918 and early 1919, was a member of the short-lived national *Sozialisierungskommission*, and Korsch was his assistant. Weil, who studied Marx with Wilbrandt in 1919, was radicalised

DOI: 10.4324/9781003336365-3

as a result (Abromeit 2011: 56). In his *Inaugural-Dissertation*, he called for 'the "union of Marxist training with free creative imagination"' (Wilbrandt)' in the spirit of Karl Korsch, who had written that the

> realisation of the idea of socialisation from a Marxist standpoint cannot be gained by pure thought or [by] gifted 'social engineers [*Gesellschaftstechniker*]' but requires rather the unification of theoretical-historical [and] practical-formative intellectual activity, whose unsurpassed role model remains Marx in almost all of his works.[3]

A year later, Weil and Korsch convened a gathering of critical Marxists, the *Erste Marxistische Arbeitswoche*, which featured presentations of ground-breaking new work by Korsch, György Lukacs, and Karl Wittfogel (Yagi 2011), all of whom would play leading roles in the escalating struggles of the ensuing decade – a decade of hyperinflation and depression, communist revolt and ultra-right death squads, and, ultimately, the menace of National Socialism. In this context, theory became much more than an ornament, or an insignia of ortho-doxy. Keenly alive to the urgency of the moment, Weil and Korsch returned from the *Marxistische Arbeitswoche* intent upon founding a new institute – one that would soon attempt the publication of 'almost all' of Karl Marx's works.

Marx's renaissance

Founded by Weil in Frankfurt with Korsch's help in 1923, the Institute for Social Research would soon forge a close working relationship with the Marx-Engels Institute in Moscow. Granted access to Marx's *Nachlass* by the German Social Democratic Party and directed, respectively, by the trailblazing Marxologists Carl Grünberg and David Ryazanov, the newborn institutes launched a massive project which is now nearly a century old – the publication of the *Marx-Engels Gesamtausgabe* (Hecker 2000).

Many seminal texts came to light for the first time in the 1920s and early 1930s, thanks to the efforts of the two institutes and their associates: the Paris manuscripts, the so-called *The German Ideology*, Marx's critique of the Gotha Program, the Zasulich letters, Marx's excerpt notes on Lewis Henry Morgan's *Ancient Society*, and much, much more. Essential works that we now date to the years of their composition (1844, 1846, 1881) were all, in reality, Weimar-era publications. But a critical edition of *Capital* was not among them. It was not, in fact, until Korsch's friend and protege Kurt Mandelbaum, a member of the Frankfurt Institute's inner circle of research associates, published Marx's letters to Nikolai Frantsevich Danielson in 1929 (Marx and Engels 1929) that it became clear that Marx regarded the French edition of *Das Kapital* – 'entirely revised by the author', as the title page explains – as in many ways the best of the editions he had prepared personally.[4]

Soon after, Valerie Kropp, who had been one of Mandelbaum's colleagues at Grünberg's institute and had since joined the staff of Ryazanov's institute, began a comparative study of the French and German editions of *Capital*.[5] The intent was to produce a communist *Volksausgabe*, which would appear on the 50th anniversary of the first edition and eclipse Kautsky's Social Democratic version. Kropp soon found that the French edition was strikingly different from the German editions and that Kautsky had made a start, but only a start, towards integrating the French and German editions. Reporting with Kurt Nixdorf on 5 February 1931, Kropp told Ryazanov that *Le Capital* – the last edition Marx himself prepared – differed in 'immensely numerous' ways from the second German edition of 1872. Hence, 'for the *Volksausgabe* [...] the basic question is how extensively the changes in the French edition should be used' (Kropp and Nixdorf 1997: 127).

Kropp and Nixdorf applauded many small improvements in the French text – the transfer of key points from the notes to the main text, the translation of nearly every foreign term, the replacement of parochial Anglicisms with intelligible local terms (e.g., *centimes* for shillings) – but what mattered most, of course, was the nature and content of Marx's changes. 'Not all parts of *Capital* are equally affected' they wrote. 'Most of the reformulations are found in the section on accumulation, which, we can safely say, Marx entirely reworked for the French translation'.[6] Hence *Le Capital* was to be taken very seriously as a potential source for the new communist edition.

What Ryazanov would have decided on this score is unknown since, a week later, he was summoned to meet Stalin to respond to the charge that he was serving a mythical conspiracy, 'the Menshevik Center'.[7] On 16 February, Ryazanov was arrested and sent into internal exile. Four days later, Vladimir Adoratsky was named to succeed him and soon Kropp, Nixdorf, and many others had been fired. Like Ryazanov, Kropp and Nixdorf had been under suspicion for some time. In 1929, amid the Stalinisation of the Comintern, Nixdorf had been 'disciplined' as a 'conciliator', that is, a partisan of anti-Nazi unity between communists and socialists. Kropp, too, was called a conciliator.[8] Nixdorf was shot in 1937, Ryazanov in 1938. Kropp's fate is unknown.[9]

Adoratsky, meanwhile, was quick to exclude Marx's 'immensely numerous' revisions from the new *Volksausgabe*, insisting that only the second Engels edition, the so-called fourth edition, could serve as the basis for a definitive edition and blasting the 'pretentious philistine' and 'renegade' Kautsky for attempting to bring *Le Capital* into the canon. Kautsky 'has dared to arrogantly change the text [...] as published by Engels', thus proving to be, yet again, 'a falsifier of Marxism, an enemy of the revolutionary proletariat' (Adoratsky 1933, cited by Tarcus 2017: 18).

Hidden in plain sight

What made *Le Capital* such an outlier among Marx's texts? Nearly every archival discovery was greeted with acclaim, and nearly every fact or rumour was warmly embraced, yet Marx's own final edition of his undisputed masterpiece was disputed, or ignored. Engels, we know, was unfriendly to *Le Capital* from the start and, unlike Danielson and Friedrich Sorge, had not been kept fully abreast of Marx's plans for new editions. But in 1894 even Paul Lafargue, Marx's son-in-law, who had co-translated the preface to *Capital* into French as far back as 1868,[10] published a curious volume (Pareto and Lafargue 1894) which featured a refutation of *Capital* by Vilfredo Pareto paired with a selection of French 'extracts' which Lafargue drew, in most instances, from Engels' fourth German edition. Even Kautsky, a decade after publishing his *Volksausgabe*, sponsored a volume of select French translations (Marx 1924) from the fourth German edition.[11] Korsch, when he published a new edition to honour the second German edition on the occasion of its 50th anniversary (Marx 1932), entirely ignored the French edition.

Finally, in 1983, on the centenary of Marx's death, a new *Le Capital* appeared, which a team of translators drew entirely from the fourth German edition. How that translation compares to Marx's original we may judge, for example, from a passage Marx had just added to the 1872 German edition, which he now rendered as follows:

> J'ai le premier mis en relief ce double caractère du travail représenté dans la marchandise. Comme l'économie politique pivote autour de ce point, il nous faut ici entrer dans de plus amples détails.
>
> (Marx 1875: 16; 1989: 25)

In other words, 'I was the first to highlight the double character of the labour represented in the commodity. Since political economy pivots around this point, we must now go into more detail'.

Compare the new version: 'J 'ai été le premier à mettre le doigt, de manière critique, sur cette nature bifide du travail contenu dans la marchandise. Comme c'est autour de ce point que tourne la compréhension de l'économie politique, il convient de l'éclairer un peu plus ici'.

> (Marx 1983: 47)

In other words: 'I was the first to put my finger, in a critical manner, on the bifurcated character of the labour contained in the commodity. Since it is around this point that the comprehension of political economy turns, it is worth clarifying a little more here'.

Neither of these translations misses the point. Marx's version is obviously superior – clearer, simpler, easier to interpret and unpretentious – but his latter-day ventriloquists convey much the same message. In fact, whatever we may think of the merits of the different editions, they are all, in most respects, monuments to scholarship and penetrating, humane critique. Engels, as we will see, missed many opportunities to produce the legacy volumes that Marx had hoped for (and, in part, had already written), but his editions nonetheless inspired and educated generations of readers. Many of his defenders, though, have been uncharitable towards Marx's *Le Capital*. Jacques d'Hondt, writing in 1985, went far beyond the charge of 'dangerously compromised' precision which Louis Althusser had lodged against *Le Capital* a decade and a half earlier. Bent on defending Marx's posthumous editor, d'Hondt says that the French edition – which he calls 'the Roy translation' – moves from mistakes and modifications to 'important falsifications', perhaps, he adds charitably, 'without fraudulent intent'. Any claim to higher insight derived from this text is hence baseless: 'The certificate of validity, too generously granted by Marx, is certainly not valid for such use of the Roy translation!'

(d'Hondt 1985: 133)[12]

Le Capital redivivus

Capital, clearly, has always been a hotly contested text, with critics across the ideological spectrum.[13] But the Engelsian orthodoxy of traditional Marxism has receded since the fall of the Soviet Union. Russia and China, like many of their former satellites in eastern Europe and Asia, have embraced the profit motive.[14] This has cleared the path for a new era of dissident, anti-authoritarian Marxism, which, though still in its infancy, now has many fresh scholarly resources to draw upon. Most relevant, here, is Thomas Kuczynski's remarkable new *Capital*, the *Neue Textausgabe* (Marx 2017), which, inspired by Kropp and Nixdorf, blends nearly every major variant from *Le Capital* into a composite text based on the second German edition.

Attached to the *Neue Textausgabe* is a giant appendix which, building on the MEGA[2], shows where *Le Capital* and the four German editions differ.[15] This permits a ready appreciation of the distinctiveness of *Le Capital*, which Marx intended, as he said in a preface dated on the first anniversary of the Paris Commune, for an audience of French workers. That intent led him to spend three years 'entirely revising' a text which then appeared in 44 low-cost instalments.

Kropp and Nixdorf, reporting the results of their 'sporadic' study of *Le Capital*, said that most of Part VII had been either 'completely' or 'largely' reworked – above all Chapters 22 and 24 – and that Chapters 1, 12, 14, 15, and 20 had also been significantly revised (Kropp and Nixdorf 1997: 127–8). Thanks to the *Neue Textausgabe* we can now specify this more exactly. What we learn is that Marx did, in fact, revise the text throughout and that in several places (most notably in connection with wages, machinery, and accumulation) he introduced an extraordinary number of changes, amounting, in some cases, to entirely new text.[16] And even in chapters that appear to have only a modest number of changes, those revisions are often quite significant. While very few changes appear, for example, in the chapter on 'the purchase and sale of labour power', one of those changes modifies an absolutely crucial point, namely, that labour power is unique in containing, 'from the standpoint of value, a moral and historical element'. All other commodities are valued exclusively in terms of the average socially necessary labour they embody, but the value of different units of labour power vary cross-culturally and over time, independent of the amount of labour they embody, given differences and changes in living standards. Few facts, if any, could matter more for workers, as Marx underlines in *Le Capital* when, at this juncture, he adds this critical point:

> What defines the capitalist epoch for the worker himself is that his labour-power takes the form of a commodity he owns and that his labour, thus, takes the form of wage labour. So too, it is only at this juncture that the commodity form of products becomes the dominant social form.
>
> (Marx 1875: 74)

In the second German edition this point had appeared earlier, near the end of a long, awkward passage: Until labour power is commodified the 'social production process is far from being dominated by exchange-value in its breadth and depth' (Marx 1872: 133). Engels returned this passage to its 1872 form and location, thus obscuring its cultural relevance – the implication that capitalism will not become a truly world-historical force until, in manifold diverse ways, labour power is *morally* and *historically* constituted as a commodity. And it is also worth noting that the passage in *Le Capital* made no mention of exchange value, which was consistent with Marx's practice at this point; not long before, in the second German edition, he had added this line to Chapter 1:

> When at the start of this chapter I said, in the usual manner: 'The commodity is use value and exchange value', that was, strictly speaking, wrong. The commodity is a use value or utility and a 'value'. It reveals its twofold reality when its value has its own appearance-form, *exchange value,* differing from its natural form – and it never has this form in isolation, but always only in the value or exchange relation to a second, different commodity.
>
> (Marx 1872: 36)

Marx's point here, which is essential to his entire theory, is that commodities are dualities of use-value and *value*, that is, abstract labour; but since value appears to us only in exchange, we misread it as 'exchange value' in many specific forms: seeing the value of 20 yards of linen in the form of an equivalent, a coat or coffee or cash. The issue here is what we *see*, which differs from the ulterior reality, namely, the reduction of concrete labour to abstract. And Marx is careful, in the second German edition, to reinforce this point by replacing *Tauschwerth* with *Werth* in many places – eight times in the labour power chapter alone.[17]

Marx's *Capital* and the first International

In what follows, I offer a reading of passages in *Le Capital* which introduce subtleties and nuances into Marx's account of capital accumulation, which is also, as he famously says, the accumulation of the proletariat, whether employed or unemployed. To set the stage for that reading, I will briefly situate *Le Capital* in the broader stream of Marx's systematic writings on capital and labour, which he undertook after publishing *Zur Kritik der politischen Ökonomie* (Marx 1859, 1970, 1987). That volume opened the critique of political economy with Marx's account of precapitalist value relations, which evolved from barter to monetised commerce. Soon after *Zur Kritik* appeared, in 1861–63, Marx wrote a first, unpublished version of *Capital, Volume I*, and in 1864–65, he wrote what we now call *Capital, Volume III*, and fragments of what we now call Volume II. Rosa Luxemburg exaggerated when she said, of the latter two texts, 'Here, the workers play no part' (Luxemburg 2015: 459). But even in the 1861–63 draft of Volume I, workers are present theoretically more than empirically. Only in the final chapter, on machinery, does the real-world proletariat arrive on the scene, and then only modestly (Marx 1988; see the chapter on machinery, pp. 318–46).

That would change dramatically in the fall of 1864 when Marx became a founding member of the General Council of the International Workingman's Association (IWA).

In 1865, when Marx replied in a General Council meeting to the claim, by the carpenter John Weston, that strikes and trade unions would harm workers (Marx 1898), he gave a preview of the argument in his 1864–65 manuscript that profit rates tend to decline even as total profits rise because capital, over time, is increasingly is driven by competition to substitute machinery for exploited labour, and profits derive from labour, not machinery. At this stage, the arrow of causality went from Marx's research to the General Council.[18] But soon, what Marx learned from his week-to-week involvement in the International loomed ever larger in his thinking.

The IWA, as Marx explained more than once, owed its original impetus to the stunning growth of commerce and industry in the aftermath of the crisis of 1857. That growth sparked conflicts of ever-growing scale, generating epic strikes (e.g., by building trade workers in London, by typographers in Paris) and spurring workers in countless trades to organise unions for the first time.[19] Many of these unions affiliated with the IWA, and Marx learned a great deal about their concerns.

Those concerns, which inspired many General Council debates and discussions, often pivoted around attempts by capitalists to undermine workers' wages by replacing them with machines or poorly paid, often foreign substitutes.[20] Machinery in particular had been a sore point since the late 1850s, when striking tailors and cobblers in England and Switzerland formed 'anti-machine' committees to repel the threat posed by sewing machines. As François Jarrige has shown, the resistance to mechanisation in this period was strongest in textile-producing regions, most dramatically in Roubaix, in the north of France, where a wild, riotous general strike broke out in 1867, with active support from the IWA. It was precisely in these regions that the IWA won many of its major affiliates (Jarrige 2018: 96; cf. Cordillot 2010).

It was at the IWA's Brussels Congress in September 1868, not long after the Roubaix insurrection, that machinery was most fully debated. Marx set the stage by offering a perspective on 'the influence of machinery in the hands of capitalists' which the General Council debated at three sessions in July and August, in anticipation of the Brussels meeting.[21] Much of what he said echoed *Capital*, which was then barely a year old, but that was only the starting point for a discussion which remained central to the IWA's concerns. Several General Council members shared insights based on personal experience with machine production, and Harriet Law closed the discussion with the comment that 'machinery had made women less dependent on men than they were before and would ultimately emancipate them from domestic slavery'.[22]

Much remained unresolved, but Marx's framing of the issue continues to reverberate.[23] 'Formerly', he said, at the 28 July 1868 meeting of the General Council,

> There were wealthy employers of labour, and poor labourers who worked with their own tools. They were to a certain extent free agents, who had it in their power effectually to resist their employers. For the modern factory operative, for the women and children, such freedom does not exist, they are slaves of capital.

This stems largely from the fact 'that machinery produces a constantly increasing surplus population [which] exercises a constant [...] wage lowering pressure upon the labour market'. And yet, at the same time, machinery produces 'associated organised labour', which harbours the potential for free association on a higher basis.

Thirty months later, class conflict fuelled by this and other contradictions exploded in revolutionary Paris, with consequences just as contradictory: tragic, yet heroic – a second, vastly larger edition of the Roubaix insurrection. That fall, Marx's publisher asked him to prepare a second German edition of *Capital*. In the brief time he devoted to this task, Marx focused primarily on revising the sections on commodities and money, which he felt he had dealt with cursorily, wrongly thinking that readers would consult the fuller account of those subjects in *Zur Kritik*. That left the field of revisions wide open with respect to capital *per se* and, soon after, Marx seized the opportunity presented by *Le Capital* to revise the core chapters on capital and its constituents, among them labour power and machinery.

Accumulation in production, *en route* to circulation

Marx's activities in the IWA and his work on *Capital* were not separate projects, hermetically sealed. They were, rather, two sides of the same coin, attempts to grasp the nettle of class and contradiction in the spirit of what Korsch, rather grandly, called 'the unification of theoretical-historical [and] practical-formative intellectual activity'. Marx worked on *Le Capital* in the twilight years of the IWA and beyond, incorporating a new citation into the French text as late as 12 June 1874 – a citation Engels omitted. In 1875, when the final fascicules of *Le Capital* were in press, Marx wrote his stinging critique of the Gotha

Program, which, despite its uncritical loyalty to Lassalle's 'iron law of wages', formed the basis for the new German Social Democratic Party.[24] Two years later, Marx wrote what I call the 1877–78 manuscripts – new materials that extend *Capital* 1 in ways we can most fully appreciate in the light of Marx's revisions, clarifications, and amplifications in *Le Capital*.[25]

In a word, the 1877–78 manuscript *extends* what *Capital, Volume I*, offers with respect to the theme most freshly and extensively developed in *Le Capital* – accumulation. This is clear not only substantively but formally, in the language of the closing paragraph of the introduction to the accumulation section. The standard translation of the fourth German edition renders the closing lines as follows:

> ... the simple, fundamental form of the process of accumulation is obscured both by the splitting-up of surplus-value and by the mediating movement of circulation. An exact analysis of the process, therefore, demands that we should, for a time, disregard all phenomena that conceal the workings of its inner mechanism.
>
> (Marx 1976: 710)[26]

The parallel passage in *Le Capital*, though more complex, is also clearer:

> The intermediating movement of circulation and the splitting of surplus value into diverse parts, assuming various forms, complicates and obscures the fundamental process of accumulation. So to simplify the analysis we must first set aside all those phenomena which conceal the intimate play of its mechanism *and study accumulation from the standpoint of production.*
>
> (Marx 1875: 246; Marx 1989: 488, italics mine)

The final phrase here – the reference to production – is crucial. The implication, which resonates throughout the ensuing discussion, is that Marx intends to analyse accumulation under three headings: production, circulation, and the contradictory unity of the two – in short, all three volumes of *Capital*.[27] When he spent 1874 and 1875 'completely reworking' the accumulation section of *Capital, Volume I*, Marx was laying the groundwork for what he did in 1877 and 1878 – bringing the analysis of accumulation into the realm of circulation. That was something he had done only fragmentarily in his earlier work. So, *Le Capital*, viewed in this light, figures as a stepping-stone on the path to Marx's fully realised theory of capital accumulation.[28]

After 1878, Marx widened his lens still further, to map the contours of societies not yet captured by capital. What opportunities and what obstacles do societies of that kind present to capital's global ambitions? Marx delved into myriad aspects of that question in his voluminous 'ethnological notebooks', which contain innumerable facts and themes relevant to accumulation.[29]

Marx, of course, did not live long enough to integrate his new findings into the unwritten volumes of *Capital*. But he knew well that the story of capital, globally, was far from complete. In contrast to bourgeois economists, who took capitalist relations for granted, he emphasised in *Le Capital* that even 'among the cultivators of continental Europe and North America, funds to maintain labour only exceptionally take the form of capital, that is, advances to immediate producers by capitalist entrepreneurs' (Marx 1875: 248).

The world market was growing exponentially, but world capital was still embryonic.

This critical implication is nearly invisible in the fourth German edition, which Fowkes renders as follows:

> The bourgeois economist, whose limited mentality is unable to separate the form of appearance from the thing which appears within that form, shuts his eyes to the fact that even at the present time the labour-fund only crops up exceptionally on the face of the globe in the form of capital.
>
> (Marx 1976: 714)

Why does the standard edition so rarely benefit from the clarity of the French edition? We know, as Kuczyinski has shown (2014), that Engels first became acquainted with Marx's instructions to Danielson and Sorge years after the third German edition had appeared, and that when he prepared the fourth edition, he ignored most of those instructions. Hence there are enormous differences between the editions. Kuczynski's appendix enables us to identify many of these differences: by my count, 122 passages appear in *Le Capital* which have no counterpart in the German editions; 422 passages differ so markedly from the German edition that Kuczynski felt obliged to combine them; and in many places in *Le Capital* Marx omitted lines that Engels restored in his editions (Kuczynski 2014, *passim*).

In the remaining sections of this paper, I will explore only a fraction of the passages in *Le Capital* which have no counterparts or adequate equivalents in the Engels editions, but that fraction is significant: passages from the accumulation section which illuminate what Marx, in the chapter on 'The General Law of Capitalist Accumulation', calls his primary concern, understanding the impact of accumulation on the fate of the working class.[30] I will refrain from back-and-forth comparisons between the passages I cite from *Le Capital* and the Engels editions but, suffice to say, my criterion for choosing these passages is that they differ from the German – often completely. (Passages that have no parallel in the standard editions appear ★★★ with three asterisks, below). My intent is to show what Marx contributes, uniquely and distinctively, in *Le Capital*. To that we now turn.

La vie accidentée

Marx co-translated and 'entirely revised' *Le Capital* with two sections primarily in mind: Part IV, 'The Production of Relative Surplus Value', and Part VII, 'The Process of Accumulation'. The thread connecting these sections is Marx's defining concern with machinery and the organic composition of capital – which rises when capital substitutes means of production for labour power and revolutionises production to subsume labour power fully and effectively, using machines of ever higher power and productivity.

Study of *Le Capital* brings two aspects of this problem into brighter light: the character of what Marx calls the general law of capitalist accumulation, which I will call *the falling rate of employment*, and the specific effects of the sphere of *production* on the rate of employment, which Marx frames as the main determinant of the fate, the plight, of the working class, as long as capital remains dominant.

These points are central to the interpretation of every edition of *Capital* and they will occupy our attention here for that reason. But they also lead us beyond traditional readings of Volume I, in two ways: on the one hand, they remind us of the class-historical context in which *Le Capital* was conceived – the experience of the IWA, the Commune, and early Social Democracy – and they form a bridge to Volumes II, III, and beyond.

The central thesis of the accumulation section, which is stated most clearly and fully in *Le Capital,* is intimately linked to the defining theme of the 1864–65 manuscript, that is, the falling tendency of the rate of profit. The profit rate tends to fall, Marx says, precisely because the employment rate tends to fall. The ulterior determinant of both tendencies is the rising organic composition of capital, the progressive substitution of constant for variable capital, which is driven by competition. So capital harbours within itself a dual tendency, both absolute accumulation and relative disaccumulation – and the latter, at a certain point, has the potential to overwhelm accumulation *in toto.*[31]

Increasingly, over the centuries, the rate and mass of employment thus tend to gallop away from each other – the mass rises, while the rate falls – just as the mass and rate of profit move in opposite directions. But there are also countertendencies which Marx carefully maps, always with an eye to their interactive effects on working people. Here, the workers play a central part, both passively and actively. Treated by capitalists as units of labour power, workers prove their agency whenever conditions are favourable, most notably, within the confines of capitalist production, when the demand for labour power exceeds the supply.

There are two other levels on which Marx's analysis is illumined by *Le Capital.* On the one hand, he now focuses directly on *le système capitaliste,* progressing beyond the revisions of the German edition to focus on the capitalist mode of production as a whole.[32] At the same time, Marx puts the plight of the working class front and centre – *'la vie accidentée',* the rough, hazardous lives workers lead on the uphill and downhill paths of the business cycle. To what extent, he asks, are workers captives of the labour market? To what extent do they win the capacity to limit or shake off that captivity?

Though framed more technically, Marx is now asking the very same question that he posed in the IWA concerning the influence of machinery on workers. He opens Chapter 25 with a sentence missing in German: ★★★'If the composition of capital remains the same, the progress of accumulation tends to raise the wage rate'. But what happens when the share of capital invested in labour power falls over time? That, Marx says, is his defining concern: 'We turn now to the influence of the growth of capital on the fate of the working class. The most relevant fact for the solution of this problem is the composition of capital and the changes it experiences as accumulation progresses' (Marx 1875: 269; Marx 1989: 534).

The premise for this question is the nature of the capital-labour relationship, which Marx defines in the spirit of the famous 'cash nexus' passage in the *Manifesto:*

> ★★★The official relationship between the capitalist and wage earner is purely mercantile. If the former plays the role of the master and the latter the role of the servitor, we owe this to a contract by which the latter not only serves but depends upon the former, waiving all title to his product. [[Why, Marx asks,] does the worker make this exchange? Because he owns nothing but his strength [...] while [the capitalist controls everything] he needs to actualise that power – the materials and tools needed for useful labour, [and access to the] subsistence needed to sustain labour power and convert it into productive activity'.
>
> (Marx 1875: 315; Marx 1989: 632)

Marx posits a historical dialectic, a spiral, with periodic swings from high employment to low, with matching swings in wage rates. In some periods – phases of 'relative labour surplus' – there are fewer jobs than job seekers, leaving them stranded in 'the industrial reserve army', unable to sell their labour power.[33] At other times – phases of 'relative labour scarcity' – there are more jobs than job seekers. When the demand for labour power exceeds the supply, wages generally rise; when the opposite is true, wages typically fall. Unfortunately for workers, the overall accumulation dynamic, which first concentrates labour power and means of production in the hands of competing capitalists and then centralises them under the control of the victorious competitors, relegates an ever-larger proportion of aspiring wage-earners to the industrial reserve army.

This is not simply 'economics'; it the very fabric of life for contemporary proletarians, whose precarity is inherent.

> The presence of this industrial reserve, its sometimes partial, sometimes general return to active duty, then its reconstitution on a larger scale – all this lies at the base of the rough, hazardous life *(la vie accidentée)* that permeates modern industry, with its quasi-regular decennial cycle of routine periods, high-pressure production, crisis and stagnation, [along with] other, irregular shocks.
>
> (Marx 1875: 279; Marx 1989: 555)

The general law of accumulation, then, amounts to the tendency of the *système capitaliste* to subjugate workers by keeping the demand for their labour below its supply. This is accomplished willy-nilly, in part intentionally, in part through the pressure of competition. The result is that wages

> ★★★ *rise only within limits that leave the basis of the capitalist system intact and ensure its reproduction on a growing scale. And how could it be otherwise, where workers exist only to increase, for others, the wealth they create?* Just as man is dominated in the religious world by the work of his brain, in the capitalist world it is the same with the work of his hand.
> (Marx 1875: 273; Marx 1989: 541–2)[34]

And yet, even so, Marx stresses that capital's hegemony is no solid crystal. Despite the inertia of the wage system, despite the spell cast by the value forms, workers retain the capacity to resist, even if that resistance is restricted, under ordinary circumstances, to demands for fair wages and hours.

Near the end of *Le Capital,* Marx stresses that thanks 'to the threatening attitude of the proletariat', the 'atrocious' British laws against combination had been modified as far back as 1825, though it was only recently – on 29 June 1871 – that 'the last vestiges of this class legislation' had been overcome with the legalisation of 'Trade Unions.' The phrase Marx used to clarify that English term had first appeared just three years earlier, in the French version of the International's updated Statuts Généraux: *'sociétés ouvrières de résistance'*.[35] The implication, plainly, is that resistance is inherent in the sheer fact of labour combination – in every campaign, however small.

Contradictions of the employment rate

Explaining how and why the pendulum of class power swung alternately in favour of the workers, then in favour of capital, was central to Marx's mission in Part VII. He approached this subject historically, stressing that the dialectic of capital and labour evolves through a series of stages. Initially, when money first became available to serve as variable capital, labour power was hard to pry loose from traditional lifestyles, since even expropriated farmers were reluctant to work for wages. The commodity form of labour power had not yet been established, and eudaemonist 'traditionalism' of the kind Max Weber and Werner Sombart analysed was still strong.[36] This, then, was a phase of relative labour scarcity, which enhanced the bargaining leverage of the active labour army. Since, in this phase, the relatively undeveloped state of constant capital made it difficult to replace workers with machines, capitalists sought to annex labour power by force, for example, via colonialism.

For the moment, domestically, the balance of power favoured the workers.

> The wage-earning class, which arose in the last half of the fourteenth century, formed then, as in the following century, only a very small portion of the population. The standing of the wage-earners was fortified, in the country by the independence of the yeomanry, in the city by the guild

system, and [in both places by the fact that] masters and workers were socially intimate. [At this stage,] the subordination of labour to capital was merely formal, and capital's variable element greatly outweighed its constant element. Hence, with each fresh accumulation of capital, the demand for wage labour grew rapidly while the labour supply grew slowly. Much of the national product, which would later enter into capitalist accumulation, then still entered the worker's consumption fund.

(Marx 1875: 327; Marx 1989: 655)

At times, calamities forced up wages: 'the Black Death, [...] this plague, which decimated Europe, [...] contributed in England to the enrichment and emancipation of the cultivators' (Marx 1875: 309; Marx 1989: 622).[37] The powers-that-be, however, eager to shift the costs of the calamity to the workers, relied upon naked force, not the market: 'during the genesis of capitalist production [...] the nascent bourgeoisie needed constant state intervention [...] to "regulate" wages, [...] to prolong the working day, to keep workers dependent to the desired degree'. Suppressing wages and extending the day enabled capital to grow at a time when yielding to the unfettered play of supply and demand would have benefited labour, not capital. This was already plain in the wake of the Black Death, which peaked in 1347. 'Legislation on wage labour, marked from the start by the exploitation of the worker and always subsequently directed against him, was inaugurated in England in 1349 by the Statute of Labourers of Edward III' (Marx 1875: 327; Marx 1989: 655–6).

But the pendulum continued to swing. Given the stimulus of

exceptionally favourable circumstances – the opening of new foreign markets, new spheres of internal investment, etc. – [...] the passion for gain [...] threw larger shares of the net product into the reproduction fund [and] provided employment for a greater number of wage-earners each succeeding year, so that, at a turning point, the needs of accumulation began to exceed the regular labour supply. Thereafter the wage rate followed an ascending arc. This was, in England, a subject of continual lamentations during most of the fifteenth century and the first half of the eighteenth.[38]

(Marx 1875: 270; Marx 1989: 535)

Capitalists had much to lament, since, without enough available labour power, they were unable to realise the profit opportunities which commerce and colonialism were offering them. In a now-famous passage, Marx said that, as before, the solution was 'primitive accumulation' by force:

'The discovery of the gold-rich and silver-rich regions of America, the conversion of their *indigènes* into slaves, exterminated or buried alive in mines; the conquest and pillage of the east Indies; the transformation of

Africa into a kind of commercial warren for the hunting of black skins';
all these, extending European sway globally, 'signaled the dawn of the capitalist era'.

(Marx 1875: 336; Marx 1989: 668–9)

Struggle for colonial domination led to all-out 'mercantile war with the
whole globe as its theater',[39] from early modern times to the Napoleonic
wars and

'the famous opium wars against China. The diverse methods of primitive
accumulation to which the capitalist era gave birth' – colonialism, credit,
etc. – were united 'in the last third of the 17th century into a systematic
whole [...]. Some of these methods relied on brute force, but all without
exception exploited the power of the state, the concentrated and organised
force of society'.

(Marx 1875: 336; Marx 1989: 669)[40]

The augmentation of state power, entwined with colonialism and trade, was
a powerful stimulant.

The colonial regime greatly boosted navigation and commerce. It spawned
mercantile societies and granted state monopolies [...] that served as
powerful levers for the concentration of capital. [...] Treasures from over-
seas, which were directly wrung from peoples reduced to slavery by forced
labour, extortion, pillage and murder, flowed back to the European mother
countries to serve as capital.

(Marx 1875: 337; Marx 1989: 670–1)[41]

In other words, lamentation led to legislation and violence. Ultimately, the
methods of colonial violence were applied locally as well, to farmers whose
land and labour power were coveted by capital. 'This is how the rural population, violently expropriated and reduced to vagrancy, was broken to the discipline the wage system requires – by laws of a grotesque terrorism, by whipping,
branding, torture and slavery' (Marx 1875: 326; Marx 1989: 655).

A moment of reversal came in the late eighteenth century when an interval....
of labour scarcity gave workers enhanced power. Listen, Marx says, to

the remonstrances of English manufacturers [...] on the eve of the mechanical revolution. [One], appreciating the effect that a reserve of [idled]
workers produces on those in active service, exclaims: 'Whenever from an
extraordinary demand for manufactures, labour grows scarce, the labourers
feel their own consequence, and will make their masters feel it likewise –
it is amazing; but so depraved are [...] these people, that in such cases [they]
have combined to distress the employer by idling a whole day together';
★★★ 'that is', Marx says drily, 'these 'depraved' people actually believed

that commodity prices are regulated by the 'sacred' law of supply and demand.[42]

(Marx 1875: 281; Marx 1989: 559)

But before long capital regained its advantage.

In England [today, a] worker would be punished for breach of contract if, for reasons of religious devotion, he was absent on Sunday from his factory, store, or glass works. The [authorities] show no unease about the profanation of the Sabbath ★★★when it takes place in the honor and interest of the God Capital.

(Marx 1875: 114; Marx 1989: 221)

Yet contradictions remained. Force was still needed to pry farmers from the land in the colonies and, also, to capture ex-slaves where anti-slavery struggles (by the slaves themselves, or abolitionists) had created *colonial* labour scarcity. Once again, capital and its prophets abandoned market fundamentalism, feeling an 'itch' to repress resistance by force:

> Even that fine man, the [...] eminent free trader M. de Molinari, does not hesitate to say: 'In the colonies, where the forced labour of slavery was abolished without being replaced by an equivalent quantity of free labour, we have seen [...] simple *(sic)* workers exploiting the industrial entrepreneurs, demanding wages out of all proportion to the *legitimate share* which is their due [...]. The sugar planters, unable to charge enough to cover the wage increase, had to [pay it] out of their profits, then out of their capital'.
>
> Monsieur Molinari, Monsieur Molinari! ★★★What then becomes of the Ten Commandments, of Moses and the Prophets, of the law of supply and demand, if the capitalist can reduce the worker's legitimate share in Europe but in the West Indies the worker reduces the capitalist's? ★★★And what, if you please, is this *legitimate share* which, by your own admission, the capitalist does not pay in Europe?
>
> ★★★ Come, Monsieur Molinari: in the colonies, where the workers are *simple* enough 'to exploit the capitalist', you feel a terrible itch to lend a bit of police assistance to the unhappy law of supply and demand which, you say, works so well elsewhere on its own.

(Marx 1875: 345–6; Marx 1989: 685)

Irresistible force, immovable object

If oscillations in the labour market often destabilise and disturb workers, what ultimately convinces them that the wage system – the alienation of their labour power, alternating employment and joblessness, wage hikes and cuts – is their destiny? To answer this question, Marx offers a metaphor drawn from nature.

As capitalism progresses, 'there arises an ever-larger class of workers which, by virtue of education, tradition and habit, submits as spontaneously to the demands of the regime as to the changing seasons'. In other words, workers learn to take the wage form for granted – the commodification of their personal strength seems as natural to them as nature itself, which swings from winter to summer, from autumn to spring.

> As soon as this mode of production reaches a certain level, its mechanical operation breaks down all resistance. The constant presence of a relative surplus population ensures that the laws of supply and demand for labour (and hence wage levels) remain within limits that meet the needs of capital, and the mute pressure *(sourde pression)* of economic relations completes the capitalist's despotism over the worker. Recourse is still made at times to coercion, to brutal force, but this is exceptional. In the ordinary run of things the worker can be left to the action of the 'natural laws' of society, that is to say, to dependence on capital.
> (Marx 1875: 326; Marx 1989: 655)

Critics occasionally note the tension between this powerful claim and the dramatic passage, just 16 pages later, where Marx posits the ever-growing *résistance* of the dispossessed, which will ultimately expropriate the expropriators. In other words, he appears to posit both an immovable object and an irresistible force. Can these claims be squared? If so, Marx's new metaphor – *le changement des saisons* – offers a valuable clue. Capitalism, as it universalises, comes to be regarded as a second nature; upswings and downswings, booms and busts are intrinsic to that nature, a fact which, however transient 'in the long run', is now omnipresent, a social fact of the kind that Durkheim would later say prompts fatalism. But this immutability is only apparent. When the mute pressure of the economy is disrupted, cracks disfigure the system's façade and fatalism can give way to anomie, or to a spirit of radical resolve.

In other words, labour docility is relative, too. Workers who now seek only fair wages and hours nevertheless combine to form *societes ouvrieres de résistance.* They may treat the booms and busts of the business cycle as if they were the alternating seasons, but they try to *survive* the changing seasons by uniting to defend their interests. And those interests may ultimately exceed the limits of what capital can even appear to promise.

Still, Marx's optimism is tempered. Contradictions at the level of consciousness may ultimately spiral out of control, but for the moment, after a half-millennium of slow but accelerating growth, capital reigns triumphant.

> 'Ultimately the law which balances the advance of accumulation and relative surplus population rivets the worker to capital more firmly than Vulcan's wedges riveted Prometheus to his rock'. The result, for 'the class which produces capital itself', is poverty and brutalisation – an outcome some of capital's apostles see as positive: 'the Reverend J. Townsend, light-hearted and even joyful, came to glorify this as the necessary condition of wealth: "Legal constraint" [to labour, Marx adds] "is attended

with too much trouble, violence, and noise, [...] whereas hunger is not only a peaceable, silent, unremitted pressure, but [...] calls forth the most powerful exertions". Keeping the workers hungry is thus the sole major article of his labour code, which can be left to the poor for implementation. "It seems to be a law of Nature that [...] there may always be some to fulfil the most servile, the most sordid, and the most ignoble offices in the community"'.

(Marx 1875: 285–6; Marx 1989: 568–9)[43]

Just sentences later, Marx cites Antoine Cherbuliez, who draws out the implication of this point: ★★★ 'The workers themselves [...], by cooperating in the accumulation of productive capital, thereby contribute to the eventuality in which, sooner or later, they will see their wages trimmed' (Marx 1875: 286; Marx 1989: 570).[44]

Still, however much they may have enabled their own immiseration, workers also resisted that immiseration when it arrived. Their new *sociétés ouvrières de résistance* soon angered bourgeois ideologues as much as their hunger had pleased them. English capitalists, feeling suddenly embattled, lauded Belgium for defending the 'freedom of capital' against labour's encroachments: 'There is neither the humiliating despotism of trade unions nor the oppressive oversight of factory inspectors' (Marx 1875: 296; Marx 1989: 592).

Trade union influence, which had soared after 1830, spurred innumerable attempts to emancipate capital from its dependence on workers by means of 'labour-saving' devices.

An entire history could be written about the inventions made since 1830 to defend capital against workers' disturbances. Mr. Nasmyth, the inventor of the steam hammer, enumerates the *perfectionnements* in machinery to which he was led by the long mechanics' strike of 1851: 'The characteristic feature of our modern mechanical improvements, is the introduction of self-acting tool machinery. What every mechanical workman has now to do [...] is not to work himself but to superintend the beautiful labour of the machine. The whole class of workmen [who] depend exclusively on their skill, is now done away with.'

(Marx 1875: 296; Marx 1989: 592)

Replacing labour in this way, Andrew Ure rejoiced, offered capital 'deliverance' from 'intolerable bondage'. He cited a machine 'which had been invented as the result of a strike: the horde of malcontents [soon found] their defenses rendered useless'. Of the self-acting mule, Ure says, triumphally:

This '*Iron Man*', as the operatives fitly call it, was a creation destined to restore order among the industrious classes [...] The news of this Herculean prodigy spread dismay through the *sociétés de résistance*; and [...] long before it left its cradle [...] it strangled the Hydra of sedition [...] This invention

confirms the great doctrine [...] that when capital enlists science in her service, the rebellious hand of labour will always be taught docility.[45]

(Marx 1875: 188; Marx 1989: 375)

Yes, the nectar with which political economy inebriates itself is this phil-
anthropic theorem: that after a period of transition and more or less rapid
growth, the factory regime bends more workers under its iron yoke than it
had originally starved by forced joblessness.

(Marx 1875: 193; Marx 1989: 385)

Harnessed to capital

Had Ure been writing 40 years later, he might have been less self-assured. Marx,
writing in 1875, saw a world which had changed considerably since Ure's time,
given the rise of trade unions and the example of the International and the
Commune. But the axial issue remained much the same: whether the falling
rate of employment would spur relatively more, or less, labour docility.

The forces at work were seemingly straightforward: unions organise workers,
reducing labour supply, while machines displace them, reducing labour demand.
But the broader context, as always, was shaped by the dynamics leading to relatively increased investment in constant capital relative to variable capital. Capitalists
often have pressing reasons to enhance machinery for immediate reasons of class
and conflict: the Iron Man grinds down mortal men. But recomposing capital by
transferring investment from the wage relation to the expansion and refinement
of machinery is not, ultimately, a choice. Capitalists who wish to survive the com-
petitive wars, to keep their armies on the march, have no other options: accumu-
late on an escalating scale, or go bankrupt. That, too, is Moses and the Prophets.

It was in connection with this premise that Marx cited an 1874 article that
had appeared in *Engineering*, a trade publication for industrial engineers. This was
the most recent citation to appear in *Le Capital,* and one of the most significant.
Even Adoratsky, in the communist *Volksausgabe*, felt constrained to include it,
though he omitted nearly everything else which Marx had newly woven into *Le
Capital*.[46] Engels, for reasons unknown, omitted this passage. Marx wrote:

> 'Above all, we need to clarify the conditions under which [capital accumulates],
> which so far we have considered only in the special phase when capital
> increases though its technical composition remains stationary. But at a cer-
> tain stage the advance of social labour's productive powers becomes the most
> dynamic lever of accumulation on the basis of *le système capitaliste*'.

> This precedes the passage omitted by Engels, which opens with a
> comment by Marx:

★★★'At the birth of large industry, a method of using coke to convert molten
iron into wrought iron was discovered in England. This process, which is
called *puddling* and consists in refining the molten iron in special furnaces, gave

rise to immensely enlarged blast furnaces [and] such an increase in the tools and materials employed by a constant quantity of labour that iron was soon delivered cheaply and abundantly enough to *drive stone and wood out of* a host of uses. Since iron and coal are the great levers of modern industry, the significance of this innovation cannot be overstated. But since the puddler, who refines the iron, is a manual worker, the size of the batches he can handle is limited by his personal faculties. It is this limit which now halts the marvelous progress the metallurgical industry has made since 1780, when puddling was invented'.

Marx now turns to the article: **★★★** 'The fact is', exclaims *Engineering,* one of the organs of English engineers, 'the fact is that the old process of hand-puddling is little better than a barbarism [....] The whole tendency of our iron industry is towards dealing, in every stage of the manufacture, with larger and larger quantities of materials. Thus, almost every year witnesses the introduction of larger blast furnaces, heavier steam hammers, more powerful rolling mill machinery, and larger and more powerful tools for dealing with the manufactured material in the workshop. Amidst all this growth' – increase in the means of production in relation to the labour employed – 'one stage only – that of puddling – has remained practically stationary', and today places intolerable obstacles to industrial movement. Hence all large factories are now *en route* to the substitution of furnaces capable of handling, by *révolutions automatiques,* colossal batches entirely beyond the reach of manual work'.[47]

The anonymous author adds (1874: 432), in a passage Marx did not cite: 'we believe that the majority of our leading ironmasters are so fully alive to the desirability of a change, that when once [...] mechanical puddling has been proved to be commercially successful, class prejudices' (that is to say, worker resistance) 'will not be permitted to interfere with its rapid and extensive adoption'.

Marx goes on: **★★★** 'Thus, after puddling revolutionised the iron industry and immensely extended the tools and mass of materials required per quantum of labour, it has become, in the course of accumulation, an economic obstacle which is now being replaced [...]. This is the history of all the discoveries and inventions driven by accumulation, as we have shown by tracing the march of modern production from its origin to our time. [...] Hence, in the progress of accumulation, there is not only a quantitative and simultaneous increase in the diverse real elements of capital: the progress of the productive powers of social labour which this progress engenders is also shown by qualitative changes [...] in the technical composition of capital, in which the scale of the objective factor gradually gains in proportion to the subjective factor. That is to say, the mass of tools and materials increases more and more relative to the sum of the workforce needed to use them. Thus, to the degree that capital growth raises labour productivity, it reduces the demand for [labour] in proportion to its own magnitude'.

(Marx 1875: 273–4; Marx 1989: 542–4)

Ambivalence, or the dialectic of consciousness

The bourgeois of Marx's day had good reason to be wary of factory inspectors, who reported countless awkward facts which were 'passed over in silence by official political economy'. Marx underlined, in particular, the contributions of the Children's Employment Commission, which brought a fateful contradiction in class consciousness to the surface. On the one hand, it was a 'great fact' that adult male workers had forced the employers to shorten labour times for women and children.[48] That was positive. But on the other side of the coin, Marx called attention to recent factory reports which revealed 'truly revolting slave-trader [*esclavagiste*] practices on the part of certain parents in the sordid traffic of their children' (Marx 1875: 171; Marx 1989: 339).

Marx went on, in another passage overlooked by Engels:

> ★★★In the *Bulletin de la Société industrielle de Mulhausen* (31 mai 1837), Dr. Penot says: 'Poverty sometimes stirs in the fathers of families an odious spirit of speculation on their children, and heads of establishments are often solicited to receive [young] children in their workshops' (Penot 1837, T. 10: 482 n. 1). This aggravated a situation which was already dire: ★★★ 'In French working-class towns the mortality rate for workers' children under one year of age is 20-22% *(Roubaix figure)*. In *Mulhouse* it reached 33% in 1863. It always exceeds 30% [...]. In a work presented to the Académie de Médecine, M. [Charles] Devilliers showed [...] that childhood mortality in wealthy families is 10%, while that for the children of wage-earning weavers is at least 35%[49]
>
> (Marx 1875: 171; Marx 1989: 340–1)

All this unfolded, Marx stressed, under the shadow of mechanisation, which destabilised workers' life chances. The response, in Émile Durkheim's terms, could be anomie or fatalism, solidarity or egoism.[50] In Roubaix, one year after Devilliers reported his findings, chaotic resistance broke out. But servility and its evil twin, the *esclavagiste* spirit, were also very much alive.

The part of *Capital* which Marx revised most extensively for the French edition was, unsurprisingly, the section on the industrial reserve army of labour. Nothing bore down on the working class more heavily. Marx explained:

> ★★★The absolute demand for labour from a given capital corresponds not to its absolute size but to its variable element, which alone is exchanged for labour power. The relative demand for labour, i.e., the ratio between the size of a given capital and the amount of labour it absorbs, depends on the relative dimensions of its variable fraction.
>
> Now, what is the effect of this movement on the fate of the working class?
>
> Clearly, to answer this question, we must first see how [...] a decrease in the relative demand for labour affects the absolute or effective labour demand. As long as a given capital does not change in magnitude, any

proportional decrease in its variable share is at the same time an absolute decrease.

It could only be otherwise if an increase in the sum total of the advanced capital-value [*valeur-capital*] balanced the relative decrease. The variable part [...] which serves as a wage fund thus decreases [in] inverse proportion to the simultaneous increase in the entire capital.

(Marx 1875: 277; Marx 1989: 550)

In other words, wages can rise absolutely while falling proportionately, but under all circumstances, as the value composition of capital rises, the 'wage fund' falls proportionally, relative to overall capital. The consequence is an ever-growing army of candidate workers whose labour power is held in abeyance unless or until capital needs more heads and hands. And if the total investment does not increase at a rate faster than the falling rate of employment, the wage fund will fall absolutely as well as relatively. There are, Marx says, sequential ★★★'phases in which the masses of social capital in the different spheres of production pass successively, one after the other, often in different directions; from the standpoint of social accumulation, the forms [these phases] take are determined' by the ways in which these possibilities are realised or blocked (Marx 1875: 277; Marx 1989: 550).

In some factories

an increasing sum of materials and tools has been deployed by a constant number of workers. There, increases spring only from the extension of the constant share of capital, causing the *proportional* size of its variable share – the relative mass of exploited labour power – to decline by the same amount, but without changing its absolute magnitude.

(Marx 1875: 277; Marx 1989: 550)

In equally capitalised and productive industries, employment can rise in some cases and fall in others. The difference is a function of the degree to which increased productivity in one industry stimulates job-creating growth in another:

... some great branches of industry [...] have had absolute decreases in employment while [...] others have had increases, though all are equally marked by increasing capital and productivity. In England from 1851 to 1861 the personnel [in] the manufacture of long wool [fell] from 102,714 to 79,249, and in silk factories from 111,940 to 101,678. Yet in the same period the personnel in cotton spinning and weaving rose from 371,777 to 456,646, and in iron manufacture from 68,053 to 125,711.

(Marx 1875: 277; Marx 1989: 551)

★★★Finally, the other face of social accumulation – progress in a single industry which leads alternately to an increase, a decrease or a stationary state in the number of workers employed – is strikingly illustrated by the history of the adventures *(péripéties)* of the cotton industry. Over a period of several years, say, 10, we generally find that the number of exploited workers increases as social accumulation advances [...]. Hence it must be the case that the standstill or fall in absolute size of the employed labour force in some industries where capital investment significantly rises must be *exceeded* by employment increases in industries where opposite movements have been definitely defeated. This result, however, is obtained only amid tremors and under increasingly difficult conditions.

(Marx 1875: 277; Marx 1989: 551)

Self-emancipation?

The situation, in other words, is complex and calls for analysis of equal complexity, marked by sensitivity to contingency as well as necessity, to counter-tendencies as well as tendencies. 'Immiseration', plainly, is one tendency; but so too is the reverse, fuelled, above all, by the determination of *sociétés ouvrières de résistance*. The rising composition of capital is only fate if we resign ourselves to it, accepting tremors and crises of every kind, as if the sale, idling, and destruction of labour power were predestined, like the changing of the seasons.

In ordinary times, Marx ([1865] 1898: 126) wrote, though workers fight for fair pay and working conditions, they tend to take the wage system for granted. But times are often far from ordinary, and self-emancipation – the abolition of the wage system, the free association of producers – remains possible, however utopian it may seem when the juggernaut of accumulation grinds 'relative surplus labour' under its wheels. That, increasingly, is the global reality we face, as world capital extends its reach to every corner of the globe. Farmers, nearly everywhere, have lost their land, and workers everywhere are exposed to the hazards of periodic or permanent wagelessness. The working class, now as ever, is as much a precariat, suspended over the abyss of the industrial reserve army, as it is a 'proletariat' in the stereotyped, 20th-century sense. And Marx's *Capital* – not least, the 'completely reworked' account in *Le Capital* of the hazards of working-class life amid advancing accumulation – could hardly be more relevant, given precisely that over-determined reality.

When Marx translated his Inaugural Address ([1864] 1962) into German, he titled it *Manifest an die arbeitende Klasse Europa's*.[51] The 'workers of the world', at that stage, were still concentrated in just a few places. But today the working class and the industrial reserve army are global. The 'General Law of Capitalist Accumulation' is now more general than ever. So too is the need to understand that law, and its consequences.

Notes

1 On the Lassalle cult in German Social Democracy, see Bonnell (2020).
2 Mehring (1918: 507). For the first use of the phrase *'ein langsames Sterben',* see Spargo (1912: 295) and cf. Spargo (1910: 304), where he attributes the phrase 'a protracted dying' to Engels.

3 This is Weil (1921: 99–100) citing Korsch (1920) and praising the 'young Marxists', i.e., Max Adler and others who are now known collectively as 'Austro-Marxists'.

4 On 15 November 1878, Marx wrote:

> Regarding the second [Russian] edition of *Capital,* please [ensure] that the translator always carefully compares the second German edition with the French, since the latter contains many important changes and additions (although I have sometimes been forced – especially in the first chapter – to compress [*aplatir,* that is, condense, smooth] the French version...).
>
> (Marx and Engels 1929: 15)

5 Kropp was an early Frankfurt Institute associate. On 12 December 1924, she wrote to a communist functionary:

> We have here all the labour movement materials. There is a special archive for KPD party materials. As Hilde Weiß tells me, you have [...] circulars, etc. [...] You can inquire in this connection with comrades Ernst Meyer and Korsch.
>
> (Kropp 1924)

For details about Korsch, Weiß, Mandelbaum *et al.,* see Smith (2021b, 2020).

6 They note, too, that

> every other chapter is blanketed with smaller changes...There are also countless changes that knit together larger sections. Entire sentences or paragraphs have been left out, while others have been added. There can be no doubt that all these changes are the work of Marx. This is evident from the numerous remarks made by Marx to Engels, Sorge, Kaufman and Nikolai-on [Danielson] about the French edition. He keeps repeating that he completely reworked the French text.
>
> (Kropp and Nixdorf 1997: 127)

7 For colourful details about Ryazanov's brusque response, see Serge (2012: 292).
8 This was the fateful moment at which Stalin called Social Democrats 'social fascists', that is, mortal enemies.
9 For further details, see the biographical sketches in Vollgraf *et al.* (2001: 398f.).
10 Lafargue's co-translator in 1868 was Marx's daughter, Laura Lafargue.
11 This peculiar volume, though billed as Volume I, ends with the chapter on the purchase of labour power. The translator Jacques Molitor later translated many other Marx volumes as well.
12 Elsewhere d'Hondt 'denounces' *Le Capital* for its 'perverse effects' and 'puerile' epistemological biases (1985: 131, 136).
13 Hereafter, when I cite *Capital* without a volume number, I am always citing Volume I. And for the sake of consistency, though different editions of *Le Capital* differ in their spellings *(Le capital, Le Capital),* I will always cite this text as *Le Capital.*
14 On this point, see Smith (2016).
15 Kuczynski (2017). This is a PDF on an appended USB drive, which provides the most complete account yet available on the parallels and contrasts between *Le Capital* and the German editions.
16 Besides what Kropp and Nixdorf report, I find notable changes in discussion of the relationship of surplus value to labour power valuation in Chapters 11, 17, and 19

and comprehensive changes in Chapters 23 and 25 – especially the latter, which focuses intently on the plight of the working class when the rate of employment falls, as we will see below.

17 For further details, see Smith (2017: 669). I note there, e.g., that Marx's newly added line about the misleading implications of the term 'exchange value' in the second German edition – which he repeats in *Le Capital* – has been cited by just a few commentators in any language.

18 This is very clear, as well, in the inaugural address to the International (Marx 1962).

19 The London Trades Council was a direct outgrowth of the 1859 construction strike. Several of the Council's leading figures became active IWA members.

20 Ryazanov (1926) was among the first to bring scholarly expertise to the study of the IWA. See also Franz Neumann's review (1936) of *Marx and the Trade Unions* (1935) by the veteran leader of the Red International of Labour Unions, Alexander Lozovsky, who called attention to the fact that the Marx-Engels Institute had discovered and planned to publish the General Council minutes.

21 On 28 July, 4 August, and 11 August 1868. Our source for these discussions, the *Minutes of the General Council of the First International*, are readily available online and will not be cited here by page and volume numbers. Digests of those minutes were also widely circulated, at the time, in several languages in the workers' press.

22 Law is remarkably little remembered. She was, at the time, one of the leading feminists and secularists in Britain, a peripatetic debater and public figure who ultimately wrote (Law 1898) one of the first and most laudatory biographical sketches of Marx. For a few initial details, see Schwartz (2013: 49–52, 101 ff.).

23 For a superb overview of the issues here, and a sampler of the main texts that sprang from this discussion, see Musto (2014).

24 See Peter Hudis, 'The Alternative to Capitalism in Marx's Critique of the Gotha Program', in Marx (2022: 4–29).

25 For other recent discussions of *Capital* after 1867, see Roth (2018) and Vollgraf (2018).

26 In what follows, below, the Fowkes translation appears simply as 'Fowkes'.

27 Marx says he will also set aside the division of surplus value between lenders, investors, and landlords, which anchors his notion of capital fetishism and is expounded brilliantly under the heading of 'The Trinity Formula' in Marx (2016).

28 In the translation of Marx's so-called *Capital, Volume II* (1978) by David Fernbach, 230 pages derive from Marx's (1877–78) manuscripts. Of those, 130 appear in the section on 'the extended reproduction of capital', that is, on accumulation on a dynamic, geographically extended scale.

29 For details on these notebooks, which I am editing for Yale University Press, see Smith (2021a: 183–206).

30 Many other themes also appear in a new or nuanced ways in *Le Capital,* but space constraints preclude attention to them here.

31 The *locus classicus* here is the manuscript Engels called *Capital, Volume III*, which is now available in pre-Engels form (Marx 2016. On related themes, see Smith [2018, 2014]).

32 The phrase *système capitaliste* appears eight times in *Le Capital*, entirely in the later chapters. Much the same is true for the phrase 'capitalist mode of production', which appears *en passant* in the early chapters but pervasively – over 40 times – in the later chapters. In contrast, the second German edition – Marx (1872: 517) – mentions the capitalist system just once.

33 For Marx 'industrial' is an encompassing term. Capital

> appears as a value that passes through a sequence of connected [...] transform-
> ations [forming] stages of a total process. Two of these phases belong to the
> circulation sphere, one to [...] production. [...] The capital that assumes these
> forms in the course of its total circuit [...] is industrial capital – industrial here
> in the sense that it encompasses every branch of production that is pursued on
> a capitalist basis.
>
> (Marx 1978: 132)

34 This passage illustrates nicely how *Le Capital* differs from the standard edition. The
sentences in italic are new, and where Marx writes 'capitalist world' in *Le Capital,*
Fowkes (Marx 1976: 772) offers the phrase 'capitalist production'.

35 Marx (1875: 328; 1989: 658). In several passages Marx cites *'sociétés de résistance'*,
employing what was then a quasi-standard term for still unfamiliar concept of trade
unions.

36 Weber (1904, 1905) discusses this issue in detail, with respect to Sombart's views
(1902) and his own, contrasting views.

37 The plague, however, had opposite results in France, showing, Marx says, that contrary to Malthusian illusions, population is not destiny.

38 I've lightly altered the tense of this passage.

39 This phrasing might allude to Shakespeare ('the whole world's a stage') and the
Globe theatre, where his players performed.

40 In the same passage, in another variant on a well-known phrase, Marx writes:
'Indeed, *la Force* is the midwife of every society in labour with the new. Force is
an economic agent'.

41 Colonialism 'was "the strange god" who "set himself on the altar beside" the old
idols of Europe, [until,] "one fine day he elbowed his comrades aside, and crash,
bang! All the idols had fallen!"' (Marx 1983: 337; 1989: 671). See Smith (2021a: 165)
for discussion of the literary antecedents of this passage.

42 This passage follows a line in which Marx compares 'Yankee' wage rates with
Chinese wage rates – a newly added point of some significance. See again Smith
(2021a: 195) for commentary.

43 Marx generally translates non-French citations into French, but here I have
reinstated Townsend's original English.

44 Marx cites Cherbuliez (1840: 146).

45 This complex passage includes, besides many small changes, a line missing in the
standard editions of *Capital*. Marx cites this passage from the French edition of Ure
(1836: 138), with minor modifications, e.g., substituting *sociétés de résistance* for *'les
associations'*. To convey the flavour of Marx's text, I have not restored the English of
Ure's original text (1935) which differs from the French translation only in small
ways (e.g., 'refractory' rather than 'rebellious').

46 Dona Torr, 'on the authority of the [Bolshevik] *Volksausgabe'*, included Marx's
quote from the 1874 *Engineering* article in her reprint of the Moore-Aveling translation of *Capital* (Torr, in Marx 1938: 818). She also gave an accurate brief account
of *Le Capital* in an appendix.

47 Since Marx's French parallels the original English, with only slight exceptions
(omission of the word 'iron', a slight syntactic simplification), I have reinstated the
original, anonymous text from the article 'Mechanical Puddling' in *Engineering*

(12 June 1874: 432). This article opens with the observation that, since the Danks puddling furnace had been abandoned by the Roane Iron Co. of Chattanooga, 'a reaction in favour of hand-puddling' had arisen. The author hoped to prove the wrongheadedness of that reaction.

48 In principle Marx favoured children's and women's labour, but he found the subsumption of their labour under capital 'abominable', as he said in the General Council debate on machinery.

49 See respectively Boudet (1866) and *Bulletin de la Société industrielle de Mulhausen* (1833). Marx cites these texts as follows: ★★★ 'Discourse by M. Boudet at the Académie de Médecine, [...] November 27, 1866. – [...] In its 28th *Bulletin*, the Société industrielle de Mulhouse notes the "frightening decline" of the ascending generation'.

50 Durkheim (1897: 283) famously said that, while anomie and egoism reign in the sphere of trade and industry, solidarity, especially occupational solidarity, remains a credible possibility.

51 Marx's translation appeared in *Der Social-Demokrat*, n. 2, December 21, and n. 3 (Bellage), 30 December 1864.

References

Abromeit, John (2011) *Max Horkheimer and the Foundations of the Frankfurt School,* New York and London: Cambridge University Press.

Adoratsky, Viktor Vladimirovich (1933) 'Vorrede' in Karl Marx, *Das Kapital, Band I, Volksausgabe,* Vienna and Berlin: Verlag für Literatur und Politik, pp. 7–26.

Anonymous (1874) 'Mechanical Puddling', *Engineering,* June 12, p. 432.

Bonnell, Andrew G. (2020) *Red Banners, Books and Beer Mugs: The Mental World of German Social Democrats, 1863–1914,* Leiden and Boston: Brill.

Boudet, Félix (1866) 'Discours et propositions de M. Boudet, La Future Commission de l'hygiene de l'enfance', in *Gazette hebdomadaire de médecine et de chirurgie,* Paris: Académie de médecine, December 5 (Marx wrote November 27).

Bulletin de la Société industrielle de Mulhausen (1833), vol. 6, n. 25–8.

Bulletin de la Société industrielle de Mulhausen (1837), vol. 10, n. 46.

Cherbuliez, Antoine Élisée (1840) *Riche ou Pauvre,* Paris and Geneva: Librairie d'Ab. Cherbuliez.

Cordillot, Michel (2010) 'La section française de l'Internationale et les grèves de 1867', in *Aux origines du socialisme moderne,* edited by Michel Cordillot, Paris: Éditions Ouvrières, pp. 33–56.

D'Hondt, Jacques (1985) 'La traduction tendancieuse du *"Capital"* par Joseph Roy', in *L'Oeuvre de Marx, un siecle apres: 1883–1983,* edited by Georges Labica, Paris: PUF, pp. 133–9.

Durkheim, Émile (1897) *Le suicide. Etude de sociologie,* Paris: F. Alcan.

Hecker, Rolf (2000) *Erfolgreiche Kooperation: das Frankfurter Institut für Sozialforschung und das Moskauer Marx-Engels-Institut (1924–1928),* Hamburg: Argument.

Jarrige, François (2018) 'The IWMA, Workers and the Machinery Question (1864–1874)', in *'Arise Ye Wretched of the Earth': The First International in a Global Perspective,* edited by Fabrice Bensimon, Quentin Deluermoz, and Jeanne Moisand, Leiden, Boston: Brill, pp. 89–107.

Korsch, Karl (1920) 'Grundsätzliches über Sozialisierung', *Die Tat,* vol. 11, n. 12: 900–1.

38   *David Norman Smith*

Kropp, Valerie (1924) 'Unpublished letter' in *Stiftung Archiv der Parteien und Massenorganisationen der DDR im Bundesarchiv* (SAPMO-BArch) RY 1 I 3/23/13.

Kropp, Valerie and Nixdorf, Kurt (1997 [1931]) 'Der Vergleich der franzosischen Ausgabe des *"Kapitals"* mit der 2. deutschen Auflage', in *Beitrage zur Marx-Engels-Forschung. Neue Folge. Sonderband 1. David Borisovič Rjazanov und die erste MEGA*, edited by Carl-Erich Vollgraf, Richard Sperl, and Rolf Hecker, Hamburg: Argument, pp. 127–31.

Kuczynski, Thomas (2014) 'Die historisch-kritischen Editionen von *Kapital, Band* I in der *MEGA* – unabdingbarer Ausgangspunkt einer neuen Textausgabe', *Zeitschrift Marxistische Erneuerung*, n. 100. www.zeitschrift-marxistische-erneuerung.de/arti cle/1253.die-historisch-kritischen-editionen-von-kapital-band-i-in-der-mega-unabdingbarer-ausgangspunkt-einer-neuen-textausgabe.html

Kuczynski, Thomas (2017) *Historisch-kritischer Apparat zu Karl Marx: Das Kapital. Kritik der politischen Ökonomie*. Erster Band, Buch I (Online appendix to Marx, 2017).

Law, Harriet T. (1878) 'Dr. Karl Marx', *The Secular Chronicle*, July 7, n. 222: 1–3.

Lozovsky, Alexander (1935) *Marx and the Trade Unions*, New York: International.

Luxemburg, Rosa (2015) 'The Second and Third Volumes of Capital', in *The Complete Works of Rosa Luxemburg*, vol. II, *Economic Writings 2*, London and New York: Verso, pp. 453–61.

Marx, Karl (1859), *Zur Kritik der politischen Ökonomie*, Berlin: Duncker.

Marx, Karl (1867) *Das Kapital, Band I*, Hamburg: Otto Meissner.

Marx, Karl (1872) *Das Kapital, Band I*, second edition, Hamburg: Otto Meissner.

Marx, Karl (1875) *Le Capital*, Paris: Maurice Lachâtre.

Marx, Karl (1898 [1865]) *Value, Price, and Profit: Addressed to Working Men*, London: Sonnenschein.

Marx, Karl (1910 [1862–1863]). *Theorien über Den Mehrwert*, vol. 3: *Von Ricardo zur vulgärökonomie*, Berlin: Dietz.

Marx, Karl (1914) *Das Kapital, Erster Band*, Stuttgart: Dietz.

Marx, Karl (1932 [1872]) *Das Kapital. Ungekürzte Ausgabe nach der zweiten Auflage von 1872*. Mit einem Geleitwort von Karl Korsch, Berlin: Kiepenheuer.

Marx, Karl (1933) *Das Kapital, Band I*, Vienna and Berlin: Verlag für Literatur und Politik.

Marx, Karl (1938 [1889]) *Capital*, London: George Allen and Unwin.

Marx, Karl (1962 [1864]) 'Inaugural Address of the Working Men's International Association', in *Minutes of the General Council of the First International, vol. I, 1864–1866*, Moscow: Progress Publishers, pp. 277–87.

Marx, Karl (1969 [1865]) 'Wages, Price, and Profits', in Karl Marx and Frederick Engels, *Selected Works in One Volume*, Moscow: Progress, pp. 181–239.

Marx, Karl (1970 [1859]), *A Contribution to the Critique of Political Economy*, New York: International.

Marx, Karl (1975 [1861–1863]) 'Revenue and Its Sources', in *Marx Engels Collected Works*, vol. 32: *Marx: 1861–1863*, New York: International, pp. 449–66.

Marx, Karl (1976 [1890]) *Capital, Volume I*, London: Penguin in association with New Left Books.

Marx, Karl (1978 [1885]) *Capital, Volume II*, New York: Penguin.

Marx, Karl (1983 [1890]) *Le Capital, Livre I*, Paris: les Éditions sociales.

Marx, Karl (1988 [1861–1863]) 'Economic Manuscript of 1861-1863, Third Part, Capital in General', in *Marx Engels Collected Works*, vol. 30: *Marx 1861–1863*, New York: International Publishers, pp. 9–346.

Marx, Karl (1989 [1872–1875]) 'Le Capital: Paris 1872–1875', in *Marx Engels Gesamtausgabe* (MEGA²), vol. II/7: *'Das Kapital' und Vorarbeiten,* Berlin: Dietz.

Marx, Karl (2016 [1864–1865]) *Marx's Economic Manuscript of 1864–1865,* Leiden and Boston: Brill.

Marx, Karl (2017) *Das Kapital. Kritik der politischen Ökonomie. Erster Band. Neue Textausgabe,* VSA:Verlag Hamburg.

Marx, Karl (2022 [1875]) *Critique of the Gotha Program,* Oakland: PM Press.

Marx, Karl and Engels, Friedrich (1929) *Die Briefe an Danielson (Nikolai-on),* Leipzig: Liebing.

Marx, Karl and Engels, Friedrich (1989) *Marx Engels Gesamtausgabe* (MEGA²), vol. II/7: *'Das Kapital' und Vorarbeiten,* Berlin: Dietz.

Mehring, Franz (1877) *Die deutsche Socialdemokratie,* Bremen: Schunemann.

Mehring, Franz, (Ed.) (1902) *Aus dem literarischen nachlass von Karl Marx, Friedrich Engels und Ferdinand Lassalle,* vols. 1–4, Stuttgart: Dietz.

Mehring, Franz (1918) *Karl Marx,* Leipzig: Leipziger Buchdruckerei.

Minutes of the General Council of the First International (1962–1968 [1864–1872]), vols. 1–5, Moscow: Progress.

Musto, Marcello (2014) *Workers Unite! The International 150 Years Later,* London: Bloomsbury.

Musto, Marcello (Ed.) (2021) *Rethinking Alternatives with Marx,* London and New York: Palgrave Macmillan.

Neumann, Franz (1936) 'Review of Alexander Lozovsky, *Marx and the Trade Unions',* *Zeitschrift für Sozialforschung,* vol. 5, p. 297.

Pareto, Vilfredo and Lafargue, Paul (1894) *Karl Marx, Le Capital, extraits fait par M. Paul Lafargue,* Paris: Guillaumin.

Penot, Achille (1837) 'Rapport. De la commission chargée d'examiner la question relative à l'emploi des enfans dans les filatures de coton', *Bulletin de la Société industrielle de Mulhausen,* vol. 10, n. 46: 481–500.

Roth, Regina (2018) 'Editing the Legacy: Friedrich Engels and Marx's *Capital',* in *Marx's Capital: An Unfinishable Project?,* Leiden and Boston: Brill, pp. 31–47.

Ryazanov, David (1926) 'Zur Geschichte der ersten Internationale. i. Die Entstehung der Internationalen Arbeiterassoziation', in *Marx-Engels-Archiv* (Frankfurt), vol. 1, pp. 119–202.

Schwartz, Laura (2013) *Infidel Feminism: Secularism, Religion and Women's Emancipation, England 1830–1914,* Manchester and New York: Manchester University Press.

Serge, Victor (2012) *Memoirs of a Revolutionary, 1901–1941,* New York: New York Review of Books.

Smith, David Norman (2014) *Marx's Capital Illustrated,* Chicago: Haymarket.

Smith, David Norman (2016) 'Time is Still Money: Common Sense and Commodity Fetishism' epilogue in *The Hegemony of Common Sense* by Dean Wolfe Manders, San Francisco: Looking Up Press, pp. 191–259.

Smith, David Norman (2017) 'Sharing, Not Selling: Marx Against Value', *Continental Thought and Theory,* vol. 1 n. 4: 653–95.

Smith, David Norman (2018) '21st Century Capital: Falling Profit Rates and System Entropy', in *Twenty-First Century Inequality and Capitalism,* edited by Lauren Langman and David A. Smith, Leiden and Boston: Brill, pp. 321–34.

Smith, David Norman (2020) 'Anti-Authoritarian Marxism', in *Erich Fromm's Critical Theory,* edited by Joane Braune and Kieran Durkin, London: Bloomsbury, pp. 131–65.

40   *David Norman Smith*

Smith, David Norman (2021a) 'Accumulation and Its Discontents', in *Rethinking Alternatives with Marx,* edited by Marcello Musto, London and New York: Palgrave Macmillan, pp. 151–215.

Smith, David Norman (2021b) 'Capital Fetishism and the Authoritarian Personality', in *How to Critique Authoritarian Populism,* edited by Jeremiah Morelock, Leiden and Boston: Brill, pp. 108–44.

Sombart, Werner (1902) *Der moderne Kapitalismus, Bd. 1, Die Genesis des Kapitalismus,* Leipzig: Duncker and Humblot.

Spargo, John (1910) *Karl Marx,* New York: Heubsch.

Spargo, John (1912) *Karl Marx,* Leipzig: F. Meiner.

Tarcus, Horacio (2017) 'Traductores y editores de la "Biblia del Proletariado": La suerte de *El Capital* en el mundo hispanoamericano', *Revista Los Trabajos y los Días,* Año 9, Noviembre, n. 6/7: 7–66.

Ure, Andrew (1835) *The Philosophy of Manufactures: Or, Exploration of the Scientific, Moral, and Commercial Economy of the Factory System of Great Britain,* London: Charles Knight.

Ure, Andrew (1836) *Philosophie des Manufactures,* vol. 2, Brussels: Hauman.

Vollgraf, Carl-Erich (2018) 'Marx's Further Work on Capital after Publishing Volume I: On the Completion of Part II of the *MEGA²*', in *Marx's Capital: An Unfinishable Project?,* edited by Marcel van der Linden and Gerald Hubmann, Leiden and Boston: Brill, pp. 31–47.

Vollgraf, Carl-Erich, Sperl, Richard and Hecker, Rolf (Eds.) (2001) *Beiträge zur Marx-Engels-Forschung. Neue Folge. Sonderband 3: Stalinismus und das Ende der ersten Marx-Engels-Gesamtausgabe (1931–1941),* Hamburg: Argument.

Weber, Max (1904) 'Die protestantische Ethik und der "Geist" des Kapitalismus, I. Das Problem', *Archiv für Sozialwissenschaft und Sozialpolitik,* vol. 20: 1–54.

Weber, Max (1905) 'Die protestantische Ethik und der "Geist" des Kapitalismus, II. Die Berufsidee des asketischen Protestantismus', *Archiv für Sozialwissenschaft und Sozialpolitik,* vol. 21: 1–10.

Weil, Felix (1921) *Sozialisierung,* Berlin: Verlag Gesellschaft and Erziehung.

Wilbrandt, Robert (1918) *Karl Marx,* Leipzig and Berlin: Teubner.

Yagi, Kiichiro (2011) 'Was Sozialforschung an Aesopian Term?', in *The Dissemination of Economic Ideas,* edited by Heinz-Dieter Kurz, Tamotsu Nishizawa and Keith Tribe, Cheltenham: Elgar, pp. 315–36.

3 Marx's French Edition of *Capital* as Unexplored Territory

From the Centralization of Capital to Societies beyond Western Europe

Kevin B. Anderson

Marx's expressed view of the French edition

There is little question that Karl Marx held the 1872–75 French edition of *Capital* in higher esteem than did his successors, who have tended to downplay or even ignore it, beginning with his comrade Friedrich Engels.[1] According to its title page, the French edition was 'completely revised by the author' and was thus much more than a mere translation (Marx 1989a: 3). In fact, it was an extensively reworked new edition. In a postface to it dated 28 April 1875, Marx underlined the importance of this new edition of his *magnum opus*, the last one he personally brought to press: 'Whatever the literary defects of this French edition may be, it possesses a scientific value independent of the original and should be consulted even by readers familiar with German' (Marx 1976: 105). A week later, he confirmed the French edition's importance alongside the previous German ones (1867 and 1872) in another way, not for the general public but for his closest comrades inside Germany, this at the very time he was sending them what has come to be seen as one of his most important texts, *The Critique of the Gotha Programme*. In the accompanying letter of 5 May 1875, to the Braunschweig communist Wilhelm Bracke, Marx noted, after summarizing and contextualizing the *Critique* at some length:

> I shall shortly be sending you in the near future the final instalments of the French edition of *Capital*. Printing was held up for a considerable time by the French Government ban. The thing will be finished this week or the beginning of next. Have you received the six previous instalments?
> (Karl Marx to Wilhelm Bracke 5 May, 1875; Marx and Engels 1989a: 78)

This suggests that his private comments on the importance of the French edition to some of his closest comrades accorded with his public ones in the work itself.

Le Capital appeared in France in nine instalments between September 1872 and November 1875, with the long delays mainly due to state harassment of the publisher, Maurice Lachâtre, a participant in the 1871 Paris Commune who

DOI: 10.4324/9781003336365-4

had narrowly escaped execution and was managing his firm from exile in Spain. The political harassment was eventually overcome, the work also appeared in book form, and by 1879 had sold close to 700 copies out of a print run of 1,000 (Maurice Lachâtre to Karl Marx, 21 June 1879; Gaudin 2019: 174).

Engels's negative assessment creates a conceptual barrier

But the French edition was also encountering another kind of opposition from Marx's own supporters, beginning with his closest comrade, Engels, and continuing to this day. From the start, when he read some of the drafts of the French edition, Engels complained of its poor quality. In a letter to Marx of 29 November 1873, in the chapter on 'The Working Day', he wrote:

> I still felt regret at what had been lost from the beautiful chapter. Its vigour and vitality and life have gone to the devil... It is becoming increasingly impossible to think originally in the straitjacket of modern French. Everything striking or vital is removed if only by the need, which has become essential almost everywhere, to bow to the dictates of a pedantic formal logic and change round the sentences. I would think it a great mistake to take the French version as a model for the English translation.
>
> (Marx and Engels 1989b: 540–1)[2]

This attitude was taken up later, not only by German Marxists but even by many French ones. A century later, the structuralist Marxist Louis Althusser could write, in a 1969 preface to *Capital* – and he was not alone in his view – that the French edition was a simplified version of what he considered to be the German original: 'Marx, who was uncertain of the theoretical capacities of his French readers, sometimes dangerously compromised the precision of the original conceptual expressions' (Althusser 1985: 19).

But why is it assumed that the German edition of *Capital* constitutes the true, original version? Why is it that Marx, who lived more years of his life in Britain than in Germany, and who wrote important works in English (*The Civil War in France*) and French (*Misère de la philosophie,* Letter to Vera Zasulich), is usually considered to be a German thinker, rather than the cosmopolitan, trilingual one that he was?[3] These assumptions are especially odd concerning an era when the modern nation-state had not fully crystallized. Thus, one has actually to step across a conceptual barrier erected by decades of Marxism and Marx scholarship before one can even consider seriously Marx's French edition of *Capital*.

A second, more obvious conceptual barrier to grasping the importance of the French edition is the place of Engels as Marx's intellectual and political successor, including as chief editor of his friend's writings in the 12 years between Marx's death in 1883 and his own in 1895. During this period, Marxism also stepped forth as a mass movement with deep roots in the European working class, notably in Germany. For many decades, and to a lesser extent even today, a marked tendency to conflate Marx and Engels into a single authorial voice has dominated the literature on Marx. Counter to this dominant, albeit slowly abating narrative, four major strands of *Critique* of Engels have emerged over the years within Marxism and Marx scholarship: (1) Starting over a century ago with Rosa Luxemburg, but culminating in the MEGA² editions of this century, Engels's editorial choices in the creation of *Volumes II* and *III* of *Capital* from Marx's drafts have been called into question; (2) in the 1920s, Georg Lukács separated Marx from Engels on dialectics; (3) in the 1980s, Raya Dunayevskaya did so with respect to gender and to preliterate and other noncapitalist societies; (4) also in the 1980s, but with some work on this having been carried out by Maximilien Rubel in the 1960s, Dunayevskaya and others, including the present writer, did so with respect to the French edition of *Capital, Volume I.* These critiques, and the dismissals and fierce debates that sometimes surrounded them, form part of the terrain for any attempt to approach the French edition of 1872–75 today.

Before Marx's death in 1883, *Capital, Volume I*[4] went through three editions prepared for publication by the author, each of them involving substantial reworkings of the text (German 1867 and 1872, French 1872–75), as well as an 1872 Russian translation not reviewed by the author, who had just begun to learn that language. Beginning in 1883, Engels, who took upon himself the establishment of a definitive edition of *Capital*, brought to press two posthumous German editions (1883 and 1890) and was heavily involved in the first English translation (1887). Through these efforts, he did more than anyone to establish the notion of the French edition as somehow inferior to the German ones. Most visibly, the prefaces Engels contributed to these editions undercut the French edition's importance. In his preface to the third German edition of 1883, written only eight months after Marx's death, Engels indicated that he used the French edition occasionally for the lengthy part seven, the book's last part. Titled 'Accumulation of Capital', in the 1872 German edition, it included the chapters on 'So-Called Primitive Accumulation'. Engels mentions, without being very specific, notes left behind by Marx concerning the French edition in relation to the German ones and private conversations as well, indicating that he was following Marx's intentions. At this point, Engels does not even claim to have thoroughly studied the French edition.

Three years later, in his 1886 preface to the first English edition of 1887, Engels begins over a century of attacks on the theoretical depth of the French edition when he writes,

> the French text has been referred to in most of the difficult passages, as an indicator of what the author himself was prepared to sacrifice wherever something of the full import of the original had to be sacrificed in the rendering.
>
> (Marx 1976: 110)[5]

This is the most dismissive of all of Engels's public utterances on the French edition, as he suggests that it was a simplified version addressed to a readership presumably less sophisticated than a German one.

By the time Engels established the fourth German edition in 1890, which he evidently considered to be definitive, he gives somewhat more credence to the French edition. By now, he seems to have really studied it, perhaps as part of the work on the English translation. Mentioning six places where he incorporated text from it, Engels writes: 'After again comparing the French edition and Marx's manuscript remarks I have made some further additions to the German text from that translation' (Marx 1976: 110). It should be noted, however, that none of the three editions Engels produced or assisted in producing included Marx's preface or postface to the French edition, which would have alerted readers to the author's quite different assessment of the last edition of his book.

Marx's explicit and implicit differences with Engels over the French edition

For his part, Marx maintained the importance and originality of his French edition in a number of letters and in conversations, this in addition to his pre-viously cited statement in the postface about its 'scientific value independent of the [German] original' (Marx 1976: 205). In a letter of 28 May 1872 to his Russian translator Nikolai Danielson, Marx implied that the French edition should become the basis of other translations: 'It will be all the easier later on to translate the book from French into English and the Romance languages' (Marx and Engels 1989b: 385).[6] In the 1873 exchange with Engels, after, as discussed above, his friend disparaged the French edition and even the French language, Marx replies on 14 November that if Engels were to 'persevere' with the French edition, 'I think you will find that some passages are superior to the German' (Marx to Engels, 14 November 1873, Marx and Engels 1989b: 543). Five years later, in a letter to Danielson of 15 November 1878 concerning a possible second Russian edition, Marx indicates again the importance of the French edition, urging 'That the translator compare always carefully the second German edition with the French one, since the latter contains many important changes and additions' (Marx and Engels 1991: 343). He also wanted the chapters and section structure to follow the French edition, which would have meant a separate part eight on primitive accumulation, something Engels did not carry out in either of the German editions he published. And, as the Brazilian scholar Rodrigo Pinho shows in detail, Marx told the U.S. journalist John Swinton in 1880 that the French edition should be the basis for an English translation, also confirming this stance by sending him a copy along with a letter thanking him for his published article that had mentioned this preference for the French version.[7]

In short, we have here a rare instance of a fairly explicit difference of opinion between Marx and Engels on a major issue: What was the best version of Marx's *magnum opus* and in what form should the book be published?[8]

But even if it is true that Marx preferred the French edition, or at least saw it as a major, original edition of *Capital* to be read alongside the German ones, and that should become the basis of translations, was he correct to do so? In short, what is the theoretical substance of the changes he introduced into the French edition?

Some key changes incorporated by Engels from the French edition, especially on the centralization of capital

Upon Marx's death in 1883, Engels was faced with a daunting task in considering the two editions, the last German one prepared for publication by Marx in 1872 and the French edition began that same year, but whose publication was not complete until 1875. As one indicator of the scope of the problem, the MEGA² publication of the French edition includes a list comprising more than 150 pages of 'divergences' from the 1872 German one (Marx 1989a: 775–933). And this is only a list. The actual text of all the French variants would likely be even longer. To his credit, after having disparaged the French edition in his prefaces of 1883 and 1886, Engels seems to have recognized to a greater extent its importance as he was preparing the 1890 fourth German edition. As a result, he now incorporated significant material from the French edition at four key junctures.

One of Engels's additions from Marx's French edition concerns the 'metamorphosis' of money, wherein the relationship of commodity production to money is discussed at several levels. Engels incorporates here a couple of hundred words from the French edition deepening the discussion of how in commodity exchange, money and a commodity 'are displaced twice', first from money to a commodity and then from a commodity to money (Marx 1976: 212). This passage clarifies Marx's theorization of money.

In a second passage of about 700 words added by Engels to the chapter on machinery, Marx details a major tightening of workplace safety and health regulations in Britain in 1867. He also sums up nicely the way that these show,

> on the one hand, the necessity imposed by Parliament on the ruling classes of adopting, in principle, such extraordinary and extensive measures against the excesses of capitalist exploitation, and, on the other hand, the hesitation, the unwillingness, and the bad faith with which it actually puts these measures into practice.
>
> (Marx 1976: 626)

In an earlier chapter on 'The Working Day', he had already highlighted such a studied lack of enforcement of another law crucial for workers' well-being, the ten-hour-day law in France.

A third change incorporated by Engels from the French edition was much more significant, as this 1500-word addition concerned the issue of extended or expanded reproduction, wherein not only the worker but also the working class as a whole, as well as the other overall conditions needed for capital accumulation, are not only reproduced but augmented through the additional accumulation and investment of surplus value. The section included a succinct passage about labour and capital:

(1) that the product belongs to the capitalist and not to the labourer; (2) that the value of this product includes, apart from the value of the capital advanced, a surplus value which costs the worker labour but the capitalist nothing, and which none the less becomes the legitimate property of the capitalist; (3) that the labourer has retained his labour-power and can sell it anew, if he finds a another buyer.

(Marx 1976: 731)

But the key element in this added section lies in how surplus value is plowed back into production, rather than spent, with this change leading to the accumulation of capital, that is, extended or expanded reproduction:

Nor does it matter if reproduction is replaced by reproduction on an extended scale, by accumulation. In the former case the capitalist squanders the whole of the surplus value in dissipation, in the latter he demonstrates his bourgeois virtue by consuming only a portion of it and converting the rest into money.

(Marx 1976: 732)

Marx writes further that this is the result of a 'dialectical inversion' (Marx 1976: 734) (or 'metamorphosis' in the French text) (Marx 1989a: 509), as some aspects of commodity production transform into their opposite. Thus, 'Only where wage-labour is its basis does commodity production impose itself upon society as a whole; but it is also true that only there does it unfold in all its hidden potentialities' (Marx 1976: 733). The concept of extended reproduction was a major theme in what became *Capital, Volume II*, drafted mainly in the 1860s but published posthumously by Engels in 1885. Here in the French edition of *Volume I*, it seems, Marx wanted to add the major theme of extended reproduction to the first volume so that it would be available sooner to his readers.

These three additions incorporated by Engels from the French edition clarified points, or in the case of the third one, added in *Volume I* a point that had been left for the next volume of the work.[9] But the fourth major passage incorporated by Engels concerned the centralization of capital, here conceptualized in a totally new way that could not be found either in the 1872 German edition of *Volume I* or the drafts for what became volumes II and III.

In this addition of nearly 1000 words, Marx conceptualizes a kind of final limit to the centralization of capital, that of a single capitalist entity: 'In any given branch of industry centralisation would reach its final [*dernière*] limit if all the individual capitals invested there were fused into a single capital'.[10] At this point, Engels adds a footnote to the effect that Marx here predicted the rise of trusts, of monopolies. But the really new notion is arguably in the next sentence, which Engels provides without further comment: 'In a given society its final [*dernière*] limit would be reached only when the entire national [*national*] capital was united in the hands of either a single capitalist or a single capitalist company' (Marx 1976: 779).[11] Here we have a kind of absolute development of capitalist centralization all the way to an abstract final limit that may or may not be realized but is here conceptualized as a powerful tendency within capitalism.

These four added passages cannot be found in the 1887 English translation of *Capital*, based upon the 1883 German one published by Engels, but they were included in the 1906 Chicago-based Kerr Publishers English edition, which updated the earlier translation on the basis of Engels's 1890 fourth German edition (Marx 1919).[12] The publisher, closely linked to the Socialist Party, did not comment on these changes, nor did the Kerr edition include Marx's preface or postface to the French edition, which would have alerted readers to that edition's importance. In 1939, Moscow-linked International Publishers issued what came to be known as the 'Dona Torr' edition of *Capital*. Torr was associated with the British Marxist Historians Group that included E.P. Thompson and Christopher Hill, among others. The main text was a reprint of the 1887 English edition, but in a 58-page appendix, editor Torr provided the text of the changes introduced from the French edition by Engels discussed above from the French edition, as well as, for the first time, a translation of Marx's preface and postface (Marx 1939: 801–58).[13]

These passages caught the attention of the 'Johnson-Forest Tendency', a group of heterodox and fiercely anti-Stalinist Marxist intellectuals in the U.S. In their 1950 book, *State Capitalism and World Revolution*, the Tendency's leading theorists, C.L.R. James, Raya Dunayevskaya, and Grace Lee Boggs, used the passage on the centralization of capital as a major part of their theorization of the Soviet Union as a totalitarian state capitalist society that was part of a new stage of global capitalism that also included fascism and Franklin Roosevelt's New Deal: 'At this point, it is convenient to summarize the abstract economic analysis of state-capitalism … It is just this that Marx indicated with his addition to *Capital* dealing with complete centralization of capital "in a given country"' (James et al. 2013: 40). In a 1958 theorization of the impact of the Paris Commune on the final structure of *Capital*, Dunayevskaya saw the passage on centralization as among the 'important additions that were introduced after the Commune into the final part, on "The Accumulation of Capital"', holding that the addition's ultimate importance 'lay not in its prediction of state capitalism but in the fact that nothing fundamental is changed in the relationship of classes by such an extreme development' (Dunayevskaya 1958: 102). In these ways, the passage was crucial to a wide-ranging debate over state capitalism, seen as a new stage beyond monopoly capitalism but where alienation and exploitation of labour remained in force.

In neither these appendixes by Torr nor in the discussions in the U.S., which ran from 1939 to 1958, was it ever suggested that Engels had left out anything important; rather, the focus was on the conceptual development of *Capital* from its first edition of 1867 to its final form, under the assumption that Engels had included everything of importance from the French edition. The creation of a separate section on fetishism in the first chapter, not yet present in the 1867 edition, was a prime example for Dunayevskaya of the important changes Marx introduced after the Paris Commune of 1871. Marx had also introduced this particular change into the 1872 second German edition, but the emphasis in these discussions in the English-speaking world was on the changes between the first German one of 1867 and the final French edition prepared by Marx, which were assumed to have been incorporated by Engels.

Some important passages from the French edition excluded or ignored by Engels, especially on globalization and multilinear development

The French edition has in recent decades been taken up in another way, not only in terms of its distinctiveness from the 1867 edition but also from what was thought for many decades to have been the definitive fourth German edition established by Engels in 1890. How extensive and how numerous are the changes that Engels did not include? The short answer is that they are very extensive and very numerous. The MEGA² reprint of the fourth German edition contains a 60-page appendix listing the changes 'not taken up in the 3rd and 4th German editions', suggesting the magnitude of the problem (Marx 1991: 732–83).

What are the theoretical stakes of these omissions by Engels and the absence of these texts from most editions of *Capital* outside France? Let us examine a few passages where it seems pretty clear that Marx has improved and deepened his argument.[14] One notable passage not taken up by Engels considers the effects of colonialism on wages inside colonial powers like Britain. It also links the globalization of capital to increases in the severity and frequency of crises, this in the middle of a discussion of permanent mass unemployment inside industrially developed societies:

> But only after mechanical industry has struck root so deeply that it exerted a preponderant influence on the whole of national production; only after foreign trade began to predominate over internal trade, thanks to mechanical industry; only after the world market had successively annexed extensive areas of the New World, Asia, and Australia; and finally, only after a sufficient number of industrial nations had entered the arena – only after all this had happened can one date the repeated self-perpetuating cycles, whose successive phases embrace entire years, and always culminate in a general crisis, which is the end of one cycle and the starting-point of another. Until now the duration of these cycles has been ten or eleven years, but there is no reason to consider this duration as constant. On the contrary, we ought to conclude, on the basis of the laws of capitalist production as we have just expounded them, that the duration is variable, and that the length of the cycles will gradually diminish.[15]
>
> (Marx 1976: 786)

In this way, Marx ties the creation of a large mass of unemployed inside the industrially developed societies – a 'relative surplus population' as a 'necessary condition for modern industry' – to the global market created by colonialism and to the greater frequency of crises. (Marx 1976: 786)

A second passage not incorporated by Engels takes up wage differentials among various countries, with Marx again expanding the scope of the discussion to include non-European societies. In the 1872 German edition, Marx recounts how ideologists of capitalism, noting the much lower wages in France and the Netherlands as compared to England, were declaring 'that England's historical mission is to force down English wages to the French and Dutch level' in order to grow the economy (Marx 1976: 748). In the French edition, Marx adds the following:

> Today we have to a large extent gone beyond these aspirations, thanks to the global [*cosmopolite*] competition into which the development of capitalist production has thrown the workers of the whole world. It is no longer a question of reducing English wages to those of continental Europe, but of lowering, in the near or distant future, the European level to the Chinese. Here is the opinion that Mr. Stapleton, an English member of parliament, has just put forward to his constituents in an address on the price of labour in the future. 'If China should become a great manufacturing country, and glut the markets of the world with her fabrics, I do not see how the manufacturing population of Europe could sustain the contest without descending to the level of their competitors'.[16]
>
> (Marx 1989a: 522)

Again, Marx is globalizing further his theory of the accumulation of capital. While these two passages extend Marx's argument, two additional ones not included by Engels rework *Capital's* theoretical argument or at least clarify it in ways that cut against what have been the dominant interpretations of the work. These third and fourth passages point towards what has been termed Marx's increasingly multilinear approach to social development in his last years. They show that Marx, at least by the 1870s, no longer seems to believe that all societies of his time were destined to industrialize in the capitalist manner, or at least not via the process he called the 'primitive accumulation of capital'. This suggests a change of perspective from the time of the *Manifesto of the Communist Party* of 1848, when he and Engels imply that such a unilinear process is an inevitability, as they write of China and other non-European societies being forcibly incorporated into the global capitalist system, as part of the unfolding of historical necessity.

In this respect, in a third, brief but very significant passage added in the French edition, Marx makes a change to the 1867 preface, but without indicating he has done so. In an oft-cited sentence on the relationship of industrialized to non-industrialized societies, the standard English and German editions of the 1867 preface read: 'The country that is more developed industrially only shows, *to the less developed*, the image of its own future' (clause subsequently rephrased in italics) (Marx 1976: 91).[17] Some have seized upon this sentence to term Marx a 'unilinear' and 'determinist' thinker. Citing it as evidence, Russian scholar Teodor Shanin writes in a still influential work, *Late Marx and the Russian Road*, that the 'main weakness' of *Capital* 'was the optimistic and unilinear determinism usually built into it' (Shanin 1983: 4).[18] But in the same sentence in the French edition, overlooked by Shanin, Marx rephrases this clause in such a way as to alter the sentence's meaning in important ways: 'The country that is more developed industrially only shows, *to those that follow it up the industrial ladder,* the image of its own future' (rephrased clause italicized) (Marx 1989a: 12).[19] In so doing, he has essentially bracketed out those vast parts of the world that in the 1870s were not yet beginning to industrialize. Thus, whatever 'laws' and tendencies Marx elaborates here would apply only to industrial capitalism, in short, at that time only to Western Europe and North America. This is not a unilinear perspective, but the opposite of one.

A fourth passage added in the French edition and not incorporated by Engels is also on the question of multilinear development. It occurs in the last part of the book, 'Primitive Accumulation of Capital'. But before citing that passage two other things should be noted about this last part of the book. First, the French edition was where Marx for the first time separated the chapters on primitive accumulation from the seventh part of the book on 'Accumulation of Capital', forming them into a separate part eight of the work and thus making these chapters more prominent. Second, Marx dropped the modifier 'so-called' from the title of the section, 'The So-Called Primitive Accumulation of Capital'. The first of these changes was adopted in the 1887 English edition but not the 1890 fourth German one, while the second change was not adopted in either of these editions.

As against the nearly unnoticed alteration to the 1867 preface discussed above, this fourth key passage not incorporated by Engels in the primitive accumulation part has been very visible, though not always remarked upon, for over a century. After describing the brutal process of primitive accumulation of capital, in which the English peasantry was separated from its means of production, the land, and driven out of subsistence farming to become formally free proletarians living in precarious circumstances, later evolving into the urban proletariat. Marx writes:

> The expropriation of the agricultural producer, of the peasant, from the soil, is the basis of the whole process. The history of this expropriation assumes different aspects in different countries, and runs through its various phases in different orders of succession, and at different historical epochs. *Only in England, which we therefore take as our example, has it the classic form.* [text later altered by Marx in italics]
>
> (Marx 1976: 876)[20]

This passage concludes chapter 26, 'The Secret of Primitive Accumulation', where Marx introduces the overall theoretical framework of the six-chapter eighth part of the book on primitive accumulation. In this brief chapter, Marx gives only Western European examples, in a discussion of the transition from feudalism to capitalism. Thus, this passage could have been – and was – read as a global and unilinear process of capitalist development, with England exhibiting the 'classic form' of a process that the whole world was destined to experience now that the capitalist mode of production had appeared in Europe. Considering also the unilinear language of the *Manifesto of the Communist Party*, this was how many have read and still read this passage, if not the whole of *Capital*.

In the French edition, Marx extends and reworks this passage considerably, expressly limiting his analysis to 'Western Europe'. Although Marx subsequently referred at least twice in his correspondence to the following passage from the French edition, it has yet to make it into any of the standard English editions of *Capital*:

> But the basis of this whole development is the expropriation of the cultivators. So far, it has been carried out in a radical manner only in England: therefore this country will necessarily play the leading role in our sketch. *But all the countries of Western Europe are going through the same development, although in accordance with the particular environment it changes its local colour, or confines itself to a narrower sphere, or shows a less pronounced character, or follows a different order of succession.*
>
> (Marx 1989a: 634, altered text italicized)[21]

This altered text made clear, as far as Marx was concerned, that his narrative of primitive accumulation was meant as a description of Western European development, nothing more, and hardly a global grand narrative.[22]

Engels may not have noticed our third example of an important change, the altered sentence in the 1867 preface. But in not incorporating this fourth textual variant, he seems to have violated Marx's explicit wishes, which were available to him in written form. For in an outline Marx made for what became the third German edition of 1883, he writes that this passage was 'to be translated from the French edition' (Marx 1989b: 17). Engels's omission here may well have been deliberate, since in his 1883 preface he indicates, as discussed above, that he has consulted 'notes left by the author' in preparing the third German edition, some of which he decided not to implement (Marx 1976: 110).

Multilinear social development and revolutionary prospects

Besides Engels's general scepticism about the French edition, another factor may have been at play here, his relative lack of interest, at least as compared to Marx, in the peripheries of capitalism, in Russia and the colonized societies of Africa and Asia. Recall in this regard that after Marx's death in 1883, Engels lived until 1895, years that saw the emergence of modern imperialism. This was shown in brutal and dramatic fashion when Africa was carved up by the major European powers at the 1884 Congress of Berlin, but Engels did not write much about these kinds of developments. The serious examination of imperialism would have to await the next generation of Marxists, most notably Rosa Luxemburg and V.I. Lenin, with the latter theorizing imperialism as part of a new monopoly stage of capitalism. And while it would go beyond the scope of this essay to delve into these developments, a related issue within Marx's own writings should at least be taken up briefly.

When Engels found Marx's notes on anthropological works from the years 1879–82, he quickly published in 1884 *Origins of the Family, Private Property and the State*, his own analysis based upon the part of the notes on Lewis Henry Morgan's *Ancient Society*. Engels's book, although it has rightly been criticized for schematism and unilinear evolutionism, exhibited both originality and a strong commitment to gender equality and women's liberation.[23] However, Engels focused primarily on Native American societies and those of Greece and Rome, leaving aside what Marx also took up at length in his notes: contemporary colonized societies like Algeria, India, and Egypt, as well as Russia and its villages.[24]

In any event, Marx quoted this fourth altered passage in the part of *Capital* on primitive accumulation more than once in his interactions with Russians in his last years. In a letter thought to have been written in late 1877 to a Russian journal but never sent, he quotes the passage from the French edition after writing, 'The chapter on primitive accumulation does not pretend to do more than trace the road by which in Western Europe the capitalist economic order emerged from the entrails of the feudal economic order' (Karl Marx to Otechestvenniye Zapiski, presumably November 1877, Marx and Engels 1989a: 199). In this letter, he is also at pains to deny that he has developed 'a historical-philosophical theory of general development, imposed by fate on all peoples' (Karl Marx to Otechestvenniye Zapiski, presumably November 1877, Marx and Engels 1989a: 200).

Then, in his 8 March 1881 letter to Vera Zasulich, Marx quotes the passage again, in response to her question about whether agrarian Russia's 'rural commune' was 'capable of developing in a socialist direction', or if it 'was destined to perish', followed by capitalism, a working class, and only then the possibility of socialism (Shanin 1983: 98). Marx writes:

> In analysing the genesis of capitalist production, I say: 'At the core of the capitalist system, therefore, lies the complete separation of the producer from the means of production ... the basis of this whole development is the *expropriation of the cultivators*. So far, it has been carried out in a radical manner only in England ... But *all the other countries of Western Europe* are going through the same development' (*Capital*, French ed., p. 315). Hence, the 'historical inevitability' of this process is *expressly* limited to *the countries of Western Europe*.
>
> (Marx and Engels 1989a: 370)[25]

In this way, Marx employs the French edition in an important theorization of his position on the social transformation of societies outside Western Europe.

He adds that the village commune need not be uprooted, but could become 'the fulcrum of social regeneration in Russia' if it could be defended from the 'deleterious influences which are assailing it from all sides', here probably referring to capitalist encroachments (Marx and Engels 1989a: 371).

A year later, in an 1882 preface to a new Russian edition of the *Manifesto of the Communist Party* that was Marx's last published text, he and Engels write in the spirit of the letter to Zasulich, but in a manner that also speaks to the need for a Russian peasants and European workers to unite or at to at least operate in parallel fashion: 'If the Russian Revolution becomes the signal for a proletarian revolution in the West, so that the two complement each other, the present Russian common ownership of land may serve as the starting point for a communist development' (Marx and Engels 1989a: 426).

After Marx's death the following year, Engels did not attempt to extend or develop this argument about the revolutionary potential of the Russian village commune. Moreover, he may not have been familiar with the 1881 letter to Zasulich and its drafts, which, along with their preface to the *Manifesto*, could have alerted him to the crucial importance for Marx of the related passage in the French edition. Be that as it may, Engels never included this fourth passage in his 1890 German edition. The result was that readers of *Capital* in most editions around the world have been deprived of a crucial argument that Marx himself stressed as an important one for societies outside Western Europe and North America.

Concluding remarks: Centralization, globalization, and multilinearity

What large themes emerge from these considerations of the French edition of *Capital*, the last one Marx himself brought to press? Most of the passages taken up above concern Marx's widening of the scope of his *magnum opus*, whether to take fuller account of the centralization of capital, or of its expansion globally, or of the fact that most of the world had not yet come under the full domination of the capital relation. In viewing these new passages as a whole, all written after the Paris Commune and even after the second German edition of 1872 had appeared, one can trace the further development of *Capital* as a work under constant revision and expansion, right up through the year 1875. The changes on which the present essay has focused concern a number of passages that are more than alterations of emphasis, inconsequential updates, or slight expansions of already existing arguments.

First, there were important and original changes introduced to the French edition – and that were incorporated by Engels by 1890 – concerning the centralization of capital. These changes point towards the tendency of an entire national capital to coalesce into a single entity. Here, Marx began to theorize not only the possibility of a complete and total monopoly capitalism but also suggested that of a state capitalism into which both the state and the economy were rolled into a single, centralized apparatus of exploitation and domination.

Second, there were the equally important changes – here not incorporated by Engels – around the globalization of capital. The most original of these was the notion that that capital's globalization was very incomplete and that therefore whole swathes of the world economy were not yet subject to its laws, to its tendencies. These new passages offer a new, multilinear perspective on social development and revolution in the agrarian societies at the time like Russia, with implications for what is today termed the Global South.

If one also considers the major changes Marx introduced between the German editions of 1867 and 1872, like introducing a separate section on and expanding his discussion of commodity fetishism, then a new vista opens up, one that allows us to view the development of Marx's *Capital* across an entire eight-year period, 1867–75.

Why has there been so little research on or theorization of this kind of development of *Capital, Volume I*, which after all concerns his most important text? Recall that a huge literature has considered the development of his thought during the nine-year period from the *Grundrisse* (1857–58) to *Capital*, first published in 1867. As stated at the outset of this essay, two main reasons for this neglect of the changes in *Capital, Volume I* as a lens into the development of Marx's thought are (1) the unwarranted assumption that Marx was a German thinker rather than a cosmopolitan one who wrote easily in three languages, and that therefore the German-language versions of his work must invariably be the true originals, and (2) the equally unwarranted assumption that Engels's editorial decisions concerning Marx's writings were the equivalent of Marx's own.

Thus, in order to get at the very important but neglected issue of the development of Marx's *Capital*, 1867–75, but especially 1872–75, one needs first to peel away layers of interpretation that create a conceptual barrier blocking the consideration of such a project as a meaningful and important endeavour. The first step in going beyond that conceptual barrier is to take seriously the French edition of *Capital*, both because Marx himself consistently told his readers and other interlocutors to do so and because an examination of the text of this edition reveals important treasures, some of them already found and some of them still to be found. To enhance this effort, which is crucial to a deeper understanding of *Capital*, the French edition should be translated into as many languages as possible, in order for the text of Marx's last version to become available to general readers across the world. Or, failing that, *variorum* editions of the work should be produced so that readers can see for themselves the alternate texts left aside by Engels.[26]

Notes

1 I would like to thank Peter Hudis, Karel Ludenhoff, and Rodrigo Pinho for their comments on this chapter.

2 See also Outhwaite and Smith (2020) who suggest that Engels's disparagement of the French edition may have concerned Roy's translation, not the final version of the French edition as considerably altered by Marx. But see below the discussion

of Engels's negative comments on the French edition even after the translation was revised by Marx and published.

3 D. Levine (1995), in his *Visions of the Sociological Tradition*, rightly considered the Marxian tradition as a separate strand from the various national sociological traditions, whether German, British, French, or Italian.

4   Henceforth in the text of this chapter, *Capital* without a designated volume number will refer to *Volume I*, while references to other volumes will always carry volume numbers.

5 At the same time, Engels acknowledges openly that he was using only 'sparingly' a list Marx sent to their comrade Friedrich Sorge in the U.S. concerning how to use the French edition for an English one, because, he wrote, these instructions were older than his conversations with Marx (1976: 110).

6 He did, however, indicate that in chapter one he had decided to *aplatir* (water down) the French version for greater readability. But even here, his use of the word *aplatir* leaves some ambiguity, as it could also carry the meanings of 'make plain' or 'smooth out', i.e., clarify.

7 Pinho (2021: 38–9) has provided the most detailed examination to date of what Marx and Engels each said about the French edition.

8 The only dispute between the two men of which I am aware that reached this level of serious and sustained disagreement, and also on an important question, occurred during their correspondence during the first years of the U.S. Civil War. In this period, Engels underestimated the capacities of the industrial North in its struggle against pro-slavery secessionists who had gained the loyalty of most of the nation's top military officers. For a discussion, see my 2010 book (Anderson 2010: 79–114), chapter 3.

9 Marx intended to shape all of what became *Volumes II* and *III* into what he referred to as a second volume of *Capital*.

10 The bracketed French word *dernière* (final) replaces the current English translation's term 'extreme limit' (based probably on Engels's translation of the French as *äusserste Grenze*), which seems slightly less dramatic than what Marx wrote. See Marx (1989a: 548; Marx 1991: 563).

11 Again, 'extreme' has been replaced by 'final', plus 'social capital' (based probably upon Engels's translation of the French as *gesellschaftliche Kapital*) has been replaced by 'national capital', also in keeping with the French. See Marx (1989: 548; 1991: 563).

12 Ernest Untermann, who updated the 1887 English edition based upon Engels's 1890 German one, refers in his 1906 editor's note to 'about ten pages of text not hitherto rendered into English' (Marx 1919: 10).

13 In Stalinist fashion, this edition did not refer to the earlier Kerr edition.

14 To be clear, it is not a question of assessing each altered passage in the French edition as necessarily 'better' than in the 1872 German one. Just as with the 1844 *Economic and Philosophical Manuscripts* or the *Grundrisse*, one could easily claim that some earlier texts are philosophically richer than later ones on similar issues. Regarding the 1872 German and the 1872–75 French edition of *Capital*, one instance where Marx cuts short a phrase might be seen as problematic. This occurs in chapter one, where he writes in the German edition that in capitalist production, 'social relations ... appear as what they are ... as *material relations between persons and* social relations between things', but he removes the phrase here placed in italics from the French edition – (Marx 1976: 166; 1989a: 54). In this example, it is unclear if the new version is shallower, or rather simply clearer in its parsimoniousness. In another passage,

however, Marx writes in the German edition of a 'dialectical inversion' whereby the 'means of production' come to dominate the very workers who created them, and at the same time 'they degrade him [the worker] to the level of an appendage of a machine' and 'they alienate from him the intellectual potentialities of the labour process' (Marx 1976: 799). Again in the French edition, the passage is slightly shortened, removing the phrase 'dialectical inversion' and the clause about alienated labour (Marx 1989a: 567–8). This passage, it could be argued, lacks the philosophical depth of the German version. But this should not lead us to conclude that the French edition is shorn of dialectical language. For Marx kept lots of Hegelian language in the French edition, whether in his use of the phrase 'negation of the negation' in the discussion of working class revolution in the penultimate chapter, or in his inclusion of those parts of the postface to the 1872 German edition where he discusses 'my dialectical method' (Marx 1976: 929, 102; 1989a: 679, 696).

15 This passage was incorporated into the 1976 English edition in a footnote even though it had not appeared in Engels's 1890 German edition. For Raya Dunayevskaya (1982: 139–51), in her *Rosa Luxemburg, Women's Liberation, and Marx's Philosophy of Revolution*, this and other alternate texts from the French edition became the basis for one of the first critiques of Engels's failure to incorporate fully the French edition, in a section of a chapter titled 'Capital: Significance of the 1875 French Edition of Volume 1'. Up until now, Dunayevskaya does not appear to have been aware that Engels had left out any major passages from the French edition. Personal note: It was during this period, that Dunayevskaya, who was my mentor, urged me to write what became my first article on the French edition (Anderson 1983: 71–80). For another early critique, see Arthur (1996: 173–209).

16 According the MEGA[2] editors, the quotation is from the unknown George Potter's letter to the editor of the London *Times* article of 9 September 1873, not from MP Stapleton (1215-apparatus).

17 Because of the importance of this and the next altered passage, I have included in the notes the respective German and French versions. In the original German, this passage reads: 'Das industriell entwickeltere Land zeigt dem minder entwickelten nur das Bild der eignen Zukunft' (Marx 1991: 8).

18 This passage has also troubled Marxists. Leon Trotsky wrote in 1939, 'Under no circumstances can this thought be taken literally' – see Trotsky (2006: 39) – and Dunayevskaya (1958: 259) ventured with regard to this sentence, 'The same, it must add, is true in reverse'.

19 In the original French, this reads: 'Le pays le plus développé industriellement ne fait que montrer a ceux qui le suivent sur l'échelle industrielle l'image de leur propre avenir'. Curiously, this change is not noted in either MEGA[2], volume I/7 or MEGA[2] volume II/10, even though the editors of MEGA[2] volume II/7 do note several other changes to the 1867 preface in the French edition. It is hard to believe that so significant an alteration in so widely discussed a sentence went unnoticed by the editors. But here it should be noted that MEGA[2] volume II/7 appeared in 1989, when the MEGA[2] edition was still being published under the auspices of the Institutes of Marxism-Leninism of the USSR and East Germany, which may have been a constraining factor.

20 In the original German, this reads:

> Die Expropriation des ländlichen Producenten, des Bauern, von Grund und Boden bildet die Grundlage des Ganzen Processes. Ihre Geschichte nimmt

in verschiedenen Ländern veschiedene Färbung an und durchläuft die veschiedenen Phases in verschiedener Reihenfolge und in verschiedenen Geschichtsepochen. Nur in England, das wir daher als Beispiel nehmen, besitzt sie klassische Form.

(Marx 1989a: 634)

21 In the original French, this reads:

Mais la base de toute cette évolution, c'est l'expropriation des cultivateurs. Elle ne s'est encore accomplie d'une manière radical qu'en Angleterre: ce pays jouera donc nécessairement le premier rôle dans notre esquisse. Mais tous les autres pays de l'Europe occidentale parcourent le même mouvement, bien que selon le milieu il change de couleur locale, ou se resserre dans un cercle plus étroit, ou présente un caractère moins fortement prononcé, ou suivre un ordre de succession différent.

(Marx 1985: 169)

22 Maximilien Rubel was one of the first Marx scholars to call attention to this alteration in his Marx (1963: 1701), *Oeuvres I. Économie,* where he notes that this passage 'is not included in the German edition' but that Marx cited it in his 1881 letter to Vera Zasulich. To be discussed below.

23 For a recent Marxist critique that stresses Engels's differences with Marx, see Brown (2012); see also Dunayevskaya (1982), for the first feminist critique of Engels that differentiated him from Marx on gender.

24 For an overview of Marx's last years, see Musto (2020); see also Anderson (2010). On the Marx's last research notes, on Egypt, see Smith (2021: 151–215).

25 Emphasis and ellipses are Marx's. He wrote the letter in French and the MECW translation has here been slightly altered for consistency. The first sentence before the first ellipsis is not an exact quote and seems to be Marx's a summary of a longer sentence that precedes the remainder of the quoted passage. The rest of the quoted passage can be found in Marx (1989: 634).

26 At present, French is the only language in which both Engels's 1890 German edition and Marx's 1872–75 French edition have been published (the former by a group actually seeking to undercut Marx's French edition (see Marx 1983), while a translation of the French edition is currently underway in Brazil. A *variorum* edition based on Engels's German edition but with marginal variants from the French edition was published in Persian by Hassan Mortazavi and his colleagues in Iran (Marx 2008). The entire printing of 10,000 copies sold out quickly and a reprint has not been permitted. For background, see Afary (2011: 215–32). Thomas Kuczynski's edition (Marx 2017) incorporates into an accessible German edition all of the changes that editor Kuczynski ascertains Engels should have included. Even though it does not let readers easily see the textual variants for themselves in the ways that a *variorum* edition would allow, this is a remarkable achievement of rigorous scholarship.

References

Afary, Frieda (2011) 'A New Persian Translation of *Capital*', in *Beiträge zur Marx-Engels Forschung Neue Folge*, pp. 215–32.

Althusser, Louis (1985) 'Avertissement aux lecteurs du Livre I du *Capital*', in Karl Marx, *Le Capital*, Paris: Flammarion, pp. 7–30.

Anderson, Kevin B. (1983) 'The "Unknown" Marx's *Capital*, vol. I: The French Edition of 1872-75, 100 Years Later', *Review of Radical Political Economics*, vol. 15, n. 4: 71–80.

Anderson, Kevin B. (2010) *Marx at the Margins: On Nationalism, Ethnicity, and Non-Western Societies*, Chicago: University of Chicago Press.

Arthur, Christopher J. (1996) 'Engels as Interpreter of Marx's Economics', in *Engels Today: A Centennial Appreciation*, London: Macmillan, pp. 173–209.

Brown, Heather (2012) *Marx on Gender and the Family: A Critical Study*, Leiden, Brill.

Dunayevskaya, Raya (1958) *Marxism and Freedom. From 1776 until Today*, New York: Bookman Associates.

Dunayevskaya, Raya (1982) *Rosa Luxemburg, Women's Liberation, and Marx's Philosophy of Revolution*, New Jersey: Humanities Press.

Gaudin, François, ed. (2019) *Traduire Le Capital: une correspondance inédite entre Karl Marx, Friedrich Engels et l'éditeur Maurice Lachâtre*, Rouen: Presses Universitaires de Rouen et du Havre.

James, C.L.R., Dunayevskaya, Raya, and Boggs, Grace Lee (2013) *State Capitalism and World Revolution*, Oakland: PM Press.

Levine, Donald N. (1995) *Visions of the Sociological Tradition*, Chicago: University of Chicago Press.

Marx, Karl (1919) *Capital: A Critique of Political Economy*, vol. I, Chicago: Charles H. Kerr & Co.

Marx, Karl (1939) *Capital: A Critical Analysis of Capitalist Production*, vol. I, New York: International Publishers.

Marx, Karl (1963) *Oeuvres I. Économie,* Paris: Éditions Gallimard.

Marx, Karl (1976) *Capital: A Critique of Political Economy*, vol. I, London: Penguin.

Marx, Karl (1983) *Le Capital*, vol. 1, Paris: Messidor/Éditions Sociales.

Marx, Karl (1985) *Le Capital. Livre I. Sections V à VIII*, Paris: Éditions Flammarion.

Marx, Karl (1989a) *Le Capital Paris 1872-75*, in *Marx Engels Gesamtausgabe* (MEGA^2) vol. II/7, Berlin: Dietz Verlag.

Marx, Karl (1989b) *Das Kapital Kritik der politschen Ökonomie Erster Band Hamburg 1883*, in *Marx Engels Gesamtausgabe* (MEGA^2), vol. II/8, Berlin: Dietz Verlag.

Marx, Karl (1991) *Das Kapital Kritik der politschen Ökonomie Erster Band Hamburg 1890*, in *Marx Engels Gesamtausgabe* (MEGA^2), vol. II/10, Berlin: Dietz Verlag.

Marx, Karl (2008) *Capital: A Critique of Political Economy* [Persian], Tehran: Agah Publishing House.

Marx, Karl (2010) '*Capital*, vol. I', in *Marx Engels Collected Works*, vol. 35, London: Lawrence & Wishart Ltd.

Marx, Karl (2017) *Das Kapital: Kritik der politischen Ökonomie,* Hamburg: VSA Verlag.

Marx, Karl and Engels, Friedrich (1989a) *Marx Engels Collected Works*, vol. 24, *Marx and Engels 1874–83*, New York: International Publishers.

Marx, Karl and Engels, Friedrich (1989b) *Marx Engels Collected Works*, vol. 44: *Letters 1870-1873*, Moscow: Progress Publishers.

Marx, Karl and Engels, Friedrich (1991) *Marx Engels Collected Works*, vol. 45: *Letters 1874-1879*, Moscow: Progress Publishers.

Musto, Marcello (2020) *The Last Years of Karl Marx: An Intellectual Biography*, Stanford: Stanford University Press.

Outhwaite, William and Smith, Kenneth (2020) 'Le Capital', *Review of Radical Political Economics*, vol. 52, n. 2: 208–21.

Pinho, Rodrigo (2021) 'The Originality of the French Edition of Capital: An Historical Analysis', *The International Marxist-Humanist*, September 3, pp. 1–45.

Shanin, Teodor, Ed. (1983) *Late Marx and the Russian Road*, New York: Monthly Review Press.

Smith, David Norman (2021) 'Accumulation and Its Discontents: Migration and Nativism in Marx's *Capital* and Late Manuscripts', in *Rethinking Alternatives with Marx: Economy, Ecology and Migration*, edited by Marcello Musto, New York: Palgrave Macmillan, pp. 151–215.

Trotsky, Leon, ed. (2006) *The Essential Marx* [*The Living Thoughts of Karl Marx*], New York: Dover Books.

4   The French Edition of *Capital* and the Question of Colonialism

Jean-Numa Ducange

Introduction

The relationship of Karl Marx and of Marxism more generally to the colonial question is an important field of research – and one that has attracted renewed interest over the last 15 years, amidst the buzz surrounding postcolonial studies. While it is important to emphasise the plurality of such studies, it is clear that many of them take a critical perspective on the history of socialism and especially of Marxism, considering these as Western ideologies that have proven incapable of structurally grasping the particularities of colonised societies. The critical reference in this regard is Edward Said's *Orientalism*; this work has been followed by a number of articles and books which have taken up the thesis that Karl Marx remained a fundamentally white, Western thinker, steeped in Orientalist prejudices, who had little capacity to think about non-European societies (Saïd 1978: 12).

These critiques have prompted responses from several scholars who – drawing on their own considerable erudition with regard to Marx – show, citations in hand, that these conclusions are too narrow and take into account only a limited body of his writings. Among the most significant works that strike down the most caricatural aspects of Said's argument are the studies by Kevin Anderson (Anderson 2010) and, more recently, Marcello Musto (2020). Both show that, especially in his final years (1880–83), Karl Marx made an important shift, devoting close attention to non-European societies and to their possible future paths of development. In particular, Anderson points to the emergence of a genuine 'multilinear theory of history' in Marx from the 1850s onwards.

In this context, the present article intends to review the particular developments relating to colonisation in Joseph Roy's French translation of *Capital, Volume I*. Indeed, in this translation we can see some significant turning points, which are also foregrounded by today's historiography in order to demonstrate Marx's evolution on this subject. Marx's famous sentence in the postface to the French translation emphasises that this Lachâtre edition of Roy's translation has an autonomous value of its own. Can this general comment be applied to the question of colonisation? Answering this question implies going beyond the usual conclusions about the changes included in the French edition of *Capital, Volume I*.

DOI: 10.4324/9781003336365-5

Indeed, to answer this question it is necessary to situate Marx's work concerning France in a longer-term perspective, and moreover to study the 1872–75 edition as close as possible as a connection to the French realities that may have influenced the textual changes authorised by Marx. Until now, studies on the Roy translation have often remained internal to the text and have solely focused upon a comparison with the German-language editions of *Capital, Volume I* (especially the first one). Yet it seems that the internal study of the texts of *Capital, Volume I* tends to lay exaggerated focus on certain factors, to the detriment of others.

The Roy translation and the colonial question: A clarification

First of all, it is necessary to note some key points of comparison between the German edition of 1867 and the French edition of 1872–75. The critical apparatus of the *Marx Engels Gesamtausgabe* for the volumes concerned (published in 1989; these were among the last volumes of the MEGA^2 published in the German Democratic Republic) gives a series of precise indications (Marx 1989). It is first worth emphasising that several passages (on Malthus or the physiocrats, for example) were reworked better to suit the French readership. While there had been 25 chapters in the 1867 edition, there are 33 in the French edition, many of them subsequently integrated into the third German edition. The introduction also stresses the importance of the additions or deletions to the final chapters on primitive accumulation (Marx 1989: 33). In particular, it is mentioned that, compared to his earlier 1867 line of argument, Marx here placed more emphasis on the different rhythms of this accumulation in different countries. Without delving into the question in greater detail, the MEGA^2 does point to the importance of these changes, illustrating Marx's desire to better grasp different people's stages of development. In support of this idea, it cites the case of Russia and Marx's exchanges with Vera Zasulich, in particular a March 1881 letter that mentions the French edition. But there is no particular elaboration on the passages concerning colonial questions.

Yet, as Kevin Anderson notes, given the passages in the French translation in which Marx does adopt a new orientation on this question of different peoples, this edition marks a significant milestone in his reading of the colonial question. Anderson notes the 'considerable alterations' (Anderson 2010: 173) in this French edition. Kolja Lindner (2010) also highlights this in a landmark text on Marx and non-European societies. This is of particular interest for understanding Marx's development, as the third German edition of *Capital, Volume I* – which includes some of the changes made in the French edition – was mainly prepared by Engels and published after Marx's death. Marx himself supervised the changes, as he recalled in a 28 May 1872 letter to Danielson, the translator of the Russian edition:

> Although the French edition [...] has been prepared by a great expert in the two languages, he has often translated too literally. I have therefore found myself compelled to rewrite whole passages in French, to make them

palatable to the French public. It will be all the easier later on to translate the book from French into English and Romance languages.

(Marx 1987: 385)

Marx attached great importance to the changes he had introduced into the French edition and especially those in the section on 'primitive accumulation' (Anderson 2010: 176–7). Indeed, in the 1867 edition, the history of primitive accumulation appears as part of Western European history. In the French edition, he contemplates the question at a more general level, potentially including the history of all humanity; thus, the work loses its 'Western-centric' aspect.

Indeed, the deletion of certain sentences illustrates the important changes that were made between the two editions. First worthy of attention is a deleted sentence that had appeared in the preface to the 1867 edition, emphasising the direction of history: 'The country that is more developed industrially only shows, to the less developed, the image of its own future' (Marx 1989: 12).

Another example is this sentence in the chapter on the primitive accumulation of capital: 'These idyllic proceedings are the chief moments of primitive accumulation' (Marx 1989: 668). The 'chief moments [*Hauptmomente*]' are a Hegelian formula ('Hauptmomente'). Anderson (2010: 188) points out 'that Marx removed this sentence for more substantive reasons, to avoid merging India and the Americas – and China as well – into a single totality in which all societies could be seen as necessarily following the same pathway'.

For Anderson, these few alterations make it clear that Marx distanced himself from unilinear approaches. Drawing on Marx's other parallel works, he notes, for example, that Marx had enthusiastically supported Irish independence since 1869–70 and made a greater opening towards geographical areas such as Russia. Anderson concludes from this that the French edition of *Capital, Volume I* represents an important turning point, such as could already be noted in the *Grundrisse* and the *Critique of Political Economy*, and which would later be continued.

Utopian socialism: The source of socialist colonialism?

Anderson's demonstration is of great value in understanding little-known aspects of Marx. But as far as the particular character of the French edition is concerned, it seems to take too little account of Marx's longer-term relationship with France. Upon revisiting Marx's overall approach in *Capital, Volume I*, it is indeed necessary, to quote David Harvey, to have three sources in mind:

[his] new scientific method is predicated on the interrogation of the primarily British tradition of classical political economy, using the tools of the mainly German tradition of critical philosophy, all applied to illuminate the mainly French utopian impulse in order to answer the following questions: what is communism …? How can we both understand and critique

capitalism scientifically in order to chart the path to communist revolution more effectively?

(Harvey 2020: 6)

In the preparations for the French edition, which Marx wished to tailor to a particular audience, so-called 'utopian socialism' was thus an essential concern, for it had a profound impact on the partisans of socialism in that country, at least up till the end of the nineteenth century. France was, in large measure, the happiest hunting ground for utopian socialism (with the likes of Saint-Simon, Etienne Cabet, and Charles Fourier). Of course, Marx was already influenced by this concern in preparing the German edition of 1867, but his many contacts with Joseph Roy, and especially with publisher Maurice Lachâtre,[1] show that, in the aftermath of the Commune of 1871, Marx fully immersed himself in a French context with which he had become closely familiar during a stay in Paris between 1843 and 1845. Indeed, one of Marx's avowed aims in the aftermath of the Commune was to fight against the influence of Proudhonism, which was particularly influential in the International Workingmen's Association, and of the various socialisms inherited from utopianism, which seemed to him to be incapable of responding to the challenges of the present. Marx always thought that the political wealth of French socialism was inversely proportional to its capacity to grasp political economy and the functioning of capitalism.

While it is difficult to arrive at any exhaustive view of what Marx knew about French socialism and its relationship to the colonies, it is not insignificant to note that, in *The Civil War in France*, Marx never mentions the unrest in Algeria during the Commune, particularly in Kabylia. However, there was a movement in Algiers which called itself the 'Commune', in explicit reference to 1792–93. Here, it is worth noting a few facts on this subject. The historian Quentin Deluermoz recently underlined that there are indeed extant traces of the mobilisation in Algeria in spring 1871 – mobilisations that were mentioned at the time in the French press (Deluermoz, 2020: 143). Led by colonists who wanted to strengthen their local power as well as republicans and utopian socialists, the Algiers Commune was the first to be created in France's colonial empire. Then, with the proclamation of the Paris Commune, the Algiers radicals sent an address of congratulations and support for the Commune. One of the leading figures of the movement in Algiers, Alexandre Lambert, was even promoted to the rank of Algeria's delegate to the Commune, before he became 'head of office at the Interior Ministry'. The Commune movement was not exempt from having to address the colonial problem. But these realities were of little interest to the various socialist currents of the time – apart from those active on the ground there – nor to Marx, who would not write about Algeria until the twilight of his life (Musto 2020: 115).

Most importantly, the socialists of the time, of whatever sensibility, had next to no critical relationship with colonisation. However, this did not mean that they had no interest in it – quite the contrary. Algeria was considered a French territory, and the colonisation of such a territory was seen as legitimate, or even as a unique opportunity to realise the utopian aspirations of socialism. There is no precise record of how Marx specifically perceived French colonisation in the early 1870s, nor indeed of his assessment of French socialist opinion on the subject. But, studying more closely the French socialist literature on colonial issues from the early 1840s to 1872–75, it is impossible that Marx was unaware of it. Marx read the utopian socialists' writings, as evidenced by several of his works but also by his many notes recently published as part of the MEGA[2] (Marx 2015). In the mid-1840s he associated with several French socialist leaders who had a particular relationship to colonial issues – a fact that is widely underestimated across all works regarding Marx's relationship to France.

In his study of the republicans of the first half of the nineteenth century, who shared many points in common with the early socialist currents, Philippe Darriulat (2001: 42) has pointed out that these 'patriots' attributed France a particular mission, which was fully able to include colonial dimension. As for the 'utopian socialists' to whom historiography has devoted numerous studies – and who themselves greatly inspired Marx and Engels – only recently has the importance of their conceptions regarding the colonies been demonstrated. It is thus necessary to emphasise that 'the nascent socialist movement massively favoured the colonisation of Algeria' (Marçot 2014: 79) in the 1830s and 1840s. This is a fact rarely underlined by historical overviews, even though it is very much visible in the sources of the time. Without doubt, the social question soon marginalised the colonial question, making the latter less visible. But it was impossible to escape it completely.

Here, it is worth noting the example of Charles Fourier, read and contemplated by Marx. He was initially strongly pro-war and in favour of colonial conquest. In February 1823, Fourier communicated to the Paris Geographical Society a plan intended 'to devote all the savage and man-eating tribes to the sudden adoption of big industry and civilised mores' (Fourier 1823). Many socialists were the pioneers and architects of the notion of 'French Algeria', which would in the twentieth century become a nationalist and reactionary idea. The term 'colonial' is also very much present in Prosper Enfantin's *Colonisation de l'Algérie*. For Enfantin (1843: 488), Algeria is 'an excellent testing ground for several great social questions that are troubling France'. The book was published in 1843, the same year that Marx arrived in Paris.

Enfantin's concerns reflected those of many socialists who believed that the colonial project should be built on a collectivist system that would ensure its success. Colonisation was taken as a political solution to a major economic problem of the nineteenth century: the destitution caused by the social question. In Marx's extant manuscripts and notes from this period, there is no trace of the writings and controversies on the colonial question that occupied the French socialists at the time. Marx appears to have been totally uninterested in the question when he read and frequented the utopian socialists.

This is fully confirmed, for example, by his relationship to the work of Théodore Dezamy. Dezamy is rarely mentioned in histories of socialism in the 1840s, but several studies have highlighted his central role in the development of early Parisian communism (Maillard 1999: 50). He is even sometimes recognised as having played a central role in the later evolution of the German emigrants in Paris. In the *Holy Family*, Marx and Engels explicitly mention him as having 'developed the teaching of *materialism* as the teaching of *real humanism* and the *logical* basis of *communism*' (Marx and Engels 1975: 388). Among his works that bore great influence in the 1840s and at least up till the end of the nineteenth century is his *Code de la Communauté*. Moses Hess began the translation of this *Code* for a 'Library of Leading Socialist Writers' which he planned together with Marx and Engels, but it never saw the light of day.

At the end of 1842, Dezamy also published, together with other communists, an *Almanach de la Communauté pour 1843 par divers écrivains communistes* [*Community Almanac for 1843 by various communist writers*]. He also published a pamphlet, *Gardera-t-on Alger?* [*Will We Hold Onto Algiers*]. Many studies relating to these 'neo-Babouvists' and their influence on Marx do not mention the question of French Algeria. Yet it was very much central to current affairs during his stay in Paris. And communists like Dezamy were in favour of the colonisation of Algerian territory. In the *Almanach*, Dezamy damned the British aristocracy's manoeuvres against France, aimed at conquering Algerian territory. Louis-Philippe – the then-reigning French king – was said to have made a pact to turn popular opinion against French Algeria. The appalling repression against the Algerians was said to be the result of a 'pact of solidarity' among aristocrats: the British threatened to wage war against France and thus demanded Algeria. As a result, the French elites were supposedly doing their utmost to turn their own population against French Algeria, in accordance with a secret agreement with the British. Perhaps this reading of Algeria constitutes one of the sources of Marx's 'orientalist' formulas in the 1840s.

But what about the time when *Capital, Volume I* was written, and more particularly the time of the French translation? Kevin Anderson rightly describes this period as a turning point in Marx's positions. It is possible to supplement this by suggesting that one hypothetical explanation for why he distanced himself from this 'colonial socialism' may lie in the distance he took from French socialism from 1848 to 1850. In Marx's estimation, this socialism had not lived up to its historical task in 1848. Its pro-colonial positions could thus also be considered mistaken. This is a plausible suggestion, especially seeing as from London Marx continued to take an interest in French political life and especially in the development of Napoleon III's Second Empire. In the 1860s, the Saint-Simonians (some of whom supported the Emperor) were preoccupied with the question of the development of Algerian territory, a question on which they published numerous texts. Marx could not have failed to read texts referring to this question; he must have seen how determined many were to build up French Algeria.

'Colonisation': The realities of the early 1870s

The fact remains that the French colonial world was of only marginal interest to Marx when he was preparing *Capital, Volume I*. But what exactly was the situation in the aftermath of the Paris Commune? Marx was still in London, but he followed French affairs especially closely during the Commune and its immediate aftermath. What place did the idea of 'colonisation' have in the French press and opinion at that time? Firstly, it is worth emphasising the continual extension of the French Empire: New Caledonia was conquered in 1852, and most importantly the repression of the revolt in Kabylia in 1857 reinforced French domination. On 7 July 1864, a decree placed the civilian authorities under the supervision of military officers in Algiers. An analysis of the contemporary French press at the end of the 1860s shows that colonial policy occupied an important place, even without being the single main issue (Masson 1962: 368). The elites at odds with Napoleon III mobilised themselves in this regard to the point where 'criticism of the colonial administration was the battle horse of the defenders of the colonies' (Masson 1962: 374). It should be noted that at the level of general public opinion, including that of the workers and the popular classes, if colonial questions were of relatively little interest, those more specifically regarding Algeria did have a certain echo. Significantly, in the political lexicon of the time, the words 'Algerian question' are scattered throughout political life (while for example, there is no reference in this vocabulary to a 'Caledonian question' or similar ones regarding other peoples under French rule). Yet there was an abundance of criticism, including from the Bonapartists, who considered the maintenance of order in Algiers to be particularly badly run and costly. The numerous criticisms of this administration hardly encouraged consideration of the colonial order as immutable and untouchable, and it was not uncommon to read articles praising the greater merits of Britain's administration of its colonies, as compared to the French (Masson 1962: 426).

Marx probably followed suit on this point, noting the difficulties of the French colonial enterprise and its uncertain future. Thus, the shift in emphasis in the French edition, as highlighted especially by Kevin Anderson, ought to be put into perspective. This readjustment perhaps also took account of the particular French context: Algeria was directly integrated into France and its system of *départments* and stood in the immediate vicinity of the metropole, unlike the British colonies which were much more remote. In this sense, it seems exaggerated to see this as a real jumping-off point towards grasping the particularities of the colonial world.

Nevertheless, there did remain a certain sensitivity to this question in Marx, certainly also owing to the Russian edition of *Capital, Volume I.* Marx took much more interest in colonial questions, albeit without making them a central focus. It is worth noting a certain counter-intuitive aspect of this development: Marx evolved on this question by being 'scientific' and less 'utopian'. *Capital, Volume I* was less colonial than the young Marx's French acquaintances had been. In the Paris of 1843, the socialists were fascinated by the colonial endeavour, whereas the Marx of the 1860s was not. In today's historiographical context, marked by the rehabilitation of utopianism as against 'scientific socialism', it seems important to underline this point. It was the most 'scientific' part of Marx's work – *Capital* as reworked for the French edition – which showed a certain change of orientation on this question.

A 'question of method': 'Marxology' and *Capital*

Beyond the intrinsic interest of Marx's changing position on this point, the place of colonisation in the French edition of *Capital, Volume I* seems to provide an excellent example of the problems posed by so-called 'Marxology'. In the French context, this latter saw particular development thanks to Maximilien Rubel, editor of Marx's works in French in the 1960s and 1970s in the prestigious 'La Pléiade' collection published by Gallimard, one of France's most important publishers (Abensour and Janover 2008: 13). Rubel wanted to publish a Marx counterposed to Marxism – at the time essentially meaning, Soviet-style 'Marxism-Leninism', which in Rubel's view had distorted Marx's writings and arguments. He also founded – and long ran – the *Études de marxologie* journal, published from 1959 to 1994. Marxology aims to be as close as possible to Marx's text and the context in which it was written, as against subsequent Marxism. Such an approach has made it possible to unearth and highlight texts by Marx that were previously little known or unavailable and has invited work on the different versions of *Capital, Volume I*. From this point of view, Rubel's work was indeed useful. But it is striking to note that Rubel did not reckon with Marx's evolution on several subjects, including the colonial question, about which he wrote very little.

Above all, it seems that this Marxological approach remains limited in at least two essential aspects. First, while the philological, internal study of Marx's texts does make it possible to understand certain logics, it sometimes prevents us from resituating them in a wider context. Indeed, a study so focused on the texts can sometimes leave out essential factors; thus, the approach promoted by Rubel can in some ways lead to results at odds with his initial ambitions. For example, a close analysis of the changes between the various editions of *Capital, Volume I* shows that there are indeed considerable changes in the colonial question. But the focus on an almost line-by-line study of the text overlooks the fundamental reasons why, despite everything, colonisation is not at the heart of *Capital, Volume I*, but rather at the margins, within an overall context that also has particularities of its own. Understanding the changes that took place in Marx's references to the colonial question would require a longer-term understanding of the French socialist movement, whose texts Marx read and which he sometimes physically encountered. Without this, it seems that we will miss the essential point: namely, that Marx's views on colonisation remained largely dependent on other positions which did not, as such, appear in *Capital, Volume I*. It seems that authors such as Kevin Anderson and Kolja Lindner proceed in continuity with Rubel's approach, which, although useful on certain points, can sometimes prove problematic. It is significant that, while rejecting the most caricatural aspects of Rubel, Kevin Anderson paid a tribute to his method in a 1992 article, at a time when he had already published numerous contributions on Marx.

While criticising certain caricatural aspects of Rubel's work (notably the total dissociation between Marx and Engels) Anderson emphasises that

> after putting those points to the side, one can begin to appreciate some of the important and pioneering scholarly work Rubel has done to unearth unknown writings of Marx, and to show omission or flaws in the editing of known ones.
>
> (Anderson 1992: 89)

The second aspect concerns the Marxism so castigated by Rubel, which is also widely criticised by Anderson in his book. According to Anderson, many Marxist authors and thinkers have based their reflection on the *Manifesto of the Communist Party*, which he understands as a largely European-centred text, totally external to non-European problematics. Mechanistic Marxism is said to have taken up this idea of a socialism that had to be created primarily in Paris, London, Berlin, and Vienna. Within this framework, it follows, there is no possibility of a 'multilinear' theory of history. But what is factually true in the context of the time – certainly in 1848, Marx and Engels were wagering on European events – prevents us from thinking of the full potential impact of a text as vivid and disruptive as the *Manifesto of the Communist Party*, even outside of its initial framework. Indeed, in the twentieth century, most of the Third World leaders who looked to Marx for arguments in support of the fight against colonial domination largely drew on his best-known and yet 'European-centred' texts, such as the *Manifesto of the Communist Party*. Analyses that tend to systematically counterpose *Capital, Volume I* to the 'unilinearism' of the *Manifesto of the Communist Party* also seem dubious. This is again the problem of Marxology and the tradition it represents, which sees Marxism, taken as a whole, as merely a distorting ideology. This is, in fact, to underestimate its power to mobilise in the name of Marx. From this point of view, the *Manifesto of the Communist Party* has certainly contributed much more to 'de-Orientalising' Marxism than the passages on colonisation in the French edition of *Capital*, even though they are more significant in substance.

This is, moreover, how Marxist currents thought and perceived this question in the decades when Marx's thought was most widely read internationally, that is, in the 1970s. Take, for example, the selection of texts by Marx and Engels (1960) titled *On Colonialism,* later translated into multiple languages by Moscow's Foreign Languages Publishing House. Widely distributed throughout the world in the 1970s, the French translation (Marx and Engels 1977) enjoyed especially wide circulation in Francophone Africa, in the former French colonies. Several excerpts from *Capital* can be found therein. Roy's translation is included, and the anthology includes many passages where Marx's change of orientation is clear. For example, in the passages on primitive accumulation, this edition reflects the deletion of some overly 'Hegelian' formulations. However, in the general introduction to the collection, there is a strong emphasis on Marx's sharpest and most clear-sighted texts in opposition to the colonial order, in particular regarding the Sepoy Revolt in India in 1857. As concerns *Capital*, it is soberly stated that 'Excerpts from Marx's *Capital* dealing with the problems of colonialism are also included in the collection' (Marx and Engels 1977: 7). No mention is made of the changes introduced in the Roy translation.

Prior to scholarly studies such as the one offered by Kevin Anderson in 2010, there was no substantial tradition of analysis which read *Capital, Volume I* in Roy's translation as an important moment for the Marxian critique of the colonial order. Further studies remain to be carried out on whether there was a tradition of analysis of Roy's translation of Marx in the French-speaking colonial world. For instance, there seems to be no evidence that attentive commentators on Marx who read him in French, such as Leopold Senghor or Franz Fanon, noted the particularities of these extracts from *Capital, Volume I* (Yala Kisukidi 2014: 62). The fact remains that if a real turning point on the colonial question is to be identified, it seems to come later, really in the very last Marx. On this point, Marcello Musto has shown that, far from Marx's stay in Algiers being merely anecdotal, during it he made some empathetic notes about the native population (Musto 2020: 108). Here Marx abandoned, albeit without explicitly theorising it, the attachment to 'French Algeria' that had been a constant among socialists since the 1830s. He was initiating a shift which was increasingly felt in French socialism ten years later when, for the first time at a workers' party congress in France, a motion against colonial policy was passed. In Romilly, in 1895, the French Workers' Party adopted a text sharply hostile to colonial policy, a first in the history of French socialism (Ducange 2020: 79). The slight point of departure that could be seen in the Roy translation had finally found a concrete political outlet, even if it was still tentative.

Note

1 See the letters written by Marx, and edited by Patrick Camiller, included in Part IV of this volume titled 'Letters on *Le Capital*'.

References

Abensour, Miguel and Janover, Louis (2008) *Maximilien Rubel: pour découvrir Marx*, Paris: Sens et Tonka.

Anderson, Kevin (1992) 'Rubel's Marxology', *Capital and Class*, n. 47: 67–91.

Anderson, Kevin (2010) *Marx at the Margins – On Nationalism, Ethnicity and Non-Western Societies*, Chicago: University of Chicago Press.

Darriulat, Philippe (2001) *Les patriotes. La gauche républicaine et la nation (1830–1870)*, Paris: Seuil.

Deluermoz, Quentin (2020) *Commune(s). Une traversée des mondes au XIXe siècle*, Paris: Seuil.

Ducange, Jean-Numa (2020) *Jules Guesde. The Birth of Socialism and Marxism in France*, New York: Palgrave Macmillan.

Enfantin, Prosper (1843) *Colonisation de l'Algérie*, Paris: P. Bertrand, libraire.

Fourier, Charles (1823) 'Lettre du 23 février 1823 à la Société de Géographie de Paris', Bibliothèque Nationale de France, Archives de la Société de géographie de Paris, 6bis (2054).

Harvey, David (2020) *A Companion to Marx's 'Capital'*, London: Verso.

Lindner, Kolja (2010) 'Marx's Eurocentrism. Postcolonial Studies and Marx Scholarship', *Radical Philosophy*, n. 161: 27–41.

Maillard, Alain (1999) *La communauté des égaux. Le communisme néo-babouviste dans la France des années 1840*, Paris: Éditions Kimé.

Marçot, Jean-Louis (2014) 'Les premiers socialistes français, la question coloniale et l'Algérie', *Cahiers d'histoire. Revue d'histoire critique*, n. 124: 79–95.

Marx, Karl (1987) 'Marx to Nikolai Danielson. 28 May 1872' in *Marx Engels Collected Works,* vol. 42: *Letters 1864–1868*, London: Lawrence and Wishart, p. 385.

Marx, Karl (1989) '*Le Capital*, Paris 1872–1875' in *Marx Engels Gesamtausgabe* (MEGA²), vol. II/7, Berlin: Akademie Verlag.

Marx, Karl (2015) 'Exzerpte und Notizen Juli 1845 bis Dezember 1850' in *Marx Engels Gesamtausgabe* (MEGA²), vol. IV/5, Berlin: Akademie Verlag.

Marx, Karl and Engels, Friedrich (1960) *On Colonialism*, Moscow: Progress Publishers.

Marx, Karl and Engels, Friedrich (1975) *The Holy Family*, in *Marx Engels Collected Works*, vol. 4: *Marx and Engels 1844–45*, London: Lawrence and Wishart.

Marx, Karl and Engels, Friedrich (1977) *Textes sur le colonialisme,* Moscou: Éditions du Progrès.

Masson, André (1962) 'L'opinion française et les problèmes coloniaux à la fin du Second Empire', *Revue d'histoire d'Outre-Mer*, n. 176–7: 366–437.

Musto, Marcello (2020) *The Last Years of Karl Marx, 1881-1883: An Intellectual Biography*, Stanford: Stanford University Press.

Said, Edward (1978) *Orientalism*, London: Routledge and Kegan Paul.

Yala Kisudiki, Nadia (2014) 'Vie éthique et pensée de la libération. Lecture critique des usages senghoriens de Marx à partir de Fanon', *Actuel Marx*, n. 55: 60–72.

5 Engels and *Le Capital*

The Politics of the Fourth Edition of *Das Kapital* (1890)

Terrell Carver

Introduction

The relationship between Friedrich Engels and political economy – taking this term in a very wide and overtly politicised sense – was a very long-standing one, starting in his teenage years and finishing with his death. Yet this conjunction of man, ideas and activities is rarely considered as a self-driven, lifelong set of interests. Famously during his lifetime Engels involved himself with Karl Marx in various ways, and in that blinding glare his self-sustaining trajectory gets rather lost.[1] Overwhelmingly Engels's relationship to history, and to us, is manifested in and through his posthumous, textual relationship with Marx.[2]

In life the two were not quite the double-act-duo that Marx's reception has made them, and indeed Engels set the terms for that, casting himself as junior partner. Their array of venues and associates was always very multilateral in both directions, but many if not most of those associates, interlocutors and sparring partners now appear as walk-ons in Marx's and Engels's lives and as bit-players in their conjoined biographies.[3] Overwhelmingly the genre-tropes of biography control the contextualisations through which the two are understood as intellectuals thinking thoughts, albeit with occasional biographical nods to actions and activities. Their lived experiences, even when library-based, were in fact the other way round.

That 'second fiddle' (Ryazanov 1927: 216–7) relationship of Engels to Marx was of course highly variegated and notably varied with time and circumstance, and in any case over forty years there really wasn't 'a relationship' as such. The present volume focuses on political economy and on Marx's monumental critique, so Engels appears conventionally as an adjunct: adviser, reviewer and editor. After Marx's death Engels haunted himself with the great man's spectre, and ever since so has everyone else.

Possibly, though, there is another way of looking at this. And perhaps Engels's work on the fourth German edition of *Capital, Volume I*, published only five years before his death, is a good place to start (Marx 1996a). While not the swansong represented by his editorial work on *Capital, Volume III* (Marx 1998),[4] the fourth German edition of Volume I was a career-ending and, in a significant sense, career-spanning effort. In the political terms of the time that

DOI: 10.4324/9781003336365-6

book was a major German socialist and proto-Marxist project, and the most important volume to get right by far. It was not only introductory but also the only volume that the author himself worked on through successive editions.[5] And in that process, it became something of a synecdoche of the whole political project, since it is likely that Marx realised that manuscript drafts of further volumes would remain as such. Marx died intestate, and there were no explicit instructions on what to publish and how to do it. Engels and Marx's daughter Eleanor were left to sort it all out and get on with it (Kapp 1972: 277–86).

From later scholarly perspectives, getting any volume right is a matter of fidelity to the author as 'last hand' (Carver and Blank 2014). And it follows that editors should respect that norm of bibliographical science with all due care and restraint. But that is not how it looked to Engels at the time. And it is that political perspective which frames this account of his self-consciously standardising edition.

Thinking politically about the economy

As with Marx, Engels's interest in political economy was never purely intellectual in an academic sense, since that was not his background or his milieu. Both men approached these published studies and studious discussions as predominantly of an ideological character, limited by class or 'material' interests (Marx 1987a: 261–5).[6] The purported science was thus seldom other than misleading and deceptive, whatever empirical facts and theoretical insights were being produced. Yet Marx's classical education, university training and formative associations were very heavily academic, whereas Engels's were decidedly different.

Engels's interests were manifested in activisms that in his own time were conversational and epistolary in ongoing ways, but after his death these necessarily ceased. Since then, what we have of Engels the political activist survives as memoir recollections, massive though incomplete correspondence, and many volumes of published and unpublished writings, including notebooks and drafts. Activist and scholarly efforts to memorialise, summarise, condense, understand and explore his *oeuvre* began with his literary executor, the socialist politician Eduard Bernstein (Kapp 1976: 574–99). Since Engels's death in 1895 these enquiries have expanded to gargantuan proportions and fostered global iconologies.

Suppose – just to take a fresh angle – we approach the question posed in this chapter from an alternative point of view: what was Engels doing *politically* by publishing *Das Kapital, Band I*,[7] in a fourth edition (Marx and Engels 2004)? While the socialist activisms of the 1880s into the 1890s are necessarily understood from an Engels-centric perspective, because Marx had died in 1883, this is an endpoint, rather than a beginning. It follows that to start out in an Engels-centric way, and to consider his self-driven politics as the frame for what we now have on the record, we need to begin at the beginning. This is very likely going to jar with today's forensic examinations of his editorial relationship – faithful or otherwise – to Marx's authorial intentions. That is precisely because the test in this chapter will not be an editor's fidelity (or otherwise) to the extant editions and manuscript materials authored by Marx. The test used in discussion below will be a different one: how can we reimagine and appreciate Engels as a political activist?

After all, Engels's association with political activisms – of highly varied kinds – took place in the industrialising, commercial economies of the late eighteenth and early nineteenth centuries. His activisms began very early in life, well before he agreed to a joint authorship arrangement with Marx. Their inaugural joint intervention, *The Holy Family* (Marx and Engels 1975a) – published in Paris and Brussels in 1845[8] – was authored by Engels and Marx, in that order on the title page. In Marx-centric terms that is where the senior-junior story begins. Most bibliographies and collections list this work with the authors in Marx-centric order, just to make their biographical history of the great man and his junior partner begin correctly.

There is a reason why Engels was the lead in this project of hyperbolic critique, even if – as he commented to Marx in a letter ca. 20 January 1845 – Marx's enormous energies had consumed the volume and dwarfed his contributions (Marx and Engels 1982: 18). Unlike Marx, Engels was a highly accomplished political activist, publishing in both German and English. He was also fluent in French, and rather boastfully claimed further linguistic competencies (Friedrich Engels to Marie Engels [sister], 28 September 1839, Marx and Engels 1975b: 470). Virtually all of this work, even if apparently of merely literary interest and directed at *litterateurs* of the time, was politically motivated. However, this was always in the coded idioms in clandestine circulations that faced-off censorship and repression in the monarchical-authoritarian regimes of the day.[9] For Engels that was a lifelong situation and political practice.

The fourth edition of *Das Kapital, Band I,* was self-evidently produced as a posthumous memorial to Marx, yet even more importantly at the time, it was self-consciously promoted as a political intervention. This was directed into the German-speaking politics of central Europe and therefore into far-flung diasporic communities of the Americas, west Asia, sub-Saharan Africa and doubtless elsewhere. The new edition was produced under Engels's direction and published with his new introduction. And it bore prominently his editorial imprimatur as a political partner, family friend and personal confidante of the author. By then Engels was known very widely as an international activist for communism and socialism, broadly defined, and – though least noted in this context – as a long-standing commentator on modern industry and commercial relations, modest denials along the way notwithstanding.[10]

In the conventional contextual story of the published volumes in Marx's *Critique of Political Economy*, Engels starts out well but then steadily declines in the eyes of biographers, scholarly commentators and socialist-activists alike. So there are several puzzles here. One is whether or not Engels's editorial work in this crucial fourth edition of *Das Kapital, Band I,* is a positive development in relation to the previous three German editions, or whether – since Marx saw those volumes through the press – the third (1883) or perhaps the second (1872) is to be preferred as the authentic text of the authorial 'last hand'.

Another puzzle arises in relation to that one: what is the status of the French translation and edition *Le Capital, tom I* (1872–75), which also bears the intriguing participation of the author as corrective-translator, as well as authoritative editor and reviser of his own text, albeit in a different political culture and linguistic idiom. Marx had been continually struggling with his ideas and expositions since his work on the first German edition, *Das Kapital, Band I,* published in 1867 (Marx and Engels 1983a). That complicated bi-lingual and multi-functional Franco-German puzzle is of course the subject of the chapters in this volume.

There is yet another puzzle here: what are the consequences of accepting the prevailing view that Engels's talents as a political economist steadily declined along his career trajectory, particularly when we get to his editorial advice in relation to *Das Kapital, Band I,* and its posthumous English translation, *Capital, Volume I,* published in 1887 (Marx and Engels 1990)? And similarly to the succeeding *Das Kapital, Band II,* published in 1885 (Marx and Engels 2008) and *Das Kapital, Band III,* published in 1894 (Marx and Engels 2004), which he edited from manuscript materials?

For a final puzzle there is this one: to what extent do Engels's political concerns, and not just his concerns with political economy, explain his editorial decision-making in relation to Marx's text in French translation (Marx and Engels 1989) when he worked on the fourth German edition?

Scholarly research and commentary on Engels since that time, and increasingly in recent years, has generally concluded, with more than a little anachronism, that Engels was out of control as an editor, overly creative and prone to mistakes, tired and distracted, arrogant and muddling. He is generally credited only with getting the volumes to the press at all in some sort of shape. Thus he was not reproducing Marx's famously never-finished explorations of empirical, ideological and intellectual materials, undertaken to make his critique as sharply thorough as he could.[11] At least Engels moved swiftly, even if he broke things.

Or did he? Maybe there are rationales and explanations lurking here that scholarly values have missed or marginalised? What was going on from Engels's point of view, and what might that mean for readers today? To answer those questions this chapter will present Engels as a character personality in his own right, follow his political 'take' on commercialism and industrialisation, and thus on the self-styled science of political economy. We will then consider how '*that* Engels' looks when we get to the socialist politics of the 1880s.

Begin at the beginning

It is hard to know exactly when Engels's involvement with commercialism, and thus with the practicalities of political economy, got started, other than to say, as all the biographers do, that he was born into a family of factory-owners. These were manufacturing and trading enterprises founded by his great-grandfather and located on much the same sites as his parental home, just opposite his grandfather's. Generally, this is treated as biographical detail that is merely juvenile, simply there to be rejected in due course, as the young liberal, then socialist, then communist *Bildungsroman* will have it. And indeed that account follows what Engels said himself.

Moreover, from the conventional point of view, that narrative also sets up a rather worrying biographical contradiction between Engels's politics and his lifestyle, since he maintained contact, and indeed financial relationships, with family members all his life. In that way, he lived out what biographers variously construe as self-sacrifice – his nearly twenty post-revolutionary years amidst the grinding and grimy commercialism of Salford. Or they view him as the fox-hunting champagne-fancier with a political double-life – the same twenty years, though in more salubrious Manchester.[12]

In the German states of Engels's youth, his kind of commercial-manufacturing background was unusual, though not unintelligibly eccentric. It was rather more than merely middle-class-going-on wealthy, yet rather lower in the social scale than those of independent means in property ownership, or those educated into the professional classes. By school-leaving age at sixteen, Engels was already thoroughly versed in the commercial practicalities, and practice-laden theories, of his manufacturing and trading milieu. Home life and trade life were all much the same in Barmen and Elberfeld, the twin towns of the Wupper Valley, an early industrial-commercial district strung out along a tributary of the Rhine.

Notably, this physical reality was reinforced and licenced by the anti-intellectualism – and 'hard-work-ism' – of evangelical Pietism, a strictly fundamentalist Protestant cult. After some time in the family's local enterprise, Engels was packed off to Bremen to learn the practical essentials of the international export–import trade. In relation to the raw materials and machine-tools essential to textile manufacture, this was inward-looking. But it was also outward-looking in relation to partnership opportunities abroad, specifically in the world's most advanced manufactories in the north of England. The teenage Engels was taken there on a business trip by his father.[13]

Generally in biographical terms, even when the presentation is Engels-centric, this background commercialism is set up to be rejected, ruptured and transcended. Here we treat it as formative and consider it a high point, as Engels did himself at the time. He was sent away to Bremen to learn the business. In the culturally richer and relatively liberal world of the Hanseatic free city and trading port – worlds away from the narrow-minded, and physically narrow home patch – this was liberation. Engels's excited letters to home at the time tell us as much.

But within the whirlwinds of Engels's correspondence with family and friends, as it is preserved, we see a solid core of commercial experience being acquired in the office, at the port and in the town. His own caricatures of colleagues and self-satires of laziness notwithstanding, he was learning a lot. Engels grounded his worldly knowledge by reading the world's newspapers at the traders' reading room. He knew how commercialism worked, and he was enthusiastic about technology. And he had an economist's experiential understanding of productivity in relation to prices, competition and market share. When he was sent further afield to work at an associated enterprise in Manchester (and to be a commercial spy on an unreliable partner) he fitted right in (Carver 2020b: 55–81).

While it is certainly true that Engels rejected commercialism and the trading mentality from an early age, this was inward, or hinted at only to trusted correspondents. Or it was the stuff of *succès de scandale*. This happened when his pseudonymous *Briefe aus dem Wuppertal* [Letters from Wuppertal] (Engels 1975a) appeared in an important literary journal published in Leipzig in 1839, when he was only eighteen. Surely, though, this personal and political rejection of commercialism, and of the attendant theoretical-religious-ideological underpinnings, is rather more of a Hegelian *Aufhebung* than a complete *volte-face*. Engels could not possibly have *unlearned* what was so valuable to his liberalising, reforming and revolutionary political projects. There was always a considerable amount of memory to draw on, not simply a reservoir of things to forget.

Engels's youthful political project was the revolutionary liberalism of popular sovereignty, constitutional rule of law, representative and responsible government, and the rights of man and the citizen. His sentiments along those lines are clear from his Bremen letters. His enthusiasm for Chartism when he got to Manchester was self-declared and pursued in two languages. He reported on the semi-clandestine public meetings that were threatened by police surveillance, and he exported this information into the German states while evading censorship and prosecution. Those reports could be read there in two ways: exotic events happening abroad from which German readers were thankfully protected. Or alternatively, and as he advised, a tale from the future that wasn't a fanciful fiction but rather a vector of on-rushing commercialism and social change. England's Lancashire and nearby Yorkshire were portrayed as the Wupper Valley and nearby Ruhrgebiet of the German future (Carver 2020b: 117–52).

However, as was and is necessarily true of many activists, Engels's grasp of what he could see, hear, smell and deduce was rooted in personal experience, moral revulsion and literary fluency. Moving up a notch, he had access in Manchester to political economy in the classic English and French works, to socialist 'takes' on the subjects raised there and also to expert contacts and formative experiences (Claeys 1984). From that milieu, we have the work that kicked off Marx's *Critique of Political Economy*, namely Engels's *Outlines of a Critique of Political Economy* (1975b), published in the *Deutsch-Französische Jahrbücher* [German-French Annals] in Paris in 1844.[14] We know from a hastily noted down and generally overlooked short 'Summary' (Marx 1975) – written on receipt of Engels's manuscript article – that Marx was electrified.

At this point, it is vital to resist Marx's magnetic pull on any narrative and keep to the Engels-centric point of view. The *Deutsch-Französische Jahrbücher*, where Engels's 'Outlines' was published, was edited – let us note – by Arnold Ruge and Karl Marx, in that order. Anachronistic and Marx-centric bibliographical revisions and citations again miss this important contextual-political point.[15] In the German states, Engels was certainly not Ruge's equal as a peripatetic publicist of liberal (i.e., radical, subversive and treasonous) French ideas of revolutionary constitutionalism. Marx was obviously Ruge's rather lucky junior partner, since the elder man had a considerable reputation as the founder-editor of the subversive, censored and suppressed *Hallische Jahrbücher* (Steadman Jones 2016: 74–8, 144–50).

Engels, though, was the one contributor who had a perfect grasp of not just the practice but also the theory of the emerging world order that was barely visible over the horizon west of the Rhine. Few if any of the Young Hegelians had any English. And of those very few who – as Marx was – were inclined to think about the social question of poverty and inequality, none had anything like Engels's grasp of the issues at home and abroad (Breckman 2010). Engels's apprenticeship in nitty-gritty commercialism, and his reading-room knowledge of practical political economy, were very substantial gifts to this community. In the eyes of some, indeed Marx more than Ruge, this represented a chance for political traction.

Within the broadly liberalising political thinking, and the necessarily discreet activisms available, the Young Hegelians of the *Deutsch-Französische Jahrbücher* could play it both ways. This had indeed been the *raison d'être* of the ill-fated *Rheinische Zeitung* [*Rhenish Gazette*] – published in 1842–43 from Cologne – where Engels had already authored several articles, well in advance of Marx's latter-day editorship and subsequent self-publication (Carver 2020b: 118–23). The owners' first and founding choice for the editorship of their newspaper, with 'Politics, Trade and Business' in a banner masthead, was Friedrich List, author of the very first introduction to political economy in the German language: *Das nationale System der politischen Ökonomie* [*The National System of Political Economy*], published in Stuttgart and Tübingen in 1841. List turned them down (Steadman Jones 2016: 106).

However, the Young Hegelians could also play the political card the other way, and indeed this tactical possibility reflected their varied views. They were a very loose and malleably in-and-out radicalising 'groupuscule' of intellectuals, and intellectually minded self-styled radical modernisers. The more socialistically and communistically inclined, in some instances, were also more economically inclined, and thus more inclined to view commercialism with suspicion. From that critical perspective commercialism was a vision of the near-future in the German-speaking states and central Europe, and simultaneously slated for transcendence to a better one (Steadman Jones 2016: 135–44).

The form of this transcendence was suitably vague for some, and prospectively determined for others. Engels's Chartist experiences with working-class activisms put him in the vanguard of these radical aspirations. His knowledge of political economy, from original-language sources, or at least his very close acquaintance with the ideas of the emerging science of commercial society, put him similarly in the lead. He was even working on a full-length book on the social question, for which he had secured a publisher. The object was to tell both stories in German: a theoretically informed but vivid politics of problems, protests and aspirations. This was indeed published within months of his editorial meeting with Ruge and Marx in Paris.

Ruge, Marx and others had been working to get their radicalism printed for clandestine distribution over the Rhine. Engels's book, conceived and written entirely independently of Marx, was *The Condition of the Working Class in England* (Engels 1975c). His subtitle tells the story: *From Personal Observation and Authentic Sources*. It was legally published in Leipzig.

Scholarly focus has been much more on Engels's 'Outlines' than on his book. And indeed in terms of Marx's project – certainly a political intervention in its iterations but admittedly a highly intellectualised one – it is not hard to see why.[16] Marx had never done anything like Engels's on-the-ground study, hence Marx-centric scholarship does not find the book all that interesting beyond noting that Marx acknowledged it in conjunction with his published critique. Again, even in the activist reception of Marx's work, the interest has been in the opening sections of the published critiques that set out what appear to be the building blocks of 'economics' (Heinrich 2004). The title *Capital* itself suggests that reading, and the opening sections are devoted definitionally to the concepts value, commodity and money. So-called empirical and historical material then comes in along the way. Later on in the published volume, Marx considers topics such as modern industry, machinery and factory-work, dispossession and colonisation, citing a hugely impressive of sources. But eye-witness is not a notable feature.[17]

In that way, both Engels's early 'takes' on modernity – the 'Outlines' and *The Condition of the Working Class in England* – get marginalised: his *Critique of Political Economy* is considered unsophisticated compared to Marx's work, which was written twenty-odd years later (Hollander 2011). And his anecdotal and unsystematic observations are methodologically discounted, rather misjudging the genre.[18] Moreover, his copy-paste of official records and newspaper reports is rather snobbishly picked over (Henderson 1976).

The book was well reviewed, widely circulated and something of a success in a very unfamiliar genre. The author, publishing for the first time under his own name, was just twenty-four, though how many readers would connect his real name with the pseudonymous writers of earlier scandalous notorieties we do not know. What we do know, though, of Engels himself at sixteen years of age isn't at all dissimilar to the Engels of almost ten years later. There is little reason to imagine that this formative decade of his life somehow vanished when he took up with Marx in the spring of 1845. Engels was a critical-political economist, and in his own outlook – *rather than his contribution to Marx's* – he had a huge advantage. He knew the people, knew the places, knew the languages and knew the politics. This is quite a solid basis from which to work, on his own bat or in tandem with Marx, and indeed throughout life he did both.

However, that line of argument also poses the question: how different from Engels was Marx? We have just pointed out Engels's positioning with respect to political agitation and political economy, but that move calls for an adjustment in Marx's reception. Maybe he, and his work and activities, were more like Engels's activisms? Maybe he was more like that than like the dogmatic and deeply philosophical (or at least super-theoretical) bookworm that biographers have repetitively focused on?

A contribution to the *Critique of Political Economy*

Having absorbed what Engels had to say about political economy, having been escorted on his first-ever trip abroad in 1845 and having had tutorial English lessons from Engels in studious conjunction with the classics of British political economy that summer, Marx embarked – as he said he would in his 'Summary' of late 1844 – on his sole-authored critical-political studies. Engels's role in that regard began – over and above his very proximate contributions to setting up the project – in correspondence of 1845, just when Marx obtained his first contract for such a work, accompanied by a very useful cash advance (Gabriel 2011: 110).

Engels's letters on this subject, from that time forward, have been closely studied, so there is no need to review this correspondence in the usual detail.[19] The usual discussion is Marx-centric, in that he is conceived in intellectual-biographical terms as (already) a great man, a great mind, a great writer, making ideas in history that are worth unravelling and revisiting. Assessing Engels-in-relation-to-Marx in that manner, which is not only Marx-centric but great-ideas-centric, sidelines what is admittedly a quite repetitive mantra by Engels. He directed this to Marx throughout the next four decades: get on with it, get it written and get it out!

It is easy for scholarly commentators to identify with the Marxian intellect at work, and the annoyance that friends, publishers and family were causing by trying to short-circuit the processes of research, analysis and synthesis that creativity requires. Engels, though, had his mind and energies prioritised in a different but complementary direction. This was very much on political inter-vention, journalistic activism and keeping up the pressure. Marx could certainly do this, too, though his focus was rather more varied and harder to fathom now (and then, too, according to some).

Rather frustratingly for Marx his high points (which is how they look now) were at the time almost low points, that is, the *Manifesto of the Communist Party* – published in 1848 in London, and *The Eighteenth Brumaire of Louis Bonaparte* – published in 1852 in New York. Those pamphlet works did not have much circulation or make much impact at the time outside a few concentric circles of German, mostly émigré socialist-activists. His take-down of Pierre-Joseph Proudhon, written in French, *The Poverty of Philosophy,* published in Paris and Brussels, did not bring that great European figure down or grind his ideas into dust as Marx intended: the disciples and ideas were still his targets in succeeding decades.

Marx had rather more success, though, with the circulars and speeches authored within the International Working Men's Association in the later 1860s, a very positive part of his biographical story, though rather neglected by theory-minded commentators.[20] Marx's engagement with the personally libellous claims detailed in *Herr Vogt* – published in London in 1860 – is generally regarded as a distinctly negative moment, certainly by Engels (and *Frau* Marx).[21] Possibly, though, Marx gained some politically useful notoriety.

This political angle on Marx's life and works thus sets up the conundrum presented by his *Critique of Political Economy* as a great work intended to develop a great politics. For both Marx and Engels the *métier* of choice was the political pamphlet, the newspaper article, the personal letter. After *The Condition of the Working Class in England* Engels never wrote another full-length study, and he continued – as he had started in his teenage years – in the 'short work' mode.[22] It is worth noting here that *The Condition of the Working Class in England* had an English-language 'Preface' addressed 'To the Working-Class of Great Britain' (Engels 1975d), as well as a much less inflammatory 'Preface' for German readers (Engels 1975e). Those readers would not have been working-class, other than perhaps an unrecorded few. Engels had the considerable experience to draw on in evading the censors in the German states, evidently banking on the near-certain knowledge that they could not read English or anyway cared little about politics in a foreign country.

From the beginning, though, Marx's critique was conceived as an exploratory and vastly erudite enterprise, which – as became obvious – controlled him rather than the other way round. Engels's more immediately political perspective – reiterated and repetitive – was rather different. This is not to say, however, that there was some great spoken or unspoken difference that nagged at the two. But rather to say that we know from Engels's letters to Marx that his urging Marx on to quick publication and immediate intervention was to some extent at odds with what Marx had in mind. Of course, this can be viewed as a mere difference in emphasis, since Engels was more than enthusiastic about Marx as an intellect and about the political worth of his critique – *if only* it would appear in German and from there get into widespread translation. And of course the two were busy, as opportunity and circumstance permitted, making politics in ways that each had under control, separately and together.

The upshot is that in commentary on Marx's critique, Engels's prodding is noted but set against the Marx-centric view that intellectual values – which is what posterity has valued – are transcendent. From that perspective, quotidian politics is ephemeral, recoverable only by historians and politically interesting only in retrospect. Most of that bio-story of Marx's political career is one of failure, missed opportunity, betrayal, misappropriation and false hopes. That leaves scholars, activists and scholar-activists with limited scope, though the exciting prospect of a general theory of capitalism has been a great motivator. Hence the continuing and increasingly provocative political interest today in the critique of global political economy, in Marx's version of it, and what those ideas have to offer – at least as inspiration, even if some of the concepts, propositions and analytical relationships fail to convince.[23] From that perspective, which is politics-centric as well as Engels-centric, we return to the problem at hand: the *politics* of the *Critique of Political Economy*.

Brave new world?

Shortly after the pamphlet publication of 'The Poverty of Philosophy', and as the international politicking within the aspirationally titled 'Manifesto of the Communist Party' proceeded, Marx and Engels were suddenly swept up into the European revolutions of 1848–49. They swiftly revived the *Rheinische Zeitung* of the 1840s and used it – and other papers – to report on the political upheavals from Brussels to Budapest. The aftermath was tragic, not least for Marx, who was forced into emigration in a distinctly foreign environment. Stateless in England he was under surveillance as a convicted and/or suspected revolutionary against the lawful monarchical order in the United Kingdom and in the Kingdom of Prussia. His critique was decidedly on the back-burner, given more immediate tribulations, but by the later 1850s his situation had improved somewhat, and – in conjunction with his journalistic researches – he fired himself up with revolutionary expectations (Steadman Jones 2016: 249–374; Gabriel 2011: 175–260).

Those expectations arose within the international commercialism of the day, and in particular the financial crash that began in late 1856 and continued for some months. That is when Marx returned to his grand project and began drafting in earnest. Those materials are now rather split up in the so-called *Grundrisse* collection (Marx 1993) but also transcribed as 'notebooks' within the MEGA[2] edition, *Abteilung* IV.[24] This is where Engels's letters to Marx revisit a familiar theme, though in a political and intellectual context somewhat different from the Franco-German socialist cliques and 'groupuscules' of the 1840s.

Political economy and indeed the industrialising, commercialising economies of the German states were now both much more visible as realities rather than prophecies. Perhaps, then, the recent memories of revolutionary action – highly successful in toppling monarchs and setting up constituent assemblies – would revive? And perhaps, then, the penetration of commercial relations and modern industries into rural, neo-medieval locales was such that a political *Critique of Political Economy* would make much more sense?

Hollander (2011) provides a very workable run-through of Engels's epistolary involvement with Marx's critiques in the post-revolutionary 1850s and on through the various editions and volumes of *Das Kapital*. As mentioned, his interest is textual – relating ideas of Marx and Engels, variously, to various texts in political economy. The focus here by contrast is on the political motivations and plans through which Marx's recursive drafting activities, and eventual published texts, were conceived and executed. And, again by contrast, the perspective here is Engels-centric, that is, what *he* was doing with Marx's activities to make *Das Kapital* political.

The constant thread in the Engels-Marx correspondence, as indicated above, is Engels's insistence on publication, and his assessment of the quotidian impact that would produce. Engels's letter to Marx, written in early October 1844 (the first letter extant in their correspondence), kicks off the genre: 'See to it that the material you've collected [towards a *Kritik der Politik und National-Ökonomie* – "Critique of Politics and Political Economy"] is soon launched into the world.

It's high time, heaven knows!' (Marx and Engels 1982: 6, 568 n.5). He followed-up swiftly, writing to Marx 20 January 1845:

> But what we need above all just now are a few larger works to provide an an adequate handhold for the many who would like to improve their imperfect knowledge, but are unable to do so unassisted. Do try and finish your political economy book even if there's much in it that you yourself are still dissatisfied with, it doesn't really matter; minds are ripe and we must strike while the iron is hot [...] it is now high time. So try and finish *before* April, do as I do, set yourself a date by which you will *definitely have finished*, and make sure it gets into print quickly. If you can't get it printed in Paris, have it done in Mannheim, Darmstadt or elsewhere. But it must come out soon.
> (Marx and Engels 1982: 17–18, emphasis in original)

In the same letter Engels has already got the picture, noting Marx's voracious writing and dilatory perfectionism:

> The fact that you enlarged the *Critical Criticism* [subtitle of *Die heilige Familie: Kritik der kritischen Kritik* – 'The Holy Family'] to twenty [printer's] sheets surprised me not a little. But it is all to the good, for it means that much can now be disseminated which would otherwise have lain for heaven knows how long in your *escritoire* [...] I have as yet heard nothing [...] about the publication of the book, which I most eagerly await.
> (Marx and Engels 1982: 18)

Years later, after Marx returned to his project, the situation is almost exactly the same. Engels writes on 21 October 1858:

> What's the position about the manuscript [on political economy] for [the publisher] Duncker? NOW'S YOUR TIME.[25] Come what may there'll be a new ministry [in the Kingdom of Prussia] which will probably be rather more hesitant about making its *début* with the confiscation of a *scientific* work. I hope that it has gone off [to the publisher]. But let me know for sure.
> (Marx and Engels 1983: 349)

Marx's reply by return on 22 October 1858 was also in the genre: 'The manuscript has not gone off yet and [...] [it] will be weeks before I am able to send it' (Marx and Engels 1983: 351). And in the following month in a letter of 24 November 1858 he explained himself to Engels and thus also to their émigré associates in 'the Party':

> the material was to hand and all that I was concerned with was the form. But to me the style of everything I wrote seemed tainted with liver trouble. And I have a twofold motive for not allowing this work to be spoiled on medical grounds:

1. It is the product of 15 years of research, i.e., the best years of my life.
2. In it an important view of social relations is scientifically expounded for the first time, Hence I owe it to the Party that the thing shouldn't be disfigured by the kind of heavy wooden style proper to a disordered liver.

My aim is not to produce an elegant exposé but to write as I usually do [...] I believe that even if someone less intelligent than you were to acquaint Mr Duncker with this state of affairs, he could not but sanction a mode of conduct, which so far as a publisher was concerned, merely signified the endeavour to give him the best value for his money. I shall have finished about 4 weeks from now, having only just begun the actual writing.

(Marx and Engels 1983: 354)

During the following weeks, Marx explained that his wife was copying his manuscript for the publisher; his handwriting was notoriously bad, and he always required, so far as we know, someone to prepare 'fair copy' for the printers. And on 16 December 1858, he reported on what was then to be the first 'half-volume' of his grandly planned critical study, *A Contribution to the Critique of Political Economy* (Marx 1987b), published in 1859 in Berlin: 'the manuscript has gone off, but I'll be blowed if anyone else in similar circumstances and with as rotten a liver could have got it done as soon' (Marx and Engels 1983: 361). But after a number of false dawns, including lack of money to pay the postage (for which Engels obliged), Marx wrote again on 26 January 1859 that the manuscript had gone off (Marx and Engels 1983: 371). Rather typically the now very famous 'Preface' (Marx 1987a) was not dispatched till 23 February, as we learn from Marx's letter of 23 February 1859 to Franz Duncker, his publisher (Marx and Engels 1983: 390). Shortly thereafter on 25 February 1859 Marx wrote to Engels:

In my Preface I have done you a few *honneurs*, and thus it is all to the good if you yourself [with the topical pamphlet *Po und Rhein* – 'Po and Rhine' (Engels 1980a) – published in Berlin in 1859] take the stage immediately afterwards.

(Marx and Engels 1983: 393)

At this point, and concluding this indicative vignette of the Engels and Marx publishing and politicking partnership, we can *segue* to the pair's post-publication ambitions and plans as recorded in an excited correspondence. Marx's 'Preface', and Engels's review of Marx's little book (Engels 1980b), were both printed in the German émigré weekly *Das Volk* [*The People*]. This paper was published during 1859 in London and was edited from within the German Workers' Educational Society, very much the Engels-Marx milieu. They were involved with such groups in various locales for political agitation from the 1840s onwards, when possible.

On 13 August 1859 Marx writes to Engels: 'The *Volk* already wields considerable influence in the United State. For instance the Preface to my book has been reprinted from the *Volk* and variously commented on by German papers from New England to California' (Marx and Engels 1983: 482). Later in the year on 5 October 1859, Marx writes to Engels again:

> The thing [i.e., the 'half-volume' 'Contribution'] appears to be selling despite the *conspiration de silence*. Otherwise I wouldn't have received this indirect request from Duncker [about publishing further instalments] [...] Your *articles* on my affair [i.e., Engels's two-part review] have been reprinted in German papers from New York to California (with the tiny little *Volk* we hooked the whole of the German-American press). I enclose a cutting of the advertisements [for the book] in the Vienna [daily paper *Die*] *Presse*. BY THE BY I am giving lectures about the first instalment to a *select* circle of artisans. It seems to interest the chaps a great deal.
>
> (Marx and Engels 1983: 502, emphasis in original; see also 639 n. 483)

This quite vivid picture of the imbrication of socialist agitation and political critique with Marx's *Critique of Political Economy* sets up the strategy and tactics through which *Das Kapital* subsequently appeared. While the international politics of London-based socialism had altered and expanded in important ways, not least with the foundation of the International Working Men's Association in 1864, the Engels–Marx *modus operandi* was very substantially the same as it had always been, and it persisted through Marx's declining years. The second German edition (1872) and the French edition/translation (1872–75) were similarly positioned, albeit in the much altered political context of post-Napoleonic and post-monarchical France, still in turmoil after the Prussian occupation of 1870–71.

The twenty-five years between the revived *Critique of Political Economy* in the later 1850s, on to Marx's declining years in the run-up to the third German edition (1883), warrant detailed historical study. But the pattern of activities and ambitions was already set, and indeed its origins are in the early days of co-residence in Brussels. In that formative period, the two were publishing for German-French and occasional (usually via Engels) English-language reportage. Much of the circulation was clandestine, and with all of it they had to have regard to the proclivities of censors and publishers. With that picture in mind, we can turn to the years after 1883 with Engels in sole charge, and a new German edition of *Das Kapital* on the horizon.

Das Kapital as a political intervention

The fourth edition of Marx's *magnum opus* (Marx and Engels 1991) was far more than a way of getting fresh copies into the bookshops, though that was certainly an aim. The third edition of *Das Kapital* (1883) had sold out (Marx and Engels 1991: 705). And the project was far more than an editorial tidying-up operation, as Engels explains in his 'Preface' of 25 June 1890 (Engels 1996), noting his emendations to his copy-text, which was the third edition. These corrections, amendments and clarifications were selectively and variously derived from the French edition/translation *Le Capital* (1872–75, published in Paris), which incorporated original work by Marx himself, and from the English translation *Capital* (1887, published in London), on which Engels himself had assisted.

However, Engels gave no overall or detailed rationale for these changes, something that has intrigued and infuriated commentators ever since. Instead most of his 'Preface' is devoted to rehearsing, over several tedious pages, the ongoing counter-responses to a very old anonymous complaint, dating from 1872, that in his book Marx had both carelessly and deliberately misquoted important source material. Those allegations, as Engels tells the story, emanated rather conspiratorially from academic socialists (*Kathedersozialisten*) who were viewed, by Marx in his time, and also by Engels to date, as a continuing unhelpful influence in the German socialist movement (Engels 1996).

There is something odd going on here. Where exactly is the political substance? What is the relationship between this book in its 1890 edition, its theoretical and empirical content, and Engels's ongoing socialist politicking? He had been doing this, as we have seen, ever since his teenage years as a liberal revolutionary, proto-socialist and calculating class warrior. The answer lies in the *Sozialistengesetze* (*Anti-Socialist Laws*), which Otto von Bismarck, Reichskanzler of the imperial government, presented to the Reichstag for passage in 1878. After a failed attempt, he successfully secured its passage, making much of a second (failed) assassination attack on Kaiser Wilhelm. He had little difficulty using these crimes as a pretext for his conservative policies. And in particular the law licenced restrictions, prohibitions and prosecutions designed to suppress socialist ideas and publications, and to repress such political activity as would otherwise be legal. Even deportation was eventually used as a threat (Steadman Jones 2016: 555–9).

Rather familiarly in the context of Engels's life, a politics of democratising ideas and agitation, particularly when advocating representative institutions and accountable power-sharing with working-class (male) political parties, was associated by the conservative ruling orders with revolutionary terror and bloody outrages in France. This time it was the Paris Commune of 1870–71, which was a civic uprising against Prussian occupation and French collaborators. Some German socialists had been publicly on-side and so were tried and sentenced for treason (Lidtke 2016).

The anti-socialist laws were time-limited and had been successively renewed as recently as 1888. Engels was clearly going for legal publication for his fourth edition, in order to obtain wide circulation. Hence in his 'Preface' he was playing up Marx's work in relation to scholarly and scientific standards, presumed to be apolitically objective and useful. Outlining the socialist message and its political import in clear terms was out of the question, as was also the case with Marx's own careful yet rather more daring rhetoric in the book.

In his 'Preface to the Second German Edition', published in 1873, Marx addressed his message to 'the practical bourgeois', helpfully showing how 'the contradictions inherent in the movement of capitalist society' will result in a 'universal crisis' (Marx 1996b: 20). To the casual eye this might sound rather helpful, even if better-informed readers, then and now, can see what the author is really getting at. At the time of writing his own 'Preface' in 1890, Engels stuck to textual corrections in a boring list and to a coded politics of defending Marx's scholarly reputation.

While the law was in process of repeal from early 1890, it was still in force until 30 September. Writing in June of that year, Engels couldn't be entirely sure that it wasn't coming back, and he wanted no hitches in speedy publication, which was announced on 15 August (Marx and Engels 1991: 706, 709). At nearly seventy years of age, in deteriorating health, and burdened with the very incomplete manuscripts destined for *Das Kapital, Band III* (*Capital, Volume III*), published in 1894 in Hamburg (Marx 1998), Engels knew that this was his last chance to work on Volume I and that his edition had to last for years in order to do its job.

What exactly was this job? By September 1889 Engels regarded the publication of a new edition as a 'necessity' (Engels to Kautsky, 15 September 1889, Marx and Engels 2001: 375). *Das Kapital, Band I,* had been playing quite a role in socialist agitation, at first legal and then clandestine, in the new imperial Germany of the early 1870s. Besides the Engels–Marx efforts to publicise the content of the work accessibly in reviews, notices and topical articles, Marx in particular cooperated in the production of a second edition in 1876 of a short conspectus titled *Kapital und Arbeit* (*Capital and Labour*), published originally in 1873.

Engels also spent some time in 1886 correcting Karl Kautsky's popularisation, *Karl Marx's Ökonomische Lehren* (*Karl Marx's Economics*). This was published in 1887 in a didactic book series *Internationale Bibliothek* (International Library), a medium for workers' education at the time. Among the source material that Engels cites, in conjunction with his editorial work, was Marx's own register of textual differences between the second German edition and the subsequent French translation/edition, notable here for the fact that Marx drew it up in preparation for a planned but abortive American edition (Nietzold et al. 1991: 706, 708–9). Even if something didn't happen, we can understand how it fits a pattern.

Conclusion

Taking an Engels-centric and career-long view puts his editorial work in preparing the fourth edition of *Das Kapital,* and seeing it through the press, into a different perspective. Writing to Marx's daughter Laura Lafargue on 9 September 1889, Engels mentioned that a fourth edition is 'impending' (Marx and Engels 2001: 373). And he wrote to Friedrich Adolph Sorge (in Hoboken, New Jersey) on the 26th that an edition 'was wanted' but needed 'only a few alterations and additional notes', adding that great care would of course be taken with these (Marx and Engels 2001: 378).

After a bout of ill-health, evidently compounded by his labours on the third volume of *Das Kapital,* Engels broke off those labours and addressed himself to the new edition of the first. On 12 October 1889, and evidently speeding up, he wrote to Sorge: 'the quotations are all having to be revised to conform to the English edition [...]. After that I shall buckle down to the 3rd [volume of *Das Kapital*]' (Marx and Engels 2001: 388). This is the story that Engels tells in his 'Preface', where in great rapidity he describes his editorial changes in just a few paragraphs (Engels 1996: 37–8). This is where the scholarly controversies about his editorship arose. It is also where the somewhat more politicised issues as to his authorial (rather than merely editorial) status have arisen. And rather similarly the status of his imprimatur as Marx's political and intellectual partner comes into question.

This chapter does not attempt to circumvent those issues or to take sides in those debates as they are generally framed, oftentimes in polarising ways (Blackledge 2019: 1–20, Kangal 2020: 9–37). Rather the perspective offered here is less text-oriented and more action-oriented. The intention is not to excuse Engels's editorial work or indeed to assume that the relevant standards by which to judge it as defective are the standards of today. Nor is it to claim that there aren't issues here and that simply 'being Engels' settles everything.

Rather the perspective offered here looks at these texts and editorial practices as interventions into political contestations which those involved took very seriously. There is thus more than one way to understand and evaluate the texts that we have sitting on our shelves and accessed by our screens. The legal publication of the fourth edition of Marx's *Das Kapital, Band I,* was an intervention into a hostile, avowedly illiberal and distinctly anti-democratic political environment, only rather minimally reformed from medieval monarchism to an authoritarian constitutionalism. There were certainly risks here, but also urgency and steady purpose. Engels's working methods weren't entirely about his increasing years and declining health running up against mammoth editorial tasks undertaken single-handedly. From today's perspective in reading the correspondence and testimony, the political situation doesn't look all that tense. But to those involved it certainly was. Engels was the one producing the book and doing the politics.

Authenticity to an authorial 'last hand' won't tell us everything we might want to know about what a text might mean. Indeed how a text makes meaning for readers over time is an important part of what it does. And in that way what a text was meant to do in the first place, over and above just sit on a page, is an important interpretative question. Part of that interpretive question involves a relationship between quotidian politics, editorial practice and strategic timing. Having started work in October 1889, Engels wrote again to Laura Lafargue barely a month later on 16 November: 'The 4th edition [of] Vol. I is in the press and I am back to my Vol. III [of *Das Kapital*]. No easy job, but mun [*sic*] be done as they say in Lancashire' (Marx and Engels 2001: 409).

Notes

1 Samuel Hollander's (2011: xiii) very thorough examination of Engels as a political economist is self-confessedly undertaken from a Marx-centric perspective through

which Engels is understood as an influence, though at many points Hollander's appreciation of Engels in various respects is noteworthy.

2 Hollander (2011: 1–7) also provides quite an even-handed overview of the ways the Marx–Engels relationship has been framed in various receptions, noting no instances where anyone has tried the reverse perspective.

3 Mary Gabriel (2011) is something of an exception, as the book proceeds diary-like from a Marx-family point of view.

4 For a meticulous account of Engels's editing of Marx's manuscripts, see the editorial matter and discussions in MEGA², volume II/15 (Marx and Engels 2004).

5 For an overview, see Heinrich (2004).

6 For this contextualisation, see Marx (1987a: 261–5).

7 This is the edition taken as the basis for many subsequent editions and translations, including Karl Marx, *Capital, Volume I* (Marx 1996a); I use the German title from here on to refer to this particular edition (1890) so as to avoid confusion with subsequently edited versions and translations, and similarly for other specific German-language editions (1867, 1872, 1883) and for the French edition (1872–1875) *Le Capital.*

8 From here on I am using italic for German and French titles, because that is the political context under discussion; I then give the English titles, as rendered in *Marx and Engels Collected Works*, though using single quotes for short or pamphlet-style works, and italic only for full-length books, because that again relates to the kind of political intervention that Engels or Marx was attempting. For that reason, again, I give not just dates of first publication but also places of publication, since those facts relate to the local censorship regimes within which Engels and Marx had to negotiate for publishers willing to take on the risks involved, whether for legal or clandestine circulations. That way I draw attention to the significance to Engels and Marx of various target audiences, noting though that sometimes within particular political interventions each looked forward to translations and wider international readerships.

9 For this point, and a discussion of the way that politics functioned during Engels's youthful years, see Carver (2020a: 12–16).

10 See Hollander's (2011: 1–24) thoughtful discussion and evaluation in Hollander, *Friedrich Engels.*

11 Hollander (2011) offers a readable review of the situation; the MEGA² II volumes present research that arises from the strict, scholarly point of view; see also van der Linden and Hubmann (2018).

12 As biographers Blackledge (2019) and Hunt (2010) gravitate towards opposite poles of this contradiction.

13 The episode is recounted in Carver (2020b: 68–9).

14 Hollander (2011) is usefully, though rather typically as a scholar, more interested in the short work's deficiencies in relation to its predecessors in political economy and to Marx's subsequent work on his own critique.

15 The sole volume or number of this journal included quite a number of contributors and contributions other than Marx's and Engels's essays (two each), yet it has never been republished or translated as a historical document in its own context; rather it is viewed anachronistically from the Marx-centric biographers' perspective.

16 For a lucid consideration of *Capital, Volume I,* as a political intervention, see Roberts (2017: 158–63 and *passim*).

17 For a reading of *Capital* that highlights Marx's work on the historical evolution of capitalism, see Cleaver (2000).

18 While praising the work as literature, Steven Marcus (2017), the literary historian, inadvertently confirms the allegation.

19 Hollander's (2011) commentaries on the correspondence are the most detailed because they are the most focused on economic points, though those biographers telling a story, such as Steadman Jones, present the most material; there is an old but useful collection (Marx and Engels 1983) of letters-in-exchange on *Capital* translated into English.

20 For an excellent documentary collection and discussion, see Musto (2014).

21 For a rare discussion of *Herr Vogt* that isn't dismissive, see Carver (2010).

22 Note that many of Marx's and Engels's pamphlet-type publications have become honorary books on the shelf and listed in italics in bibliographies.

23 For an exemplar, see Saito (2017).

24 For the MEGA^2 structure plan, see https://mega.bbaw.de/de/struktur (accessed 26 May 2022).

25 I follow the convention for these translations that words and phrases originally in English appear in capital letters.

References

Blackledge, Paul (2019) *Friedrich Engels and Modern Social and Political Theory*, Albany: State University of New York Press.

Breckman, Warren (2010) *Marx, the Young Hegelians and the Origins of Radical Social Theory: Dethroning the Self*, Cambridge: Cambridge University Press.

Carver, Terrell (2010) 'Marx and the Politics of Sarcasm', *Socialism and Democracy*, vol. 24, n. 3: 102–18.

Carver, Terrell (2020a) *Engels Before Marx*, Cham: Palgrave Macmillan.

Carver, Terrell (2020b) *The Life and Thought of Friedrich Engels*, Cham: Palgrave Macmillan.

Carver, Terrell and Blank, Daniel (2014) *A Political History of the Editions of Marx and Engels's 'German Ideology Manuscripts'*, New York: Palgrave Macmillan.

Claeys, Gregory (1984) 'Engels' *Outlines of a Critique of Political Economy* (1843) and the Origins of the Marxist Critique of Capitalism', *History of Political Economy,* vol. 16, n. 2: 207–32.

Cleaver, Harry (2000) *Reading Capital Politically*, Chico: AK Press.

Engels, Frederick (1975a [1839]) 'Letters from Wuppertal', in *Marx Engels Collected Works*, vol. 2: *Frederick Engels 1838-42*, London: Lawrence and Wishart, pp. 7–25.

Engels, Frederick (1975b [1844]) 'Outlines of a Critique of Political Economy', in *Marx Engels Collected Works*, vol. 3: *Marx and Engels 1843-1844*, London: Lawrence and Wishart, pp. 418–43.

Engels, Frederick (1975c [1845]) 'The Condition of the Working-Class in England', in *Marx Engels Collected Works*, vol. 4: *Marx and Engels 1844-1845*, London: Lawrence and Wishart, pp. 295–583.

Engels, Frederick (1975d) [1845]) 'To the Working-Classes of Great Britain', in *Marx Engels Collected Works*, vol. 4: *Marx and Engels 1844-1845*, London: Lawrence and Wishart, pp. 297–301.

Engels, Frederick (1975e) [1845]) 'Preface', in *Marx Engels Collected Works*, vol. 4: *Marx and Engels 1844-1845*, pp. 302–4.

Engels, Frederick (1980a [1859]) 'Po and Rhine', in *Marx Engels Collected Works*, vol. 16: *Marx and Engels 1858-1860,* London: Lawrence and Wishart, pp. 211–55.

Engels, Frederick (1980b [1859]) 'Karl Marx. A Contribution to the Critique of Political Economy', in *Marx Engels Collected Works*, vol. 16: *Marx and Engels 1858-1860,* London: Lawrence and Wishart, pp. 465–77.

Engels, Frederick (1996 [1890]) 'Preface to the Fourth German Edition', in *Marx Engels Collected Works*, vol. 35: *Karl Marx, Capital, Volume I,* London: Lawrence and Wishart, pp. 37–42.

Gabriel, Mary (2011) *Love and Capital: Karl and Jenny Marx and the Birth of a Revolution,* New York: Little, Brown.

Heinrich, Michael (2004) *An Introduction to the Three Volumes of Karl Marx's Capital,* New York: Monthly Review Press.

Henderson, W.O. (1976) *The Life of Friedrich Engels,* 2 vols, London: Frank Cass.

Hollander, Samuel (2011) *Friedrich Engels and Marxian Political Economy,* Cambridge: Cambridge University Press.

Hunt, Tristram (2010) *The Frock-Coated Communist: The Revolutionary Life of Friedrich Engels,* Harmondsworth: Penguin.

Kangal, Kaan (2020) *Friedrich Engels and the Dialectics of Nature,* Cham: Palgrave Macmillan.

Kapp, Yvonne (1972) *Eleanor Marx,* vol. I: *Family Life,* London: Lawrence and Wishart.

Kapp, Yvonne (1976) *Eleanor Marx,* vol. II: *The Crowded Years,* London: Lawrence and Wishart.

Lidtke, Vernon L. (2016) *The Outlawed Party: Social Democracy in Germany 1878-1890,* Princeton: Princeton University Press.

Marcus, Steven (2017 [1974]) *Engels, Manchester and the Working Class,* Milton Park: Routledge.

Marx, Karl (1975 [1844]) 'Summary of Frederick Engels' Article "Outlines of a Critique of Political Economy"', in *Karl Marx Frederick Engels Collected Works*, vol. 3: *Marx and Engels 1843-1844,* London: Lawrence and Wishart, pp. 375–6.

Marx, Karl (1987a [1859]) 'Preface' to 'A Contribution to the Critique of Political Economy. Part One', in *Marx Engels Collected Works*: vol. 29, *Marx: 1857-1861,* London: Lawrence and Wishart, pp. 261–6.

Marx, Karl (1987b [1859]) 'A Contribution to the Critique of Political Economy. Part One', in *Marx Engels Collected Works*, vol. 29: *Marx: 1857-1861* , London: Lawrence and Wishart, pp. 257–417.

Marx, Karl (1993 [1939–1941]) *Grundrisse: Foundations of a Critique of Political Economy,* Harmondsworth: Penguin.

Marx, Karl (1996a) [1867]) 'Capital, Volume I', in *Marx Engels Collected Works*, vol. 35: *Capital, Volume I,* London: Lawrence and Wishart.

Marx, Karl (1996b [1873]) 'Preface to the Second German Edition', in *Marx Engels Collected Works*, vol. 35: *Capital, Volume I,* London: Lawrence and Wishart.

Marx, Karl (1998) [1894]) 'Capital, Volume III', in *Marx Engels Collected Works*, vol. 37: *Capital Volume III,* London: Lawrence and Wishart.

Marx, Karl [sic] and Engels, Frederick (1975a [1845]) 'The Holy Family, Or Critique of Critical Criticism', in *Marx Engels Collected Works*, vol. 4: *Marx and Engels 1844-1845,* London: Lawrence and Wishart, pp. 5–211.

Marx, Karl and Engels, Frederick (1975b) *Marx Engels Collected Works*, vol. 2: *Engels 1838-1842,* London: Lawrence & Wishart.

Marx, Karl and Engels, Frederick (1982) *Marx Engels Collected Works*, vol. 38: *Marx and Engels 1844-1851 Letters* , London: Lawrence and Wishart.

Marx, Karl and Engels, Frederick (1983a) *Marx Engels Collected Works*, vol. 40: *Marx and Engels 1856-1859 Letters*, London: Lawrence and Wishart.

Marx, Karl and Engels, Friedrich (1983b) *Marx Engels Gesamtausgabe* (MEGA²), vol. II/5, *Das Kapital. Kritik der politischen Ökonomie. Erster Band, Hamburg 1867*, Berlin: Akademie Verlag

Marx, Karl and Engels, Friedrich (1989) 'Le Capital, Paris, 1872-75', in *Marx Engels Gesamtausgabe* (MEGA²), vol. II/7, Berlin: Akademie Verlag.

Marx, Karl and Engels, Friedrich (1990) 'Capital. A Critical Analysis of Capitalist Production, London 1887', in *Marx Engels Gesamtausgabe* (MEGA²), vol. II/9, Berlin: Akademie Verlag.

Marx, Karl and Engels, Friedrich (1991) 'Das Kapital. Kritik der Politischen Ökonomie. Erster Band, Hamburg 1890', in *Marx Engels Gesamtausgabe* (MEGA²), vol. II/10, Berlin: Akademie Verlag.

Marx, Karl and Engels, Frederick (2001) *Marx Engels Collected Works*, vol. 48: *Marx and Engels Letters 1887-1890*, London: Lawrence and Wishart.

Marx, Karl and Engels, Friedrich (2004) 'Das Kapital. Kritik der politischen Ökonomie. Dritter Band, Hamburg 1894', in *Marx Engels Gesamtausgabe* (MEGA²), II/15, Berlin: Akademie Verlag.

Marx, Karl and Engels, Friedrich (2008) 'Das Kapital. Kritik der politischen Ökonomie. Zweiter Band, Hamburg 1885' in *Marx Engels Gesamtausgabe* (MEGA²), vol. II/13, Berlin: Akademie Verlag.

Musto, Marcello (Ed.) (2014) *Workers Unite! The International 150 Years Later*, London: Bloomsbury Academic.

Nietzold, Roland, Focke, Wolfgang, Skambraks Hannes (Eds.) (1991) 'Entstehung und Überlieferung', in *Marx Engels Gesamtausgabe* (MEGA²), vol. II/10, Berlin: Akademie Verlag. pp. 705–12.

Roberts, William Clare (2017) *Marx's Inferno: The Political Theory of Capital*, Princeton: Princeton University Press.

Ryazanov, David (1927) *Karl Marx and Friedrich Engels*, edited by Alexander Trachtenberg, London: Martin Lawrence.

Saito, Kohei (2017) *Karl Marx's Ecosocialism: Capital, Nature and the Unfinished Critique of Political Economy*, New York: Monthly Review Press.

Steadman Jones, Gareth (2016) *Karl Marx: Greatness and Illusion*, Princeton: Princeton University Press.

van der Linden, Marcel, and Hubmann, Gerald (Eds.) (2018) *Marx's Capital: An Unfinished Project?* Leiden: Brill.

Part II
The Making of *Le Capital*

6 Le Capital

A Transnational, Family and Personal Endeavour

Kenneth Hemmerechts and Nohemi Jocabeth Echeverria Vicente

Introduction

The publishing process of the French version of *Das Kapital* was an international effort of various geographically separated individuals in Western Europe (see Bottigelli 1972: 12–31). Many people were involved in the process of writing, translating, editing and printing *Le Capital*, published in 44 instalments arranged in series[1] (see Uroyeva 1965: 124–80): Karl Marx (the author, residing in London), Joseph Roy (the translator, living in Bordeaux), Maurice Lachâtre (the refugee editor, living consecutively in Spain, Belgium and Switzerland), Juste Vernouillet and Adolphe Dervaux (working for the editor's company in Paris), the printer Lahure (in Paris) and Adolphe Quêst (the court-appointed administrator). Additionally, relatives and friends of Marx, such as Friedrich Engels, Jenny Marx (mother), Jenny Marx (daughter), Paul Lafargue, Laura Marx, Eleanor Marx and Charles Longuet, participated to some extent in the publishing of this edition.

In this chapter, we will describe the participation of Marx and others involved in *Le Capital* from December 1871, when Marx received Lachâtre's publishing offer, until the publication of the last instalments in November 1875. The focus lies not on the content of the French edition of *Capital, Volume I,* but on an overview of the contribution made by Marx and others to the publishing process. The chapter provides evidence that this edition was a family and personal endeavour of a transnational nature and delivers a history without focusing solely on Marx's involvement.

We present an examination of the publishing process of *Le Capital* without a sole focus on correspondence written by Marx and include correspondence from connections who were previously overlooked, such as relatives, friends and people working in Lachâtre's company. This approach sheds light on other people's role and contributions to the publication of this French edition, instead of giving a narrow depiction of Marx's intellectual work. By doing so, we aim to provide a nuanced representation of Marx's work on the French edition and how it intersected with his network of contacts.[2]

DOI: 10.4324/9781003336365-8

The role of Karl Marx, his relatives and his friends in the making of *Le Capital*

Accounts of the publishing process of *Le Capital* have several shortcomings. First, they tend to underestimate Karl Marx's involvement in *Le Capital*, particularly the extent to which the final product, including the translation of the French edition, was Marx's own creation (e.g., D'Hondt 1985: 131–7). Second, the literature tends to downplay the contribution of relatives and friends, such as the help provided by Marx's daughters (e.g., Lefebvre 2016: xxiii–lviii). Marx, as we will show, drew on this network for support in the editorial work and translation of this edition. In some cases, these contacts provided other types of assistance, including advice, financial support or help in finding suitable people for certain roles in the publishing process, such as editor or translator.

Karl Marx

The initial arrangements regarding the publishing process included various stages that started and finished with Marx's input: (1) Marx had to provide manuscript pages to the translator, who would then translate the manuscript and send it to Paris, (2) Marx would correct proofs of the translated material and (3) afterwards he would give his approval for printing. However, after receiving the first documents to be proofread around the end of April 1872, it became clear that the translation was not as expected. This created problems during the publishing process since Marx had to spend considerable time improving it.[3] After the difficulties with the quality of the translation emerged, the publishing process was changed, and Marx, who was proficient in French,[4] would directly receive the translator's work which – only after checking it – he would send to Paris, adding an extra stage, in which he was involved, to the publishing process (Karl Marx to Juste Vernouillet, 15 August 1872, Marx and Engels 1989b: 423).

  Marx rewrote the text to make it more accessible to the reader and to render the translation less literal (see Karl Marx to Nicolai Danielson, 28 May 1872, Marx and Engels 1989b: 385–6; Karl Marx to Friedrich Adolph Sorge, 21 June 1872, Marx and Engels 1989b: 398–400).[5] The work on the translated manuscript and proofs, however, proved to be laborious. Jenny Marx (daughter), for example, wrote of 'the revision of the French translation, which unfortunately is so very imperfect that Mohr [Karl Marx] has been obliged to rewrite the greater part of the first chapter' (Jenny Marx [daughter] to the Kugelmann family, 27 June 1872, Marx and Engels 1989b: 582–3). In July 1874, Marx also emphasized the burden of work, and that help from French contacts was limited to wording. Furthermore, Marx was adding new material to the edition and thus fundamentally deciding what to incorporate:

> It is not, as you appear to imagine, merely a question of details and of minor corrections of style; rather I had, indeed am still having, to do virtually the whole thing over again. Once condemned to this thankless task I added

here and there some important new developments, which will give the French edition – as I shall incidentally point out in the afterword – a value not possessed by the German original. As to my French friends, they can only be of use on a few points of phraseology.

(Karl Marx to Maurice Lachâtre, 23 July 1874,
Marx and Engels 1991: 25–6)

Amid assiduous revisions of translation and content, Marx experienced setbacks, with health and family problems. In the period of 1872–75, two of his grand-children died (Jenny Marx (mother) to Thomas Allsop, 12 September 1874, Hecker and Limmroth 2014: 486–8; Jenny Marx [daughter] to the Kugelmann family, 23 December 1872, Marx and Engels 1989b: 583–5), and he travelled to spas, for example, Karlsbad in 1874 (Karl Marx to Ludwig Kugelmann, 4 August 1874, Marx and Engels 1991: 31) and 1875 (Karl Marx to Friedrich Engels, 21 August 1875, Marx and Engels 1991: 82–6), to improve his health. He would eventually take until 1875 to finish his work on the French edition (Karl Marx to Juste Vernouillet, 28 April 1873, Gaudin 2019: 142, 147).[6]

The 'Reader's notice' – dated 28 April 1875 – placed at the end of the French edition is an abbreviated account of the publishing process that gives further insights into how it occurred. First, Marx gave a positive appreciation of the translator's literal and accurate translation but also commented that he revised the translation because he wanted a reader-friendly text. Second, Marx commented that the publishing process took place sequentially in instalments that received different levels of attention, possibly introducing style changes over time (see Marx 1875: 348). Third, Marx also emphasized differences compared to the German second edition: simplifications and additions.

The 'Errata' section at the end of the book also included Marx's view of the publishing process as cumbersome, due to the geographical distance between himself, the editor, the printer and the translator, which resulted in errata (see Marx 1875: 351). The specific nineteenth-century technological conditions – that is, fewer communication tools, lack of copying technology and the less strict translation standards mentioned by Lefebvre (2016: xxviii, xxxi and xl) – also need to be considered as part of the context in which the edition was produced.

Marx was actively and crucially involved in the publishing process of this edition. In discussing the drafts of *Capital, Volume II,* in 1883, Engels wrote that Marx 'weighed every word' (Engels to Becker, 22 May 1883, Marx and Engels 1995: 25–7). When he was unwell or could not work, the publishing process stalled. Furthermore, Marx would rework and add material to this edition besides revising the translation. In this sense, the published version of *Le Capital* is an edition that Marx approved and made as he saw fit.

Laura Marx and Paul Lafargue

The start-up of the published version of *Le Capital* relied not so much on efforts made by Marx but rather on the intervention of those in his close environment. Relatives laid the foundation for the publication of this edition when they met the future editor, Maurice Lachâtre. In December 1871, Laura Marx and her husband Paul Lafargue (Karl Marx to Friedrich Engels, 18 March 1868, Marx and Engels 1987: 553–4) wrote to Marx and Engels respectively that they had an offer for Marx to publish a French edition of his book (Lafargue to Engels, 12 December 1871, Marx and Engels 1989a: 393–4). Marx received this news after Lafargue and Laura Marx, in San Sebastian (Spain), met with Maurice Lachâtre, 'a first-rate French publisher, who is very anxious to publish "Das Kapital"' (Jenny Marx [daughter] to Ludwig Kugelmann, 22 January 1872, Marx and Engels 1989b: 573–5). He, just like Laura Marx and Paul Lafargue, had fled France due to the events of the Paris Commune (Jenny Marx [daughter] to Ludwig Kugelmann, 3 October 1871, Marx and Engels 1989b: 562–4) and 'was most desirous of being useful to the "cause"' (Laura Marx to Karl Marx, 12 December 1871, RGASPI 1.5.2667). This meeting would eventually offer Marx an opportunity to publish a French translation of *Das Kapital*, as Laura Marx wrote that Lachâtre 'declares himself ready & delighted to publish your book' (Laura Marx to Marx, 12 December 1871, RGASPI 1.5.2667). Laura Marx and Paul Lafargue's contribution was, however, not limited to the finding of a suitable editor: from the start, Marx was in contact with them to discuss the publishing stipulations for *Le Capital*. He, for example, communicated to Laura Marx that 'in every respect a cheap popular edition' was his preference (Karl Marx to Laura Marx, 18 December 1871, Marx and Engels 1989b: 283–4).

Lafargue also helped pay for *Le Capital* (Lafargue to Engels, 29 May 1872, Frederick Engels, Paul and Laura Lafargue 1960: 444–51) and would also help with the revision of the translation, given his proficiency in French (Jenny Marx (mother) to Eleanor Marx, dated in Hecker and Limmroth 2014: 468–9 as 25 March 1873; Karl Marx to Maurice Lachâtre, 9 January 1873, Gaudin 2019: 74–9). Not only Lafargue but others too would help Marx to revise the French translation, as will be shown below.

August Philips

Before signing a contract with the editor's company to publish the edition, Marx received legal advice after giving a draft contract to August Philips, a family member knowledgeable in the law.[7] In a letter dated 26 January 1872, Philips gave his opinion on the contract. He wrote to Marx that he should not sign the draft contract, which stipulated that 2,000 Francs should be invested by the author and that Marx risked losing the money. Marx probably also asked Philips to participate in the financing of this publication, which he declined to do, giving two reasons, one ideological and one financial: 'Mainly because I do not want to support propaganda for the International; but also because I see no advantage for you in this publication [...]. I will not do this for your political or revolutionary goals' (August Philips to Karl Marx, 26 January 1872, Gielkens 1999: 72 and 225).[8]

Friedrich Engels

From the start of this endeavour, Marx's relatives and friends were kept up to date on the state of the French edition and collaborated with him. Engels – for example – wrote in May 1872 to Liebknecht that new material for the second German and French edition would come out soon and proofreading was happening (Friedrich Engels to Wilhelm Liebknecht, 7 May 1872, Marx and Engels 1989b: 364–7).[9]

During the publishing process, Engels was a reader of *Le Capital* and would write to Marx about his impressions of the French edition of Volume I. In November 1873, Marx left with Eleanor Marx to Harrogate, a spa town near Manchester (Friedrich Engels to Friedrich Adolph Sorge, 25 November 1873, Marx and Engels 1989b: 536–9). Engels would write to Marx there that he had read a chapter of *Le Capital*.[10] Engels was critical of the translation of *Das Kapital* declaring that 'its vigour and vitality and life have gone to the devil' (Friedrich Engels to Karl Marx, 29 November 1873, Marx and Engels 1989b: 539–41). Although there are not many letters between Engels and Marx in which they discuss their views of the translation of *Le Capital*, this should not be taken as evidence that Engels was disengaged from the publishing process of this edition. By this time, Engels lived near Marx in London, they were close friends and collaborators, and the French edition was likely a discussion topic when they met in person. Engels was proficient in French,[11] so could help Marx with proofreading the translation. From two handwritten notes by Engels, it can be inferred that Engels helped Marx with the second German and French editions and that changes he suggested were incorporated into the French edition.[12]

Jenny Marx (mother and daughter), Charles Longuet and other communards

Once the editor was willing to publish Marx's work in French, the translator Joseph Roy, a resident of Bordeaux, was appointed (Karl Marx to Laura Marx, 28 February 1872, Marx and Engels 1989b: 327–8). We again see that Marx's connections played key roles in the initial arrangements. The Frenchman Charles Longuet, who also fled the Commune and later married Marx's daughter Jenny, was instrumental in arranging this translator (Charles Longuet to Karl Marx, 13 January 1872, Gaudin 2019: 81).[13] Longuet wrote to Marx about Roy: 'I am happy to inform you that I have just received a letter from the friend in Paris I had written to about your future *traductore* [translator] who I trust will not be your *traditore* [traitor]' (Charles Longuet to Karl Marx, 13 January 1872, Gaudin 2019: 81).

Earlier, towards the end of 1871, Jenny Marx (mother) also tried to locate Charles Keller, a previous translator who had been working on a translation of *Das Kapital*.

> Möhmchen [Jenny Marx (mother)] is just trying to find out the where-abouts of Keller. She has written for that purpose to his sister. If he is not to

be found (and in due time), the translator of Feuerbach [i.e., Joseph Roy] would be the man.

(Karl Marx to Laura Marx, 18 December 1871,
Marx and Engels 1989b: 283–4)

Keller would ultimately not become the translator of the published French edition.[14]

Moreover, there is evidence that both daughter and mother Jenny Marx along with Charles Longuet helped in the next steps of the publishing process. In a letter dated 1 May 1872, Jenny Marx (daughter) wrote to Charles Longuet that:

Papa has read the preface & first pages of Das Kapital with Mützchen [Jenny Marx (mother)] who, it appears, has thoroughly studied the book. He found fault with some of the first sentences in the preface which certainly are not so well translated as the rest.

(Jenny Marx [daughter] to Charles Longuet,
1 May 1872, Meier 1982: 111–2)

Another letter from Jenny Marx (daughter) to Charles Longuet commented on the deficient translation and her contribution:

Papa is calling me – he wants me to read through the second part [livraison] with him, which has just arrived. [...] I regret to say that the translation of the first part of the second *livraison* is most negligently done – very carelessly indeed. It is necessary to make many corrections. Papa is very sorry he cannot consult you as to these corrections and almost feels inclined to go to Oxford on purpose [where Longuet then lived]. However, as you are coming to London on Saturday there will be some time for you to look them over with him.

(April 1872, Meier 1979: 149–50, Meier 1982: 110–1)

Other letters also contain evidence of the involvement of Jenny Marx (daughter) and Charles Longuet. According to Engels, Marx spent several days in November in Oxford where he checked the French translation with the Longuet family (Friedrich Engels to Friedrich Adolph Sorge, 16 November 1872, Marx and Engels 1989b: 446–51).[15] Marx wrote from there to the editor (Karl Marx to Maurice Lachâtre, 14 November 1872, Baronian and Rieucau 2020: 21–2) that he made changes to two 'placards' to improve the translation.

In April and the beginning of May 1874, Marx was in Ramsgate to improve his health (Karl Marx to Ludwig Kugelmann, 18 May 1874, Marx and Engels 1991: 17–19), from where he wrote to his daughter Jenny about French proofs that he was going to send to her and that he would like Longuet to check. The letter shows that at this time Marx received help from his daughter Jenny and Charles Longuet with the proofreading of *Le Capital*; nevertheless, he had the last word on the proofs as he then stated that 'I shall then make a definitive version of the copy to be sent to Paris' (Karl Marx to Jenny Marx [daughter], undated but according to Marx and Engels (1991: 15): 'between 20 and 24 April 1874').

Besides Lafargue and Longuet, Marx would also receive help from: 'Vaillant, Lissagaray and other competent Communards' (Karl Marx to Maurice Lachâtre, 1 May 1872, Gaudin 2019: 100).[16] There was a flow of political refugees, fleeing the Paris Commune to European capitals including London (Forster 2019). In a letter to the editor in 1874, Marx noted that help with the translation was provided by others, but this help was certainly limited to language (Karl Marx to Maurice Lachâtre, 23 July 1874, Marx and Engels 1991: 25–6).[17]

Other contributions to the publishing process of *Le Capital*

In contrast to the role of Marx's relatives and friends, other people involved in the publishing process in various capacities are now receiving more attention in the literature (see Gaudin 2019). The focus tends to be primarily on the translator and editor, and others who were not relatives or friends of Marx, such as the printer Lahure, are mentioned less frequently in reconstructions of the publishing process. These other contacts, who have gone largely unnoticed, were in fact essential to ensure the circulation of manuscripts and proofs, and to keep the publishing process moving. The description given in the following sections of their roles in this process will shed light on these aspects, with a view to enabling an informed assessment of the extent of their contribution.

Joseph Roy

After Marx had received news that Lachâtre wished to publish a French translation of *Das Kapital*, he contacted Charles Keller, who had been working on a French translation of the first German edition. However, Keller was then occupied with other work and since Marx felt that the editor wanted to publish quickly, he chose Roy who, unlike others, was available (Karl Marx to Maurice Lachâtre, 9 January 1873, Gaudin 2019: 74–9).[18]

In early February 1872, the translator Joseph Roy received from Marx the first material to translate, namely a (at least partly) handwritten manuscript (Roy to Marx, 2 February 1872, Marx and Engels 1989a: 395) based on the second German edition of *Das Kapital* (Karl Marx to Maurice Lachâtre, 30 January 1872, Baronian and Rieucau 2020: 18–19).[19] To his daughter, Laura, Marx had specified that he would send 'the old one [i.e., the first edition of *Das Kapital*] with the changes inserted' (Karl Marx to Laura Marx, 18 December 1871, Marx and Engels 1989b: 283–4).[20] Initially, the translator would send his translated manuscript directly to Paris: 'Today I have written him to send at once to Paris what manuscript may be ready' (Karl Marx to Laura Marx, 28 February 1872, Marx and Engels 1989b: 327–8). Later, after receiving the first proofs at around the end of April 1872, Marx would directly receive Roy's translated manuscript to check it (Karl Marx to Laura Marx, 28 February 1872, Marx and Engels 1989b: 327–8).

In March 1872, Roy had highlighted challenges involved in translating *Das Kapital*, such as the difficulty of translating the work into French and the linguistic differences between the French and German languages that made the translation process lengthier:

> It is not that the translation presents serious difficulties, but it does present very many small problems that are constantly holding us up. First of all, French, because of its Latin origins, contains a multitude of words which look and sound very different, although their meaning is similar. As a result, the relationships between the ideas are not reflected in the language, and in this respect German is far superior. You know this as well as, even better than, I do; but despite your perfect knowledge of our language, you may not be as aware as us of another difficulty that is not easily overcome. In a work such as yours, the same words are necessarily repeated very often. This repetition shocks the ear in French infinitely more than in German, because it is not so easy to place the words where one would like.
>
> (Joseph Roy to Karl Marx, 14 March 1872,
> Marx and Engels 1989a: 398–9)

Immediately after the first proofs of *Le Capital* arrived near the end of April 1872, the translator was criticized by the editor, even claiming that Roy was not French. It would be the first and not the last time that there were complaints about Roy and the translation (Maurice Lachâtre to Karl Marx, 29 April 1872, Marx and Engels 1989a: 406–7). Lachâtre, particularly, criticized the quality of the translation on many occasions (e.g., Maurice Lachâtre to Karl Marx, 30 May 1872 and 13 August 1872, Marx and Engels 1989a: 414–15 and 415–16).

At first in May 1872, Marx defended the translator, commented on the literal quality of the translation and stressed that Roy was a native speaker (Karl Marx to Maurice Lachâtre, 1 May 1872, Gaudin 2019: 100). However, in 1873, Marx pinpointed the translation as problematic and found that the translator was inadequate for the task. Marx made strenuous efforts to bring the publication up to his expectations and became overburdened with the reworking of the French edition and revision of the translation, having little time to focus on other projects (Karl Marx to Maurice Lachâtre, 9 January 1873, Gaudin 2019: 74–9).

Previously, Marx thought that the translator was suited to the job, since Roy had translated Ludwig Feuerbach *Religion. Death – immortality – religion* and *Essence of Christianity*, in 1864, and he had given his own positive appraisal of the translation of the first pages of the first chapter (Karl Marx to Maurice Lachâtre, 11 February 1873, Gaudin 2019: 123–7).[21] Marx wrote that this had deceived him because Feuerbach's work had previously been translated by another translator, and this made Roy's translation of Feuerbach less difficult:

I was misled at first by the praise I had heard for his translation of Feuerbach (there is a reason for this: Feuerbach had been translated by Everbeck before Roy, and it is much easier to work on such a basis)

(Karl Marx to Maurice Lachâtre, 11 February 1873,
Gaudin 2019: 123–7)

His trust in the translator declined during the proofreading phase of the publishing process. In May 1872, Roy admitted that the translation might be too literal:

The translation is perhaps too faithful, I mean at times stays too close to your text, in accordance with the genius of our language, however I believe that the reading of it will not present more difficulties than are inherent to the subject matter.

(Joseph Roy to Karl Marx, 2 May 1872,
Marx and Engels 1989a: 407–9)

There may have been a conflict between what Marx wanted from a translation and Roy's work. The fact that the beginning of the work is more difficult to translate was also mentioned in Lefebvre (2016: xxxvii) and by Marx in a letter dated 11 February 1873. This difficulty was perhaps felt more strongly because the aim was to make the work 'more accessible to the reader' ('Reader's notice', see also the facsimile of Marx's letter in the first instalment). Roy also indicated problems with an instalment (Joseph Roy to Karl Marx, 8 May 1872, Marx and Engels 1989a: 412; see also Adolphe Dervaux to Karl Marx, undated, IISH D 1016) for which he blamed the printer. In 1873, Roy also admitted mistakes when he wrote to Marx: 'You can count on my accuracy and less faulty work' (Joseph Roy to Karl Marx, 26 March 1873, IISH D 3852).

Besides the quality of the translation, the geographical distances between people working on the publication set back the publishing process. Near the end of 1872, Marx noted that sending the proofs to Roy, who frequently changed addresses, created delays (Karl Marx to Juste Vernouillet, 5 November 1872, Gaudin 2019: 113 and 117).[22] In a letter written in March 1873 to Marx, the translator communicated his difficult living circumstances and his dissatisfaction about the lack of payment when he heard that there were comments about his slow translation speed (Roy to Marx, 26 March 1873, IISH D 3852). He also had not yet received a published series of the edition (Karl Marx to Juste Vernouillet, 29 March 1873, Gaudin 2019: 134 and 138), which meant that he could not see and learn from the published work and improve his future translation, as Marx wrote to Vernouillet and the editor (Karl Marx to Maurice Lachâtre, 29 March 1873, Gaudin 2019: 135, 139).

The translation was a lengthy and cumbersome process. Near the end of October 1873, almost two years after starting the translation, Marx received the last remaining translated manuscript pages from Roy (Karl Marx to Juste

Vernouillet, 28 October 1873, Gaudin 2019: 146 and 151). This marked the end of Roy's involvement in the publishing process of *Le Capital*.

Maurice Lachâtre

The editor was heavily involved in the French edition. First, he had an influence on how the edition would look and be published. The first instalment contained a printed facsimile of a letter of 18 March 1872 from Marx to Lachâtre (Marx 1875: 7; Rubel 2019: 91; Marx 1989b: 9), repeating the stipulation in the contract between the editor's company and Marx that the publication would be in instalments. The editor wished to receive a letter to this effect from Marx, which would be followed by his response. Marx was of the opinion that Lachâtre was delaying the publication and felt it necessary to correct the editor's letter (Karl Marx to Paul Lafargue, 21 March 1872, Marx and Engels 1989b: 346–52). As arranged in the contract with Marx, the work was printed in double columns and in instalments of eight pages.[23]

Second, the editor also took part in the organizing of the publishing process, including a letter setting out steps in the process. (1) Marx could send the to-be-translated manuscript to the translator; (2) the translator could give the translated manuscript to Marx to check the quality of the translation. These points were formulated tentatively by the editor, and it was up to Marx to arrange how this initial stage of the translation would take place; (3) this translation should be given to the publisher in Paris who gave it to the printer; (4) printed proofs would be simultaneously sent to various people: the editor, Marx and the translator (the name of Lafargue is also mentioned as optional); (5) the corrected versions of these sheets would be sent as new printed proofs to the author and the translator; (6) when there were new corrections after this round of proofreading, new printed proofs would be sent to the author and the translator; (7) the author should then prepare and approve the final version; (8) the translator was paid after Marx approved printing and after each instalment (Maurice Lachâtre to Karl Marx, 12 March 1872, Marx and Engels 1989a: 397–8).[24] Third, he proofread and sought to influence Marx on the content of the text (e.g., Maurice Lachâtre to Karl Marx, 9 May 1872, IISH D 2815, Maurice Lachâtre to Karl Marx, 9 April 1873, IISH D 2835).[25] Lachâtre, for example, noted in a letter dated 4 May 1875 that he did the 'proofreading of instalments 36 to 44' (Maurice Lachâtre to Karl Marx, 4 May 1875, Gaudin 2019: 159).

In May 1872, the use of notes in the edition was also discussed by the editor. Lachâtre found the notes too long and too numerous and felt that they would annoy the reader. Lachâtre suggested numbering the notes and placing them at the end of the volume. In the published work, the notes, however, were not placed at the end of the volume and are ordered with a number which restarts at each column of the double-columned pages (Maurice Lachâtre to Karl Marx, 14 May 1872, IISH D 2816).[26] This shows that Marx also had an influence on editorial decisions, such as the way footnotes were presented.

Another discussion point was the use of non-French and dead languages (Maurice Lachâtre to Karl Marx, 5 May 1872, Gaudin 2019: 101–3). In May 1872, Marx preferred to have a French translation of all foreign language terms. However, Lachâtre preferred to clearly provide all non-French and dead language citations with a French translation in an italic font and brackets. The editor's preference was eventually not followed.[27]

As seen in his enquiries about the terminology in the edition, Lachâtre was an editor who advised Marx and wished to publish the work in as accurate a form as possible (Maurice Lachâtre to Karl Marx, 30 November 1872, IISH D 2827). While doing his editorial work, Lachâtre would often criticize the work of the translator. In May 1872, for example, he commented the following to Marx: 'I am sending you a short extract from a letter I have received from Paris, so that you can see I am not the only one to find the translator's style incorrect in several passages' (Maurice Lachâtre to Karl Marx, 4 May 1872, Marx and Engels 1989a: 409–10) and 'it is clear to me that the translation work leaves much to be desired' (Maurice Lachâtre to Karl Marx, 30 May 1872, Marx and Engels 1989a: 414–15).

Lachâtre would stay involved through the entire publishing process (e.g., Maurice Lachâtre to Karl Marx, 24 June 1874, IISH D 2842). Notwithstanding this editorial involvement, Lachâtre often indicated that Marx had the final say on the edition (e.g., Maurice Lachâtre to Karl Marx, 17 February 1872, Gaudin 2019: 83–4). For example, in a letter dated 15 February 1875, the editor noted that

> This morning I received instalments 33-34 and 35 to check your corrections; I still found a good number of mistakes, please take a look at the new corrections, and if you approve them, be so kind as to send the proofs back to the printer in Paris.
>
> (Maurice Lachâtre to Karl Marx, 15 February 1875,
> Gaudin 2019: 158)

His advisory role continued, and near the end of the publishing process in 1875, the editor felt that Marx made the book too long and commented critically on the table of contents presented in the proofs: it was too detailed and pages were missing (Maurice Lachâtre to Karl Marx, 11 June 1875, Gaudin 2019: 160–1). Lachâtre was also not happy with Marx's criticism of the translation and the edition in the 'Reader's notice' and the note in the 'Errata' and advised Marx to remove them: 'You are doing the critics' work in advance and denigrating your own book' (Maurice Lachâtre to Karl Marx, 11 June 1875, Gaudin 2019: 160–1). The published version still contains a note in the 'Errata' and the 'Avis au lecteur', but it is unclear whether Marx removed or revised text in these parts of the book. A shortening or removal of the postface was also recommended by the editor. Although the published work still contains an 'extrait' of the postface of the second German edition (Maurice Lachâtre to Karl Marx, 18 June 1875, IISH D 2851), it is uncertain whether Marx followed the advice of the editor.

The printer Lahure

The printer Lahure oversaw the receipt of the translated manuscript and produced proofs. This process did not always go smoothly. In May 1872, the translator noted that the composition of the proofs was not optimal (Joseph Roy to Marx, 8 May 1872, Marx and Engels 1989a: 412).[28] The editor asked the printer Lahure to change the workers who were doing the composition, echoing Roy's criticism (Maurice Lachâtre to Karl Marx, 30 May 1872, Marx and Engels 1989a: 414–15).

In the beginning of 1873, Marx blamed the printer for delays in the publishing process (Karl Marx to Maurice Lachâtre, 9 January 1873, Gaudin 2019: 74–9).[29] One problem was the loss of a proofread, translated manuscript including chapter VII, which Marx claimed to have sent directly to the printer on 8 October 1872 (Karl Marx to Maurice Lachâtre, 19 October 1872, Gaudin 2019: 107–8). After Marx started reworking the supposedly lost manuscript, he found out that the old manuscript was not really lost and that proofs had been printed but not received by him.

Marx also complained that proofs were not immediately sent according to his instructions (i.e., in two copies) and in a more orderly and timely manner. The proofs also continued to give rise to (new) issues and Marx thus kept revising them. Marx was clearly dissatisfied with the printer's work and even spoke of 'bad faith'. Lachâtre did not agree that there had been bad faith regarding the publication: 'Believe me, there were no hidden political or other reasons for delaying publication' (Maurice Lachâtre to Karl Marx, 14 February 1873, IISH D 2831).

Near the end of 1874, after a hiatus when Marx was in Karlsbad to recover his health, he again sent manuscript pages to Paris (Karl Marx to Maurice Lachâtre, 12 November 1874, Baronian and Rieucau 2020: 22). At the beginning of 1875, Marx was dissatisfied with the lack of communication from the printer and the printing progress: 'you seem to want neither to answer my letters, nor to send proofs, nor to proceed with the printing until such time as you choose (…)' (Karl Marx to the printer Louis Lahure, 20 January 1875, IISH C 410). The printer Lahure had not replied to Marx concerning the receipt of a manuscript, and the editor blamed the printer's young age and workload.[30]

The printer's work was stalled; it was not until 2 February 1875 that the printer Lahure informed Marx that they had received approval to restart and proofs would be sent: 'We have received permission to continue the composition of Le Capital, which we had to suspend' (the printer Louis Lahure to Karl Marx, 2 February 1875, IISH D 2887). This specific delay can be attributed to the administrator, who now managed the editor's company and had to give authorization to continue with the publishing process, as described below. It might also be that after a long period of receiving no translated manuscripts from Marx, the printer had become involved in other projects.

Adolphe Dervaux

Working for the editor's company, Dervaux's role was to receive translated material (Karl Marx to Juste Vernouillet, 15 August 1872, Marx and Engels 1989b: 423), receive and send proofs and make suggestions about how the publishing process should be organized (Adolphe Dervaux to Karl Marx, 11 May 1872, Gaudin 2019: 104) and to proofread (Maurice Lachâtre to Karl Marx, 30 May 1872, Marx and Engels 1989a: 414–15). Dervaux also made suggestions about the translation of foreign language words in the edition, reflected on the use of punctuation marks (Adolphe Dervaux to Karl Marx, 20 June 1872, IISH D 1018) and acted as an intermediary between the printer and Marx.

In the first instalment of *Le Capital*, a portrait and facsimile of a letter from Marx were printed at the request of Lachâtre (Karl Marx to Maurice Lachâtre, 30 January 1872, Baronian and Rieucau 2020: 18–19). Marx had to arrange the portrait with Dervaux, who was involved in the engravings of the French edition (Maurice Lachâtre to Karl Marx, 17 February 1872, Gaudin 2019: 83–4).[31] Jenny Marx (daughter) mentioned that the portrait resulted in delays: 'the fact is that it is owing to the likeness which had to be first taken, then engraved, that a great delay has been occasioned' (Jenny Marx [daughter] to Ludwig Kugelmann, 3 May 1872, Marx and Engels 1989b: 578–9).

In May 1872, Dervaux wanted to make the publishing more efficient and wrote about the possibility of reorganizing the publishing process, in which Marx received the proofs from Lachâtre and Roy with their corrections (Adolphe Dervaux to Karl Marx, 3 May 1872, IISH D 1015B).

Later in May 1872, Dervaux wrote that it would also be better if Marx first received Roy's translation of manuscript pages, which he would then be able to correct and send back to Dervaux. According to Dervaux, this would facilitate the process by producing better first proofs: 'it will mean less trouble and less money' (Adolphe Dervaux to Karl Marx, 11 May 1872, Gaudin 2019: 104).

Towards the end of May 1872, Lachâtre wrote about the possibility of Roy sending the translated manuscript to Marx directly to be revised before it was sent to Paris, echoing Dervaux (Maurice Lachâtre to Karl Marx, 30 May 1872, Marx and Engels 1989a: 414–15). This seemed to be the new way of working, as seen in Marx's letter to Vernouillet dated 15 August, in which Marx reports that he has sent manuscript pages of the second section to Dervaux (Marx and Engels 1989b: 423). Dervaux's involvement stopped in August 1872 and Vernouillet replaced him in the publishing process.

Juste Vernouillet

At the beginning of the publishing process, in February 1872, Juste Vernouillet – who was in charge of the editor's company in Paris – sent Karl Marx a clean copy of the contract between Marx and the editor's company for the publication of *Le Capital* (Juste Vernouillet to Karl Marx, 13 February 1872, IISH D 4374).

In the summer of 1872, Vernouillet became more involved in the publishing process (Maurice Lachâtre to Karl Marx, 13 August 1872, Marx and Engels 1989a: 415–16). Until then, Dervaux received the manuscript pages from Marx and sent the proofs from the printer to Marx. According to the editor, Dervaux stopped fulfilling this role. Instead, the printer had to send the proofs immediately to Marx who then sent them to the printer (including Roy's translated manuscript pages).[32] The flow of proofs and translated manuscripts now had to be arranged between the printer and Marx.

Perhaps after the bad experience when the printer Lahure presumably lost one of Marx's manuscripts in October 1872, letters from November 1872 indicate that Vernouillet was receiving translated manuscript pages from Marx, which he gave to the printer (e.g., Vernouillet to Marx, 2 November 1872, Gaudin 2019: 112). Marx also complained to Vernouillet that he had not been provided with new proofs of instalments 8 and 9 (Karl Marx to Juste Vernouillet, 5 November 1872, Gaudin 2019: 113 and 117).[33] Vernouillet thus fulfilled an intermediary role between Marx and the printer. He would also receive complaints from Marx (Juste Vernouillet to Karl Marx, 6 November 1872, IISH D 4380) about the number of copies of proofs sent by the printer (Marx wanted two copies of proofs, not single copy) (Karl Marx to Juste Vernouillet, 18 November 1872, Gaudin 2019: 114 and 118) and was also prompted by Marx to ask the printer to send proofs to him (e.g., Juste Vernouillet to Karl Marx, 20 November 1872, IISH D 4381).[34]

Vernouillet also acted as an intermediary between the translator and Marx. He contacted Roy in February 1873 when there were no further manuscript pages left for Marx to revise: 'I wrote to Mr Roy today to tell him that you had no copy left' (Juste Vernouillet to Karl Marx, 17 February 1873, IISH D 4386).[35]

Later in 1873, Marx sent proofs and manuscripts directly to the printer (e.g., Karl Marx to Juste Vernouillet, 10 July 1873, Marx and Engels 1989b: 517–18).[36] However, there is evidence that Vernouillet acted as an intermediary in February 1875, when Marx wrote a complaint to him about the printer Lahure when the publishing process was stalled. Vernouillet claimed that he had asked the printer to reactivate the process and send the proofs to Marx for correction (Juste Vernouillet to Karl Marx, 5 February 1875, IISH D 4392).

Adolphe Quêst

At the beginning of 1875, the editor informed Marx that the French government had placed his publishing house under the supervision of a court-appointed administrator in the person of Adolphe Quêst (Maurice Lachâtre to Karl Marx, 12 January 1875, IISH D 2845) who, in the wake of the Paris Commune, would manage Lachâtre's company.

In July 1875, this administrator was blamed when problems arose concerning the publication of the last 14 instalments of the work (Maurice Lachâtre to Karl Marx, 20 July 1875, Gaudin 2019: 163–4). According to Vernouillet – who was fired by the administrator – (Juste Vernouillet to Karl Marx, 11 July 1875, IISH

D 4393) the publication was ready to be finished but the administrator did not wish to finalize it and did not give authorization to the printer Lahure to continue. Financial reasons were stated by Quêst but disputed by Vernouillet and Lachâtre (Juste Vernouillet to Karl Marx, 21 July 1875, IISH D 4395).

In the middle of July, the last instalments were thus ready to be printed. The printer wrote to Marx that they were only waiting for a printing authorization (the printer Louis Lahure to Karl Marx, 14 July 1875, IISH D 2889). According to the administrator, the printer had received this authorization in January 1875 but took until June 1875 to finalize the composing of the last instalments. Other printing jobs and a library debt of 20,000 francs (disputed by Lachâtre and Vernouillet) then further postponed the decision to print. The administrator wrote that at the end of August, it would be possible to finalize the printing of *Le Capital*:

> At the end of August I shall be less busy. If, therefore, Sir, it were possible for you to wait for that time I would be very grateful, and I formally undertake to have M. Lahure complete the last instalments of Le Capital.
>
> (Adolphe Quêst and Plantez to Karl Marx,
> 15 July 1875, IISH D 3690)

Near the end of October 1875, news arrived that the printer would finally print the remaining instalments (Juste Vernouillet to Karl Marx, 28 October 1875, IISH D 4396). On 15 November, the administrator informed Marx that the order had been given to the printer: 'I have indeed instructed M. Lahure in due course to edit the rest of the book' and that he would receive the remaining instalments on that day (Adolphe Quêst and Plantez to Karl Marx, 15 November 1875, IISH D 3692). Later in November, Quêst wrote to Marx that he did not know that he was legally obliged to send 100 copies of the last instalments to him and that he would send them (Adolphe Quêst and Plantez to Karl Marx, 25 November 1875, IISH D 3693).[37] In 1876, Marx commented that the printing was delayed by the administrator and that he had to threaten him with legal proceedings and financial costs: 'It is only through the force of such threats that he has finally ordered the printing' (Karl Marx to Pyotr Lavrov, 7 October 1876, Marx and Engels 1991: 153–4).

Conclusion

From the start of this publishing venture, Marx's initiative was emphasized. Although the translator and the editor did influence Marx, for example, on the format of publishing in instalments and on the translation, Marx had the final say on the work. Marx was closely involved in the content of *Le Capital*, and it can be rightfully called his own edition. A title page of the French edition states that the translation was 'entirely revised by the author' (Marx 1875). This announcement was published in the first instalment of the edition on 17/18 September 1872 (Maurice Lachâtre to Karl Marx, 19 October 1872, Marx and

Engels 1989a: 418–19, Juste Vernouillet to Karl Marx, 18 September 1872, IISH D 4378), and, as shown in this chapter, this statement holds for this entire work. *Le Capital* is, in this sense, Marx's *personal endeavour*.

As the publishing process unfolded, Marx and the editor would evaluate Joseph Roy's translation in a negative light. The revision of the translated work would cost Marx time and effort, resulting in an overburden and a strain on his health, which in turn further delayed the publication of this edition.

Additionally, and after the initiation of the French edition in the wake of the Paris Commune in December 1871, the geographical distance between the actors involved and the persecution related to the Commune had to be overcome.[38] Marx and the editor were both persecuted and living in exile due to unrelated circumstances (Maurice Lachâtre to Karl Marx, 17 February 1872, Gaudin 2019: 83–4, Karl Marx to Friedrich Engels, 23 August 1849, Marx and Engels 1982: 212–13, Maurice Lachâtre to Karl Marx, 24 December 1873, Gaudin 2019: 152–3, Maurice Lachâtre to Karl Marx, 3 May 1875, IISH D 2848). This had several implications: (1) the editor could not travel to his company in Paris and lived consecutively in Spain, Belgium and Switzerland during the publishing process, (2) Marx also could not travel to France to, for example, physically deliver material, thus, (3) from the start *Le Capital* was *a transnational endeavour* for which all communication needed to take place from a distance. Both, however, had the support of other people in Lachâtre's company and had access to the postal system. Vernouillet, other members of the editor's company and the printer could meet in person to have easier communication. Finally, the appointment of the administrator Quêst also seems to have frustrated the publishing process near its end.

Another feature of this process is that primordially Marx's networks of relatives but also other connections were closely involved with the work on the French edition, making it a *family endeavour*. Both networks helped to initiate and further support the publishing process. Although little is said about them in the accounts of work on *Le Capital*, their involvement is not unimportant, as shown in this chapter. Moreover, looking at their contribution sheds light on Marx's working process, closely interconnected with networks of relatives and friends, intermingling work with more private life. Finally, the present chapter also shows the need for historical reconstructions of Marx's work from a plural rather than a singular perspective, distancing themselves more from the author and investigating his close environment in order to distill additional information on how the publishing process unfolded. Marx's relatives and friends thus constitute a valuable source of knowledge on the author and on the context of this specific intellectual project.

Notes

1 The contract concerning the publication of *Le Capital*, concluded between Karl Marx and Maurice Lachâtre et Cie (dated 13 February 1872), states: '2 Columns and

ten centimes for an eight-page instalment' (See Annex I in Gaudin 2019: 178–9). Gaudin's book contains printed colour scans of primary sources. See also Marx 1875.

2 We made use of (un)published German, French and English letters, biographical testimonies and other documents of the period, including primary sources to be found in the International Institute of Social History (IISH in Amsterdam, 'Karl Marx / Friedrich Engels Papers' (https://zoeken.iisg.amsterdam/Record/ARCH00 860#A6608ac22f8), the Russian State Archive of Socio-Political History (RGASPI in Moscow), the Public Library (New York), the Paul Lafargue archive (Paris), the Musée de l'Histoire vivante (Montreuil) and the British Library (London). Nicolas Rieucau sent us the primary sources discussed in their article Baronian and Rieucau (2020).

3 Marx also improved the editor's letter published in *Le Capital* (Karl Marx to Paul Lafargue, 21 March 1872, Marx and Engels 1989b: 346–52). See also Marx (1987).

4 Marx published, for example, Marx (1847). See also Wilhelm Liebknecht's reminiscences (Liebknecht 1896: 36–7). Liebknecht also gave the example of the just cited work.

5 Lefebvre (2016: l) noted that revising a translated version of the work is more difficult than translating the work from scratch.

6 Gaudin identifies the addressee of the letter as Lachâtre. It is actually Vernouillet: Marx asked for Roy's address, which seems more likely to be available to Vernouillet, who responded to Marx with the information (IISH 4387, 2 May 1873).

7 See August Philips' 'Specimen historico-juridicum de dominio rei mobilis, ad artic. 2014 cod. civ. neerl'.

8 Philips also suggested that Marx should add another stipulation to the contract which, however, was not inserted in the final contract.

9 Later Engels wrote to Liebknecht that Marx 'has a terrific amount of work to do on the French translation; much has to be altered in the opening part. And then he has also to read the proofs of the 2nd German edition' (Friedrich Engels to Wilhelm Liebknecht, 15/22 May 1872, Marx and Engels 1989b: 373–7).

10 Namely on 'Fabrikgesetzgebung'. This refers to chapter fifteen, subsection nine: 'Législation de fabrique', part of the already published sixth series (Juste Vernouillet to Karl Marx, 26 September 1873, IISH D 4390).

11 Engels moved to London in September 1870 (Jenny Marx [daughter] to the Kugelmann family, 19 November 1870, Marx and Engels 1985: 118–21, and Jenny Marx [daughter] to the Kugelmann family, 18 April 1871, Marx and Engels 1985: 187–9). On 16 September 1870, Marx still sent a letter to Engels, so he had not yet settled in London (Karl Marx to Friedrich Engels, 16 September 1870, Marx and Engels 1989b: 84). See also Bernstein (1918: 166–7) and Lafargue (1904–05: 558); Paul Lafargue also commented on the extensive language skills (including French) of Friedrich Engels (Lafargue 1904–05: 559–60). In the reminiscences of Eleanor Marx on Engels, a similar statement is made (Marx Aveling 1890: 4).

12 See Marx (1989a: 3, 799–800; 803–4, 961, 963–4). The first note (IISH A 62) contains text with references to the second German edition, some changes to which can be found in the French edition. In the note, Engels wrote for example: '387. 15 Jahre (Nota) jetzt 20 Jahre' (i.e, five years after the publication date of the first German edition). The corresponding note in the second German edition (Marx 1872: 387), third German edition (Marx 1883: 376) and first German edition (Marx 1867: 358) says 'Erst seit ungefähr 15 Jahren (…)'. In the French edition (Marx 1875: 162)

fifteen was changed to 'Ce n'est que depuis 20 ans environ (...)'. A similar, but not identical change can be found in the fourth German edition edited by Engels (Marx 1890: 337 'Erst seit ungefähr 1850 (...)'. In the English edition: 'It is only during the last 15 years (i.e., since about 1850) (...)' (Marx 1889: 368). A second example is '396. Spinnmaschine _Vorspinn_ M. näher drawing frame' in the note. In the French edition 'drawing frame' was used on page 165 in the corresponding passage. In the first, second, third and fourth German edition (respectively pages 367, 396, 385 and 345), this word was not present in the passage. In the English edition 'drawing frame' was used on page 377 in the corresponding passage (Marx 1889). The second note contains text with references to the first German edition (see Marx 1989a: 963–4 with a facsimile on page 961), changes were listed that are also in the second German edition (e.g., 'unentgeldlich' in the first German edition, p. 315 versus 'unentgeltlich' in the second German edition, p. 342 and 'raçe' in the first German edition p. 243 versus 'race' in the second German edition p. 268).

13 The name of Vaillant was also mentioned Marx to Lachâtre, 9 January 1873 (Gaudin 2019: 74–9).

14 It is, however, likely that Keller had an influence on Marx and this French edition (Karl Marx to Paul Lafargue, 18 October 1869, Marx and Engels 1988: 359–60), as there is evidence of discussions on the translation of words (Keller to Marx, 23 November 1872, IISH D V 62).

15 Marx most certainly also asked Paul Lafargue and Charles Longuet for help with *Le Capital*. See, for example, the letter from Engels to Sorge (07-12 (or 09)-1872, Marx and Engels 1989b: 453–5). There is also an undated letter where it is said that 'Yesterday Mohr looked through a mass of placards with Longuet (...)' (Jenny Marx (mother) to Eleanor Marx, Hecker and Limmroth 2014: 470–1). The date is given in the book as 1 April 1873. See also Karl Marx to Maurice Lachâtre, 9 January 1873 (Gaudin 2019: 74–9).

16 We also obtained a facsimile of the letter.

17 Despite a lack of direct evidence, Eleanor Marx may also have helped in the publishing process of *Le Capital* (Weissweiler 2018 and Kapp 2018). As seen in letters of the time, she lived with Marx (Eleanor Marx to M^{rs}. Liebknecht, 23 October 1874, Eckert 1963: 417–19). She, moreover, had the linguistic skills to help with the translation part of the publishing process, since she was able to translate French into English or German into French. See her French to English translation of Lissagaray's book on the Paris Commune, when Marx was still alive (Lissagaray 1886: v) and her translation of Liebknecht's German presentation in the Reichstag into French in 1874, despite her reservations about her level of proficiency in German (Eleanor Marx to Wilhelm Liebknecht, 20 November 1874, Eckert 1963: 419–20; Eleanor Marx to Wilhelm Liebknecht, 28 November 1874, Eckert 1963: 421). The case of Eleanor Marx highlights a difficulty when investigating contributions from relatives or friends. There is little documentation on the help received for *Le Capital* or *Das Kapital* from people living, at certain times, in the same house as Marx or in his immediate vicinity. Nevertheless, this should not be taken as evidence of no involvement. Letters were evidently only written between people who were not living close by. We can thus only know of the help provided by people living close to him, such as Eleanor Marx, Jenny Marx (mother) or Friedrich Engels, when they write to each other when not together, or when they write to others. Alternatively, other people could also have recorded it or there could be a specific manuscript documenting the help provided.

18 Although Marx wrote '1872', this letter deals with the second series and fits 1873.

19 See also the editor's letter and Marx's letter in the French edition.

20 See also Karl Marx to Laura Marx, 28 February 1872, Marx and Engels 1989b: 327–8. In a letter dated the beginning of May, Roy wrote 'Erster Abschnitt', a book division not used in the first edition, but added in the second edition, while he used the page numbers of the first edition. Roy received a first German edition document with changes derived from work on the second German edition (Joseph Roy to Karl Marx, 2 May 1872, Marx and Engels 1989a: 407–9). Roy also criticized the editor about the use of engravings, the facsimiled letter from Marx and the editor's letter in the edition. He felt that these were unnecessary and did not like to have two printed columns on each page.

21 Pp. 14 and 15 were mentioned. Marx's comment in the letter was foreshadowed in Lefebvre (2016: xxxi). Lefebvre wrote that translations at the time of Marx were 'in general quite distant from the original text' and 'Marx could have seen this for himself by comparing Roy's translation of Feuerbach in 1861-1864 with that published by Ewerbeck in 1850'.

22 According to Gaudin, this letter was sent to Lachâtre. It should be Juste Vernouillet, as the latter responded in a letter dated 6 November 1872 (IISH D 4380).

23 See Annex I in Gaudin 2019: 178–9. The editor and Dervaux reflected on the use of punctuation marks. In a letter from Dervaux to Marx (20 June 1872, IISH D 1018), there is evidence that Marx wanted to have full stops after the titles in the French edition. Lachâtre and Dervaux did not want full stops after the titles. Dervaux said it could be changed. In the published edition there are, however, no full stops after the titles.

24 See also Lefebvre (2016: xxxiii). Lefebvre notes that the order of operations is different from the one Roy suggested. Roy suggested to Marx in a letter dated 2 February 1872 that it would be easier for Marx if he only received the proofs instead of the translated manuscript (Marx and Engels 1989a: 395). In the letter from Marx to Laura Marx (dated 28 February 1872), Marx said that he had allowed Roy to send the translated manuscript directly to Paris (Marx and Engels 1989b: 327–8).

25 A case in point is the use of 1867 as the preface date. At the end of April 1872, the editor advised against printing this date because it would give the impression that the French edition was an old version of the text. However, the date 1867 was eventually printed in the French edition (Maurice Lachâtre to Karl Marx, 29 April 1872, Marx and Engels 1989a: 406–7).

26 The editor also wrote to Paul Lafargue about the notes and asked him to influence Marx to place them at the end of the volume (Maurice Lachâtre to Paul Lafargue, 14 May 1872, Marx and Engels 1989a: 413–4). In an undated letter (IISH D 1016), Dervaux also communicated to Marx that the editor and Lafargue thought endnotes were better than the current notes system.

27 In the book, foreign citations were not always translated into French (see, e.g., Marx 1875: 14 and 33).

28 Marx was also critical of typographical errors made by the printer (see Karl Marx to Maurice Lachâtre, 11 February 1873, Gaudin 2019: 123–7).

29 Although Marx wrote '1872', this letter deals with the second series and fits with 1873. See also Karl Marx to Maurice Lachâtre, 11 February 1873, Gaudin 2019: 123–7.

30 Marx also sent manuscript to the printer Lahure (e.g., Karl Marx to the printer Louise Lahure, 20 January 1875, IISH C 410).

31   Marx also corrected the editor's letter printed in the edition (Lachâtre to Marx, 24 March 1872, Marx and Engels 1989a: 401–2). The engravings in the first instalment resulted in delays (Dervaux to Marx, 25 April 1872, IISH D 1015A).

32   In a letter from the printer Lahure, Marx was asked to send proofs to the printer at '9 Rue de Fleurus', who also would send them directly to him (14 August 1872, Gaudin 2019: 105), and in a letter from Marx to Vernouillet (dated 15 August 1872): 'According to a letter received yesterday from M. Lachâtre, I will have to send the proofs to M. Lahure in the future'. Marx and Engels (1989b: 423).

33   This last letter was sent to Vernouillet, as seen in his response in IISH D 4380. Vernouillet continued to receive manuscript pages from Marx (e.g., Marx to Vernouillet, 1 November 1872, Gaudin 2019: 109–11). Gaudin wrote that this letter went to Lachâtre, which is not correct. There is a mention of the French post giving the manuscript to Lachâtre (who, however, lived in Spain while Marx was in England). Sending the manuscript to Spain would mean that Lachâtre then needed to resend it. Vernouillet was currently receiving manuscripts. In January, Vernouillet also received a manuscript: Marx to Vernouillet, 13 January 1873, Gaudin 2019: 80 and 82). Marx wrote '1872' but this letter clearly precedes the letter from Juste Vernouillet dated 15 January 1873 (Gaudin 2019: 122). Vernouillet acknowledged receipt of the manuscript, which was transferred to the printer.

34   Gaudin wrote that the letter of 18 November is addressed to Lachâtre, but for reasons already disclosed in this text, it was sent to Juste Vernouillet. The letter is about manuscripts sent by Marx – he wished to know when they were received. Juste Vernouillet to Karl Marx (IISH D 4381) is a response to Marx's letter.

35   See also Karl Marx to Juste Vernouillet, 15 February 1873, Gaudin 2019: 128–9: Marx sent proofs to the printer Lahure and asked for Roy's address.

36   Vernouillet wrote to Marx that no new manuscripts had been received by the printer, in a letter dated 26 September 1873, IISH D 4390.

37   In a letter dated 04 December 1875, Quêst wrote to Marx who had not yet received these instalments (Adolphe Quêst and Plantez to Karl Marx, IISH D 3694).

38   In 1875, Marx noted that the geographical distances made the publishing process difficult (in the original edition on p. 351).

References

Baronian, Laurent and Rieucau, Nicolas (2020) 'Pièces inédites de Marx: lettres et projet de contrat pour la publication française du capital', *Cahiers d'économie politique*, vol. 2, n. 78: 7–26.

Bernstein, Eduard (1918) *Aus den Jahren meines Exils. Erinnerungen eines Sozialisten*, Berlin: Erich Reiß Verlag.

Bottigelli, Émile (1972) 'La première édition française du *Capital*', *Cahiers de l'institut Maurice Thorez*, vol. 6, n. 28: 12–31.

D'Hondt, Jacques (1985) 'La traduction tendancieuse du Capital par Joseph Roy', in *1883-1983. L'œuvre de Marx, un siècle après*, edited by Georges Labica, Paris: Presses universitaires de France, pp. 131–7.

Eckert, Georg (1963) *Wilhelm Liebknecht Briefwechsel mit Karl Marx und Friedrich Engels*, The Hague: Mouton & co.

Engels, Frederick, Lafargue, Paul and Laura, Marx (1960) *Correspondence*, vol. 3: *1891-1895*, Moscow: Foreign languages publishing house.

Forster, Laura (2019) 'The Paris Commune in London and the Spatial History of Ideas, 1871-1900', *The Historical Journal*, vol. 62, n. 4: 1021–44.

Gaudin, François (2019) *Traduire Le Capital. Une correspondance inédite entre Karl Marx, Friedrich Engels et l'éditeur Maurice Lachâtre*, Mont-Saint-Augnan: Presses Universitaires de Rouen et du Havre.

Gielkens, Jan (1999) *Karl Marx und seine niederländischen Verwandten. Eine kommentierte Quellenedition*, Trier: Schriften aus dem Karl-Marx-Haus n. 50.

Hecker, Rolf and Limmroth, Angelika (Eds.) (2014) *Jenny Marx. Die Briefe*, Berlin: Karl Dietz Verlag.

Kapp, Yvonne (2018) *Eleanor Marx. A Biography*, London and New York: Verso Books.

Lafargue, Paul (1904-5) 'Persönliche Erinnerungen an Friedrich Engels', *Die Neue Zeit*, vol. 23, n. 44, pp. 556–61.

Lefebvre, Jean-Pierre (2016) *Marx, Karl Le Capital livre 1. Traduction de la 4e édition allemande entièrement révisée par Jean-Pierre Lefebvre avec un nouvel avant-propos*, Paris: Les éditions sociales.

Liebknecht, Wilhelm (1896) *Karl Marx zum Gedächtniß. Ein Lebensabriß und Erinnerungen*, Nürnberg: Wörlein & Comp.

Lissagaray, Prosper-Olivier (1886) *History of the Commune of 1871*, London: Reeves and Turner.

Marx Aveling, Eleanor (1890) 'Friedrich Engels', *Sozialdemokratische Monatsschrift*, n. 10–11: 1–8.

Marx, Karl (1847) *Misère de la philosophie. Réponse à la philosophie de la misère de M. Proudhon*, Paris and Brussels: Frank and Vogler.

Marx, Karl (1867) *Das Kapital. Kritik der politischen Oekonomie. Erster Band. Buch I: Der Produktionsprocess des Kapitals*, Hamburg: Verlag von Otto Meissner.

Marx, Karl (1872) *Das Kapital. Kritik der politischen Oekonomie. Erster Band. Buch I: Der Produktionsprocess des Kapitals. Zweite verbesserte Auflage*, Hamburg: Verlag von Otto Meissner.

Marx, Karl (1875) *Le capital par Karl Marx (traduction de M. J. Roy, entièrement revisée par l'auteur*, Paris: Éditeurs, Maurice Lachatre et cᶦᵉ.

Marx, Karl (1883) *Das Kapital. Kritik der politischen Oekonomie. Erster Band. Buch I: Der Produktionsprocess des Kapitals. Dritte vermehrte Auflage*, Hamburg: Verlag von Otto Meissner.

Marx, Karl (1889) *Capital: A Critical Analysis of Capitalist Production*, London: Swan Sonnenschein & co.

Marx, Karl (1890) *Das Kapital. Kritik der politischen Oekonomie. Von Karl Marx. Erster Band. Buch I: Der Produktionsprocess des Kapitals. Vierte, durchgesehene Auflage. Herausgegeben von Friedrich Engels*, Hamburg: Verlag von Otto Meissner.

Marx, Karl (1987 [1872–1873]) 'Das Kapital. Kritik der politischen Ökonomie. Erster Band Hamburg 1872', in *Marx Engels Gesamtausgabe* (MEGA²), vol. II/6, Berlin: Dietz Verlag.

Marx, Karl (1989a [1883]) 'Das Kapital. Kritik der politischen Ökonomie. Erster Band. Hamburg 1883', in *Marx Engels Gesamtausgabe* (MEGA²), vol. II/8, Berlin: Dietz Verlag.

Marx, Karl (1989b [1872–1875]) 'Le Capital, Paris 1872-1875', in *Marx Engels Gesamtausgabe* (MEGA²), vol. II/7, Berlin: Dietz Verlag.

Marx, Karl and Engels, Friedrich (1982) *Marx Engels Collected Works*, vol. 38: *Letters 1844-51*, Moscow: Progress Publishers.

Marx, Karl and Engels, Friedrich (1985) *Marx-Engels-Correspondance*, vol. 11: *Letters juillet 1870-décembre 1871*, Paris: Les éditions sociales.

Marx, Karl and Engels, Friedrich (1987) *Marx Engels Collected Works*, vol. 42: *Letters 1864-68*, Moscow: Progress Publishers.

Marx, Karl and Engels, Friedrich (1988) *Marx Engels Collected Works*, vol. 43: *Letters 1868-70*, Moscow: Progress Publishers.

Marx, Karl and Engels, Friedrich (1989a) *Marx-Engels-Correspondance*, vol. 12: *Letters janvier 1872-octobre 1874*, Paris: Les éditions sociales.

Marx, Karl and Engels, Friedrich (1989b) *Marx Engels Collected Works*, vol. 44: *Letters 1870-73*, Moscow: Progress Publishers.

Marx, Karl and Engels, Friedrich (1991) *Marx Engels Collected Works*, vol. 45: *Letters 1874-79*, Moscow: Progress Publishers.

Marx, Karl and Engels, Friedrich (1995) *Marx Engels Collected Works*, vol. 47: *Letters 1883-86*, Moscow: Progress Publishers.

Meier, Olga (Ed.) (1979) 'Les filles de Karl Marx. Lettres inédites', in *Collection Bottigelli*, Paris: Éditions Albin Michel.

Meier, Olga (Ed.) (1982) *The Daughters of Karl Marx. Family Correspondence 1866-1898*, London: Andre Deutsch Limited.

Rubel, Maximilien (2019) *Marx, Karl. Le capital. Livre I. Édition établie et annotée par Maximilien Rubel*, Paris: Éditions Gallimard.

Uroyeva, Anna (1965) *For All Time and All Men*, Moscow: Progress publishers.

Weissweiler, Eva (2018) *Lady liberty. Das Leben der jüngsten Marx-Tochter Eleanor*, Hamburg: Hoffmann und Campe Verlag.

7   From Moscow to Paris

The Russian Roots of the First French Translation of Marx's *Capital*

Guillaume Fondu

Introduction

The first French translation of *Capital* (Marx 1989), proof-read – and largely rewritten – by Marx himself, is subject to different assessments among commentators of Marx's work. This translation into French was indeed used by Marx as an opportunity to *de-hegelianize* his work (Lefebvre 2016: LV–LVIII), an attempt that started with the second German edition (Marx 1987). Readers have interpreted Marx's revisions either as an honourable but momentary effort at popularization, necessary given the French readership's lack of theoretical knowledge, or, on the contrary, as a sign of Marx's progression towards a more scientific approach to his subject (Bidet 2007: 8–9).[1]

It is beyond the scope of this article to settle this question. Rather, the aim is to simply take the first steps towards a more thorough study of the intellectual context of the French translation, which followed directly from the completion of the second German edition of *Capital*. Marx's rewriting of his work was indeed a continuous process, and it is likely that the French edition of *Capital* contains a number of additions that Marx could not include in the second German edition (either because of lack of time or because he had not yet thought of them). However, there is a more interesting aspect of this transition into French, that is, the confrontation with a foreign language, which Marx had perfectly mastered; it was also an opportunity for him to step away from the langue of German philosophy and its accompanying logic.

The hypothesis put forward here is that this distancing from an overly speculative position takes place in a context in which Marx, in particular due to his discovery of the Russian *Narodnik*[2] current (broadly understood), questioned the exact scope of his work. The question, in other words, is whether Marx described a universal trajectory or simply one that could be followed by countries that are already partly capitalist? We know that towards the end of his life, Marx put the universality of *Capital's* analyses into perspective by pointing to the possibility of alternative historical paths and by substituting the analysis of an historical evolution with that of synchronic relations of domination between nations (e.g., the relations between Ireland and England).[3] This article aims to show that the proofreading and rewriting of the French version of *Capital* is

DOI: 10.4324/9781003336365-9

part of this trend – a trend which is reflected in a number of textual clues that can be followed thanks to the editorial work carried out by the MEGA² team.[4] Simultaneously, this shift away from universalism comes into tension with Marx's desire to provide a thorough, if intermittent, critique of Proudhonism, which he believed was powerful in France. Marx regarded the anarchist current as a type of utopian socialism that failed to appreciate the systematic dimension of the capitalist mode of production. Hence the hesitations in this French version caught between Marx's questioning of the scope of his work, on the one hand, and his desire to destroy Proudhonian socialism, on the other.[5]

This article begins by briefly outlining the context in which Marx undertook the revisions, in particular his discovery of the social realities and thinkers of the Russian world, before looking at the changes made to the French version compared to the second German edition. Finally, one of the important additions to this French edition will be discussed, namely Marx's critique of Mill, which was partly absent from the second German edition.

The discovery of Russian Narodnism

Among the many texts that Marx was reading at the end of the 1860s, the ones that most evidently influenced the rewriting for the French edition (excluding statistical material) were those concerning the Russian world. It was mainly in the late 1860s when Russian activists came into contact with him that Marx's attitude towards Russia changed.[6] On 30 September 1868, Nikolai Danielson, a Narodnik activist, wrote to him about his project to translate *Capital* into Russian and sent him a book by Flerovski on the situation of the working classes in Russia.[7] Marx then decided to learn the Russian language, which by March 1870 he could 'read somewhat fluently with the aid of a dictionary', and was struck by the quality of Flerovski's work (Marx to Laura and Paul Lafargue, 5 March 1870, Marx and Engels 1987: 450). In the course of his research, Marx discovered other supporters in Russia (Utin in particular) and took an interest, among other works, in Chernyshevsky's articles about Russian rural communities as well as in his critical notes on Mill. At the time, the Russian movement was questioning whether it was possible to build socialism on traditional institutions (the land community, the *mir*, and the peasant cooperative, the *artel*) without going through an intermediary capitalist phase.

These questions aligned with a process that was already maturing in Marx's own thought which was the path he described as universal, as he wrote in the first German edition of *Capital*, according to which 'the country that is more developed industrially only [shows] to the less developed, the image of its own future'? (Marx 1983: 12). Or, on the contrary, should he consider the possibility of alternative paths towards socialism and, consequently, limit the scope of *Capital* to the countries that were already capitalist? As early as 1871, there were moments in Marx's correspondence that hinted at such questions. For example, E. Tomanovskaya addressed the following reply to Marx that is clearly a response to a letter by Marx on the same issue:

Regarding the alternative you foresee for the question of the fate of communal land ownership in Russia, unfortunately, its decline and transformation into small property is more than likely. All the government's measures – an atrocious and disproportionate increase in taxes and charges – have the sole aim of introducing individual property through the annihilation of solidarity.[8]

Marx thus seemed to have put forward the hypothesis of the specificity of the Russian rural commune. And this is not due, contrary to Marx's understanding of Herzen (see Mervaud 2012), to an ahistorical specificity peculiar to the Russian people but to Slavic historical backwardness. This is, as we know, Chernyshevsky's thesis, which in a certain sense secularizes the idea of a properly Russian agrarian socialism and underlines its historical determinations while fighting against the Slavophile idea of a Slavic or Orthodox collectivist essence. This thesis can be found in the changes to *Capital* that were already present in the second German edition. First, Marx removed a passage against Herzen that is present in the first German edition:

> If, on the continent of Europe, the influence of capitalist production, which subverts the human race through overwork, the division of labour, the subjugation to machines, the crippling of immature and female bodies, bad living, etc., develops, as hitherto, hand in hand with competition in the size of the national soldiery, national debts, taxes, elegant warfare, etc., then the rejuvenation of Europe through the knout and obligatory infusion of Kalmyk blood, so earnestly prophesied by the half-Russian and entirely Muscovite Herzen, would likely become inevitable after all (this belletrist, by the way, did not make his discoveries about 'Russian' communism in Russia, but in the work of the Prussian Government Counsellor Haxthausen).
>
> (Marx 1983: 635)

This statement complemented Chapter VI, which in the first German edition was devoted to the tendencies of capitalist accumulation. Marx saw Herzen as a typical representative of a reactionary and identitarian rejection of history and social development. Five years later, in the second German edition, this passage was removed. This could be an indication of Marx's change of heart about the Russian commune, or at least of an ambivalence. This appears to be the case as Marx added a positive reference to Chernyshevsky, who was considered to be a supporter of Herzen's ideas and the defender of the idea that Russia could avoid capitalist development to build socialism on a communal basis:

> The Continental revolution of 1848-9 also had its reaction in England. Men who still claimed some scientific standing and aspired to be something more than the mere sophists and sycophants of the ruling classes tried to harmonise the Political Economy of capital with the claims, no longer

to be ignored, of the proletariat. Hence a shallow syncretism of which John Stuart Mill is the best representative. It is a declaration of bankruptcy by bourgeois economy, an event on which the great Russian scholar and critic, N. Chernyshevsky, has thrown the light of a master mind in his 'Outlines of Political Economy according to Mill'.

(Marx 1987: 703)

This reference to Chernyshevsky is particularly important: the Russian intellectual's critique of Mill, as we shall see, inspired Marx to make a number of observations on the state of post-Ricardian bourgeois economics and on the question of the historicity of capitalism. And Marx, possibly due to a lack of time, began his critique of Mill in the second German edition, but only completed it in the French version. It was in the French version that he asked N. Danielson to use the second Russian edition, with some reservations:

In regard to the second edition of Capital, I beg to remark:

1) I wish that the divisions into chapters – and the same holds good for the subdivisions – be made according to the French edition.
2) That the translator compare always carefully the second German edition with the French one, since the latter contains many important changes and additions (though, it is true, I was also sometimes obliged—principally in the first chapter—to '*aplatir*' [simplify] the matter in its French version).

(Marx to Nikolai Danielson, 15 November 1978,
Marx and Engels 1991: 343)

And then he added the following a few days later:

The two first sections ('Commodities and Money' and 'The Transformation of Money into Capital') are to be translated exclusively from the German text.
There, p. 86, line 5 from bottom READ: 'And, as a matter of fact, the value of each single yard is but the materialised form of a part of the social labour expended on the whole number of yards'.
In Chapter XVI of the French edition (not contained in Chapter XIV of the German edition) the added passage on J. St. Mill, p. 222, column II, line 12 from bottom, should read: 'I always assume, he says, the actual state of affairs which predominates wherever workers and capitalists are distinct classes, etc.!'
★ The following two sentences, viz.:★ 'It is a strange optical illusion to see everywhere a state of affairs which as yet exists as an exception in this world of ours! But to continue'—★ are to be struck out, and the following sentence is to be read thus: 'Mr. Mill would like to think there is no absolute

necessity that such should be the case—even in an economic system where workers and capitalists are distinct classes'.

(Marx to Nikolai Danielson, 28 November 1978,
Marx and Engels 1991: 346)

In light of this, the hypothesis that there is a link between Marx's gradual discovery of Russian Narodnism, his ongoing work on the second German edition, *and* his revisions for the French version of *Capital* seems founded. However, if, as Marx acknowledges above, the most theoretical chapters of the French version have been 'simplified', to what exactly does this simplification entail?

Simplifying or historicizing?

It is well established that Marx criticized Roy's translation for being often too literal and therefore artificial sounding to French ears (see, e.g., Marx to Sorge, 21 December 1872, Marx and Engels 1989: 460). However, the main consequence of Marx's rewriting is the removal of a certain number of elements of Hegelian discourse that are present in the first two sections of *Capital* in German. Those changes are important because the point is nothing less than the logic at work in the deductive movement of the capitalist categories – the commodity, money, and capital – which seem to arise from one another in the German text. While this movement is obviously still perceptible in the French version, which also aimed to debunk the Proudhonian 'utopias' where categories are autonomous, Marx's discourse is indubitably inflected. Rather than seeing this as a mere simplification, perhaps we should read it as a sign of Marx's hesitation to the status of his argument, which echoed the concerns of the Russian Narodniks, that is, does *Capital* propose a universal theory of bourgeois society? And how does the germ of the commodity inevitably give rise to generalized capitalism? As the 1857 introduction seemed to theorize, does it theorize a historically specific society produced by the contingent encounter of diverse dynamics?

A first indication of this hesitation can be found in the translation of a German term that is recurrent throughout *Capital*, that of '*bürgerliche Gesellschaft*' [civil society]. The first time it appears, in the preface to the first German edition, Marx inserts a small addition by speaking of 'société bourgeoise actuelle [current bourgeois society]'[9] (Marx 1989: 12). The addition of *actuelle* may seem like a minor point, but it is a significant one: Marx places the society he is talking about in a determined space-time and is less categorical than in the German version. This Marxian desire to embed his words with 'deictics' can be found on several occasions (see Marx 1989: 62). In addition, the German term is rendered as 'société civile' on two occasions. It is well known that in French, the translation of the term '*bürgerliche Gesellschaft*' is problematic since it refers both to the idea of '*bourgeoisie*', that is, to a certain structure of production, but also to the idea of 'civility', that is, to the constitution of new modalities of social interaction, characterized in particular by a certain horizontality. This is simply the way Hegel, after others, translated the English 'civil society' into German. And he had already pointed out that the German term '*bürgerlich*' was ambiguous, sometimes meaning 'bourgeois' and sometimes meaning 'citizen' – an ambiguity that was the focus of some of Marx's early texts. This category is all the more important because it is the one that Herzen used to diagnose the disease of the Western democracies after 1848, the bourgeois spirit having led the elites to disassociate themselves from the people and to join the aristocracy in its bloody repression of revolutionary movements. The German term therefore crystallized a conceptual problem that had to be dealt with differently in French. Marx achieves this by specifying that the society he is talking about is a historically existing society, in all its dimensions, and not a purely logical product resulting from a categorical deduction that is reduced to its economic mechanism.

A still more notable 'simplification' of the French translation of *Capital* is visible in the treatment of logical categories derived from Hegelian discourse. For example, we can point to the notable absence of one of the terms used in the German versions to define capital: that of 'subject' ('automatic subject', 'subject of a process', etc.), which is evacuated or replaced by the French term '*substance*'. This is not insignificant since the tripartite structure, 'relation – substance – subject', was explicitly conceptualized, in the first version of *Capital*, as a logical matrix for understanding the central categories of the capitalist mode of production, 'commodity – money – capital'. These three realities formed, in Marx's eyes, three degrees of increasing autonomization of value, that is, of the objectification of human labour whereby commodity exists only in relation to others, unlike money that embodies value in a substantial way. Finally, capital accomplishes this process of fetishization of human activity by adopting the features of a subject, that is, an autonomous entity with its own dynamics. This tripartite structure was all the more important because it was mobilized as a weapon against Proudhonism, which sought to preserve commodity production without money and thus lost sight of the logical process engendering capitalist relations. Again, this logical genesis suggested that the capitalist mode of production developed autonomously once its presupposition, commodity production, was present. However, if, in the French version, the distinction between 'subject' and 'substance' cannot be made, then the Hegelian triad evaporates.

This is not the only place where Marx sets aside Hegelian systematicity. Marx defined his endeavour as an '*analyse du capital*' (Marx 1989: 132), whereas in German it is much more explicit: 'analysis of the primary form of capital, the form in which it determines the economic organization of modern society' (Marx 1976: 266).[10] This is the 'simplification' Marx referred to and explains why he favoured the use of the second German edition for subsequent translations. Perhaps Marx simply wanted the French text to be less daunting and more readable. Yet this desire for a pedagogical approach may not be the only reason. Indeed, the changes reflect Marx's hesitation of how to arbitrate between the logical relations of generation, on the one hand, and historical causality, on the other. If we consider the French version as a location where Marx thought this question through, then one can read it not as a linear path from logic to history but rather as a process marked by hesitations.

This is all the more likely since the historical part of the text, the passages devoted to primitive accumulation, also underwent some modifications. Again, these are not substantial changes, but rather a few details which may suggest hesitations. The passage that summarizes Marx's historical account is written in French as follows:

> Au fond du système capitaliste il y a donc la séparation radicale du producteur d'avec les moyens de production. Cette séparation se reproduit sur une échelle progressive dès que le système capitaliste s'est une fois établi; mais comme celle-là forme la base de celui-ci, il ne saurait s'établir sans elle. Pour qu'il vienne au monde, il faut donc que, partiellement au moins, les moyens de production aient déjà été arrachés sans phrase aux producteurs, qui les employaient à réaliser leur propre travail, et qu'ils se trouvent déjà détenus par des producteurs marchands, qui eux les emploient à spéculer sur le travail d'autrui. Le *mouvement historique* qui fait divorcer le travail d'avec ses conditions extérieures, voilà donc le fin mot de l'accumulation appelée « primitive » parce qu'elle appartient à l'âge préhistorique du monde bourgeois.
>
> (Marx 1985: 632–3)

Its German equivalent in English is the following:

> The capital-relation presupposes a complete separation between the workers and the ownership of the conditions for the realization of their labour. As soon as capitalist production stands on its own feet, it not only maintains this separation, but reproduces it on a constantly extending scale. The process, therefore, which creates the capital-relation can be nothing other than the process which divorces the worker from the ownership of the conditions of his own labour; it is a process which operates two transformations, whereby the social means of subsistence and production are turned into capital, and the immediate producers are turned into wage-labourers. So-called primitive accumulation, therefore, is nothing else than the historical process of divorcing the producer from the means of production. It appears as 'primitive' because it forms the pre-history of capital, and the mode of production corresponding to capital.[11]
>
> (Marx 1976: 874–5)

Apart from the fact that the historicity of the process is explicitly underlined in French, the Hegelian logical vocabulary disappears here too ('presupposes', 'process', 'turn into'). Moreover, the condition stated in French is simply a necessary one, whereas the German text suggests that it is a sufficient one, which is the main question that animates Russian Narodnism at the time: does the separation of workers and means of production, which is then underway, necessarily mean the adoption of a capitalist path or is it possible to resist it? In the rest of his French remarks, Marx continued to insist more than in the German text on the properly factual dimension of this development, which is not seen as the mere condition for the unfolding of a logical process as much. The very terms used to conceive change are not the same in French and German. And above all, the French versions raised far more questions about the protagonists of capitalism (*'producteur'*, *'affranchis'*, *'capitalistes entrepreneurs'*) than about systems ('a change in the form of this servitude'). The conclusion of the chapter is even more explicit, the French version reads as follows:

> [L'accumulation primitive] ne s'est encore accomplie d'une manière aussi radicale qu'en Angleterre: ce pays jouera donc nécessairement le premier rôle dans notre esquisse. Mais tous les autres pays de l'Europe occidentale parcourent le même mouvement, bien que selon le milieu il change de couleur locale, ou se resserre dans un cercle plus étroit, ou présente un caractère moins fortement prononcé, ou suive un ordre de succession différent.
>
> (Marx 1989: 634)

The German version in English reads:

> The history of this expropriation assumes different aspects in different countries, and runs through its various phases in different orders of succession, and at different historical epochs. Only in England, which we therefore take as our example, has it the classic form.[12]
>
> (Marx 1976: 876)

Here, Marx thus underlined the geographical embeddedness of his subject, Western Europe, and we can see an intent not to present the process of capitalization of the economy as a universal logic but as a singular history, albeit potentially generalizable. It is the French edition that Marx quotes in his letter to Vera Zasulich, usually considered one of the major texts indicating Marx's hesitation about the status of his topic:

> In analysing the genesis of capitalist production I say: 'At the core of the capitalist system, therefore, lies the complete separation of the producer from the means of production [...] the basis of this whole development is the expropriation of the agricultural producer. To date this has not been accomplished in a radical fashion anywhere except in England [...] But all the other countries of Western Europe are undergoing the same process' (Capital, French ed., p. 315).

Hence the 'historical inevitability' of this process is expressly limited to the countries of Western Europe. The cause of that limitation is indicated in the following passage from Chapter XXXII: 'Private property, based on personal labour [...] will be supplanted by capitalist private property, based on the exploitation of the labour of others, on wage labour' (i.e., p. 341).

(Marx to Vera Zasulich, 8 March 1881,
Marx and Engels 1992: 71)

Everything Marx quotes here is very different from the German version, and we can assume that in 1872 he was already thinking about these discussions with the Russian Narodniki, whom he had been reading and frequenting. Later, these changes cause Engels much difficulty, and he hesitated to incorporate them in his editing of the 'definitive' *Capital*. For instance, in the last German edition, Engels did not keep the clause limiting the validity of Marx's predictions to 'Western Europe' (see Marx 1991: 644).[13] Consequently, the French edition of *Capital* represents a stage in Marx's intellectual trajectory and its status is just as problematic as the various German editions since it is a testament to the evolutionary character of Marx's thought.

Marx on Chernyshevsky's Mill

The additions to this French version are easier to integrate since they do not replace an existing text. They also show the work done by Marx in the course of the various drafts of *Capital*. Such is the case for the passage on Mill mentioned by Marx in the letter to Danielson quoted above. As already suggested, it was possibly the reading of Chernyshevsky that prompted Marx to take up his commentary on Mill to whom he had only devoted a brief passage in the *Theories of Surplus Value*.[14] The Russian theorist indeed gave Mill a special place in the history of political economy, since, according to him, Mill represented the symptom of the final crisis of the discipline and of the egoistic anthropology upon which he relied. A first addition, already present in the second German edition, concerned progress and is a direct echo of Chernyshevsky's remarks. Marx quoted Mill:

> It is questionable if all the mechanical inventions yet made have lightened the day's toil of any human being.

He wrote further in a footnote:

> Mill should have said, 'of any human being not fed by other people's labour', for, without doubt, machinery has greatly increased the number of well-to-do idlers.

(Marx 1987: 362)

Chernyshevsky, in his commentary on Mill, had already emphasized this passage, similar to Marx, in order to level criticism of the alleged benefits of technical progress:

> Supporters of the prevailing theory are advised to pay particular attention to the lines at the very end of the extract quoted here. Mill frankly says that

it is doubtful whether technical inventions have so far brought any support to the people. They have increased the comfort of the middle class, he says, and increased also the number of rich capitalists, but have not yet begun to produce that improvement in human destiny which they should produce in their nature. When we say this, the dabblers in political economy reproach us with not knowing their theory. But here they can read the same idea in the pen of the most remarkable of Adam Smith's disciples. Should we not then accuse Mill himself of ignorance? For, in essence, we are only saying what the reader has just read from his pen. Although., in fact, the people who see a difference between his words and ours are right. This observation, which he makes in passing, has almost no influence on the course of his thinking. We, on the other hand, keep this fact in mind all the time in order to draw conclusions from it, which he did not bother to do.

(Chernyshevsky 1949: 642)

Later in his text, Chernyshevsky points out that capitalism and its specific use of technical progress cannot represent a general progress for human societies and therefore must be fought. In other passages, Chernyshevsky gives Mill credit for his frankness, and here too, the resemblance between his statement and Marx's is visible. The Afterword to the Second German Edition of *Capital*, in addition to the passage quoted above, contains another general assessment of Mill, who is described as 'attempting to reconcile irreconcilables' (Marx 1987: 703), that is, the acceptance of capitalism and the desire for social progress. But what distinguishes the French edition, in terms of its relation to Mill, is the presence of a lengthy discussion of the nature of profit in Chapter XVI, 'Absolute and relative surplus value'. This discussion constitutes a historical excursus that intends to show the way contemporary economists, after having placed the origin of profit in the 'productive force of labour' (following Ricardo), evade further discussion by cancelling the difference between capitalists and workers. Mill is an excellent example of this position. Marx brought up his polemic against mercantilism, which described the exchange as a source of profit. Ricardo's statement and its contemporary interpretations, of course, represent a kind of 'progress'. However, the remainder of Mills's text is an attempt to reduce 'the different forms of social production' to the capitalist mode of production alone:

'I assume, throughout, the state of things which, where the labourers and capitalists are separate classes, prevails, with few exceptions, universally; namely, that the capitalist advances the whole expenses, including the entire remuneration of the labourer'.

Strange optical illusion to see everywhere a state of things which as yet exists only exceptionally on our earth. But let us finish – Mill is willing to concede,

'that he should do so is not a matter of inherent necessity'. On the contrary: 'the labourer might wait, until the production is complete, for all that part of his wages which exceeds mere necessaries: and even for the whole, if he has funds in hand sufficient for his temporary support. But in the latter case, the labourer is to that extent really a capitalist in the concern, by supplying a portion of the funds necessary for carrying it on'.

Mill might have gone further and have added, that the labourer who advances to himself not only the necessaries of life but also the means of production, is in reality nothing but his own wage-labourer. He might also have said that the American peasant proprietor is but a serf who does enforced labour for himself instead of for his lord.

After thus proving clearly, that even if capitalist production had no existence, still it would always exist, Mill is consistent enough to show, on the contrary, that it has no existence, even when it does exist.

(Marx 1989: 447–8)

Here again, this addition does not fundamentally alter Marx's point. Indeed, the reproach levelled at economists for lacking historicity and for confusing the general categories of all economies with those specific to the capitalist economy is a recurrent one. However, it is undoubtedly significant that he adds to this French version a discussion specifically on the question of the necessary dispossession of the worker that it requires. Indeed, the essence of Mill's argument is to consider the worker and the capitalist only as two subjects of an exchange, the capitalist holding their own function by lending the worker their means of existence, in the form of a quasi-loan. Mill noted that this is the case everywhere – thereby refusing to recognize the historically singular phenomenon of Western primitive accumulation – but also that it could be otherwise if workers had sufficient means of existence from which to provide the necessary advances for themselves, thereby becoming capitalists. Mill's reasoning is flawed in two ways: on one hand, it makes a historically singular situation absolute, and, on the other hand, it refuses to account for the systemic dimension of the relationship between worker and capitalist once the latter has been established. Marx's project was exactly the opposite: to point out the specificity of capitalism, but also its systematicity, that is to say, to study not its presumed omnipresence but the dynamics of its potentially (but only potentially) universal development. It is therefore not insignificant that Marx took the trouble to specify his project negatively in this way in relation to an author he rediscovered through Chernyshevsky's critique.

On this point, Mill and Proudhon are subjected to similar criticisms. Indeed, we do not find the idea that Marx developed here in Chernyshevsky's work. Chernyshevsky is mainly interested not in Mill's definition of profit, but in the dynamic tendencies he pointed out, in order to show its conflictual relationship to social welfare. In this, Marx takes advantage of this brief passage devoted to the history of economic thought to take up an old criticism of Proudhonism, which he considered to be a by-product of left-wing Ricardianism that was incapable of linking exchange to accumulation and thus of grasping the reproductive dimension of exploitation.[15] Here again, the difference between Marx and Chernyshevsky is easy to explain: while, in his work, Chernyshevsky aimed to denounce the falsity of capitalist progress and the ideology of its Russian importers, Marx intended to correct the false criticisms of capitalism that failed to conceive of it as a system. This appears to be due to the uncritical endorsement of the sole paradigm of exchange, which levels all situations and finally allows the wage-earner to be considered a capitalist:

> 'And even in the former case' (when the workman is a wage labourer to whom the capitalist advances all the necessaries of life, he the labourer), 'may be looked upon in the same light', (i.e., as a capitalist), 'since, contributing his labour at less than the market-price, (!) he may be regarded as lending the difference (?) to his employer and receiving it back with interest, &c'.
> In reality, the labourer advances his labour gratuitously to the capitalist during, say one week, in order to receive the market price at the end of the week, &c., and it is this which, according to Mill, transforms him into a capitalist. On the level plain, simple mounds look like hills; and the imbecile flatness of the present bourgeoisie is to be measured by the altitude of its great intellects.
>
> (Marx 1989: 448)

Marx's reading of Chernyshevsky thus provided him with the opportunity to take up a critique of Mill that he had previously initiated elsewhere and to put it to the service of the essential purpose of *Capital*, and even if the specific tasks that the French edition had to fulfill, that is to finish off the war against Proudhonism already begun in 1857 (see Marx to Engels, 10 January 1857, Marx and Engels 1983: 90).

Conclusion

Marx constantly revisited Volume I of *Capital* and was still working on it at the time of his death. The French edition, written between 1872 and 1875, represents an important part of this work. As this article has sought to show, it is a testament to the way that Marx integrated his different readings and the new questions he had encountered. The reality of the Russian context and the thinkers who analysed it played a central role in this endeavour. The questions linked to the development of Russian socialism − whether to rely on communal traditions or to accept capitalist development − resonated strongly with Marx, who at the time had begun to question the philosophy of universal history. Of course, the French edition of *Capital* is also linked to other circumstantial problems more specific to its intended audience, French workers, while this problematization of the exact meaning of *Capital*'s analyses follows on from a previous critique of Proudhonism. Nevertheless, it is one of the pieces to be added to the study of the relationship between logic and history in *Capital* and, more generally, in the thought of the late Marx.

The richness of Marx's thought comes precisely from the fact that it was in constant evolution, thanks both to the materials Marx had accumulated but also to the struggles he had to wage in the field of political ideas. The French edition of *Capital* demonstrates this double movement and the tensions that run through it. Indeed, the project of the critique of political economy was aimed first and foremost in an effort to demonstrate the systematicity of capitalist realities, against any attempt to autonomize them (as with the commodity, in Marx's reading of Proudhon). However, this systematicity does not constitute a developmental scheme directly applicable to any society subject to commodity exchange. Thus, Marx had to fight both against those who, in France, claimed to be defending an already outdated reality (small-scale commodity production against capitalism) and against those who, outside Western Europe, preached capitalism and the bourgeois society as the only medium-term political perspective.

These questions were central to the Russian reception of *Capital*. Indeed, the book was to be read according to opposite interpretations: Marxist Narodniks would see it as the description of a repulsive situation from which Russia could still escape, while the so-called 'orthodox' would consider that the book prophesied Russia's imminent capitalist future. Of course, these debates were inseparable from more philosophical considerations, on the nature of historical determinism, and more political ones, on the revolutionary subject and therefore the authentic target of the political message (the peasantry or the working class). However, these debates were always based on a reading of *Capital*. It was not until 1899 that Danielson's 1872 translation was replaced by a new one, which incorporated the achievements of later French and German editions (Marx 1899). Tellingly it was Petr Struve, a legal Marxist and a firm believer in the Marxist philosophy of history, who edited the volume and was therefore responsible for integrating the historicizing remarks of the French version.

Notes

1 On the debates that accompanied the different French translations, see this author's own article co-written with A. Bouffard and A. Feron (Bouffard, Feron and Fondu 2017).

2 Built on the Russian word for 'people' (*narod*), the term designates a Russian political current defending the interests of the working classes, especially the peasants, against tsarism but also against the liberal bourgeoisie (then very weak in Russia). Despite a great theoretical diversity, the current was built around the idea that Russia could have its own form of socialism based on the country's peasant traditions.

3 Thus we find in his later writings the seeds of what would be more explicitly theorized by Trotsky in the idea of 'uneven and combined development' (see Anderson 2010: 177 ff.). For a more detailed account of the last years of Marx's intellectual life, see Musto (2020).

4 The project of the MEGA^2 (*Marx Engels GesamtAusgabe*) is to publish the complete texts of Marx. Section II, devoted to *Capital* and its drafts, includes all the versions of the text revised by Marx or Engels and offers exhaustive comparative indexes between the different versions.

5 I have tried to clarify this link between the systematicity of the categories of *Capital* and Proudhon's critique in my article (Fondu 2017). I can roughly summarize the argument here by saying that the critique of Proudhonism is based on the idea that the market cannot exist without capitalism and that socialism presupposes the socialization of the means of production to the level of concentration permitted by capitalism.

6 Marx was put in touch with Russian activists in the context of the First International. It was probably A. A. Serno-Solovievich, a member of the Association as early as 1867, who drew Marx's attention to the importance of Russian Narodnism.

7 This news came as a surprise to Marx. It was part of a wider project to translate recent Western social science books into Russian.

8 I have not found the original and translate from the Russian version given by Haruki Wada in the article referred to above.

9 From now on, when quoting Marx's *Capital*, we will give Roy's French translation and Ben Fowkes's English translation of the German edition (we give the German original text in endnotes).

10 'Analyse der Grundform des Kapitals, der Form worin es die ökonomische Organisation der modernen Gesellschaft bestimmt' (Marx 1987: 180).

11 Das Kapitalverhältniß setzt die Scheidung zwischen den Arbeitern und dem Eigenthum an den Verwirklichungsbedingungen der Arbeit voraus. Sobald die kapitalistische Produktion einmal auf eignen Füßen steht, erhält sie nicht nur jene Scheidung, sondern reproducirt sie auf stets wachsender Stufenleiter. Der Prozeß, der das Kapitalverhältniß schafft, kann also nichts andres sein als der Scheidungsproceß des Arbeiters vom Eigenthum an seinen Arbeitsbedingungen, ein Proceß, der einerseits die gesellschaftlichen Lebens- und Produktionsmittel in Kapital verwandelt, andrerseits die unmittelbaren Producenten in Lohnarbeiter. Die sog. ursprüngliche Akkumulation ist also nichts als der historische Scheidungsproceß von Producent und Produktionsmittel. Er erscheint als 'ursprünglich', weil er die Vorgeschichte des Kapitals und der ihm entsprechenden Produktionsweise bildet (Marx 1987: 645).

12 Ihre Geschichte nimmt in verschiedenen Ländern verschiedene Färbung an und durchläuft die verschiedenen Phasen in verschiedener Reihenfolge. Nur in England, das wir später als Beispiel nehmen, besitzt sie klassische Form (Marx 1987: 646).

13 Thomas Kuczynski, on the other hand, has included it in his recent edition of *Capital*, which aims to deliver a work as close as possible to Marx's final intentions (see Marx 2017: 646).

14 We leave aside here the long passages Marx devotes to Mill in his early work.

15 This link was made very explicitly in the *Contribution to the Critique of Political Economy* (see Marx 1980: 157) and is repeated, albeit in an abbreviated form, in the various versions of *Capital*.

References

Anderson, Kevin (2010) *Marx at the Margins. On Nationalism, Ethnicity and Non-Western Societies*, Chicago: University of Chicago Press.

Bidet, Jacques (2007 [2000]) *Exploring Marx's* Capital. *Philosophical, Economic and Political Dimensions*, Leiden: Brill.

Bouffard, Alix, Feron, Alexandre and Fondu, Guillaume (2017) 'Les éditions françaises du *Capital*', in *Ce qu'est le Capital de Karl Marx*, edited by Michael Heinrich, Paris, Les éditions sociales, pp. 91–145.

Chernyshevsky, Nikolai (1949 [1860]) 'Очерки из политической экономии (по Миллю)' [Essays on Political Economy (by Mill)], in *ПОЛНОЕ СОБРАНИЕ СОЧИНЕНИЙ В ПЯТНАДЦАТИ ТОМАХ* [*Complete Works in 15 Volumes*], Moscow: Gosudarstvennoe izdatel`stvo khudozhestvennoy literatury, pp. 337–725.

Fondu, Guillaume (2017) 'La critique de l'économie a-t-elle encore un sens', in *Que reste-t-il de Marx*, edited by Catherine Colliot-Thélène, Rennes: Presses Universitaires de Rennes, pp. 77–92.

Lefebvre, Jean-Pierre (2016 [1983]) 'Introduction de l'édition de 1983', in Karl Marx, *Le Capital*, Paris: Les éditions sociales, pp. XXIII–LVIII.

Marx, Karl (1899) *Капитал* [*Capital*], Saint Petersburg: O. N. Popovoï.

Marx, Karl (1976) *Capital*, London: Penguin Books.

Marx, Karl (1980 [1859]), 'Zur Kritik der politischen Ökonomie', in *Marx Engels Gesamtausgabe* (MEGA²), vol. II/2, Berlin: Dietz Verlag, pp. 95–245.

Marx, Karl (1983 [1867]) 'Das Kapital', in *Marx Engels Gesamtausgabe* (MEGA²), vol. II/5, Berlin: Dietz Verlag.

Marx, Karl (1987 [1872]) 'Das Kapital', in *Marx Engels Gesamtausgabe* (MEGA²), vol. II/6, Berlin: Dietz Verlag.

Marx, Karl (1989 [1875]) 'Le Capital', in *Marx Engels Gesamtausgabe* (MEGA²), vol. II/7, Berlin: Dietz Verlag.

Marx, Karl (1991 [1890]) 'Le Capital', in *Marx Engels Gesamtausgabe* (MEGA²), vol. II/10, Berlin: Dietz Verlag.

Marx, Karl (2017), *Das Kapital*, Hamburg: VSA Verlag.

Marx, Karl and Engels, Friedrich (1974) *La Russie*, Paris: 10/18.

Marx, Karl and Engels, Friedrich (1983) *Marx Engels Collected Works*, vol. 40: *Letters. 1856-1859*, Moscow: Progress Publishers.

Marx, Karl and Engels, Friedrich (1987) *Marx Engels Collected Works*, vol. 43: *Letters. 1868-1870*, Moscow: Progress Publishers.

Marx, Karl and Engels, Friedrich (1989) *Marx Engels Collected Works*, vol. 44: *Letters. 1870-1873*, Moscow: Progress Publishers.

Marx, Karl and Engels, Friedrich (1991) *Marx Engels Collected Works*, vol. 45: *Letters. 1874-1879*, Moscow: Progress Publishers.

Marx, Karl and Engels, Friedrich (1992) *Marx Engels Collected Works*, vol. 46: *Letters. 1880-1883*, Moscow: Progress Publishers.

Mervaud, Michel (2012) 'Le conflit avec les "marxides": note sur les rapports de Herzen et de Marx', *Revue des études slaves*, vol. 83, n. 1: 163–83.

Musto, Marcello (2020) *The Last Years of Karl Marx: An Intellectual Biography*, Stanford: Stanford University Press.

Wada, Haruki (1981) 'Карл Маркс и революционная Россия' [Karl Marx and Revolutionary Russia]. See: http://gefter.ru/archive/24390 (accessed on 15 March 2022).

8 Reading *Le Capital*

Marx as a Translator

Paul Reitter

Introduction: Divergent reading

What kind of a translator was Karl Marx? Those who have addressed this question, including Marx himself, have tended to do so with reference to the original French edition of *Capital, Volume I*. This makes sense, of course. Skilled in French, and disappointed by what he called the 'literalness' of Joseph Roy's attempt to render *Capital, Volume I,* into that language (Gaudin 2019: 78), Marx subjected Roy's work to an overhaul – so much so that the finished product is as much a self-translation by Marx as it is a translation of Marx by Roy. Furthermore, as he revised the form and content of *Capital, Volume I*, for *Le Capital*, breaking up chapters to create a new textual structure and adding new passages, Marx also translated – or retranslated – in a way that seems to combine translation and revision. He may have had a term for this practice. In an often-cited letter to Nikolai Danielson, who translated *Capital, Volume I,* into Russian, Marx wrote that at times he had to '"smooth out [*aplatir*]" the matter in the French version' (Marx 2010: 343).

The difficulty here is that the French term Marx used in the letter, '*aplatir,*' can denote both 'smooth out' and 'flatten' or 'simplify', and neither Marx's letter to Danielson nor his other exchanges about *Le Capital* provides much useful context for interpreting his statement. Certainly, Marx thought that *Le Capital* was in some ways better than the German source text. But the claims he made to that effect, including his famous remark about *Le Capital* serving as a crucial reference point for future translations of *Capital, Volume I*, seem to turn more on the material added to the French edition, and the structural changes the edition features, than on the quality of the French translation.

Over the 150 years that have passed since that translation appeared, some scholars and critics have advanced the view that it does in fact simplify its source text, namely, the 1872 German edition of *Capital, Volume I.* Here is one example[1] that appeared very recently and thus suggests that the tradition to which it belong persists in the present day. Kyle Baasch characterized the abovementioned line from Marx's letter to Danielson in the following terms: 'he [Marx] admitted that he was forced to "aplatir", or flatten, the complex German presentation' (Baasch 2020). Baasch then employed his reading of

DOI: 10.4324/9781003336365-10

Marx's self-assessment as a hermeneutic key, moving from the idea that Marx's use of the word '*aplatir*' constitutes a confession to the claim that with respect to rigor, the French translation doesn't match the German text – doesn't match it at important moments, that is, ones where important conceptual framing occurs. He maintained that 'the French edition is highly inconsistent in its translation of the more idiosyncratic terms that decorate the opening chapters' (Baasch 2020). To illustrate this point, Baasch considered how Marx and Roy rendered the word '*Träger* [bearer]' into French. As he observed, they translated it in different ways, even where the term's signifying function in the German source text appears not to change. Sometimes '*Träger*' is rendered as 'carry [*porte*]' and sometimes as 'support [*soutien*]'. In a couple of cases, it is simply dropped.

Baasch called such inconsistencies 'shortcomings' of the French translation, and they matter, according to him, because they have obscured meanings that play a central role in the text. He saw this as happening when '*Träger*' is rendered as 'support'. Whereas '*Träger*' helps develop the theater metaphor that pervades *Capital, Volume I*, which keeps evoking the 'actor's masks' that people and things wear or bear under capitalism, 'support' pulls against it. The latter term promotes an architectural metaphor instead, which in turn implies relations of non-transferability, that is, a situation where the actor's masks can't come off. One of the aims of Baasch's essay is to show that this shift from theater to architecture has negatively affected some of the most consequential readings of *Capital* in the twentieth century.

For other scholars, however, Marx and Roy's *Le Capital* rises to a level above 'mere translation', as one of them has put it (Anderson 1983: 72). Here one encounters the view that readers should see their edition as an original, 'authentic' work, or a kind of super-translation. The thinking behind this view is that Marx made very liberal use of the self-translator's prerogatives not only by producing a translation that strays so much from the structure of the source text and, again, features entirely new passages but also by translating with the goal of improvement. Marx clearly wanted to enhance *Capital, Volume I,* as much as he could as worked on *Le Capital*, and this holds for his work on the translation, too. In other words, the thinking here has been that Marx translated 'upward' in *Le Capital* – that his mode of translating bordered on rewriting in the sense of emending. So, for example, in his recent article 'The Originality of the French Edition of Capital', Rodrigo Maiolini Rebello Pinho has framed Marx's French translation as a revising effort that took place within the context of an intellectually ambitious project of rewriting. According to Pinho, 'the fact that it [*Capital, Volume I*] was completely rewritten by the author himself, as he revised the translation in great detail, means that it [*Le Capital*] became an original work' (Pinho 2021; see also Anderson 1983).

Pinho noted that Engels expressed reservations about the French translation: as is well known, Marx's friend and writing partner worried that modern French wasn't compatible with Marx's dialectical thought. Hence the French edition wouldn't be able to preserve that fundamental component of *Capital, Volume I*. But Pinho registered this critical perspective mainly to explain why

Engels didn't go further in honoring Marx's wish that the changes in the French edition be integrated into posthumous German editions of his *magnum opus*, which is a way of pointing up the value of *Le Capital*. Pinho reminded us that the content of *Le Capital* still differs from that of the existing German editions of *Capital, Volume I* – it has remained a unique text, and since it is the last edition whose publication Marx oversaw himself, it has remained uniquely authoritative. Moreover, if in his recent account of *Le Capital* Baasch invoked Marx's self-characterization of his self-translating ['*aplatir*'], Pinho cited no less an authority than Raya Dunayeskaya, and her invocation of Marx himself, to stress the significance of Marx and Roy's French translation. Pinho wrote about Dunayeskaya that 'she referred to it [*Le Capital*] as the "crucial, famous, irreversible French edition, 1872"' and 'emphasized that "Marx had informed us in the Afterword to the French edition of Capital (28 April 1875) that it" possesses a scientific value independent of the original and should be consulted even by readers familiar with German'. 'The philosopher', Pinho added, 'also analyzed, in-depth, changes in the commodity-form concept and law of capital centralization and concentration, among others' (Pinho 2021).

Unlike Baasch, then, Pinho wasn't inclined to see terminological movement or alterations of metaphor in the French edition as potentially damaging deviations from the source text. His is a hermeneutics of the benefit of the doubt, at least when it comes to *Le Capital*. He encouraged readers to treat lexical shifts in the translations as authorial revisions from which they might gain special insight, or whose importance, in other words, he essentially presupposed. Consider how quickly Pinho went from identifying an instance of metaphorical movement to describing its significance as he pointed out that Engels neglected to include this change in later German editions of *Capital, Volume I*:

> In the Preface to the first German edition, Marx wrote: 'The country that is more developed industrially only shows, *to the less developed*, the image of its own future'. Marx modified even the text in the Preface to the first German edition, and the passage was changed in an important way. The final wording in the French edition was: 'The most industrially developed country only shows *those that follow it on the industrial ladder* the image of their own future'.
>
> (Pinho, 2021)

A common hermeneutic framework

Despite how differently Baasch and Pinho assessed Marx's performance as a translator in *Le Capital*, their essays exhibit a notable interpretive commonality. Both operate with a narrow hermeneutic framework that rests on very limited contextualization. Based on a line from a letter to a fellow translator of *Capital*, a translator whom Marx was perhaps trying to encourage by criticizing his own translation effort (if that's what he was doing), or to whom he was saying, in effect: you, Nikolai Danielson, could produce the best translation of *Capital, Volume I*, Baasch treated the inconsistencies in the French translation with suspicion. Making a great deal of the same ambiguous line from Marx's letter to Danielson, and also some claims Dunayeskaya made about *Le Capital*, Pinho approached each lexical change as a likely revision upward. Neither scholar seemed interested in entertaining other interpretive possibilities, which is a problem, since the kinds of changes in *Le Capital* they pointed to can arise for a variety of reasons.

Terminological inconsistency, for example, need not have to do with flattening. Where a term in the source text has connotations and resonances that its closest match in the target language lacks, a translator might decide that lexical variation is the best option. The consistency in the source text will be lost, but loss in the service of preservation is part of translation. As it happens, the term '*Träger*' has a range of architectural connotations: unlike '*porte*', it can mean 'beam', 'pillar', or 'transom'. Perhaps in using both '*soutien*' and '*porte*' as he translated '*Träger*', Marx was trying to convey resonances and thus nuances that readers of *Le Capital* wouldn't experience if he had rendered the German word into French more consistently. As for the dropped occurrences of the term, Marx's style in *Capital* is conspicuously compressed – '*gedrungen*' is how Engels once described it (Engels 1989: 58).[2] Since translation generally entails producing a text that is longer than the original, Marx may have been engaging in a kind of holistic mode of translation. By leaving out words where he could, he may have been trying to compensate for compression he couldn't retain elsewhere in the text. Perhaps this, too, is a case of loss in the service of preservation, rather than another effect of a program of *aplatir*.

Similarly, Pinho took for granted that Marx was acting on a program of revision when he, Marx, introduced the term 'ladder' in translating the Preface to the first German edition of *Capital*. Why else assume, as Pinho did, that with the introduction of 'ladder', the passage where the word occurs was 'changed in an important way'? But many words are casually used as metaphors – 'ladder' is a good example – and thus most translations introduce metaphorical elements that aren't present in the source text. These new elements do affect the meaning of the translation, which is one of the reasons why a translation of a text like *Capital, Volume I*, can only ever be a new text with its own unique constellation of images. But its images won't all matter equally, and one of the ways a reader develops a sense of what the text might be saying is by deciding how much importance she should ascribe to the different images it contains. To develop an informed sense of how the ladder image added to *Le Capital*, it is of course necessary to do some actual exegesis, for example, examine whether it reinforces or counterbalances patterns of metaphor, but it is also helpful to think further about the principles guiding the French translation.

We could expand the two traditions or hermeneutic frameworks under discussion simply by combining them. For as opposing as they are, they are not mutually exclusive. *Capita, Volume I*, is a very large book, after all, and I suspect that as he helped translate it into French, Marx was looking to simplify the text in some cases and smooth it out or improve it in others. But what we really need is the additional orientation for making sense of Marx's translation moves in *Le Capital*, since even when we take them together, flattening and translating upward leave us with a narrow base of contextualization. The main part of this article will seek to expand that base by examining how Marx translated before he became a self-translator and thus gained the self-translator's motivations and license that scholars have stressed in their analyses of his French translation. Marx did a lot of translating before he worked on *Le Capital*, and if we analyze his earlier practice of translation, we will be much better equipped to ask an important question as we consider *Le Capital* – important because of its potential to affect how we read *Le Capital* and compare it to other editions of *Capital, Volume I*. Was Marx pursuing an agenda peculiar to his interests and position as a self-translator, or was he employing his customary translation strategies and proceeding as he had before, even in cases where we might be tempted to think that he was following a specific strategy of *aplatir*? Was he perhaps operating with his typical, though not necessarily programmatic, bold strokes, and neither simplifying nor translating upward?

Marx as a translator

The text to investigate to get a sense of Marx as a translator, rather than a self-translator, is in fact *Capital, Volume I*. In Marx's correspondence with Engels, Engels was the one who tended to raise questions about how Marx's work was being translated. This holds not only for *Le Capital* but also a French translation of *The Eighteenth Brumaire of Louis Bonaparte*. For the most part, Marx brushed off his friend's concerns, declining the numerous invitations to discuss how well basic features of his writing might be communicated in French, given not so much the syntactical possibilities of that language, as its overall ethos. In *Capital, Volume I*, however, Marx showed that he was quite interested in how language systems differ with respect to what he treated as their guiding inclinations. He observed in an early footnote,

> Seventeenth-century English writers still tended to use 'worth' for use-value and 'value' for exchange-value, which is very much in the spirit of a language with an affinity for expressing unmediated things with Germanic words and reflected things with Romance ones.
>
> (Marx 2024)

He also remarked, or lamented, 'Less forcefully than the Romance term *valere, valer, valoir*, for instance, the German word "*Werthsein* [to be worth]" expresses that equating commodity B to commodity A is commodity A's value expression' (Marx 2024). In a footnote toward the end of the book, moreover, Marx offered some comments on producing a responsible translation. He took issue with a bibliographical practice that made it hard to tell whether a text was a translation, and he criticized a particular translation for failing to include some of the material contained in the source text (Marx 1987: 516).

More important, Marx's *magnum opus* abounds with his own translations of the English-language writings he cited, among which theories of how to organize industrial production, works of political economy, and factory inspectors' reports bulk especially large. (Generally speaking, Marx translated citations for the body of the text and left quotes in footnotes untranslated.) Below are sample English-to-German translations from *Capital, Volume I*, preceded by the corresponding part of the English source text and followed by an analysis of the translation. The examples given are representative in the limited sense that they feel representative to the author of this article. The tools of digital humanities might soon help us make such choices more systematically and provide documentation in support of them. But for now, with *Capital* being as big and as varied as it is, you would still be basically asking readers for the benefit of the doubt even if you presented them with pages of examples. Ultimately, a very large survey is needed.

The passages given here come from the *Report of the inspectors of factories to Her Majesty's Principal Secretary of State for the Home Department for the half-year ending 31st October 1848*. Marx made no secret of how much he appreciated the work of the civil servants who spent their professional lives documenting industrial labor conditions in England. Not only did he acknowledge that they provided him with the statistical material he needed for his analysis of capitalist production, but he also remarked on the professionalism, the commitment to getting to the truth, that they brought to their task, praising it in emphatic terms. Above all, though, what expresses Marx's debt to the factory inspectors' work is the sheer extent to which he relied on their reports in attempting to evoke the lived reality of the modern capitalist system, which is one of his major goals in *Capital, Volume I*, even if it isn't explicitly framed as such there. Of all the sources Marx cited in *Capital, Volume I*, quotations from the factory inspectors' reports occur with by far the greatest frequency, and many of the quotations are quite long, as is the case with the second of the two passages that follow. Marx, then, did much of his translating with this particular material as his source material. Both passages are from Chapter 8 of the 1872 edition, 'The Working Day'. The first passage is itself a quotation – the inspectors' report is citing a 'counter-petition' against the Ten Hours Bill that, according to Marx, manufacturers pushed the parents of child workers to sign, although he also indicates that they probably didn't need much pushing.

> That your petitioners, who are parents, conceive that an additional hour of leisure will tend more to demoralize their children than otherwise, believing that idleness is the parent of vice
>
> (Marx 1987: 1,318)

> Eure Bittsteller, Eltern, glauben, daß eine zusätzliche Mußestunde weiter keinen Erfolg haben kann, als die Demoralisation ihrer Kinder, denn Müßiggang ist allen Lasters Anfang
>
> (Marx 1987: 236)

This sentence doesn't contain major instances of ambiguity or syntactical complexity. Hence a German translator can simply move through it without altering the order of its clauses, which is what Marx in fact did. At the same time, when we compare the two versions of the sentence, some of his translation decisions stand out, inviting us to examine them. I am not thinking of how the verb 'demoralize' is rendered as a noun (*Demoralization*), or how the repetition of the central term 'parent' gets dropped. The German verb '*demoralisieren*', perhaps the most direct match for 'demoralize', was used much less commonly than the noun form of the word, and if Marx was aiming to avoid obscure and recondite words in a translation of a workers' petition, that goal should hardly be surprising – or controversial. At the end of the sentence, Marx simply employed a folksy colloquial expression to translate another colloquial expression in a political context where rhetoric mattered a great deal, a conventional thing to do and thus also hardly surprising. What, then, stands out? Marx's translation compresses the original text while also giving its propositional content a more emphatic air.

The phrase 'who are parents' becomes 'parents'. 'Believing that' is elided, which at once compresses the prose and amplifies the effect of assertiveness, since the connection between idleness and vice goes from being presented as something that the parents have views about to being framed as a statement of fact: Marx's translation of 'believing that idleness is the parent of vice' could be back-translated into English as 'for idleness is where all vice begins'. Similarly, Marx dropped the term 'conceive', which introduces the claim that follows it as a subjective position, and he made the almost tentative formulation 'will tend more to demoralize their children more than otherwise' into what we can back-translate as: 'cannot do anything except demoralize their children'.

Here, the voice of the text translated, with its more *gendrungen* and decisive style, edges closer to the voice of the translator, which is, of course, a widespread tendency in translation and something we should expect to happen when a strong-voiced writer like Marx functions as a translator. But there may be another reason why Marx's translation features this kind of movement. Marx's challenge wasn't to produce a translation that would sound about as assertive as the source text. It was to use the resources of German to produce a text that would sound about as assertive as the source text sounded to him. For a text doesn't sound assertive to this or that degree independent of readers, and the best Marx could do was convey in another language how he experienced the source text, which is ultimately the best any translator can do. Given how appalling Marx found moral justifications for exploiting child labor, how clearly their hypocrisy and brutality affected him, and how extensively he cataloged them in *Capital, Volume I*, it seems safe to say that Marx was hardly a typical reader of the parents' petition. On the other hand, if as he listened to the sentence under discussion Marx drew on his contextual knowledge, and thus experienced a forcefulness that the English phrasing doesn't immediately evoke for most readers, he would have been doing what translators – and readers in general – do when they make sense of individual passages in a text. Namely, they orient themselves by situating individual passages and texts within larger discursive contexts and their patterns of meaning. If a translator forces a passage to conform to such a pattern, then she is translating irresponsibly, or perhaps not translating at all. But while Marx's translation of the petition might be a bit freewheeling, or perhaps 'assertive' is a better word for how he proceeds, it is not coercive in any obvious way.

A second sample

Let's now consider how Marx translated a passage from the inspectors' report where the report isn't, for the most part, quoting an outside text.

> The factories in which the children of these parents are employed, are small flax spinning mills scattered along the streams on the borders of these two counties; and from the innumerable particles of the dust and fibre of the raw material with which the air in these factories is loaded, it is extremely disagreeable to remain in one of them, even for ten minutes; for you cannot do so without experiencing a sensation of considerable distress, in conse-quence of the eyes, ears, nostrils, and mouth being filled with the clouds of flax dust from which there is no escape on any side. The employment, by reason of the rapid motion of the machinery, requires the untiring exercise of great dexterity and activity, under the guidance of incessant vigilance; and it appears somewhat hard that their own parents should apply the term 'idleness' to the condition of children who are kept working a good ten hours (over and above meal times), at such an employment, in such an atmosphere... I do not see, nor do these poor people allege any reason, why they apprehend danger to their children's morals, simply because they do not perform a longer day's work that their neighbours, who are employed as labourers and journeymen in the ordinary occupations of country village... then this uncharitable talk about idleness and vice is deservedly to be denounced as mere cant and hypocrisy... They who, some twelve years ago, were startled by the confidence with which it was gravely proclaimed to the public, under sanction of high authority, that the *net profit* of the master was derived from the 'last hour' of work, and that if the hours of working should be reduced by one hour per day, *net profit* would be destroyed; will scarcely be less surprised to find that the original discovery of virtues of the 'last hours' has been so far improved upon as to make it comprehend *morals* as well as *profits*, so that if the duration of children's labour be reduced to ten hours' active employment, *their* 'morals' must be destroyed, together with the 'net profit' of their employer; both depending upon the last − final hour.
>
> (Marx 1987: 1, 318−19)

Die Atmosphäre der Flachsspinnereien, worin die Kinder dieser tugendhaft-zärtlichen Eltern arbeiten, ist geschwängert mit so unzähligen

Staub- und Faserpartikelchen des Rohmaterials, daß es außerordentlich unangenehm ist, auch nur 10 Minuten in den Spinnstuben zuzubringen, denn ihr könnt das nicht ohne die peinlichste Empfindung, in dem Auge, Ohr, Nasenlöcher und Mund sich sofort füllen mit Flachsstaubwolken, vor denen kein Entrinnen ist. Die Arbeit selbst erheischt, wegen der Fieberhast der Maschinerie, rastlosen Aufwand von Geschick und Bewegung, unter der Kontrole nie ermüdender Aufmerksamkeit, und es scheint etwas hart, Eltern den Ausdruck 'Faullenzerei' auf die eignen Kinder anwenden zu lassen, die, nach Abzug der Essenszeit, 10 volle Stunden an solche Beschäftigung, in einer solchen Atmosphäre, geschmiedet sind... Diese Kinder arbeiten länger als die Ackerknechte in den Nachbardörfern... Solch liebloses Gekohl über, Müßiggang und Laster' muß als der reinste cant und die schamloseste Heuchelei gebrandmarkt werden... Der Theil des Publikums, der vor ungefähr zwölf Jahren auffuhr über die Zuversicht, womit man öffentlich und ganz ernsthaft proklamirte, unter der Sanktion hoher Autorität, daß der ganze,Reingewinn' des Fabrikanten aus 'der letzten Stunde' Arbeit fließt, und daher die Reduktion des Arbeitstags um eine Stunde den Reingewinn vernichtet; dieser Theil des Publikums, sagen wir, wird kaum seinen Augen trauen, wenn er nun findet, daß die Original-Entdeckung über die Tugenden der 'letzten Stunde' seitdem soweit verbessert worden ist 'Moral' und 'Profit' gleichmäßig einzuschließen; so daß wenn die Dauer der Kinderarbeit auf volle 10 Stunden reducirt wird, die Moral der Kinder zugleich mit dem Nettogewinn ihrer Anwender flöten geht, beide abhängig von dieser letzten, dieser fatalen Stunde.

(Marx 1987: 236–7)

Here, too, Marx draws the voice in the source text closer to his own voice, in this case making the language not only more forceful, and amplifying the effect of critique, but also making the prose more vivid and saltier. Most striking of all is the addition of the combination of adjectives '*tugendhaft-zärtlichen*', which means 'virtuous and delicate', and gives the passage an ironic note that the corresponding phrase in the source text doesn't seem to have – the parents being criticized for their 'hard' talk about their children are obviously anything but delicate (no adjectives modify the first instance of 'parents' in the original English version of the passage). While we might occasionally encounter such irony in a factory inspectors' report, we find quite a bit of it in *Capital, Volume I*, where Marx wrote, for example:'What is the basis of this absurd compensation theory? Beyond an honest desire to conceal what is actually happening, there is also' (Marx 2024: 239).

Furthermore, whereas the air is 'loaded' with particles in the source text, it is 'pregnant [*geschwängert*]' with them in Marx's translation. Whereas the factory inspector described the motion of the machinery as 'rapid', in the translation it has intensified into a 'feverish haste [*Fieberhast*]'. And where the source text speaks of the children 'kept at' their work, Marx's translation has the inspector saying that they are 'bolted to it [*geschmiedet an*]', a phrase that occurs frequently in *Capital, Volume I* – Marx employed it to evoke the fate of specialized workers tied to a single specialized task – and one that, like 'pregnant' and 'feverish haste', amounts to a suggestive new metaphorical moment in the passage. Clearly, Marx wasn't shy about introducing such moments as he pursued his core strategies as a translator.

He also amplified the critical tone of the inspectors' report by rendering the decorous term 'uncharitable' with a blunt and more damning word, 'loveless', so that the parents' 'talk' about the morality-destroying idleness of their children sinks in terms of its own moral standing: surely it is worse for a parent to speak about their children lovelessly than uncharitably. In addition, whereas the inspector opined that the parents' talk 'is deservedly to be denounced as mere cant and hypocrisy', Marx has him say what we might back-translate into English as the superlative-heavy admonition: the talk 'must be denounced as the purest cant and most shameless hypocrisy'.

This isn't to say that Marx's translation dramatically amplifies the critical character of the source text. Superlatives are used more freely in German than they are in English, and Marx may have felt that the source text features a kind of biting understatement – 'deservedly to be denounced' can be read that way – that was less common in German, and thus more likely to go unappreciated by readers of a German translation. The fact that Marx translated the key term 'idleness' in two different ways in one quotation – as '*Faulenzerei*' and '*Müßiggang*' – suggests not so much carelessness on his part but a desire to preserve connotations of 'idleness' that neither German term encompasses on its own. Perhaps other such liberal moves were carried out in a preservationist spirit.

Conclusion

Given the size of *Capital, Volume I*, and the sheer number of Marx's translations it contains, one would need to marshal much more evidence in order to convincingly make the case that Marx's renderings of the reports are indeed representative of the translation strategies in the book. Still, those renderings suggest that in translating prior to his work as a self-translator in *Le Capital*, Marx tended to move in several directions at once, enhancing his source material – Marx also compressed the second passage, eliminating, for example, the superfluous words after 'escape' – and boldly assimilating it to his own style to some extent, while exhibiting a sense of responsibility toward the source text, so that it isn't easy to say whether the moments in his translations that stray most conspicuously from the source texts are functions of his readerly position, that is, creative attempts draw out of texts elements that might be less apparent to other readers, or creative attempts to navigate the differences between languages systems – or some combination of those two things. What should be clear, however, is that in the translations we examined, Marx employed techniques associated with his self-translation independent of his work as a self-translator. Thus, when we encounter those techniques in *Le Capital*, we should not assume that they proceeded only from his self-translator's agenda, that they have to do primarily with simplifying or translating upward, or *aplatir* in one sense or another.

Given the intellectual stakes here, returning to the translations in *Capital, Volume I,* seems eminently worthwhile. After all, most of the people who read Marx's writings read them in translation. This means that we will be hard pressed to adequately comprehend the reception and appropriation of Marx's writings and, thus, the shape of the modern world, unless we engage with the topic 'Marx and translation' seriously and thoroughly. Thanks to the burgeoning interest in translation studies, particularly global approaches to the translation histories of individual works, and the active efforts of certain Marx scholars to draw attention to the importance of translation for Marx scholarship, the topic has finally begun to get the kind of attention it deserves.[3]

Notes

1   It was chosen because it was published in 2020 and it is very recent.
2   In *Le Capital,* Marx doesn't translate instances of other key words, too. This some-times happens with '*sachlich*', for example. *Sachlich,* an adjective, can denote quite a few qualities: 'professional', 'objective', 'factual', 'material', and more. In *Capital, Volume I,* Marx employs it in different ways. Most notable, however, is his use of the term toward the end of Chapter 1, to evoke what capitalism does to the relation between people and the things they make – *Sachen.* Here Marx is building up to the chiasmus where he speaks of the 'personification of things and the reification of people' ['*Personificierung der Sache*' and '*Versachlichung der Personen*'] (Marx 1987: 138), as well as to his climatic definition of capital, which reads, 'Capital isn't a thing [*Sache*]. Rather, it is a relation among people that is mediated by things' (Marx 1987: 685). Marx writes of '*sachliche Verhätnisse der Menschen* and *gesellschaftliche Verhälntisse der Sachen*' (Marx 1987:104). *Le Capital* mostly drops this chiasmus, but not necessarily to spare the reader, that is, simplify, or refine Marx's thinking, that is, smooth it out. In this case, Marx may have simply wanted to avoid misleading – the phrase 'to prevent misconceptions' occurs quite a bit in *Capital, Volume I* – by dropping an occurrence of Marx's phrase '*sachlich*', which, as Marx is using it, lacks a good match in French – and also English. The standard English translation of Marx's phrase '*sachliche Verhälntnisse*', 'material relations', does in fact mislead readers, since Marx is describing 'relations [*Verhältnisse*]' in which things play a particular role – that is, relations of a very par-ticular kind – rather than general 'material relations'. Of course, it is easier for a self-translator to omit to translate a key word or phrase than it is for a 'regular' translator. This is especially so when the text being translated has become a classic.
3   The Marx scholars I have in mind are Marcello Musto and Babak Amini (2023), the co-editors of a monumental handbook that will appear in 2023.

References

Anderson, Kevin (1983) 'The Unknown Marx's *Capital, Volume I*: The French Edition of 1872-75, 100 Years Later', *Review of Radical Political Economics,* vol. 15, n. 4: 71–80.
Baasch, Kyle (2020) 'The Theatre of Economic Categories: Rediscovering *Capital* in the Late in 1960s'. See www.radicalphilosophy.com/article/the-theatre-of-economic-categories (accessed on 10 February 2022).

Engels, Friedrich (1989) 'Vorwort zur Dritten Auflage', in Karl Marx, *Kapital: einen Kritik der politischen Ökonomie, Bd. 1* (1883), in *Marx Engels Gesamtausgabe* (MEGA²), vol. II/8, Berlin: Dietz, pp. 57–62.

Gaudin, François (2019) *Traduire Le Capital: une correspondance inédite entre Karl Marx, Friedrich Engels et l'éditeur Maurice Lachâtre*, Rouen: Presses universitaires de Rouen et du Havre.

Marx, Karl (1987) *Kapital: einen Kritik der politischen Ökonomie, Bd. 1* (1872), in *Marx Engels Gesamtausgabe* (MEGA²), vol. II/6, Berlin: Dietz.

Marx, Karl (2024 forthcoming) *Capital: A Critique of Political Economy, Volume 1*, Princeton: Princeton University Press.

Marx, Karl and Engels, Friedrich (2010) *Collected Works*, vol.45: *Letters 1874-9*, London: Lawrence and Wishart.

Musto, Marcello and Amini, Babak eds. (2023 forthcoming), *The Routledge Handbook of Marx's 'Capital': A Global History of Translation, Dissemination and Reception*, London and New York: Routledge.

Pinho, Rodrigo Maiolini Rebello (2021) 'The Originality of the French Edition of *Capital*'. See https://imhojournal.org/articles/the-originality-of-marxs-french-edition-of-capital-an-historical-analysis (accessed on 1 March 2022).

9 An Unfinished Project

Marx's Last Words on *Capital*

Michael R. Krätke

A book project too big for a lifetime

Although many Marxists still ignore this simple truth, Marx's lifelong project of a *Critique of Political Economy* has never been completed. What is more and worse: we know that Marx was not content with the result of his many efforts to improve the text of the first volume of *Capital* until his very last days. While still working on his manuscripts for Volumes II and III, he revealed his intention to thoroughly rework and rewrite the first volume of the book on several occasions. Not in public, but in private letters to close friends. After nearly forty years of work – from the spring of 1844 until March 1883 – the biggest project of his life remained unfinished, although he kept working on it until his very last days. All the intensive studies on a wide range of topics related in one way or another to his *Critique of Political Economy* notwithstanding, the project was never finished. Engels, who was longer and more closely involved in this project than anybody else, had been left in the dark about its actual state for a long time. Marx knew from experience that he had to keep Engels at a distance if he did not want to be harassed on a daily base to finally come to an end and publish. Engels had already succeeded once, persuading Marx to publish Volume I separately, before finishing the manuscripts for Volumes II and III. Engels took over, he managed to publish a third and a fourth German edition of *Capital, Volume I*, in 1883 and 1890, respectively, and he accomplished the task of making something out of the large number of unfinished manuscripts that Marx had left.

But we don't have a final and complete version of Marx's work on *Capital*, not even of those parts which he managed to complete and to rework and amend before his death. Not for the second and third volumes of Capital for which we only have a big heap of manuscripts from Marx's hand and two volumes of text, edited, arranged, and revised by Engels. We are not even allowed the pleasure of reading a final version of the first volume of Marx's masterpiece – although Volume I had been published three times during Marx's lifetime. Hence, Marx's *Critique of Political Economy*, even in its reduced form of the three volumes of *Capital*, not to mention a version of the original plan of six books, much vaster in scope and much more ambitious in its high claim

DOI: 10.4324/9781003336365-11

to revolutionise a whole science and set a new standard for the social sciences, remains an unfinished project.

Marx did not complete *Capital* – for many reasons. One important reason was that he did spend a lot of time and efforts on preparing a second German edition and a French edition of Volume I and giving instructions to the translators and editors of a second Russian and an American edition. That could be justified if he still made progress on his manuscripts.

For Marx, the French edition was an important station in his quest for a perfect presentation of his theory, but not more than that. As he wrote in a letter to his friend Adolph Sorge, dated 21 June 1872, the phrase 'entièrement revisée par l'auteur' (completely revised by the author) which appeared on the front page was no exaggeration. The second German edition was presented as 'Zweite verbesserte Auflage' [second improved edition], and it offered a lot of alterations and additions, including a completely revised division of the text. On the front page of the third German edition, it says 'Dritte vermehrte Auflage' [Third extended edition]. Marx had, directly advising the editors in private letters or indirectly by means of detailed lists of alterations and additions, been involved in all of these – as well as in the preparation of two Russian and one American edition. None of these completely satisfied him. *Capital,* including *Volume I,* remained very much a work in progress in Marx's view. Although he did not leave us a final version of *Capital,* he bequeathed some last words to us, and quite a lot of them.

The French edition of *Capital, Volume I*

It took Marx nearly eight years, from the moment when he delivered the manuscript of *Capital, Volume I,* to the editor Otto Meißner in Hamburg in May 1867 until January 1875, when he had finished all the corrections of the text, before a complete French edition of his book was ready to see the light. After all, he had published his first book on political economy, his polemic against Proudhon in French in 1847. His *Misère de la philosophie. Réponse à la philosophie de la misère de M. Proudhon* had raised great expectations from friend and foe, albeit not from Proudhon who dismissed it outright. Already in 1859, after the publication of *A Contribution to the Critique of Political Economy*, Marx had envisaged a French edition of that book, but dropped the project as he convinced himself that he had to change his whole plan and start anew. But now, with the first part of his long-awaited masterpiece on the *Critique of Political Economy* ready and published, he would be able to resume the struggle against the influence of Proudhon and win. As he wrote to Ludwig Büchner in a letter dated 1 May 1867, he wanted

> to have the thing [*Capital, Volume I*] published in French as well, in Paris, after its publication in Germany. […] I consider it to be of the greatest importance to emancipate the French from the erroneous views under which Proudhon with his idealized petty bourgeoisie has buried them.
>
> (Marx 1987a: 368)

He regarded the numerous crowds of followers of Proudhon in France and other countries in Southern Europe as the most serious adversaries of the kind of scientific socialism he and Engels stood for. If only the admirers of Proudhon in the French-speaking world would be able to read his work in their own language, it would be possible to counteract their influence. Hence, Marx was delighted to report to Ludwig Kugelmann in a letter dated 30 November 1867: 'In France (Paris) there are the best prospects that the book will be discussed in detail (in the *Courrier français*, a Proudhonist paper unfortunately!) and even translated' (Marx 1987a: 490).

From the very beginning of the project, Marx saw it as a chance to improve, even partially rewrite *Capital, Volume I*. Responding to his friend Victor Schily who had found some suitable candidates for the French translation, Marx wrote on 30 November 1867: 'In a translation, I would indicate certain changes to be made in several parts and, at the same time, reserve the right to carry out the final revision myself' (Marx 1987a: 488). Engels, who was involved in the project of the French translation from the very beginning, issued early warnings. Be careful whom you entrust with the arduous task of 'condensing' and 'Frenching' the book, he wrote to Marx in a letter, dated 2 February 1868. 'It is really your fault; if you write strictly dialectically for German science, then afterwards, when it comes to the translations, particularly the French, you fall into evil hands' (Engels 1987: 533, 534). Eventually, after some detours, in February 1872 Marx found a translator whom he trusted, Joseph Roy, and a publisher, Maurice Lachâtre, who supported the project wholeheartedly. At that time, he had already done a lot of work for the planned second German edition of the book; the most important changes to the text, in the first section on 'Commodity and Money', were written between December 1871 and January 1872. For his work on the second German edition, Marx had drawn up a long list of changes and additions, more than forty pages in handwriting – a document that had first been published in the MEGA² (cf. Marx 1987b). And that was not the end of it.

In April 1872, when the first copies of the second German edition were rolling off the printing press, Maurice Lachâtre had asked Marx to write for him a short text for a prospectus to bang the advertising drums for the book. Marx was quick to comply with his request and provided a text (first published in the MEGA², cf. Marx 1987c).[1] In this short text, he emphasised that he had treated political economy 'from a completely new point of view' and opposed both the views held by economists and the socialists. He had proven that 'the laws of capitalist production are like the laws of the antique and feudal mode of production the adequate form of a certain phase of historical development' and he had explained them 'with regard to their historical origin' and pointed to the 'economic upheaval' which capitalist production, 'freely developed' would generate from itself 'with necessity'. Regarding the changes made, he added that this second edition had been 'revised throughout' by the author himself, as well as improved in essential points' and had been provided with 'many new additions'; the unwieldy and sometimes confusing structure of the book had been thoroughly amended. Unfortunately, he could not resist the temptation to overstate his case: Apart from its theoretical content, the book was of the utmost importance because it was the only one providing 'the development history of modern industry and the modern land ownership since the beginning of the sixteenth century in their basics and according to the sources' (Marx 1987c: 55). That was another pledge to be met in the future.[2]

Apart from political reasons like his specific antagonism to Proudhon and his followers, Marx had other reasons to plunge into the arduous work of translating, revising, extending and partly rewriting *Capital, Volume I*. Inspired by his achievement to finally publish the first volume of his great work, Marx delved into his work on the second and third volumes again. Within less than two years' time, he produced several manuscripts, starting with new drafts for the first chapter of Volumes III and II, respectively, continuing with longer drafts on surplus value and profit, a first draft on the 'general laws of the rate of profit' and ending with another long draft of the first and second chapter of Volume II (the so-called Ms IV).[3] At the end of 1868, he started anew writing down a second draft for Volume II, this time covering all the topics of the planned book. Two years later, he had finished this draft – a large manuscript (the so-called Ms II) of more than 500 pages in printing.[4]

After the first draft for this volume which he had completed in the summer of 1865 and left untouched until the winter of 1867, this was his second attempt to come to grips with the highly complicated matter of the circulation process of capital. Still, he had not managed to realise his plan, dating from 1862, to surprise friend and foe with another, Marxian version of Quesnay's *tableau économique* and to show the world how the enigma of capitalist dynamics and growth could be analysed instead of mystified. His analysis of the reproduction and accumulation process of *Capital* was far from finished, he had to admit to himself, that his original plan to publish Volumes II and III of *Capital* shortly after the publication of *Volume I* had failed. The events of the Franco-Prussian war, the Paris commune and his many pressing obligations to the General Council of the IWA did not help. So, when he started to work on the second German edition of Volume I in late 1871, and, shortly after, engaged himself with the French translation, that shift provided a welcome break from the work on the still largely unfinished manuscript for Volume II. Marx was aware of its shortcomings, as his correspondence shows. In a letter to Danielson, he explained why his friends and admirers should not expect the second volume to be published soon. He had worked hard on it, but 'I have decided that a complete revision of the manuscript is necessary' (Karl Marx to Nikolai Danielson, 13 June 1871, Marx 1989a: 152).[5] He did not anticipate that he would only return to his work on Volume II in 1876.

The new editions of *Capital, Volume I*, took up the better part of his time and energy for several years. His correspondence with his publisher Maurice Lachâtre, not yet available in English, clearly shows how he tried to explain his intentions to him and to the translator.[6] Eager as he was to see the French edition to be published,[7] Marx did not just engage with the task of finding acceptable French equivalents for the new technical terms he had either inherited from the Classics or coined himself, but soon started to reformulate whole passages and to rewrite whole sections, sometimes rather long ones. However, one can argue that he did not go far enough and allowed far too much leeway to Joseph Roy, who abused his trust and produced a French version which was often false and misleading, even tendentious as Jacques D'Hondt put it (cf. D'Hondt 1985).

The main problem was not to translate German philosophical terms into French (cf. Fondu and Quétier 2018). Marx's terminology in *Capital* was not philosophical, although he used terms that might have sounded philosophical in the ears of readers still familiar with the German, and in particular Hegelian tradition. Elaborating the analysis and critique of modern capitalism further than any of his predecessors, trying to demystify the economic categories in full sway in everyday economic life of capitalist societies, he had to invent his own technical terms and analytical categories. Terms and categories which did not yet exist – neither in German nor in French. Categories like surplus value, labour power, constant and variable capital, organic composition of capital did not exist before; others like use-value, exchange-value, money, capital, accumulation, and so on, did exist before in classical political economy but were transformed by Marx into new economic concepts with a very specific meaning, making sense only within the context of Marx's theory. Regarding prospective French readers of his book, Marx did not worry about associations with Hegelian parlance that the text might arouse. What is more, in the French text Marx had avoided what he himself had called 'flirting with Hegelian phrasing – and this very quality can be and has been regarded as one of the great merits of the French version (cf. Bidet 1985). Quite in contrast to the views of many of his admirers, Marx was aware of the problem of philosophical jargon and had already removed some of the most striking 'dialectical' phrases from the text of Volume I when preparing the second German edition.[8]

Some of the extensions mentioned by Marx and Engels can and should be considered as valuable additions to the text indeed. For instance, the passage on John Stuart Mill. If anything, this clearly shows Marx's intention to refute basic tenets of classical economics in a way professional economists would understand and appreciate. In *Capital* he did so many times, often in footnotes. He attacked Mill, the author of the *Principles of Political Economy*, the most widely read textbook on economics in the English-speaking world until World War I, because he wanted to demonstrate that even from the pure technical point of view his analysis of the inner mechanisms of a capitalist economy was superior.

In the last section of the book, he made numerous extensions and additions, on the changing composition of capital, on the different forms of accumulation and their laws, on the dynamics of the industrial business cycle and on the impact of the world market – all very fine and correct. But all these extensions were anticipations of analyses which at the end of Volume I he could by no means properly perform. Hence, the publication of the extended French edition marked an epoch – for the history of Marxist thought and the publication of Marx's writings in France (Lindner 2009). But the French version was not a totally original work (as Bouffard, Feron and Fondu (2018) would have it). Rather, and together with the second German edition which served as its base, it marked another important but still partial progress on the long road towards the analysis and critique of modern capitalism that Marx had in mind since the 1840s. For this progress – both in terms of clarification of his arguments and re-arranging the exposition – Marx's work on the text for the second German edition was decisive because it was in this version that he had the most important alterations for the first time (For an overview of these alterations see Jungnickel 1990).

Marx and Engels in disagreement

In the end, Marx was pleased with the final result of all his efforts. As a matter of fact, he had not just corrected or improved Roth's translation, but rewritten whole passages, sometimes comprising several pages, in French himself. He changed the structure of the book again, and he had added quite a lot of text, in particular in the last sections. All in all, he regarded this version as an improvement. Engels did not share his view. Their correspondence shows a clear disagreement about the quality of the French version.

As usual, Engels had been involved in the project from the beginning to the end. Marx sent him larger chunks of the translated and revised text in French and asked for his opinion and advice. Engels did not attempt to hide his misgivings. In a letter dated 29 November 1873, he bluntly expressed his criticism:

> Yesterday, I read the chapter on factory legislation in the French translation. With all due respect for the skill with which this chapter has been rendered into elegant French, I still felt regret at what had been lost from the beautiful chapter. Its vigour and vitality and life have gone to the devil. The chance for an ordinary writer to express himself with a certain elegance has been purchased by castrating the language. It is becoming increasingly impossible to think originally in the strait-jacket of modern French. Every striking or vital is removed if only by the need […] to bow to the dictates of a pedantic formal logic and change round the sentences.

He did not keep his conclusion for himself: 'I would think it a great mistake to take the French version as a model for the English translation' (Engels 1989a: 540–1). Marx responded immediately: 'Now that you are taking a look at the French translation of Capital, I would be grateful if you could persevere with it. I think you will find that some passages are superior to the German' (Karl Marx to Friedrich Engels, 29 November 1873, Marx 1989a: 543). Engels took the hint and agreed, although only with respect to the parts that had been rewritten by Marx:

> More soon on the French translation. Up to now I find that what you have *revised* is indeed better than the German, but neither French nor German has anything to do with that. Best of all is the note on Mill, *quant au style.*
> (Friedrich Engels to Karl Marx, 5 December 1873,
> Engels 1989a: 545)

Obviously, Engels had acknowledged some improvements in the French version but remained sceptical regarding its literary quality.

As Marx had rewritten a lot of the text in French himself, we can assume that he felt at least a little piqued by Engels' remarks on the shallowness of it compared to the German original. We should remember that Engels had not shied away from criticising even the original text of the first German edition. In two letters to Marx, dated 16 June and 23 August 1867, focussing on the first chapters, he taunted him with the poor quality of the exposition compared even with the earlier version of 1859. In his view, Marx had failed to use the mass of historical material at his disposal to make the development of money understandable. According to Engels, it was a 'serious mistake' not to clarify his abstract argument by means of a large number of sections with their own headings (Engels 1987: 382). Although Engels praised the lucidity of Marx argument, he did not like the structure of his exposition: 'But how could you leave the *outward* structure of the book in the present form?' (Engels 1987: 405–6). He found the exposition difficult to read, sometimes unclear, even confusing. Again, he recommended subdividing the text frequently and using headings to make the different sections stand out clearly (Engels 1987: 405–6). Marx accepted his criticism, although he did not heed the advice completely. With respect to the structure of the book – the division in sections and chapters, the insertion of numerous headings and sub-headings – he did so extensively, but only for the second German edition.

Engels might have hurt his pride, but in his correspondence with others, he expressed some doubts about the results of his efforts. 'The toil involved in revising the translation is incredible', he wrote to Danielson on 18 January 1873. 'I would probably have had less trouble if I had done the whole thing myself from the start. And moreover, such patched-up jobs are always an amateur job' (Marx 1989a: 470).[9] Even in his *Afterword to the French Edition*, dated 28 April 1875, Marx conceded that this edition might have some 'literary defects'. However, he asserted, 'it possesses a scientific value independent of the original and should be consulted even by readers familiar with German' (Marx 1996d: 24).

Beyond any doubt, the French version represents more than a translation. As Marx had told his friend Sorge in a letter, dated 4 August 1874, the revision of the French translation had 'actually amount[ed] almost to complete rewriting' (Marx 1991: 28). In the Afterword of 1875, Marx has described his part in this project in some detail: He had been modifying and revising the French text produced by Joseph Roy and doing this he was led to revise and rewrite also 'the basic original text (the second German edition), to simplify some arguments, to complete others, to give additional historical or statistical material, to add critical suggestion' (Marx 1996d: 24). Hence, he created another original version of the book. But whether this version had a 'scientific value' of its own, independent of and – as some enthusiasts seem to believe – even superior to the German original, is debatable. To support Marx's assertion, one would have to scrutinise not just single formulations – as most commentators have done so far – but consider whether Marx had actually changed some of his argumentation and done a better job substantiating it.[10]

Marx's plans for further editions of *Capital, Volume I*

The French edition was not the last one that troubled Marx and kept him away from his work on Volumes II and III, his most urgent task after all. The second German edition and the French edition had cost him the better part of nearly four years. And still, he struggled with the text as he continued to struggle with his drafts for the first chapters of Volumes II and III, which he rewrote several times during the 1870s.

For the second German edition, Marx had reorganised and to a large degree rewritten the text of the first chapters and changed the overall arrangement of the book, much clearer and much more differentiated than in the first edition. In his *Afterword to the Second German Edition,* written while he was working on the French edition, he described the major alterations he had made in this edition, referring to Chapter 1, in particular the section on the 'Fetishism of Commodities', Chapter 3, in particular the section on the 'Measure of Value', and more. In short, he mentioned several parts of the book that had been 'completely revised' or 're-written to a great extent', apart from many 'partial textual changes, which were often purely stylistic' and could be found 'throughout the book' (Marx 1996b: 12–13). Compared to the French edition, which was just starting to appear, he found that 'several parts of the German original stand in need of rather thorough remoulding, other parts require rather stylistic editing, and still others painstaking elimination of occasional slips' (Marx 1996b: 13). First, in 1871, he had worked on the text of the second German edition and on the French translation parallelly. When the second German edition appeared, he found it wanting but used its text as a base for his work on the French translation. For any further German edition, the text would have to be rewritten and revised again, as he said in the *Afterword*, and the French edition should serve as a point of reference for such an operation.

The first occasion for another revision of the text came in September 1877, when his friend Sorge informed him about the plan for an American edition. Marx was delighted and spent more than two months comparing the text of the second German and the French edition and preparing detailed lists of the changes to be made. In fact, he produced three different documents, one list of the changes for the first volume of *Capital* and two lists (one a short draft) of changes expressly intended for an American edition.[11] The largest and most elaborated of these he sent to Sorge, together with a copy of the French edition, peppered with marginalia. His instructions to Sorge (and the prospective American translator) were quite clear: The division in chapters and sections should be made according to the French edition, the translator should use the text of the second German edition as a base and carefully work through the list where he had indicated all the passages where the French text should be used instead of the German. In short, the translator must 'compare the 2nd

German edition with the *French edition* in which I have included a good deal of new matter and greatly improved my presentation of much else' (Karl Marx to Friedrich Sorge, 29 September 1877, Marx 1991: 276). He attached particular importance to the changes and additions made in the last section of the French edition, dealing with the accumulation process.

The first translation of *Capital, Volume I,* into Russian had been published in 1872 and was based upon the first German edition of 1867.[12] When Nikolai Danielson was preparing a new translation of the book into Russian six years later he asked Marx for his advice. How far should he take into consideration the changes made to the text for the second German and the French edition? Marx replied in a long letter, dated 15 November 1878, giving detailed instructions.

> In regard to the second [Russian MK] edition of *Capital*, I beg to remark:
> 1) I wish that the *division into chapters* – and the same holds good for the *subdivisions* – be made according to the French edition. 2) That the translator compare always carefully the second German edition with the French one, since the latter contains many important changes and additions (though, it is true, I was also sometimes obliged – principally in the first chapter – to 'aplatir' the matter in its French version).
>
> (Marx 1991: 343)

Furthermore, he promised to get 'some changes I consider useful' ready and send them as quickly as possible (Marx 1991: 343). So, regarding the content of the book, Marx once again stressed the importance of the changes and additions he had made for the French edition. Obviously, he had more changes in mind and was eager to further improve the text. Regarding the language, he was not afraid to use Engels's term: In the French version, at least important parts of the texts had suffered from a 'flattening'.

In 1880, the American journalist John Swinton visited Marx in his holiday resort and enjoyed the opportunity to converse with him for several hours. Referring to Marx's *Capital,* Swinton wrote in his account of the interview: 'he said that anyone who might desire to read it would find the French translation much superior in many ways to the German original' (Swinton 1985: 443).[13] But that was a much weaker statement than the claim he made in his Afterword of 1875.

Marx's marginalia and the 'marginal notes on Adolph Wagner'

Marx left quite a lot of hints for a further reworking of his book. Some in the form of detailed lists, as the ones he had prepared for Sorge in 1877. Some of these hints were to be found in his personal copies of the French edition. As was his habit, he scribbled a lot of marginalia on the pages of his books, varying from simple underlinings and marks of all sorts to single-word remarks – the insult 'asinus' was one of Marx's favourites – to longer comments. In the case of his personal copies of *Capital, Volume I*, he indicated phrases, sentences and whole passages that should be altered, replaced, augmented and extended. Engels had two such personal copies with marginalia by Marx at his disposal when he was working on the third edition. In his *Preface to the Third Edition*, he described them: 'Among the books left by Marx there was a German copy which he himself had corrected here and there and provided with references to the French edition', and there was 'also a French copy in which he had indicated the exact passages to be used' (Engels 1996a: 27).[14]

Unfortunately, the original plan for the MEGA[2] to include the marginalia, or at least a selection, in the fourth section, has been dropped. However, the marginalia remain an important source of information: first about Marx's (and Engels's) study of the work of other authors and second about revisions and amendments they had in mind for further editions of their works. Several of these copies still exist in various places (in archives in Moscow, New York, Brussels and Trier). Thomas Kuczynski has presented a full account of the marginalia in Marx's copy of the second German edition (cf. Kuczynski 2005, 2010).[15] However, Marx's marginalia were not easy to decipher and required some interpretation. Marx did not always follow his own hints, and his marginalia were far from clear and unequivocal instructions for any editor. He invented his own system of marks and symbols, sometimes using little graphs, sometimes using Greek letters like φ. The letter φ in the margin of a page meant 'to be used' for further elaboration or in another edition of the text. Once in a while, Marx wrote short comments, sometimes a few words, sometimes unfinished sentences, in the margins of his personal copies. But even those hints were just hints at what he had in mind at the moment of reading and could be changed or dropped again.

In the summer and fall of 1881, Marx was busy scribbling down about forty pages of comments on his own work, responding to an academic critic who had attacked him ferociously. He studied the second edition of Adolph Wagner's textbook on political economy with care, a weighty tome of more than 800 pages. Wagner was one of the most renowned and influential economists in the German-speaking world at that time, a leading figure of the so-called 'Younger Historical School'.[16] He had attacked Marx and his *Capital* before in one of his books (see Wagner 1870). His books reached a high circulation. In 1876, he had prepared a new textbook that should replace the then most widely used textbook by Karl Heinrich Rau, the *Lehrbuch der politischen Oekonomie* in three volumes, which had seen eight editions since it had first been published in 1826. Wagner's new textbook, titled *Allgemeine oder theoretische Volkswirtschaftslehre. Erster Theil. Grundlegung* [*General or theoretical Economics. First Part. Principles*] in the subtitle, was quite successful, a second 'improved and enlarged' edition was already published in 1879.[17] When an academic authority like Wagner deigned to read and to comment on his work in a widely read textbook, Marx could not afford to completely ignore him.[18] Regarding the context, it is highly probable that Marx bothered to read Wagner's textbook, at least the passages where Wagner took issue with his own work, not for fun. Reading one of the voluminous and verbose German textbooks on political economy was not one of his favourite pastimes. In general, he did not hold the German economists of his time in high esteem. In this case, he did start reading Wagner's book because he was already considering some revisions of the text for the next German edition of *Capital, Volume I.* We know that he did read Wagner's tome with care because his personal copy of the book has been preserved – and this copy is littered with marginalia, marks and short comments in Marx's hand-writing.[19] We don't know how exactly Marx might have used these notes for a reply to Wagner and, maybe, other critics. Regarding how much he bothered to organise an Anti-critique of Eugen Dühring, we can imagine that he might have included a similar reply to his more important academic critics in the footnotes of the next, the third German edition of Volume I.

Marx wrote these notes down in his usual manner, as a mixture of excerpts and comments, some rather short and some more elaborated, extending over several paragraphs and pages. They form the first part of one of his latest larger notebooks devoted to political economy, titled 'Economic matters in general' ('Oekonomisches in general' in the original German version).[20] Some parts of these notes have been published posthumously in a Russian translation in 1932, the full text was first published in the original German and in Russian in the 1960s. In Marx's notebook, the text came with the heading 'A. Wagner Lehrbuch der politischen Oekonomie ★ (2te Auflage) I Band', which was the main heading of the book (Marx 1881: 5). Marx's notes on Wagner have become famous and are often hailed as his 'last economic work' (Rosdolsky 1968: 544). Indeed, they do provide some kind of a penultimate statement of his views on his own method of presentation and core concepts of his theory of value. That statement, however, does not vindicate Althusser's view that this text, together with the *Critique of the Gotha Program*, are the only works of the 'mature Marx' (cf. Althusser 1971: 93–4).

In his notes, Marx explicitly rejected the view taken by Wagner, Schäffle and other German economists that his theory of value constituted the corner-stone of a socialist system. 'As I have never established a "socialist system", this is a fantasy of Wagner, Schäffle *e tutti quanti*' (Marx 1989f: 533). He insisted upon the conceptual distinction between 'exchange-values' – '(*exchange-value*, without at least two of them, does not exist)' (Marx 1989f: 534) – and value, remaining adamant about the big difference between Ricardo's theory of value and his own (cf. Marx 1989f: 534 ff.). In these marginal notes, Marx was stingy with further explanations, in particular when he would have been obliged to transcend the range and scope of Volume I. Ricardo did confuse values and production prices, but in his theory, both did not coincide as he had already pointed out in the notes to *Capital*. 'Why not? That I have *not* told Mr. Wagner' (Marx 1989f: 535).

His theory of value, Marx specified, was not meant to be a 'general theory of value', as Wagner had in his mind. The apologetic drawback of Wagner's critique was all too obvious: No production process, no economy could and would ever exist without capital, capitalists and capital profit. Wagner should have demonstrated that I am wrong considering the capitalist economy as a transitory, historical form, Marx retorted (cf. Marx 1989f: 535). He did not deal with hypothetical social forms like a 'social state', an invention of Schäffle that Wagner had planted on him. 'In my *investigation of value* I have dealt with bourgeois relations' and nothing else, he insisted (Marx 1989f: 536).

Wagner, as other German professors of economics, had been completely unable to grasp the gist of Marx's approach: He did not try a '*derivation of the concept of value*', starting with a prefabricated general concept of value. Instead, he had started with 'a *concretum, the commodity*' (Marx 1989f: 537, 538). Marx ridiculed the German professor's strong penchant for deriving economic categories from concepts, especially Wagner being prone to 'derive the *concept of value in general*' (Marx 1989f: 540, 541).[21] Following Wagner's textbook over many pages, Marx began obviously losing his patience. He got vexed when he read Wagner's false claim that he wanted to remove use-value entirely from the realm of economic science. 'All this is "drivel"', Marx exploded (Marx 1989f: 544). He felt compelled to restate his case again and actually started to outline his famous method in some detail. This last statement on method in his own words has become a point of reference for many readers and interpreters of Marx's *Critique of Political Economy*.

First, stepping up his earlier remarks, he repeated that he did 'not proceed from "concepts", hence neither from the "concept of value"' (Marx 1989f: 544). What he did do instead was proceeding from a 'concretum', as he had stated before in his notes. Now, he was making his point more precisely: 'What I proceed from is the simplest social form in which the product of labour presents itself in contemporary society, and this is the "commodity"' (Marx 1989f: 544). Eager to continue and to come to the salient points, Marx did not hesitate a moment at his own statement. It is obvious, however, that the commodity considered as the 'simplest social form' of labour products is not a 'concretum' in the sense of a palpable, empirical fact. It is an abstraction, or rather the result of several abstractions which allow him to dub the commodity the 'simplest concrete element of economics' (Marx 1989f: 545)[22]. First, the abstraction from other forms of labour products that exist in contemporary, that is, capitalist, societies: Public goods, commons, products of housework that anyone does for himself or members of his or her family. And other kinds of non-commodities that might be produced with the cooperation of family, friends or neighbours. Second, the abstraction from other kinds of commodities that are more complicated than the 'simple' commodities. Fictitious commodities (or quasi-commodities) of various kinds do exist in a capitalist economy and society. Commodities that are as essential as anything else, in some cases even more important than others, but are not entirely the product of human labour or are usually not produced by private producers for sale on a market. Like the commodity labour power, like money as a commodity in the money markets, like capital as a commodity, debts of all kinds as a commodity in the financial markets, like land and other natural resources that have been privately or publicly appropriated, like rights of all kinds that can be negotiated, portioned, bought and sold. Hence, the 'commodity' Marx was investigating must be seen as a concept – 'commodity as such' as Engels aptly called it in his synopsis of *Volume I*.[23] Or 'simple commodity' as one might call it. Because to start with Marx's abstraction makes perfect sense. To deal with the whole range of 'commodities' and non-commodities that we encounter in any commodity-producing economy and in a capitalist economy in particular, we first have to establish what all or most commodities have in common.

At any rate, even without reflecting upon the theoretical status of the first economic category he introduced, Marx wanted to emphasise that he did not derivate concepts but had performed a careful analysis of the subject matter at hand. The commodity, a specific object of scientific study, although presented in a rather laconic manner in the opening sentences of *Capital, Volume I*, had been scrutinised by him 'initially in the *form in which it* appears' (Marx 1989f: 544). In these short notes, he did not expound in detail on how he proceeded in the first chapters of *Capital*. He simply states that he had analysed, got a result and continued to analyse what he found, one step of analysis following the other. Briefly, he summarised the most salient results of this analysis: The commodity is a 'two-fold thing', rather a two-fold form, two forms, a 'natural form' and a 'social form', linked together and constituting the '*concrete social form* of the product of labour' which he calls 'commodity' (Marx 1989f: 544, 545). And he replies to Wagner's reproach that he ignores the importance of use-values by emphasising the specific, social character of use-values. Taking issue with a phrase Wagner borrowed from a more serious rival of Marx, Karl Rodbertus-Jagetzow, Marx stated that use-value, as 'use-value of a "commodity"', must possess a 'specific historical character'. In political economy, one should be aware of the different 'social character' of the use-value in different historical forms of economies and societies (Marx 1989f: 546).[24]

Against Wagner's numerous objections, Marx insisted that the topical constrictions of his analysis in the opening chapter were correct and necessary. His '*analytic* method, which does not proceed from *man* but from a given economic period of society' was completely different from and apparently incomprehensible to German professors who like deriving or rather associating – not concepts, but words (Marx 1989f: 547, 548). He emphasised – against Wagner and Rodbertus – that he had been dealing with historic-specific economies, that is, those 'where commodity production predominates' (Marx 1989f: 550). To talk about value and exchange values, one had, first, to envisage many commodities, as exchange value 'only exists where *commodity* occurs in the *plural*, different sorts of commodities' (Marx 1989f: 551). Hence, Marx amended his earlier statement: He did not analyse 'the commodity' or a single commodity, but a relation between commodities – because their exchange values can only manifest themselves in exchange and/or the preparation for exchange. Second, Marx argued that exchange value 'only occurs when at least some parts of the products of labour [...] function as "commodities"' and this did only happen 'at a definite stage of historical development' (Marx 1989f: 551). He tried to delimit the scope of his analysis of commodity, exchange value and value as a 'particular historical form of something which exists in all forms of society' (Marx 1989f: 552). The same must be true of the use-value as social use-value, Marx added. It is striking that Marx did not harp on about the value-form but criticises Rodbertus (and Wagner) who are unable to examine or grasp the substance of value (Marx 1989f: 552). These celebrities of German economics played with the magnitude of value and its measure but failed to go one step beyond Ricardo.

The last pages of Marx's notes on Wagner have usually escaped the attention of his admirers and followers. What has been ignored by Marxist philosophers is, in fact, of the utmost importance for anyone interested in the fate (and future) of the Marxian project. Because on these pages he follows Wagner's presentation of actual developments and recent changes in the capitalist (world) economy. First, he follows Wagner's description of the factors of the 'outside world' that affect '*individual enterprise and wealth*', '*especially the influence of the state of the economy*' (Marx 1989f: 554–6). Second, he follows Wagner's description of '*Chief individual elements affecting the state of the economy*' – fluctuations in the harvest yields of staple foods, changes in technology, changes in the means of communications and transport, changes in tastes, political changes, and so on (Marx 1989f: 556–8). And third, he follows Wagner's attempt to ana-lyse the '*National Income in England and France*', starting with the '*annual gross income of a nation*' and ending with the approving remark: '*Comparatively greater importance of foreign trade* nowadays' (Marx 1989f: 558–9). That Marx followed Wagner into the shallows of empirical economic research on business cycles and the correct calculation of national wealth gives another strong hint at his plans at this moment when he was still far from concluding his work on *Volumes II* and *III* of *Capital*. As anyone familiar with the text will remember, in Volume I anticipations of an analysis of the modern industrial business cycle as anticipations of a theory of capitalist accumulation and growth abound. In 1881, Marx had still not abandoned hope to come to grips with these issues.

Unfortunately, these efforts by Marx to clarify his manner of presentation and argument were not meant for publication nor has their content been communicated to others. It is possible that even Engels, scrutinising the moun-tain of excerpts and notebooks that Marx had left for him, simply overlooked it.[25] From 1859 to 1875, Marx had produced five different versions of the first chapters of *Capital*. Nonetheless, these chapters remain prone to ambiguities, regardless of which of the several versions we choose to consult. Hence, three or four different readings are possible, all buttressed by textual evidence.[26]

Marx's final words on *Capital*

Ten days after the death of wife Jenny, Marx wrote a long letter to his friend Nikolai Danielson, telling him that he would have to spend time and energy upon a new German edition of *Capital, Volume I* again.

> My German editor informs me that a third edition of the *Capital* has become necessary. This comes at a moment anything but opportune. In the

first instance I must first be restored to health, and in the second I want to finish off the 2nd volume (even if to be published abroad) as soon as possible.

And he continued explaining his plan for a third German edition:

> I will arrange with my editor that I shall make for the 3rd edition only the fewest possible alterations and additions, but, on the other hand, that he must this time only draw off 1.000 copies, instead of 3.000, as was his want. When these 1.000 copies forming the 3rd edition are sold, then I may change the book in the way I should have done at present under different circumstances.
>
> (Karl Marx to Nikolai Danielson, 13 December 1881, Marx 1992: 161)

The English translation does not completely carry the meaning of Marx's wording here. What he wrote was much stronger, rather meaning 'rework', 'rewrite' or 'revamp' than just 'change'. Marx was not afraid to radically rewrite a text that was not good enough in his view, and he had told Danielson so before (cf. Karl Marx to Nikolai Danielson, 13 June 1871, Marx 1989a: 152).

All his reserve notwithstanding, Marx did some work preparing a new, third German edition of Volume I. His intentions were clear enough: Not to make too much fuss about the third German edition and leave the real rewriting of Volume I for the future – when he would have finished and published Volumes II and III of the book.

In November 1882, when Marx was still alive, Engels reported to their mutual friend Sorge in a letter, dated 9 November 1882: 'So far as circumstances permit, the 3rd edition will now be taken vigorously in hand there and won't, I trust, occupy too much time' (Engels 1992: 368). Obviously, he and Marx had at least talked about the third German edition and made some preparations for it. Due to Marx's declining health, the work was delayed again and again. Engels did what he could to procure additional material on the progress of factory legislation in Europe, but that did not help much. The third edition of *Capital* 'will doubtless take some time yet as Marx is still ailing. [...] he can barely speak, so not much could be discussed', he reported to Bernstein in February 1883 (Engels 1992: 434). When Marx briefly resumed his work on the third German edition in October 1882, he apparently did discuss the project with Engels and asked him for help. Engels did what he could to procure the materials Marx wanted and needed, in particular the texts of the factory laws recently enacted in Germany and Switzerland. 'For the 3rd edition Marx merely intends to bring the state of factory legislation up to date by making emendations and additions; to that end he needs *the texts of the original Acts and nothing more*', he wrote to Bernstein on 4 November 1882 (Engels 1992: 359). He had asked Bernstein for more information about the actual state of the Swiss and German factory legislation before – 'Marx needs it for the 3rd edition of Volume I', he wrote to him on 27 October 1882 (Engels 1992: 347). On 6 November 1882, Engels reported to Marx that the materials he requested were on their way (Engels 1992: 364). Unfortunately, Engels did not take any notes from his conversations with Marx on the changes intended for the third edition, as he had done before, in 1873, when discussing the second German and the French editions (cf. Engels 1989b).

To imagine how Marx might have revised the text of Volume I after the completion of Volumes II and III, we can only rely on what we know about his work on the book during the last fifteen years of his life, from winter 1867/68 to March 1883. This is a serious question because Marx had been pushed hard by Engels to publish Volume I alone, contrary to his original plan and long before he had finished Volumes II and III. He claimed, though, that 'Volume I constitutes a whole, complete in itself' (in a letter to Danielson, 7 October 1868) (Marx 1988: 123). However, Volume I was far from the completed whole Marx claimed it to be. Due to Marx's very peculiar mode of presentation, the text of the book remained dotted with anticipations, open ends, inconsistencies and breaks – all of which could only be amended once the following volumes had been completed and Marx had delivered on his promise to give a comprehensive presentation and critique of modern capitalism.

Marx took his work on Volumes II and III very seriously. It might suffice to mention the fact that from 1868 to 1878 he took no less than nine different tries to produce a final version of Chapter 1 for Volume II (cf. Marx 2008: 549–697; Marx 2012: 32–43, 285–363). From 1868 onwards, he increased the range and scope of his studies – and all of those were in one way or another linked to his continuing work on *Capital*. First, he widened the scope of his statistical studies far beyond the English statistics he had used so far, paying ever closer attention to American, Russian and, last but not least, comparative European and international statistics. Second, he devoted a lot of time and energy to the study of money, credit and finance and their recent developments in the USA and in other parts of the world. Third, he spent more time than before on the comparative study of agriculture, mining and real estate in Europe and abroad, and became fascinated by the ongoing industrialisation of agriculture in several parts of the world. He understood perfectly well the challenges that developments like the financialisation of money and credit and the industrialisation of agriculture and the extractive industries at large posed for views held by classical economists as well as for his own theory. Fourth, Marx continued and intensified his studies of higher mathematics. Since 1878, he worked more intensively on his mathematical manuscripts than ever before. When he died on 14 March 1883, the last piece that lay on his desk was an unfinished manuscript on differential calculus (see for Marx's mathematical manuscripts Marx 1974; Alcouffe 1985).

Marx did not study mathematics just as a diversion as he sometimes boasted. His purpose, and a core part of his project to revolutionise political economy, was to transform it into a science that would allow for mathematical formalisation. Since 1863/64 he had experimented with that, in Volume I of *Capital* he had already introduced a lot of mathematical formulas, totally uncommon at that time. As he had learned a lot more on mathematics in the meantime, he dropped or reformulated many of the analogies to mathematics in the text of the second German edition that he had used quite liberally in the text of the first edition. However, this did not mean that he had given up his plan to present the laws of political economy in a formalised way. On the contrary, his continuing work on the last section of Volume II and on the mathematical relationships between the rate of surplus value and the rate of profit during his last years (until the summer of 1881 and the spring of 1882, respectively) shows that he was already deeply involved in the process of rethinking and reformulating core parts of his theory. Sam Moore and Friedrich Engels remained sceptical, but Marx pursued the idea of applying the 'analytical' and 'differential' method, as he called them, to political economy (see his letter to Engels, 22 November 1882) (Marx 1992: 380). Finally, there was another reason for Marx to pursue his plan. As we know by now from his notebooks, and from testimonies by his friends, like Maxim Kowalevskij, Marx was well aware of the rise of the new mathematical school in political economy. He had studied the work of Antoine Cherbuliez, an early pioneer of formalisation in political economy, and he did study several articles and books by William Stanley Jevons in the 1860s and 1870s but did not know any of the writings of Léon Walras. According to Kowaleskij, he intended to counter this new challenge (cf. Kowaleskij 1983: 352).

Engels's work on the third and fourth German editions of *Capital, Volume I*

After Marx's death in March 1883, Engels managed to prepare and publish the third German edition of *Capital, Volume I,* rather quickly. In his preface for this edition, Engels explained how he had followed Marx's intentions: 'It was Marx's original intention to re-write a great part of the text of the first volume, to formulate many theoretical points more exactly, insert new ones and bring historical and statistical material up to date' (Engels 1996a: 27). But he was forced to give up this plan and restrict himself to a much more modest scheme: 'Only the most necessary alterations were to be made, only the insertions which the French edition [...] already contained, were to be put in' (Engels Ibidem).

Even implementing this reduced scheme caused Engels some headaches. He had three copies of the first volume with marginalia from Marx's hand at his disposal – one of the first, one of the second German and one of the French edition; he probably also had one of the lists of alterations in his hands which Marx had prepared in 1877. 'I have to prepare for the 3rd edition sundry additions from the French translation which I know Mohr [Marx MK] intended inserting', he wrote to Laura Lafargue (Friedrich Engels to Laura Lafargue, 22 May 1883, Engels 1995: 29). But interpreting and implementing Marx's instructions caused him 'a tremendous amount of work. We have one copy in which Marx follows the French edition when indicating the emendations and additions to be made, but all the detailed work remains to be done', he complained in a letter to Sorge

(Friedrich Engels to Friedrich Sorge, 29 June 1883, Engels 1995: 42). In the last section on 'Accumulation' he encountered 'a case of revising almost completely the entire theoretical section' (Engels 1995: 42). What bothered him most was the task of revising and rewriting a text written in German by Marx, based on changes made in the French edition. Engels had not changed his view on the poorer quality of the French edition qua language compared to the German original: 'to some extent the French translation lacks the depth of the German text; Marx would never have written in German in that way' (Engels 1995: 42).

In 1887, the first English edition of *Capital, Volume I*, came out, edited by Engels and translated by Sam Moore and Edward Aveling, based upon the text of the third German edition. In his preface, Engels referred to 'notes left by the author' and 'changes prescribed by Marx in a set of Ms. instructions for an English translation' planned ten years ago (Engels 1996b: 33). Engels stuck to what he regarded as the 'final instructions for the third edition' from Marx's hand, and used the older instructions, dating from 1877, but sparingly (Engels 1996b: 33). However, in the English edition the French version had been referred to in some difficult passages of the text, 'as an indicator of what the author himself was prepared to sacrifice wherever something of the full import of the original had to be sacrificed in the rendering' (Engels 1996b: 33). Again, Engels made it quite clear, in spite of the tortuous expression, that he regarded the original German version (the second and third editions) as superior to the French translation.

The fourth German edition of Marx's *Capital, Volume I,* was published in 1890. It was the last edition of the text that Engels could complete. This time, Engels had all the marginalia and all the lists of alterations prepared by Marx at his disposal and could take his time to revise the text. Accordingly, he did incorporate some more of the alterations and additions which Marx had indicated in his many notes and lists of instructions. The fourth edition was the most complete German edition ever. Only Kautsky, in his popular edition of *Capital, Volume I*, published in 1914, would go any further.

Engels had set himself the task to 'establish in final form, as nearly as possible, both text and footnotes' (Engels 1996c: 37). He had made 'further additions to the German text' from the French translation – and he indicated them briefly in his preface. He had performed a 'complete revision of the numerous quotations' throughout the text, correcting and complementing Marx's original and often faulty version (cf. Engels 1996c: 33–4).

Why did Engels not follow all of Marx's instructions and hints for future editions and translations of *Capital, Volume I*

Engels did not follow all of Marx's instructions. He retained the changed structure of the second German edition of the book, the division into chapters and sections, as well as the headings and sub-headings in the third and in the fourth German editions. But he followed Marx's wish to use the structure of the French edition as the base for any future translation of the book for the English edition. In the third German edition, there are but a few 'editor's notes', the French edition is only mentioned once. In the fourth edition, we find just thirteen additional notes or additions to notes from Engels.

But Engels followed Marx's instructions regarding the incorporation of passages from the French edition quite often. Whenever he thought that the French text had a more accurate formulation to offer or represented an improvement, a precision or an elaboration of the original argument in the first or the second German edition, he carefully followed Marx's instructions. Even in those cases, a lot of the real work – the retranslation or rather reformulation of the French text in German – had still to be done by him. As for the many marginalia in Marx's copies of the German and French editions of the book, they had to be deciphered and interpreted, as they were far from unequivocal. Engels, who knew his friend Marx well enough, was aware of the fact that Marx did not always deliver on his promises, not even in the same text.

In his correspondence, Engels gave some reasons why he did not heed all of Marx's wishes. Regarding the list of changes of 1877, he wrote to Sorge on 29 April 1886:

> In most cases the notes contained in the ms. are the same as those Marx made in his copy for the 3rd edition. In the case of those which provide for more insertions from the French, I would not commit myself unequivocally 1) because the work done for the 3rd edition is of much later date, and hence, for me, more authoritative, 2) because, in respect of a translation to be made in America, i.e., outside his own orbit, Marx might have preferred some of the passages to be translated correctly from the simplified French version rather than incorrectly from the German – a consideration which no longer applies.
> (Engels 1995: 439)

For the fourth German edition, it should have weighed even less. Nonetheless, when time allowed it, he was inclined to insert more phrases, formulations and passages from the French edition as Marx has recommended. So, the number of passages from the French edition included in the German text increased from the third to the fourth edition. How far Engels has followed Marx's instructions has been meticulously listed by the editors of Volumes II/8 (third German edition) and II/10 (fourth German edition) of the MEGA². Japanese researchers have performed detailed comparisons and found out that, in the end, Engels had left out only a small portion of the changes that Marx had noted (cf. Hayashi 1975, Omura 1991, 1994).

The editors of Volume II/8 of MEGA² have made an admirable effort to list all the passages from the French edition which Engels had decided not to include into the third or fourth German edition (cf. Verzeichnis 1991). However, it should be noted that this list is not based upon the written instructions given by Marx himself. Marx did not at all recommend using all the revised and rewritten passages from the French edition into future editions and/or translations. And Engels did include some words and passages from the French into the third and fourth German editions that Marx had not even indicated.

In the eyes of a growing group of critics, Engels has committed grave errors by not including some of the passages and formulations from the French editions into the third and fourth German editions. They take Marx's assertion about the 'scientific value' of the French edition at face value and discard all possible reasons for not following Marx's numerous instructions. According to them, Engels has deprived the readers of *Capital* of valuable insights and advances made by Marx in the French edition – notwithstanding the fact that most of these insights are already to be found in the second German edition and preserved in the following third and fourth editions. The critics all agree upon the utmost importance of the passages not included by Engels, an assertion never queried by any one of them (cf. Anderson 1983, 1998; Roth 2018; Outhwaite and Smith 2020, just to mention a few). However, their most favoured examples simply show that this is debatable or outright wrong. That Engels did not replace the phrase used in Marx's Preface to the first German edition – 'The country that is more developed industrially only shows, to the less developed, the image of its own future' (Marx 1996a: 9) – by the phrase 'The most industrially developed country only shows those that follow it on the industrial ladder the image of their own future' (retranslated from Marx 1989b: 12), does not make a big difference at all. Certainly, to become a less developed industrial country, a country will first have to follow others on the path of industrialisation.[27] The important point to note here is that we can imagine different paths of industrial development in different parts of the world, although Marx did not say so, neither in French nor in German. It is correct that in the 1870s Marx wanted to restrict the validity of his analysis of capitalist development (in the section on 'Primitive Accumulation') to Western Europe and he said so several times (although in private letters or in drafts never finished and never sent). But what did that mean? Marx knew at that time that both the United States and Russia followed a different path of economic development. But the real question to ask is whether Marx's account of the origins of capitalism in Western Europe is correct or not. It is not, as most historians will agree today. The English example is rather exceptional, in other parts of Europe the transformation of land into private property, of landowners into capitalists and of peasants into free labourers followed very different roads. Marx had the right theoretical clue: *Capital* as a social and economic relation presupposes a separation between the owners of the means of production and the owners of nothing but human labour power, and this separation must have been achieved by some historical process, as it cannot be assumed to be a natural state. But wielding this clue was another matter, and playing with phrases and words will never suffice, even if those phrases have been coined by Marx himself.

Do we need another revised edition of Marx's *Capital, Volume I?*

Thomas Kuczynski certainly did think so. Hence, in 2017 he published a new edition of *Capital, Volume I*. In this edition, he tried to atone for the omissions and alleged mistakes committed by Engels. Many years before, during the work on the first MEGA at the Marx-Engels Institute in Moscow, two of David Rjazanow's collaborators had already examined the possibility of a new edition. Engels had applied the largest and most important part of Marx's textual changes for the French edition for the third and fourth editions of Volume I, but not all of them. Karl Kautsky had applied quite a lot more of the textual changes made for the French edition for his 'Volksausgabe' of *Capital, Volume I*. Still, many textual changes remained that none of them had applied. Hence, one could imagine using some of the textual changes that had been disregarded by Engels and Kautsky to produce a new version of the book (cf. Kropp and Nixdorf 1997: 129).[28] Karl Kautsky had used the second edition as a starting point and added further passages from the French edition, going much further than Engels had done for the third and fourth editions (Kautsky 1914: XV, XVII). Benedikt Kautsky used the second edition as well for the popular edition, published in 1929 (Kautsky 1929). Karl Korsch, however, took a different view: Only the second German edition could be regarded as the last edition by Marx's hand, and he used passages from the French edition only where they did not interfere with the structure and cohesion of Marx's original German text (Korsch 1996: 535–6). The editors of the Volume II/8 of the MEGA[2] deemed the third edition as the last by Marx himself, because he had been directly involved in the preparation of this edition. Some Japanese scholars (e.g., Omura 1991) disagreed. They thought the fourth German edition was the last one because Engels had heeded much of Marx's instructions.[29]

Does Kuczynski's edition offer a better, more complete edition of Marx's *Capital*? His edition can serve as a test case: If all the phrases, words, passages from the French edition that Engels did not include in his editions of the book are really representing key elements of Marx's theory that all but the readers of the French edition have dearly missed so far, then an edition in which all of these have been included must be better than all the other editions available. No one can claim to have access to Marx's spirit, and Kuczynski did not claim to present a 'final' edition like the one Marx might have produced after finishing Volumes II and III and reworking the whole book, had he lived long enough. Marx had his preferences as his correspondence shows. For him, the French version was not better throughout, some chapters and passages he liked better in the second German version.

What we get from Kuczynski's edition are, first and foremost, much longer and more complicated, convoluted sentences. For people who are a little slow on the uptake, such repetitions might be useful. For others, tortuous sentences and passages full of redundancies are not very enlightening. That is what you get when you try to blend six different texts, belonging to six different editions, into one. When dealing with lists of variations in a text, such blending is feasible, although only at a substantial loss of clarity. For an already complicated text which is already loaded with metaphors and a lot of technical terms, this operation is deadly. Some Marx specialists may enjoy it, the ordinary reader will not.

Regarding the structure of the book, the progress made is debatable. In Kuczynski's edition, we get the structure of the text according to the second

German edition, in twenty-five chapters, not thirty-three as in the French edition. Only the last two chapters are regrouped in section 8, a section which also occurs in the French edition.

Many of the changes made by Kuczynski befit a 'popular edition', and he follows a well-trodden path. Marx had not been very alert to the exactness of the quotations he made, and Engels had already corrected a lot of that. Kuczynski, as Kautsky had done before him, offers a translation of all the citations plus some explanatory notes. Some of his changes are well-meant but rather disturbing. To integrate the footnotes by Marx into the main text in order to create space for additional footnotes by the editor is not a good idea. Editor's notes should be incorporated in an appendix, not in the main text of a book written by an author who was an aficionado of footnotes himself and a master in creating very long and well-written ones.

Many readers will be impressed by the huge appendix that comes with Kuczynki's edition. Although most of that work has already been done by the editors of the volumes of the MEGA^2 dedicated to Volume I of *Capital*, and Kuczynski has widely used the work of his predecessors, we get an impressively long and detailed list of all the changes, amendments and additions ever made to the text of Volume I in any of the editions by either Marx or Engels. But that is just a tool, a device that does not solve the problem of deciding which alterations should be incorporated in the German text and which not. Both Marx and Engels had made decisions in this respect and not always the same. Kuczynski seems to think that we should incorporate as much as even possible and not be shy to overload the text with bulky, inconsistent, over-redundant phrases and passages. The only rational solution in this matter, to decide which phrase or passages would be more suitable for the problem at hand – be it a problem of exposition or a problem of theory – is avoided. Because posing such questions would inevitably mean to engage with the content of Marx's text itself, something that the author Marx and his closest friend and sometimes co-author Engels dared to do, but later editors don't.

Many among the critics dissing Engels as editor of Marx's *Capital* have succumbed to a chimera. The chimera of an authentic Marx, unequivocal and complete, splendidly overbearing all doubts and objections. One just has to forget about Engels and follow Marx's instructions and one will get a perfect Marx in Marx's own words. Kuczynski has tried something like that, a complete refurbishing of Volume I of *Capital* according to Marx's own instructions, although he did not treat Engels with the same contempt as the usual critics. But the result is a convoluted text that Marx would never have written, nor published.

Notes

1 It should be noted that the second edition of *Capital, Volume I*, was first published in nine instalments from July 1872 through March 1873, and then as a book in May 1873.

2 It should be noted that Marx continued to study the development of agriculture and industry in Russia and in the USA in much detail throughout the 1870s (cf. Krätke 2005 and 2022).

3 All of these drafts have been published for the first time in Volume II/4.3 of MEGA² in 2012 (cf. Marx 2012).

4 This manuscript, together with some others, has been published in Volume II/11 of MEGA² in 2008 (cf. Marx 2008).

5 Marx wrote 'völlige Umarbeitung' in German, which is much stronger than 'revision' and should rather be translated as 'complete reworking' or 'complete rewriting'.

6 Marx's numerous letters to Maurice Lachâtre have not yet been completely published in any of the widely used works editions (MEW, MEGA² or MECW). See for a recent edition of these letters in their original French version (Gaudin 2019). Ducange and Hecker (2022) provide an excellent overview of the recent efforts to publish this part of the correspondence of Marx and Engels.

7 Remember that the first study on political economy published by Marx was a lengthy polemic against Proudhon, written in French by Marx himself and published in French in 1847. A German version of the book was only published posthumously, in 1884/85.

8 This false reading of *Capital* as a treatise of social philosophy – or, as it is imagined in some quarters, as an example of applied Hegelian logic – has led Marxist debates on *Capital* completely astray for many years. Marx's text is also full of allusions to and paraphrases of passages from world literature (see Prawer 1976). Any claim that *Capital* is a work of literature or literary criticism, though, would be as misguided as the similar claim that it is a work of philosophy or philosophical criticism. Although the philosophers, the Neo-Hegelians in particular, don't like the idea, *Capital* is not and never was intended as a work on social philosophy, none of it, not even the first chapters, the philosopher's favourites (cf. Quante 2019 for the opposite position).

9 At the time of writing this letter, he had about finished the second section. The English translation in Collected Works does not exactly carry the sense of what Marx wrote – he talked about 'Zusammengeflicktes' and 'Stümperwerk'. A 'bungler's job' would be closer to what Marx meant.

10 In the text of the French edition, Marx was obviously beginning to change some of the views he had held before, for instance with respect to the joint-stock companies which he had highly praised in his unfinished manuscript for Volume III, written in 1864–65 (cf. Marx 1989b: 549).

11 These three lists have first been published in Volume II/8 of MEGA² (cf. Marx 1989b, 1989c, 1989d).

12 For a short history of the arrival of Marx's Capital in Russia, the translations of the work into Russian and its reception by Russian intellectuals in the 1870s and later see Resis (1970).

13 On John Swinton, see Garlin (1976).

14 The first copy of *Capital* that Engels mentioned is today in the Russian State Archives for Social and Political History in Moscow, see RGASPI, Signature f 1, op 1, de 4140. The second personal copy cannot easily be identified as there are several copies of the French edition with marginalia from Marx's hand. One of these copies is today at the Russian State Archive in Moscow, see RGASPI, Signature f. 1, op. 1, d 6983. Kautsky could use copies belonging to Engels, with marginalia from Engels, but they seem to have been lost.

15 These marginalia in Marx's copies have first been presented by the editors of Volume II/8 of MEGA² (*Capital, Volume I,* third German edition) in 1989.

16 On Wagner and the younger Historical School, see Backhaus (1997).

17 Regarding the critical comments on Marx's *Capital,* there is hardly any difference between the first and the second editions. In both editions, Wagner was only referring to the first edition of 1867.

18 It is a myth, created by Marx himself, that his work was met by a 'conspiration of silence' in German academic circles and beyond. Although his work met with sharp criticism, he was not ignored at all and many economists tried to prove him wrong. Apart from Wagner, other leading German economists criticised him, including leading representatives of the 'Older Historical School' like Wilhelm Roscher and Carl Knies. Marx read their work and was not impressed.

19 The copy is kept in Moscow today, in the Russian State Archives for Social and Political History (see RGASPI, Signature f. 1, op. 1, d. 4035).

20 This notebook will be published in MEGA², Volume IV/33. The original is to be found in the Karl Marx-Friedrich Engels Nachlass at the IISG, Amsterdam, Signature B 133/B_164.

21 An aspiration still very much alive among Marxist philosophers and votaries of a 'new reading of Marx' today.

22 What Marx wrote here in German should rather be translated as 'the simplest economic concretum'.

23 The text of this review was written in 1868 and first published in the original language in 1933 (see Engels 1985). In German philosophical parlance, the term 'Ware als solche' (commodity as such) is equivalent to 'Ware im allgemeinen' (commodity in general). In *Capital* Marx regularly invokes current economic categories as they are used by businessmen and the general public, but also by professional economists, and transforms them into concepts. Hence, the concept of money or the concept of capital is different from the categories of money or capital in everyday life or in textbook economics. Developing the right concepts is a way of criticising the economic categories of everyday life and of the conventional wisdom of businessmen.

24 Marx was switching several times from Wagner to Rodbertus as the main adversary in his notes. He took Rodbertus to task because Wagner had quoted his critique of Marx approvingly and because according to Robert Meyer, one of his disciples, Rodbertus had 'written a 'big, fat manuscript' against *Capital* (Marx 1989f: 550).

25 He must have seen it at any rate, because he created tables of content for most of Marx's notebooks, including the notebook 'Oekonomisches in general'.

26 For a detailed discussion of these different interpretations and an answer to the question why the one and only 'right' or 'correct' reading of these chapters in Marx's *Capital* does not exist, see Krätke (2022).

27 And Marx does retain the idea of a linear progress of industrial development in the metaphor of the 'industrial ladder', another point that escapes the attention of Engels's critics.

28 Kropp and Nixdorf, like most collaborators of the first MEGA project, perished in Stalin's great purges. Rjazanow, an old Marxist and the best Marxologist of his generation, was arrested in 1931 and shot in 1938.

29 Only Maximilien Rubel, in his edition of *Capital* published in 1968, went as far as to impose his very own structure upon Marx's work, dismissing some parts, introducing others from unpublished manuscripts and creating an inconsistent mixture

of texts which he presented as the 'true' version of *Capital* – the book that Marx intended to write according to Rubel's imagination. He did not intend to publish a 'popular' and abridged edition as Karl and Benedikt Kautsky did. Instead, he knew better than Marx (and dismissed Engels outright) and wanted to correct him by skipping whole passages and rearranging larger parts of the text. For a critique see Kouvelakis (1995).

References

Alcouffe, Alain (Ed.) (1985) *Les Manuscrits Mathématiques de Marx*, Étude et présentation par Alain Alcouffe, 1ᵉ traduction française, Paris: Economica.

Althusser, Louis (1971) *Lenin and Philosophy and Other Essays*, New York: Monthly Review Press.

Anderson, Kevin (1983) 'The "Unknown" Marx's *Capital, Volume I*. The French Edition of 1872-75, 100 Years Later', *Review of Radical Political Economics*, vol. 15, n. 4: 71–80.

Anderson, Kevin (1998) , 'On the MEGA and the French edition of *Capital, Volume I*: An appreciation and critique', in *Beiträge zur Marx-Engels-Forschung*, edited by Rolf Hecker, Richard Sperl and Carl-Erich Vollgraf, Berlin: Argument Verlag, pp. 131–6.

Backhaus, Jürgen (Ed.) (1997) *Essays in Social Security and Taxation. Gustav von Schmoller and Adolph Wagner Reconsidered*, Marburg: Metropolis.

Bidet, Jacques (1985) 'Traduire en allemand *Le Capital*', in *1883–1983, L'œuvre de Marx, un siècle après*, edited by George Labica, Paris: Presses Universitaires de France, pp. 139–45.

Bouffard, Alix, Ferron, Alexandre and Fondu, Guillaume (2018) 'L'édition française du *Capital*, une œuvre originale', in *Le Capital, Livre I. Présentation, commentaires et documents*, Paris: Les éditions sociales, pp. 3–8.

D'Hondt, Jacques (1985) 'La traduction tendancieuse du *Capital* par Joseph Roy', in *1883-1983, L'œuvre de Marx, un siècle après*, edited by George Labica, Paris: Presses Universitaires des France, pp. 131–7.

Ducange, Jean-Numa and Hecker, Rolf (2022) 'Marx, Engels und die französische Ausgabe von *Le Capital*. Neue Briefe an den Herausgeber Maurice Lachâtre', in *Beiträge zur Marx-Engels-Forschung*, edited by Rolf Hecker, Richard Sperl and Carl-Erich Vollgraf, Hamburg: Argument Verlag, pp. 159–80.

Engels, Friedrich (1985 [1868]) 'Synopsis of Volume One of *Capital* by Karl Marx', in *Marx Engels Collected Works*, vol. 20: *Marx and Engels: 1864-68*, New York: International Publishers, pp. 263–308.

Engels, Friedrich (1987 [1867]) *Marx Engels Collected Works*, vol. 42: *Marx and Engels: 1864-68*, New York: International Publishers.

Engels, Friedrich (1989a [1873]) *Marx Engels Collected Works*, vol. 44: *Marx and Engels: 1870-73*, New York: International Publishers.

Engels, Friedrich (1989b [1873]) 'Zusätze und Änderungen für den ersten Band des "Kapitals", in *Marx Engels Gesamtausgabe* (MEGA²), vol. II/8, Berlin: Dietz Verlag, p. 3.

Engels, Friedrich (1992 [1882]) *Marx Engels Collected Works*, vol. 46: *Marx and Engels: 1880-83*, New York: International Publishers.

Engels, Friedrich (1995 [1883]) *Marx Engels Collected Works*, vol. 47: *Engels: 1883-86*, New York: International Publishers.

Engels, Friedrich (1996a [1883]) 'Preface to the Third German Edition', in *Marx Engels Collected Works*, vol. 35: *Karl Marx: Capital, Volume I*, New York: International Publishers.

Engels, Friedrich (1996b [1886]) 'Preface to the English Edition', in *Marx Engels Collected Works*, vol. 35: *Karl Marx: Capital, Volume I*, New York: International Publishers.

Engels, Friedrich (1996c [1890]) 'Preface to the Fourth German Edition', in *Marx Engels Collected Works*, vol. 35: *Karl Marx: Capital, Volume I*, New York: International Publishers.

Fondu, Guillaume and Quétier, Jean (2018) 'Comment traduire Marx en français?', in *Marx, une passion française*, edited by Jean-Numa Ducange and Antony Burlaud, Paris: Éditions la Decouverte, pp. 111–23.

Garlin, Sender (1976) *John Swinton: American Radical (1829-1901)*, New York: American Institute for Marxist Studies.

Gaudin, François (2019) *Traduire Le Capital. Une Correspondance inédite entre Karl Marx, Friedrich Engels et l'éditeur Maurice Lachâtre* , Mont-Saint-Aignan: Presses Universitaires de Rouen et du Havre.

Hayashi, Naomichi (1975) *Investigation on the French Edition of the First Volume of 'Capital'* (Japanese), Tokyo: Otsuki-Shoten.

Jungnickel, Jürgen (1990) 'Die Stellung der 2. Auflage des ersten Bandes des "Kapitals" in der Entwicklungsgeschichte der ökonomischen Theorie von Marx', in *Marx – Engels – Jahrbuch 12*, pp. 92–125.

Kautsky, Benedikt (1929) 'Einleitung des Herausgebers', in Karl Marx, *Das Kapital. Kritik der politischen Ökonomie*, Leipzig: Alfred Kröner Verlag, pp. XV–XLV.

Kautsky, Karl (1914) 'Vorwort des Herausgebers', in *Marx. Das Kapital. Kritik der politischen Ökonomie*. vol. I Stuttgart: J.H.W. Dietz Nachf., pp. XIII–XXXV.

Korsch, Karl (1996 [1932]) 'Geleitwort zur neuen Ausgabe des "Kapital"', in *Karl Korsch Gesamtaus-gabe*, vol. 5: *Krise des Marxismus. Schriften 1928-1935*, Amsterdam: Stichting Beheer IISG, pp. 512–42.

Kouvelakis, Eustache (1995) 'Marx encore! Question d'édition de l'œuvre marxienne', *Futur antérieure*, n. 30, 31, 32: 233–49.

Kowalevskij, Maxim (1983 [1909]), 'Erinnerungen an Karl Marx', in *Mohr und General. Erinnerungen an Marx und Engels*, edited by Fritz J. Raddatz Berlin: Dietz Verlag, pp. 345–68.

Krätke, Michael (2005) 'Le dernier Marx et le Capital', *Actuel Marx*, vol. 37, n.1: 145–60.

Krätke, Michael (2006) 'Das Marx-Engels Problem. Warum Engels das Marxsche "Kapital" nicht verfälscht hat', in *Marx-Engels Jahrbuch 2006*, Berlin: Akademie Verlag, pp. 142–70.

Krätke, Michael (2017) *Kritik der politischen Ökonomie heute*, Hamburg: VSA Verlag.

Krätke, Michael (2022) *Das unvollendete Projekt. Was tun mit Marx's 'Kapital'?*, Hamburg: VSA Verlag.

Kropp, Valerie and Nixdorf, Kurt (1997 [1931]) 'Der Vergleich der französischen Ausgabe des "Kapital" mit der 2. deutschen Auflage', in *Beiträge zur Marx-Engels-Forschung*, edited by Rolf Hecker, Richard Sperl and Carl-Erich Vollgraf, Hamburg: Argument Verlag, pp. 125–32.

Kuczynski, Thomas (2005) 'Die von Marx revidierte französische Ausgabe von Band I des *Kapitals*. Ein bislang unbekanntes Exemplar mit Autorenkorrekturen', in *Marx-Engels Jahrbuch 2005*, Berlin: Akademie Verlag, pp. 222–6.

Kuczynski,Thomas (2011) 'Welche Einträge in Marx' Handexemplaren von *Kapital* Bd. I dienten derVorbereitung einer dritten deutschen Auflage?', in *Marx-Engels Jahrbuch 2010,* Berlin: AkademieVerlag, pp. 101–58.

Kuczynski, Thomas (2016) 'Marx' Eintragungen im überlieferten Handexemplar', in *Marx-Engels Jahrbuch 2015/16,* Berlin: AkademieVerlag, pp. 219–37.

Kuczynski, Thomas (Ed.) (2017) *Das Kapital. Erster Band. Neue Textausgabe,* Hamburg:VSAVerlag.

Lindner, Kolja (2009) 'Die Editionsgeschichte der Werke von Marx und Engels in Frankreich und ihr Neubeginn mit Grande Édition Marx et Engels (GEME)', in *Marx-Engels Jahrbuch 2008,* pp. 103–19.

Marx, Karl (1974 [1858–1883]) *Mathematische Manuskripte,* Kronenberg Ts.: Sriptor Verlag.

Marx, Karl (1987a [1867]) *Marx Engels Collected Works,* vol. 42: *Marx and Engels: 1864-68,* NewYork: International Publishers.

Marx, Karl (1987b [1871–1872]) 'Ergänzungen und Veränderungen zum ersten Band des "Kapitals", in *Marx Engels Gesamtausgabe* (MEGA²), vol. II/6, Berlin: DietzVerlag, pp. 1–54.

Marx, Karl (1987c [1872]) 'Prospekt zur zweiten Auflage des ersten Bandes des "Kapitals"', in *Marx Engels Gesamtausgabe* (MEGA²), vol. II/6, Berlin: Dietz Verlag, p. 55.

Marx, Karl (1988 [1868]) *Marx Engels Collected Works,* vol. 43: *Marx and Engels: 1868-70,* NewYork: International Publishers.

Marx, Karl (1989a [1871]) *Marx Engels Collected Works,* vol. 44: *Marx and Engels: 1870-73,* NewYork: International Publishers.

Marx, Karl (1989b [1872–1875]) *Le Capital,* in *Marx Engels Gesamtausgabe* (MEGA²), vol. II/7, Berlin: DietzVerlag.

Marx, Karl (1989c [1877]) 'Verzeichnis der Veränderungen für den ersten Band des "Kapitals"', in *Marx Engels Gesamtausgabe* (MEGA²), vol. II/8, Berlin: Dietz Verlag, pp. 7–20.

Marx, Karl (1989d [1877]) 'Entwurf eines Verzeichnisses der Veränderungen für eine amerikanische Ausgabe des ersten Bandes des "Kapitals"', in *Marx Engels Gesamtausgabe* (MEGA²), vol. II/8, Berlin: DietzVerlag, pp. 21–4.

Marx, Karl (1989e [1877]) 'Verzeichnis der Veränderungen für eine amerikanische Ausgabe des ersten Bandes des "Kapitals"', in *Marx Engels Gesamtausgabe* (MEGA²), vol. II/8, Berlin: DietzVerlag, pp. 25–36.

Marx, Karl (1989f [1880–1881]) 'Marginal Notes on Adolph Wagner's *Lehrbuch der Politischen Oekonomie',* in *Marx Engels Collected Works,* vol. 24: *Marx and Engels: 1874-83,* NewYork: International Publishers, pp. 531–59.

Marx, Karl (1991 [1874]) *Marx Engels Collected Works,* vol. 45: *Marx and Engels: 1874-79,* NewYork: International Publishers.

Marx, Karl (1992 [1881]) *Marx Engels Collected Works,* vol. 46: *Marx and Engels: 1880-83,* NewYork: International Publishers.

Marx, Karl (1996a [1867]) 'Preface to the First German Edition', in *Marx Engels Collected Works,* vol. 35: *Karl Marx: Capital, Volume I,* New York: International Publishers, pp. 7–11.

Marx, Karl (1996b [1873]) 'Afterword to the Second German Edition', in *Marx Engels Collected Works,* vol. 35: *Karl Marx: Capital, Volume I,* New York: International Publishers, pp. 2–21.

Marx, Karl (1996c [1872]) 'Preface to the French Edition', in *Marx Engels Collected Works,* vol. 35: *Karl Marx: Capital, Volume I,* New York: International Publishers, p. 23.

Marx, Karl (1996d [1875]) 'Afterword to the French Edition', in *Marx and Engels Collected Works,* vol. 35: *Karl Marx: Capital, Volume I,* New York: International Publishers, p. 24.

Marx, Karl (2008 [1868–1881)], 'Manuskripte zum zweiten Buch des "Kapitals" 1868–1881', in *Marx Engels Gesamtausgabe* (MEGA²), vol. II/11, Berlin: Akademie Verlag.

Marx, Karl (2012 [1863–1868]), 'Ökonomische Manuskripte 1863–1868', in *Marx Engels Gesamtausgabe* (MEGA²), vol. II/4.3, Berlin: Akademie Verlag.

Omura, Izumi (1987) 'Zum Marxschen Verzeichnis der Veränderungen für eine amerikanische Ausgabe des ersten Bandes des "Kapitals": Welche Ausgabe sollen wir für die letzte halten?', in *Beiträge zur Marx-Engels-Forschung,* Berlin: Institut für Marxismus-Leninismus beim Zentralkomitee der SED, pp. 216–22.

Omura, Izumi (1991) 'Welche Marxschen Hinweise bzw. Anweisungen benutzte Engels bei der Vorbereitung der dritten deutschen Auflage des ersten Bandes des "Kapitals"?', in *Beiträge zur Marx-Engels-Forschung,* Hamburg: Argument Verlag, pp. 103–111.

Omura, Izumi (1994) 'Zum Abschluss der Veröffentlichung der verschiedenen Ausgaben des Kapital in der MEGA²', *MEGA-Studien,* vol. 4, n. 2: 56–88.

Oppenheim, Heinrich Bernhard (1872) *Der Katheder-Sozialismus* , Berlin: Verlag von R. Oppenheim.

Outhwaite, William and Smith, Kenneth (2020) 'Karl Marx, Le Capital', *Review of Radical Political Economics,* vol. 52, n. 2: 208–21.

Prawer, Siegbert (1976) *Karl Marx and World Literature,* Oxford: Oxford University Press.

Quante, Michael (2019) 'Einleitung', in Karl Marx, *Das Kapital. Kritik der politischen Ökonomie. Erster Band,* Hamburg: Felix Meiner Verlag, pp. XI–XLIV.

Resis, Albert (1970) 'Das Kapital comes to Russia', *Slavic Review,* vol. 29, n. 2: 219–37.

Rosdolsky, Roman (1989 [1968]) *The Making of Marx's 'Capital',* London: Pluto Press.

Roth, Regina (2018) 'Editing the Legacy: Friedrich Engels and Marx's Capital', in *Marx's Capital-An Unfinishable Project?,* edited by Marcel van der Linden and Gerald Hubmann, Leiden: Brill, pp. 31–47.

Rubel, Maximilien (1968) *Karl Marx. Oeuvres. Économie II. Édition établie et annotée par Maximilien Rubel,* Paris: Éditions Gallimard.

Schäffle, Albert (1875) *Die Quintessenz des Sozialismus,* Gotha: Perthes.

Swinton, John (1880) *John Swinton's Travels: current views and notes of forty days in France and England,* New York: G. W. Carlton & Co.

Swinton, John (1985 [1880]) 'Karl Marx', in *Marx Engels Gesamtausgabe* (MEGA²), vol. I/25, Berlin: Dietz Verlag, pp. 442–444.

Verzeichnis (1991) 'Verzeichnis von Textstellen aus der französischen Ausgabe, die nicht in die 3. oder 4. deutsche Auflage aufgenommen wurden', in *Marx Engels Gesamtausgabe* (MEGA²), vol. II / 8 (Apparat), Berlin: Dietz Verlag, pp. 732–83.

Wagner, Adolph (1870) *Die Abschaffung des privaten Grundeigenthums,* Leipzig: Winter.

Wagner, Adolph (1879) *Lehrbuch der Politischen Oekonomie. Band I, Neu bearbeitet von Ad. Wagner und E. Nasse, Allgemeine oder theoretische Volkswirtschaftslehre. Erster Theil. Grundlegung,* 2, Leipzig: Winter.

Wagner, Adolph (1895) *Die akademische Nationalökonomie und der Sozialismus,* Leipzig: Winter.

Part III

The Dissemination and the Reception of *Le Capital*

10 The Contradictory Reception of the French Edition of *Capital*

Jean-Numa Ducange and Jean Quétier

Introduction and methodology: On the reception of Marx in France

Roy's translation of *Capital, Volume I*, had a peculiar fate. Overall, it cannot be said that it had a very wide-scale impact before the founding of the French Communist Party (PCF; at first called the 'French Section of the Communist International') in December 1920. Rather, its reception remained a rather more restricted affair. Nevertheless – and even admitting the need to distinguish between different periods – it cannot be concluded from this that before 1914 the reception and discussion of the French translation of *Capital, Volume I*, were entirely absent. Beyond this work itself, the various summaries and extracts drawn from it were considerable vehicles for disseminating the theses contained in *Capital, Volume I*, and these texts, too, are fully part of this history. This chapter aims to present some little-known considerations on the reception of this French edition, starting in the final quarter of the nineteenth century. It does so by returning to a nagging problem, which had emerged already in the 1870s but became particularly acute starting in the 1920s: was this French translation a reliable basis to work from? Did the translation need redoing based on the German edition, the better to grasp Marx's arguments? As we shall see, the status of this work itself changed over the years, often wavering between that of an untouchable source which bore the seal of Marx's own authority and that of an imperfect or even inadequate transposition – the laborious result of the efforts of an inept translator.

The first part of this chapter will look back at readings of *Capital, Volume I*, from before World War I, seeking to show that there was indeed an early reception of this work in France in this era, both among Marx's supporters and among his opponents. The second part will delve into the far more mass-scale circulation of this work starting in the first half of the twentieth century, highlighting the theoretical and political stakes of the publication of *Capital, Volume I*, in France, while also emphasising its international dissemination, especially in the French-speaking world.

The history of the reception of Marx and Marxism in France has been the subject of numerous major studies, which often take as their starting point

DOI: 10.4324/9781003336365-13

the first French-language translation of *Capital, Volume I.* The history of this first phase of its reception is decisive, for it represents a period in which the socialist movement was only in its infancy and had not taken on organised and structured form. Indeed, the socialist currents of this era faced the greatest difficulties in rebuilding their forces after the crushing of the Paris Commune. The first Workers' Party did not emerge until 1879; the Socialist Party was unified only in 1905 (Ducange 2019: 34).

In this context, the history of the reception of Marx largely depended (from the 1880s to 1890s) on socialist political organisations and then (after 1920) on Communist ones. The long-accepted reading tells of an 'untraceable Marxism' (Lindenberg 1975: 5); this vision based on hindsight, heavily overdetermined by the issues at stake in the debates of the 1970s, was especially advanced by Daniel Lindenberg. This perspective, which foregrounds the idea of a mediocre and badly 'digested' Marxism, is often found in overviews of various kinds. In the 1970s, 'Second Left' tendencies especially turned their fire on the Guesdist current (so named after Jules Guesde, one of the main founders of the Workers' Party), which was said to have introduced a schematic, uninteresting Marxism and, most importantly, to have prevented any kind of consequential reception of Marxism (Prochasson 2005: 426).

Yet, this reading ignores three major elements. The first is its underestimation of some of the debates that did take place around Marx's work. The second is the importance of a 'Marxism of the militants' which really did contribute to the dissemination of Marx, in popularised form. Finally worth noting is the significance of a 'Marx seen from the Right', showing that there was a critical, even hostile reception of Marx, which also needs to be integrated into our reflection. Especially when we take this third element into account, we understand that the French translation of *Capital, Volume I,* did not go unnoticed.

First read by its opponents

It is not easy to measure the real reception of the French edition of *Capital, Volume I,* outside of a few restricted circles of socialists. Some evidence would suggest that this translation went rather unnoticed, while other elements point to real attention coming from various actors.

Jacqueline Cahen has convincingly shown that a certain audience of specialised liberal economists did pay attention to Marx's *Capital, Volume I,* sensitive as they were to the strength of his arguments (Cahen 2018: 23). But – and this is highly telling – the reception of the translation in this camp seems to have been very weak: *Capital, Volume I,* was read in German, using the 1867 edition, whereas the Lachâtre edition seems to have gone unnoticed. From this, many have concluded that this edition attracted little interest outside of a few militant circles. Moreover, this was a period when the Third Republic was governed by Adolphe Thiers and then the hardline conservative Mac-Mahon. This posed obstacles to the dissemination of socialist ideas: the liberal regime which allowed texts to be more easily circulated would come only later (for instance, the law on the freedom of the press dates to 1881).

Nevertheless, the Lachâtre edition did not go unnoticed. For evidence of this, one need look only to the response which it received from the newspaper *La Patrie*, during the Second Empire one of France's two or three largest Bonapartist dailies (1852–70). It had been founded in 1841; its original director, the banker Casimir Delamarre, became an MP during the Second Empire (Anceau 2017: 30). The editorial staff included figures such as Paulin Limayrac, who was appointed prefect of the Lot département following several glowing articles about Napoleon III. The newspaper regularly reached a circulation of 30,000 in the 1860s, a considerable figure for an opinion daily in this era; it was one of the biggest titles that defended a 'hard' Bonapartist line. In summer 1870, it campaigned in favour of war. However, the paper also survived the fall of Napoleon III. In the 1870s, though remaining faithful to Bonapartism, it repositioned itself in a bid to unite the movement. Yet, while *La Patrie* was now weakened and its circulation dropped, it hardly fell out of the public gaze: indeed, the instability of the early Third Republic caused room for doubt as to whether this order would even last. This paper had always taken an interest in socialist theories, which it combatted head-on; but this was not simply a matter of invective, as several articles sought to demonstrate through detailed arguments why socialism was a harmful ideology.

In this vein, *La Patrie* published a series of critical commentaries on the French edition of *Capital, Volume I,* under the title 'Les doctrines de Karl Marx' (Gaussen 1874a: 3). The first instalment was published on 7 September 1874. It argued, among other things, that the distinction between use-value and exchange-value was 'specious'. The clear aim of these articles was to refute the French translation of *Capital, Volume I,* whose publication was still ongoing at the time; here, we shall cite some telling passages from this text. The first instalment introduced it in the following terms:

> Let us now see the first consequences which our theorist draws from highly questionable premises, and which in truth have some value only for the simple and the ignorant [...] But first of all, let us again bring out the puerility and falseness of his assertions, always leaving aside this peculiar distinction between use-value and exchange-value [...] In any case, to try to assess the value of a commodity by the amount of material labour it has necessitated, is both infantile and a gross economic error.

Many quotations of the same type could be cited. Worth noting are the author's references to the lectures which Heinrich von Sybel had given in Barmen, in refutation of Marx (Sybel 1872: 20). And while everything in this series of articles is constructed according to the logic of clear and sharp refutation, it nevertheless contained summaries of several key concepts from *Capital, Volume I*. This had the effect of allowing a summary of some of Marx's concepts to be introduced to a hardly negligible audience.

More broadly, the author related several of the theses elaborated in Marx's *Capital, Volume I,* to the development of contemporary socialism and of the organised labour movement – phenomena which the Bonapartist currents closely observed. Thus, in the 10 September instalment, we can read,

> This is where Mr. Karl Marx wanted to get to, and this is what allows him to proclaim, like most socialists, that the proletarian condition is the exploitation of man by man; that the wage-earner is the slave of capital, the industrial serf. So, for them, it is no longer today a matter, as per the sinister formula of the Lyon insurrection, of *live working or die fighting.* No! the rallying cry of most of the sectarians of the socialist army is this: *work for all, according to their productive faculties, and the sharing of products according to wealth.*

The whole argument is also directed at demonstrating the political danger of Marx's assertions. This was a matter of some concern to the author, who sensed the potential impact that this doctrine might have on a section of the working class:

> Whatever the falsity of their starting point, one can easily guess the consequences that such preaching may have; and the ravages it must bring in credulous hearts riven by envy. And yet, a single grain of good sense should suffice to understand the absurdity of such things. Who does not know, for example, that the more advanced a people's level of civilisation, the more developed are its agriculture, commerce and industry; and consequently, the more necessary it is that material labour should be directed by elite minds, endowed with sharpness, order and foresight?

In the last instalment on 12 September, the author moreover justified the length of his critiques, by citing the importance that Marx's theories were now taking on:

> May we be excused if we have expanded at such length on the doctrines of Mr. Karl Marx; but let us not forget that he is regarded, from the point of view of his economic science, as far superior to his colleagues in the International Workingmen's Society [sic], and that he bears great influence on his party. Moreover, he is considered – hard though it is to believe – by a great number of communists, as having provided scientific and irrefutable legitimation to the doctrines of this socialist sect, and as having demonstrated the absolute necessity of a liquidation of society in order to arrive at the reign of absolute equality and of true justice in distribution.

Much like how the power of the International Workingmen's Association was exaggerated by French elites upon the outbreak of the Commune (Cordillot 2010: 18), *La Patrie* saw Marx as a powerful and influential guru that he was not.

Paradoxically, this also performed certain job of introducing Marx. Despite the always sharp and inflammatory tone, here we also find brief expositions of key concepts from *Capital, Volume I*, for example, regarding labour-power and exploitation. Thus, a hostile, but relatively accurate, summary of several passages from *Capital, Volume I,* was published in the 11 September instalment:

> Then he makes his very gratuitous assumption, in coming to assert that in most cases six hours' labour would suffice, on average, to produce these means of subsistence: and to get his way, he then ends by saying: *Let us suppose that six hours' labour suffices to make a silver thaler; the normal price of labour would therefore be one thaler a day. The worker therefore sells his entire day's work to the capitalist –* we know what is meant by this word *– at this price.* And this, according to the famous communist, is the law which now governs exchange-value, and all that the worker would rightfully demand as the price for his labour.
>
> But, Mr. Karl Marx adds, the worker makes an abominable bargain, he sells his day of toil for the price of six hours' work on average. And this is what allows him to come to this conclusion: The exchange-value of labour is much lower than its use-value, which is to say, what it really produces.

The author of these texts was Maurice Gaussen (1811–90). So, *Capital, Volume I,* was indeed read and reflected upon by some Bonapartist journalists. These articles by Gaussen were later collected in the form of a pamphlet titled *La société internationale des travailleurs et ses doctrines* (1874), which had a certain circulation (Gaussen 1874b: 3). It should be noted that Karl Marx was himself aware of this pamphlet: he referred to it in a letter to Maurice Lachâtre dated 18 September 1874, while he was resting at the spa in Karlsbad, where it was possible to read the main French press.

Marx's arguments stood in continuity with the socialist doctrines that so preoccupied the government. In such a context, it is unsurprising that circles of former government supporters paid greater attention, here, than oppositionists did. Doctrinal questions were of relatively little concern to a socialist movement that had been left decimated and disorganised by the repression of the Commune.

A more exhaustive study of the analysis of socialist doctrines by the elites of the Second Empire and the early years of the Third Republic remains to be done. But the example of *La Patrie* shows the function of the Lachâtre edition. If liberal economists would discuss the German edition, French politicians had been able to lay their hands on this translation and read it.

The French translation of *Capital* and militants' Marxist culture

A few years after the publication of the Lachâtre edition was complete, an abridgement of Marx's *Capital, Volume I,* was published by Gabriel Deville, indeed in the same year as Marx's death (Deville 1883: 10). Deville, who did not read German, read the French translation and drew from it a few key concepts, which he summarised in a clear but often rushed and schematic manner. The fact remains that he contributed considerably to making *Capital, Volume I*, in Roy's translation, better known by way of quotations and summaries. Deville was no bit-part player: he was one of the representatives of 'Guesdist' Marxism at the time and played a political role in this current. This was a Marxism turned towards action, seeking above all to mobilise a militant milieu which did not have a very high level of political or theoretical training. It should be noted that Deville's publisher was Henri Oriol, who took over the collection of Maurice Lachâtre's publisher; there was thus a direct material continuity between the Lachâtre edition and the abridgement published by Oriol. The same editorial networks were at work in both cases (Gaudin 2014: 95).

This was an important moment in the reception of this work, in that this abridgement drew on and paraphrased entire passages from Roy's translation. Without this French translation, it would not have seen the light of day. And – as we know – Marx attached great importance to the introduction of his thought in France. Disappointed by the poor circulation of the Lachâtre edition, he hoped that a substantial summary would make up for this failure; his death meant that he would never see this abridged edition published. It is worth emphasising the importance of this volume, which the historiography has often dismissed. Without doubt, it overlooked major arguments elaborated in *Capital, Volume I,* and offers a questionable summary of this work. But generations of activists would read this abridged version and access Marx's *Capital, Volume I,* for the first time through it; and for many individuals, this would be their only contact with Marx's major work. There were many further editions: after the one published by Oriol in 1883, there was a reprint by Flammarion (a commercial publisher) in 1897 and then others in 1921, 1933, 1945 and 1948. There was also an edition by the Socialist Party-French Section of the Workers' International (SFIO) in 1929.

Although there are no detailed archives that would allow to estimate its exact circulation, two remarks are called for. First, this volume was widely quoted and used in the training schools of the SFIO and the PCF in the interwar period (Bouju 2010: 32). However, it was never republished by the PCF as such. It should be said that its author had himself become unpalatable: after having sided with the moderate socialists at the beginning of the twentieth century, Deville then became a minister-plenipotentiary and held various official posts, having abandoned all socialist convictions. In addition, there was a revised Belgian edition in 1905–06 and several foreign-language translations, including an English one (Deville 1905–06: 45). In other Eastern European languages, for example, Romanian, it was common to translate Marx based on French translations (Guesnier 2016: 323). In any case, there was a French-speaking milieu in Europe that had not mastered German and thus had a use for the Roy translation, and the abridgement that resulted. It remains to be established precisely what this reception was, as these few elements also point to the international importance of this translation. At the end of the nineteenth century,

French was still widely spoken among many of the elites and the cadres of the workers' movement.

Let's return to the 1870–80s. Consulting the main socialist press organs of the time also offers a more contradictory view than is usually given regarding the lack of reception of Marxism in France. We may take as an example *L'Égalité/ Le Socialiste*, a newspaper founded by the Guesdist current which served as one of the main vehicles for Marxism.[1] Clearly, this newspaper contained hardly any theoretical debates on *Capital, Volume I*. On the other hand, we regularly find, at the end of the 1870s (i.e., a few years after the publication of the Roy translation was complete), extracts from *Capital, Volume I,* being used to explain certain basic concepts to the militant-reader. We could mention, by way of examples, 'La production capitaliste' (30 December 1877, over two pages), 'L'accumulation capitaliste' (20 January 1878, over two pages) and 'L'accumulation primitive' (3 February 1878, over two pages), along with many other pieces of the same type. Also noticeable in militant pamphlets or almanacs is the repetition of quotations from *Capital, Volume I,* or from Deville's abridgement. In this latter spirit, we even find other militant summaries of certain passages from *Capital, Volume I*. For example, the article 'À travers le capital' published in the *Almanach du Parti ouvrier pour 1896* contains eight pages of summaries and citations from Marx's work.

There was thus a militant reception of *Capital, Volume I*, using considerable extracts for a popular, militant readership. These brief extracts have no *a posteriori* theoretical significance. But by analysing pamphlets, abstracts and newspaper extracts, we can see that there did indeed exist a certain Marxist political culture forged on the basis of the translated Lachâtre edition.

The interwar debates

From the first half of the twentieth century, efforts to disseminate *Capital, Volume I,* in France came up against a recurring problem, which can be summarised as follows: should the Roy translation, 'authorised' by Marx himself, be reissued in identical form, or should a new version be offered, which would, as necessary, incorporate certain contributions from the fourth German edition? Throughout this period, the proposed answers to this question sometimes varied considerably, in conjunction with often very different political and theoretical objectives. In any case, it is noteworthy that the first new edition (Marx 1924) of *Capital, Volume I,* in French in the twentieth century – published in four volumes by the Socialist activist Alfred Costes in 1924 – did not rely on the Roy translation, which was not yet in the public domain. Jacques Molitor was instead tasked with translating it, as part of a project for complete works of Marx; he showed little regard for accuracy and faithfulness to the original text and appears to have been more driven by the concern to produce a volume that was accessible to the public, as quickly as possible. His translation never became authoritative, and Costes himself finally chose to replace it with the Roy translation when he re-issued the book in the late 1940s (Bouffard, Feron and Fondu 2017: 99f).

It was not until 1938 that the Roy translation would see a new edition in France, thanks to the PCF's publishing office, the Bureau d'éditions (Marx 1938–39). However, the decision to republish it could hardly be taken for granted, and in fact came only after a long and conflict-ridden process. The project for such an edition dated back to 1933, the year of the fiftieth anniversary of Marx's death, when several of his works were meant to be republished. However, placed under direct Comintern supervision, the Bureau d'éditions had little freedom of manoeuvre and drew the wrath of the Marx-Engels-Lenin Institute in Moscow, which took a dim view of the identical reproduction of the Roy translation. In a letter dated 4 June 1933, the Institute stated:

> The Bureau d'éditions is indeed publishing *Capital* without our permission. We have no objection to the use of the La Châtre [sic] edition, which was revised by Marx, for this purpose, but it seems desirable to us to revise the French text in parallel with the original German text in order to correct certain misprints and inaccuracies.
>
> (Bouju 2018: 128)

The French Communists gave in under pressure from the Soviet researchers and abandoned the project, for a while at least.

However, the new context brought by the Popular Front changed the situation and allowed for a more open editorial policy, of which René Hilsum was one of the main architects. Hilsum succeeded in convincing the PCF leadership to finalise the republication of the Roy translation, arguing in particular that it was necessary to avoid leaving the publisher Costes with a monopoly. Turning around the argument put forward a few years earlier by the Marx-Engels-Lenin Institute, the cadres responsible for the PCF's Bureau d'éditions pointed to the fact that Marx had himself checked Roy's translation, in order to present this as an enterprise that stood above all suspicion. Although this time Hilsum carried the argument there were still differences with the Comintern. For reasons of accessibility and cost, the French Communists preferred a lightened edition, without an indigestible critical apparatus. Moscow, however, did not see things that way and forced the addition of prefaces and appendices, which were eventually entrusted to Alix Guillain (Bouju 2010: 83–116). These negotiations certainly delayed the publication of the book, but the outcome was essentially a positive one, since the Roy translation of *Capital, Volume I,* was finally able to appear, on the eve of the war.

The postwar period, from loyalty to contestation

The 1938 edition was the basis for subsequent republications by Éditions Sociales, the PCF's new publishing house after World War II. It produced a fresh run of this work in 1948. The revival of the Roy translation by Costes in the same period helped to make it the standard version. This was the edition in which a whole generation of Marxist-influenced French intellectuals would read *Capital, Volume I*, starting with Louis Althusser; he built on it in his famous 1965 seminar at Paris's École Normale Supérieure, whose proceedings would lead to the publication of *Reading Capital*. According to Althusser's book, however, the Roy translation already appears as marked by shortcomings; even if this did not mean that it should be rejected outright, this was grounds for a certain caution. The introductory chapter, titled 'From *Capital* to Marx's Philosophy', states at the outset:

> it is essential to read Capital not only in its French translation (even Volume One in Roy's translation, which Marx revised, or rather, rewrote), but also in the German original, at least for the fundamental theoretical chapters and all the passages where Marx's key concepts come to the surface.
>
> (Althusser 1970: 14)

Thus, on several points that he considered decisive, Althusser strove to highlight the greater depth of the German text, which he was thus driven to retranslate. One of the most famous examples concerned the problem of the overturning of the Hegelian dialectic, mentioned in the Afterword to the Second German Edition of *Capital, Volume I*. In an article from 1962, titled 'Contradiction and Overdetermination', reprinted in 1965 in the volume *For Marx*, Althusser clearly states that Roy 'edulcorates' (Althusser 1969a: 89) the original text in his translation, oversimplifying the long and complex operation that the transformation of the dialectic undertaken by Marx represents (Fondu and Quétier 2018: 118f.). Even so, these criticisms did not lead Althusser to deny all legitimacy to the Roy translation, to whose dissemination he directly contributed by putting his name, in 1969, to a 'Notice to Readers' set at the beginning of the latest edition published by Garnier-Flammarion (Althusser 1969b: 7–26).

On a wholly different bases, Maximilien Rubel – responsible for editing Marx's works for the prestigious 'Bibliothèque de la Pléiade' collection published by Gallimard – took the challenge even further by making direct interventions in the text of Roy's translation. Emphasising both Marx's ethical intentions – which, he claimed, structured his work from beginning to end – and its radically unfinished character, Rubel declared war on Marxist readings in which he saw so many illegitimate efforts at systematisation. Nonetheless, on numerous occasions, this general orientation led Rubel to make questionable and indeed contested editorial choices, paradoxically out of step with his declared concern for philological rigour (Le Moullec-Rieu 2018: 143). The edition of *Capital, Volume I,* contained in the first instalment of the *Œuvres* published in 1963 (Marx 1963), shows this tension very clearly. On the one hand, Rubel claimed to have 'taken into account Marx's expressed wishes' in deciding to produce a new edition of Roy's version rather than undertake a complete retranslation. The effort to 'correct the rather numerous errors which a comparison of the French version and the original text' (Rubel 1963: 539) allowed him to identify is itself quite understandable, for it simply relates to a concern similar to that visible in Althusser in this same period. But Rubel went much further than concern for the precision of the translation might seem to require. Indeed, he worked to propose not only a *corrected* version of the Roy translation but also a *reworked* and *restructured* one. In concrete terms, Rubel tried to sort the true substance of Marx's analysis, from passages deemed inessential that could be considered as mere dross. He thus states that 'certain chapters of *Capital, Volume I* ('The Working Day', 'Machinery and Large-Scale Industry' and 'The General Law of Capitalist Accumulation') are cluttered with statistical and descriptive materials which – it is rightly said – belong to history' (Rubel 1963: 540). Yet, not daring to go as far as depriving the reader entirely of the possibility of reading them, Rubel then asserted that he 'thought he was doing the right thing not by deleting these chapters, but by deferring the parts of pure documentation to the end of *Capital*' (Rubel 1963: 540–1). And Rubel did not stop there: his most striking decision was probably that of changing around the order of the final two chapters of *Capital, Volume I,* as found in the French edition. Whereas in the Roy version, chapter 32, devoted to the 'Historical Tendency of Capitalist Accumulation', preceded the final chapter 33 on the 'Modern Theory of Colonisation', Rubel decided to reverse their order. In this case, philological arguments gave way to a form of speculation that is questionable, to say the least: thus, according to Rubel, close examination 'suggests' that Marx himself switched the order of the last two chapters, 'perhaps' (Rubel 1963: 541) obeying advice from his publisher to skirt around the censor, which would have redoubled its severity with regard to a work which concluded with the prospect of the expropriation of the expropriators.

Beyond their differences, Althusser's and Rubel's efforts each expressed approaches that questioned the authority of Roy's translation. Such a challenge would make its way to Éditions Sociales itself, which constituted one of the main vehicles for this translation's circulation. During the 1970s, the PCF remained largely faithful to this version of *Capital, Volume I*, which it had fought to keep publishing since the mid-1930s. The Lachâtre edition constituted a sort of 'site of memory' that ought to be upheld, in order to set the Communists' struggles in its tradition. The centenary of this translation's publication was even a major celebratory moment, as shown in autumn 1972 by the publication of an issue of the *Cahiers de l'Institut Maurice Thorez* devoted to it. This came one year after the commemoration of the centenary of the Commune of 1871, which was particularly spectacular in France and allowed many *gauchiste* currents considerable visibility. Anxious to anchor socialism within a national perspective, the PCF thus took particular care to reappropriate this phase of socialism's history for itself: and between the Commune of 1871 and the Jaurès-Guesde pairing that had given rise to the founding of the Socialist Party in 1905; there was also a specific role for the Lachâtre edition of *Capital, Volume I.*

This issue of *Cahiers de l'Institut Maurice Thorez* was introduced by Georges Cogniot, president of this Institute and director of its journal. The dossier sought precisely to highlight the French specificity of the Roy edition. The particular aim was to present this edition as a decisive stage in the history of the struggles waged by the French working class, which the PCF's subsequent activity had, it was said, strove to pursue. The signing of the Common Programme for government, concluded with the Socialists and Radicals a few months earlier, was even said to constitute the culmination of this history

> The French Communist Party marks the hundredth anniversary of the publication of *Capital* in our language, in the most effective way and the one most worthy of Marx: by making a decisive advance in the real movement of the working class and of democracy.
>
> (Cogniot 1972: 11)

The republication of Roy's version of *Capital, Volume I,* by Éditions Sociales in 1976, with an introduction by Paul Boccara, fitted into this same approach. Although the text of the translation was left unchanged, it was used towards a political update process, linked to the 'crisis of state monopoly capitalism' (Boccara 1976: xxxvii). However, the most vigorous protest against Roy's translation thus far came from within Éditions Sociales. With the support of Lucien Sève, at the time the publisher's director, the main competing version of *Capital, Volume I,* in French — Jean-Pierre Lefebvre's — was published in 1983 (Marx 1983). It questioned the translation of certain central concepts of this book, drawing on a broader study of Marx's various manuscripts devoted to the critique of political economy. This expressed an effort to decouple questions regarding the publication of *Capital, Volume I,* from responses to immediate strategic objectives: in contrast to the approach taken by Paul Boccara a few years earlier, Jean-Pierre Lefebvre's introduction was mainly concerned with patiently tracing the tumultuous history of the relations between Marx, Roy and Lachâtre, without claiming to draw any lessons for the politics of the present day.

Another little-known element also deserves examination. Given that, for instance, many late-nineteenth-century Romanian socialists were better able to read French than German, the international reception of Roy's translation is also worth noting. In countries where French was the lingua franca, Roy's translation and Deville's summary continued to play a role. Here again, it would be necessary to conduct systematic research, at the scale of several countries. But it is possible at least to draw out some significant considerations. First of all, some research has shown that the Moscow-based Progress Publishers published Marx's texts in French not only for France, Belgium, French-speaking Switzerland and Quebec, but also and above all for the former French colonies, where the Soviets bore major influence in the 1960s and 1970s. The 'Marxism-Leninism' exported to Africa was based on translations of Marx, and the translation of *Capital, Volume I,* chosen in Moscow was always Roy's. Quotations from *Capital, Volume I,* in (Maoist-inspired) Marxist-Leninist journals and press organs in several African countries confirm as much. *Capital, Volume I,* was also disseminated through reading circles, such as the one run for a time in Dakar by the Senegalese Communist activist Amady Aly Dieng, who had been president of the Black African Students' Federation in France in the early 1960s (Blum 2018: 324).

Another significant case is the specific importance of French in some countries with ruling Communist Parties, such as Albania, between 1945 and 1990. In Tirana, the ruling Party of Labour of Albania particularly promoted the teaching of French, a language with which Enver Hoxha (who ruled the country from 1945 to 1985) was enamoured. According to the testimony of Patrick Kessel – one of the main conveyors of 'pro-Albanian' texts in France – the French translations of Marx were largely used as a basis for translating the classics of Marxism into Albanian. Thus, the Roy translation was largely used for the Albanian translation of *Capital, Volume I*, given that expertise in German was much rarer and more limited in this country.[2]

Conclusion

As we have seen throughout this chapter, understanding the history of the reception of the French edition of *Capital, Volume I,* demands particular attention to the variety of uses made of it. Its content was not simply disseminated through the Lachâtre edition itself, nor even through the later editions – altered or otherwise – to which it gave rise. From the mid-1870s onwards, this volume was also brought to readers' attention by way of the extracts cited in the press by both supporters and opponents of Marx. The example of Gabriel Deville's abridgement also illustrates how audiences in this era often read the Roy translation through a selection of passages rather than by delving into the complete text. The history of this work's twentieth-century reception also shows that the theoretical discussions it provoked within French Marxism were largely based on an ambivalent relationship with the Lachâtre edition. The apparent legitimacy conferred on upon this edition by Marx's 'authorisation' regularly came into conflict with a concern for philological and conceptual rigour, which instead led to reliance on the German version. No real consensus would ever emerge to settle the question once and for all.

While France was, obviously, the primary focus of the Lachâtre edition's circulation, it would be wrong to view its reception through this prism alone. On the contrary, we should adopt a transnational perspective on this subject, also taking into account its uses far beyond France's own borders. This is true not only for French-speaking Africa but also for Asia: top Communist leaders such as Vietnam's Ho Chi Minh and China's Deng Xiaoping each had some of their political formation in France in the 1920s. Thus, it is necessary to pay attention to the way in which Marx's ideas were at least partly appropriated via the French edition of *Capital, Volume I*, even beyond the Francophone community. Considered by Marx as a work in its own right, distinct from the German edition, the Roy edition has for instance been translated from French into Chinese (first in 1984 and then in 2018). Thus, beyond its own particular value, this edition has played a role in the worldwide dissemination of Marxism, well beyond the post-Paris Commune ambitions of Marx and Lachâtre alone.

Translated from French by David Broder

Notes

1 A full collection of the paper was republished by Hier et Aujourd'hui in 1974.
2 Interview of Patrick Kessel by Jean-Numa Ducange, December 2007.

References

Althusser, Louis (1969a) 'Contradiction and Overdetermination', in *For Marx*, London: Allen Lane, pp. 89–128.

Althusser, Louis (1969b) 'Préface', in Karl Marx, *Le Capital, Volume I*, Paris: Garnier-Flammarion, pp. 7–26.

Althusser, Louis (1970) 'From *Capital* to Marx's Philosophy', in *Reading Capital*, edited by Louis Althusser and Etienne Balibar, London: NLB, pp. 11–70.

Anceau, Éric (2017) *L'Empire libéral. Menaces, chute, postérité*, Paris: Éditions SPM.

Blum, Françoise (2018) 'Marx en Afrique francophone', in *Marx, une passion française*, edited by Jean-Numa Ducange and Antony Burlaud, Paris: La Découverte, pp. 320–9.

Boccara, Paul (1976) 'Introduction', in Karl Marx, *Le Capital. Critique de l'économie politique. Livre premier: le développement de la production capitaliste*, Roy translation, Paris: Éditions sociales, pp. VII–XLVI.

Bouffard, Alix, Feron, Alexandre and Fondu, Guillaume (2017), 'Les éditions françaises du *Capital*', in Michael Heinrich, *Ce qu'est Le Capital de Marx*, edited by Alix Bouffard, Guillaume Fondu and Alexandre Feron, Paris: Éditions sociales, pp. 91–145.

Bouju, Marie-Cécile (2010) *Lire en communiste. Les Maisons d'édition du Parti communiste français 1920-1968*, Rennes: PUR.

Bouju, Marie-Cécile (2018) 'Les maisons d'édition du PCF et Marx en France de 1920 à 1960: du politique au scientifique?', in *Marx, une passion française*, edited by Jean-Numa Ducange and Antony Burlaud, Paris: La Découverte, pp. 124–33.

Cahen, Jacqueline (2018) 'Marx vu de droite (I): quand les économistes français découvraient le *Capital* de Marx', in *Marx, une passion française*, edited by Jean-Numa Ducange and Antony Burlaud, Paris: La Découverte, pp. 285–94.

Cogniot, Georges (1972) 'Le *Capital* et notre combat libérateur', *Cahiers de l'Institut Maurice Thorez*, n. 28: 5–11.

Cordillot, Michel (2010) *Aux origines du socialisme moderne. La Première Internationale, la Commune, l'exil*, Paris: Éditions de l'Atelier.

Deville, Gabriel (1883) *Le Capital de Karl Marx. Résumé et accompagné d'un aperçu sur le socialisme scientifique*, Paris: H. Oriol.

Deville, Gabriel (1905–1906) *L'évolution du Capital*, Ghent: Volksdrukkerij.

Ducange, Jean-Numa (2019) *Jules Guesde. The Birth of Socialism and Marxism in France*, New York: Palgrave.

Fondu, Guillaume and Quétier, Jean (2018) 'Comment traduire Marx en français?', in *Marx, une passion française*, edited by Jean-Numa Ducange and Antony Burlaud, Paris: La Découverte, pp. 113–23.

Gaudin, François (2014) *Maurice Lachâtre, éditeur socialiste (1814-1900)*, Limoges: Lambert-Lucas.

Gaussen, Maurice (1874a) 'Les doctrines de Karl Marx', *La Patrie*, n. 7, 10, 11, 12 September.

Gaussen, Maurice (1874b) *La société internationale des travailleurs et ses doctrines*, Paris: Société des études pratiques d'économie sociale.

Guesnier, Lucie (2016) *La sédimentation des socialismes roumains: identités socialistes et mouvements sociaux dans le contexte de la modernisation du pays, 1878-1916*, dissertation, Paris: Université Paris 1.

Le Moullec-Rieu, Aude (2018) 'Les *Œuvres* de Marx dans la "Bibliothèque de la Pléiade": une consécration paradoxale', in *Marx, une passion française*, edited by Jean-Numa Ducange and Antony Burlaud, Paris: La Découverte, pp. 134–43.

Lindenberg, Daniel (1975) *Le marxisme introuvable*, Paris: Calmann-Lévy.

Marx, Karl (1924), *Le Capital: Le procès de la production du capital*, Paris: Alfred Costes.

Marx, Karl (1938–1939) *Le Capital. Critique de l'économique politique. Livre premier: le développement de la production capitaliste*, Paris: Bureau d'éditions.

Marx, Karl (1963) *Œuvres I – Économie I*, Paris: Gallimard.

Marx, Karl (1983) *Le Capital. Critique de l'économie politique (Quatrième édition allemande). Livre premier. Le Procès de production du capital*, edited by J.P. Lefebvre, Paris: Messidor/Éditions sociales.

Prochasson, Christophe (2005) 'L'invention du marxisme français', in *Histoire des gauches en France,* vol. I, edited by Jean-Jacques Becker and Gilles Candar, Paris: La Découverte, pp. 426–43.

Rubel, Maximilien (1963) 'Notice: *Le Capital. Livre premier* (1867)', in Karl Marx, *Œuvres I – Économie I*, Paris: Gallimard, pp. 537–41.

Sybel, Heinrich von (1872) *Die Lehren des heutigen Socialismus und Communismus*, Bonn: Max Cohen & Sohn.

11 A Tale of Two Translations

A Comparison of the Roy-Marx and Lefebvre Translations of *Capital, Volume I*

Alix Bouffard and Alexandre Feron

Introduction

The two main French translations of *Capital, Volume I,* were published more than a hundred years apart: on the one hand, Joseph Roy's translation, 'entirely revised' by Karl Marx (1872–75), and on the other hand, the collective translation directed by Jean-Pierre Lefebvre[1] (Marx 1983 and revised in Marx 2016). While the Roy-Marx translation has long enjoyed and still enjoys massive distribution (because of Marx's authority, its being in the public domain and easily publishable in paperback editions at an affordable price, etc.), Lefebvre's translation is gradually gaining importance in the French-speaking world, on its way to becoming the reference edition of *Capital*.

From the outset, the quality of the 1872–75 translation was subject to contrasting assessments. On the one hand, Marx declared in his correspondence that he had found in Joseph Roy the 'perfect translator' (Marx and Engels 2010: 347) and went so far as to state, in his 'Afterword to the French Edition', that the translation was 'as exact and even literal as possible' and that he recommended the French edition for its 'scientific value independent of the original' (Marx 2010: 24); on the other hand, he sometimes complained about the quality of the translation and the rewriting work he was obliged to do. If one compares the published text of the French edition with the second (1872) and fourth German editions (1890), in light of current translation requirements and practices, one might think that the problem was that the proposed translation took too many liberties with the German text, leaving out conceptual distinctions or translating the same concept in different ways, sometimes in the same passage – leading to an impoverished and simplified text. Strikingly, however, Marx's correspondence suggests that it is precisely the opposite: what Marx criticizes in the translation Roy sends him is its literalness and the presence of Germanisms,[2] which, according to him, are likely to hinder the French reception of his work. It is therefore reasonable to suppose that Marx, in his systematic and meticulous rewriting, is largely responsible for the discrepancies and simplifications found in the French edition of 1872–75. As Marx took the French to be a more political than philosophical people, 'ever impatient to arrive at conclusions' (Marx 2010: 23), he may have thought

DOI: 10.4324/9781003336365-14

it important to get to the point, and thus forego rendering the conceptual systematicity of semantic networks, the subtle theoretical distinctions, or the background of Hegel's philosophical framework. Later, both Marx's and especially Engels' judgement on the French translation grew much harsher. In 'How not to translate Marx' (a critique of an English translation of *Capital*), Engels formulates much more rigorous requirements for future translators (e.g., that 'a technical term has to be rendered always by one and the same equivalent' [Engels 2010: 336]) and comes closer to our current translation standards in many respects. It is in line with those standards that the team gathered around Jean-Pierre Lefebvre proposed in 1983 a new French translation of *Capital, Volume I*, based on Engels' fourth edition of 1890: their objective was to render, in a much more rigorous way than the Roy-Marx translation, the force of Marx's analyses and thus to shed new light on the theoretical depth of his work, thereby laying the foundations for new interpretations and appropriations of Marx's critique of political economy.

The aim of our chapter is to compare, not the two editions (since the texts are not identical) but the two French translations of *Capital, Volume I*.[3] With the specific difficulties involved in translating *Capital* into French in mind, our aim is to explain the different choices that were made and to evaluate the respective merits of the two translations.

We will begin by examining the way the two translations position themselves regarding the systemic character of the semantic networks at the level of conceptual construction; then we will look at the differing treatments of Marx's conceptual framework concerning the type and degree of reality of things; finally, we will present the two different options taken with respect to the Hegelian conceptual framework.

Marx' semantic and conceptual architecture

To build a rigorous conceptual network capable of analysing the capitalist mode of production, Marx is able to take advantage of linguistic possibilities specific to German. In particular, he can forge compound words by merging a noun with its determination; whereas, in other languages, the whole must remain split between a noun and an adjective. Marx is therefore able to construct conceptual networks based on semantic networks, producing a sense of parallelism and symmetry between certain concepts and phenomena. Thus, we find a rich 'horizontal' network derived from '-*form*': *Wertform* [value form],[4] *Warenform* [commodity form], *Geldform* [money form] (but also *Erscheinungsform* [form of appearance], *Existenzform* [form of existence], etc.). This network can then be complexified with the constitution of a 'vertical' chain, where the first elements are held constant while the second element varies – as we see with the chain *Warenform, Warenfunktion*, and so on (completed in the following volumes of *Capital* by *Warenkapital, Warenhandlungskapital*, etc.), or the chain *Geldform, Geldfunktion* (and then *Geldkapital, Geldhandlungskapital*, etc.). Such a network is also found in the series constituted from the prefix *Mehr-*: *Mehrarbeit, Mehrprodukt, Mehrwert*.

This is a real difficulty for any translator of a foreign language, especially French, where the ability to forge new words is particularly limited – even if this practice has tended to become more acceptable in philosophy during the 20th century. There is a great risk of making Marx's subtle semantic and conceptual architecture invisible. The Roy-Marx translation does not attempt to render the semantic network in a systematic way: while *Warenform* and *Geldform* are translated by a somewhat unusual phrase in French '*forme marchandise* [commodity form]' and '*forme argent/forme monnaie* [money form]', *Wertform* is rendered by '*forme de la valeur* [form of value]'.[5] This not only breaks the parallel but introduces an ambiguity: the formula could be understood as referring to the form that value *takes* (implying that value has a reality and an existence independent of the form it may take), whereas actually it refers to the form that value *is* (value is first and foremost a certain form). Similarly, the *Warenform* is not the form that the commodity *takes*, but the form that the commodity *is*; the *Geldform* is not the form that money *takes*, but the form that money *is* – and this is in contrast to value in the circuit of capital, which then *takes on* the *Warenform* and the *Geldform* at different moments. The team led by Jean-Pierre Lefebvre seeks to push the systematicity of the translation and the semantic parallel as far as possible. Thus, a compound word with a hyphen[6] was created to render the German compound word: *Wertform* becomes '*forme-valeur* [value-form]', *Warenform*, '*forme-marchandise* [commodity-form]', *Geldform*, '*forme-argent* [money-form]'.

From these coordinates, we can understand the debate that took place in France from the end of the 1970s concerning the translation of the crucial concept of *Mehrwert* – a neologism coined by Marx to designate the part of the value produced that exceeds the initial value invested in the production process, and which Marx explicitly presents as equivalent to the English 'surplus value'.[7] The Roy-Marx translation proposes to translate this concept as '*plus-value*', a term that had long existed in the French language to designate the extra value that the sale of a thing generates compared to its purchase. In a 1978 article, 'Plus-value ou survaleur?'[8] Étienne Balibar and Jean-Pierre Lefebvre (1978) launched the debate on the translation of *Mehrwert* by criticizing Roy-Marx's choice and proposing the neologism '*survaleur*'. They justified this proposal (which was later adopted in 1980 for the translation of the *Grundrisse* and then in 1983 for *Capital, Volume I*) by showing that *Mehrwert* is part of a double conceptual series – the one built from *Mehr-* and the one built from *-wert*. However, according to them, the French term '*plus-value*' makes us lose the link with each of these two semantic chains. The term '*survaleur*', on the other hand, sheds light on the process that starts with the existence of '*surtravail*' (*Mehrarbeit* – surplus labour), that is, work done beyond that which produces the goods whose value corresponds to the worker's wage, work which thus generates the '*surproduit*' (*Mehrprodukt* – surplus product), which can then be sold to realize the '*survaleur*' (*Mehrwert* – surplus value). In the same way, *survaleur* immediately refers to the conceptual network constructed by Marx from '*valeur*' (*Wert* – value): '*forme-valeur*' (*Wertform* – form of value), '*valeur d'échange*' (*Tauschwert* – exchange value), *'grandeur de la value'* (*Wertgröße* – magnitude of value), *'valorisation'* (*Verwertung* – valorization), and so on. The initially strange character of the neologism *'survaleur'* would also have the virtue of underscoring the originality of the Marxian concept of *Mehrwert* and what separates it from classical political economy. Lefebvre's team could thus be understood as simply following Engels' advice: 'new-coined German terms require the coining of corresponding new terms in English' (Engels 2010: 336). While this translational choice would trigger significant criticism, particularly from the translator Gilbert Badia,[9] it has since become increasingly accepted in the French-speaking world.[10]

In this way, the Lefebvre translation, though it disrupts certain habits and has much more technical allure, does represent undeniable progress in terms of conceptual rigor compared to the Roy-Marx translation. Still, the Lefebvre translation's quest for systematization is hardly complete – and some Marxian concepts remain as invisible in the 1983 translation as in the 1872–75 rendering. One example is the concept of *Warenkörper*, the 'body of the commodity', that is, the commodity as a physical material body (not as a form) – a dimension that plays a crucial role, especially in the first chapters of *Capital*, since it is this physical dimension of the commodity that will allow it to receive and express the value of another commodity (and never its own value). But neither Roy-Marx nor Lefebvre seem to identify this term as a concept, and they translate it differently in different passages.[11] As a result, this concept is largely invisible and impossible to thematise as such for a French-speaking reader.

But the most difficult term to translate systematically and coherently into French, because of its importance in Marx's analysis, is probably *Geld*, as well as its compounds and derivatives. Indeed, unlike the English word *money*, which corresponds perfectly to *Geld*, French has two words, *'argent'* and *'monnaie'*, each of which contains certain meanings of the German term, without either of them rendering it perfectly. Marx himself points out this difficulty in a footnote commenting on the choice of translating the title of section D of chapter 1, III as 'Forme monnaie ou argent [Money form]':

> La traduction exacte des mots allemands 'Geld, Geldform' présente une difficulté. L'expression: 'forme argent' peut indistinctement s'appliquer à toutes les marchandises sauf les métaux précieux. On ne saurait pas dire, par exemple, sans amener une certaine confusion dans l'esprit des lecteurs : 'forme argent de l'argent', ou bien 'l'or devient argent'. Maintenant l'expression 'forme monnaie' présente un autre inconvénient, qui vient de ce qu'en français le mot 'monnaie' est souvent employé dans le sens de pièces monnayées.[12]

(Marx 1948–50: 82)

If in economics one speaks of a *'théorie de la monnaie* [theory of money]' (or *'théorie monétaire* [monetary theory]'), *'monnaie'* most often refers either to 'change' (*'petite monnaie'*) or to 'currency' (*'devise'*) – which corresponds in part to what Marx is aiming at. Marx's analysis consists in identifying a *Geldform* at a different level of generality, one that is capable of shedding light on the functioning of capitalism as a particular mode of production or social formation. The option chosen by Roy-Marx was therefore '*d'employer alternativement les mots "forme monnaie" et "forme argent" suivant les cas, mais toujours dans le même sens* [To use the words "*forme monnaie*" and "*forme argent*" alternately, depending on the case, but always in the same sense]' (Marx 1948–50: 82). As a result, while chapter 3 is titled 'La monnaie ou la circulation des marchandises [Money, or the Circulation of Commodities]', it is the term '*argent*' and its abbreviation 'A' that are preferred in the formulas describing circulation ($W - G - W$, $G - W - G$, etc. are rendered as $M - A - M$, $A - M - A$, etc. [C – M – C, M – C – M, etc.]) and more broadly in the passages theorizing the movement of capital (thus the second section is titled 'La Transformation de l'argent en capital [The Transformation of Money into Capital]'). In the 1983 translation, the team led by Lefebvre, after bitter debate, did not depart from tradition and used alternatively '*monnaie*' or '*argent*' to translate *Geld* (sometimes in the same passage, which may well create confusion), while still preferring '*argent*'. On the other hand, in the revised 2016 version, Lefebvre not only opts for coherence but actually decides against the preference given to '*argent*' until then: *Geld* (as well as its compounds and derivatives) is systematically translated by '*monnaie*' (cf. Marx 2016: VIII–IX), which certainly does eliminate the back-and-forth, but at the cost of losing the level of generality at which Marx places his analysis, and substantially modifies the classical formulas of the market and capitalist circulation (which become $Ma - Mo - Ma$, $Mo - Ma - Mo$, etc. [C – M – C, M – C – M, etc.])

The difficulty of rendering the consistency of what is real

Now, in addition to making use of the resources of the German language to place a series of phenomena into a semantic network, like other German philosophers, Marx also relies on the existence in German of a large number of synonyms or quasi-synonyms in order to fix certain conceptual differences. By contrast, the French translator usually has only one word at his disposal to translate these German words. As such, he or she is forced either to find an artifice to make the German conceptual distinction visible or to make the distinction disappear, and thus impoverishing Marx's analysis. We will examine the different approaches to this issue taken by Roy-Marx and Lefebvre, by focusing on the problems raised in translating the vocabulary that seeks to render the consistency of things (their type of reality, their way of appearing, and their processual character).

Marx is in fact concerned with describing and precisely designating what we could call the ontological consistency of things or the different types of reality that things can have. He thus distinguishes between, on the one hand, the *Dinglichkeit* (*dinglich*) or *Sachlichkeit* (*sachlich*) – terms used as synonyms – which refer to an entity that has the mode of the reality of a physical and material thing (*Ding*), and which is consequently something tangible (*handgreifend*) or sensible (*sinnlich*), and, on the other hand, the *Gegenständlichkeit*. The latter refers to the specific type of reality social objects possess, namely a type of reality which does not belong to the order of the physical and material that we can touch or perceive by our senses (being thereby situated beyond sense experience, *übersinnlich*), and yet nevertheless has undeniable objectivity making them independent from subjects and irreducible to a simple imaginary projection or an act of belief shared by individuals. Thus Marx speaks of *Wertgegenständlichkeit* to designate the type of reality or ontological consistency of value, insofar as this *Gegenständlichkeit* of value is not that of a physical thing that can be observed (it is not by analysing the physical properties of the commodity that one will find its 'value'; the value has nothing *dinglich* or *sachlich*), but a social type of objectivity, existing and having consistency only within the commodity world (*Warenwelt*), that is, a social formation where certain material things are always already put in relation to each other and thus constituted as goods. The *Gegenständlichkeit* of a commodity is the result of a *Vergegenständlichung* of human labour, that is, of a constitution by human labour of a physical entity as a commodity, thus as a bearer of value. The commodity is thus as *Warenkörper* an entity that can be characterized as *dinglich* and therefore *sinnlich*, but as *Warenform* an entity that is *gegenständlich* and *übersinnlich* – hence its paradoxical characterization by Marx as '*ein sinnlich übersinnliches Ding*'.

This distinction plays a decisive role in the analysis of fetishism, that is, of the illusions produced by the *Wertform*, and more broadly in appreciating Marx's materialism. Yet it is not rendered by the Roy-Marx translation, which does not distinguish between *Dinglichkeit* and *Gegenständlichkeit* and in these passages usually omits any characterization of reality, or evokes in an indistinct way the '*matériel* [material]' character of entities or refers to them as '*choses* [things]'. The Lefebvre translation, on the other hand, allows the reader to distinguish between these two types of reality: *dinglich* and *sachlich* are often translated as '*matériel* [material]', whereas *Gegenständlichkeit* is systematically translated as '*objectivité* [objectivity]' (*Vergegenständlichung* as '*objectivation* [objectification]', etc.). The very status of Marx's materialism appears in a completely different light in the two translations: whereas the Roy-Marx translation may favour a reductive conception of what Marx means by matter (on the model of the physical thing), Lefebvre's translation allows for a better grasp of the specificity of historical materialism. The latter is an analysis of social and historical structures, which as social entities have an 'objectivity' that must be distinguished from the 'materiality' of the physical things that carry them. The newer translation thus makes it possible to highlight the double dimension of human labour, insofar as it forms, on the one hand, the 'materiality' of the commodity (the useful and concrete labour that produces use value) and, on the other hand, the 'objectivity' of the commodity (value that can then vary according to the variations of the labour time socially necessary to produce that commodity). In this sense, labour is indeed 'objectified' in value, but not 'materialized' in it.

However, if the commodity is both *Warenkörper* and *Warenform*, it appears to the senses only in its physical and material dimensions. One of the issues of the early chapters of *Capital* is precisely to understand how a commodity can appear *as a commodity*. This is what leads Marx to deploy a very rich and subtle analysis of the ways in which entities appear – distinctions that are largely absent in the Roy-Marx translation, whereas they are far more respected in Lefebvre's translation, even though it does not always take this systematization effort all the way. Thus, Marx, rather than using the vocabulary of being (a thing '*is*' this or that), speaks instead in terms of appearing: he writes, for example, that entities *erscheinen als* … or *zeigen sich als* …, that is, he tries to restore their *Erscheinungsformen*. Though Lefebvre always translates *erscheinen als* … as '*apparaître en tant que/comme* … [appearing as]' (whereas the Roy-Marx translation uses multiple formulations: '*s'annoncer comme* … [to announce itself as]', '*se manifester comme* … [to manifest itself as]', etc.), it ends up losing the proximity with the *Erscheinungsform* by translating this term by '*forme phénoménale* [phenomenal form]' (whereas Roy-Marx sometimes opt for '*forme d'apparition* [form of appearance]'). Marx then distinguishes this modality of appearance from what he designates with the verb *darstellen*, which refers to the way a thing presents, not one of its own determinations, but a determination belonging to another thing. Thus, a commodity is in a relation of *Darstellung* when it presents the value of another commodity by functioning as a mirror of value (*Wertspiegel*) – a relation that, both in Lefebvre and in Roy-Marx, is rendered by a great variety of formulas ('*présenter* [to present]', '*représenter* [to represent]', '*exposer* [to exhibit]', etc.). Marx further distinguishes this *Darstellung* from *Vorstellung*, that is, from an ideal or mental representation, for example, when the possessor of a commodity, in the absence of another commodity that could present (*darstellen*) its value to him, must represent to himself (*sich vorstellen*) the money value of his commodity. Thus, as a 'measure of values', the price or *Geldform* of commodities is an '*ideelle oder vorgestellte Form*', which Roy-Marx translates as '*quelque chose d'idéal* [something ideal]' (Marx 1948–50: 105), while Lefebvre is closer to the text with '*forme idéelle ou imaginée* [ideal or imagined form]' (Marx 2016: 108). In this whole passage, however, Lefebvre reduces *Vorstellung* [representation] to imagination, which then causes him to lose the distinction Marx makes from the *imaginäre Preisform*, the '*forme-prix imaginaire* [imaginary price-form]' (Marx 2016: 116): in the former case, the price is the 'expression' (*Ausdruck*) of the value of the commodity, in the latter case, one is dealing with a commodity of a particular type (such as land, water, honour, consciousness, etc.) which, not being the objectification of any human labour, does not have 'value': it is therefore necessary to 'imagine' a certain price for it. Thus, although the systematicity of Marx's conceptual distinctions for describing the modalities of appearing is not fully rendered by Lefebvre, his translation once again shows its superiority over Roy-Marx's by offering the Francophone reader much greater insight into the richness and precision of Marx's analyses.

The need to precisely render the distinctions made by Marx for describing the reality of entities and the way they appear is all the more important given the capitalist world's constant transformation. The processual and dynamic nature of Marx's analysis is a new challenge for French translators. This is evidenced first by the difficulty of translating the very term *Prozeß* (spelled '*Process*' by Marx), which is found in the very title of Volume I, 'Der Produktionsprocess des Kapitals [The Process of Production of Capital]', of the very important chapter 5 'Arbeitsprocess und Verwertungsprocess [The Labor Process and the Valorisation Process]', or the seventh section 'Der Akkumulationsprocess des Kapitals [The Process of Accumulation of Capital]' – a term that Marx makes considerable use of throughout the book. Marx points out the difficulty in a footnote of the French edition commenting on the first occurrence of the translation of *Arbeitsprozeß* as '*procès de travail* [labor process]':

> En allemand Arbeits-Process (Procès de travail). Le mot procès, qui exprime un développement considéré dans l'ensemble de ses conditions réelles, appartient depuis longtemps à la langue scientifique de toute l'Europe. En France, on l'a d'abord introduit d'une manière timide sous sa forme latine – processus. Puis, il s'est glissé, dépouillé de ce déguisement pédantesque, dans les livres de chimie, physiologie, etc., et dans quelques œuvres de métaphysique. Il finira par obtenir ses lettres de grande natur-alisation. Remarquons en passant que les Allemands, comme les Français, dans le langage ordinaire, emploient le mot « procès » dans son sens juridique. [13]
>
> (Marx 1948–50: 181)

Although Marx explicitly gives his preference here for the translation of *Prozeß* by '*procès*' (rather than '*processus*') with reference to the (common or pedantic) use of the terms at the time, the Roy-Marx translation still very often proposes other translations, when it does not omit the reference to processuality altogether. Thus, the title of Volume I becomes 'Le Développement de la pro-duction capitaliste [The Development of Capitalist Production, translating *Der Produktionsprocess des Kapitals*]', chapter 7's[14] 'La Production de valeurs d'usage et la production de la plus-value [The Production of Use Values and the Production of Surplus Value, translating *Arbeitsprocess und Verwertungsprocess*]', section 7's 'L'Accumulation du capital [The Accumulation of Capital, translating *Der Akkumulationsprocess des Kapitals*]'. While the term '*procès*' is often used to translate global processes such as the '*procès de production* [production process]' or the '*procès de reproduction* [reproduction process]', it is most often replaced when it comes to human activity, for example, when *Arbeitsprozeß* becomes '*production de valeur d'usage* [production of use value]' and *Verwertungsprozeß* becomes '*pro-duction de la plus-value* [production of surplus value]'. In other situations, *Prozeß* is rendered as '*phénomène* [phenomenon]', '*mouvement* [movement]', or even '*acte* [act]', as evidenced by the translation of the following famous passage, often cited today in writings about Marx's ecology,

> Die Arbeit ist zunächst ein Proceß zwischen Mensch und Natur, ein Proceß, worin der Mensch seinen Stoffwechsel mit der Natur durch seine eigne That vermittelt, regelt und kontrolirt. Er tritt dem Naturstoff selbst als eine Naturmacht gegenüber.[15]
>
> (Marx 1987: 192; Marx 1991: 162)

This passage (identical in the second and fourth German editions) is rendered in the Roy-Marx translation as follows:

> *Le travail est de prime abord un acte qui se passe entre l'homme et la nature. L'homme y joue lui-même vis-à-vis de la nature le rôle d'une puissance naturelle* [Labor is primarily an act that takes place between man and nature. In it man himself plays vis-à-vis nature the role of a natural power].
>
> (Marx 1948–50: 180)

Not only does the *Prozeβ* become '*acte* [act]' in French but also the analysis of what this process consists of, namely a *Stoffwechsel mit der Natur*, an exchange of material with nature, disappears entirely.

The Lefebvre translation presents an undeniable step forward in this respect. The term *Prozeβ* is always translated and always in the same way. However, whereas in 1983 Lefebvre's team chooses to respect Marx's preference for the term '*procès*' ('*Le Procès de production capitaliste* [The Process of Capitalist Production]', '*Procès de travail et procès de valorisation* [Labor Process and Valorization Process]', '*Le procès d'accumulation du capital* [The Process of Capital Accumulation]', etc.), in 2016 Lefebvre agrees with L. Hetzel (2021) in judging that the argument put forward by Marx is no longer valid today and that the use of the terms in French has even reversed in comparison to 1872–1875: '*processus*' is now the more widespread term, while '*procès*' is archaic and little used (Marx 2016: XV). Thus, *Process* is now systematically translated as '*processus*', as well as its derivatives (*processirende* by 'processual [processual]' etc.), so that the passage quoted above is rendered as:

> *Le travail est d'abord un processus qui se déroule entre l'homme et la nature, un processus dans lequel l'homme règle et contrôle son métabolisme avec la nature par la médiation de sa propre action* [Labor is primarily a process that takes place between man and nature, a process in which man regulates and controls his metabolism with nature through the mediation of his own action].
>
> (Marx 2016: 175. Emphasis added)

Here again, the translation made by Lefebvre's team proves to be more capable of restoring the way Marx analyses capitalism as a dynamic and temporal process with its own logic of development.

The status of Marx's Hegelianism in *Capital*

But the risk for any translation that aims to be scientific and rigorous is the 'over-conceptualization of language' (Bouffard 2019: 241–2), which especially involves positing that every linguistic difference is necessarily a conceptual difference that must be rendered in the translation by two distinct terms. This assumption is particularly problematic when moving from a language relatively rich in synonyms (like German, but also English) to a language that often has only one word to designate a thing (like French): the translator is then forced to forge new terms, which can make the text particularly difficult to read at times. It is therefore crucial for the translator to distinguish between true conceptual differences (which must be rendered in the translation) and mere variation in vocabulary (which need not be fixed in different terms). In the case of the translation of *Capital*, this difficulty arises in particular regarding Marx's use of Hegelian concepts. While some Hegelian conceptual distinctions are not relevant in Marx's text (e.g., the distinction between *Dasein* and *Existenz*, *Realität* and *Wirklichkeit*), others are certainly present, even if it may not be easy to identify their status. Are they simple 'coquetries'[16] paying homage to the 'dead dog' that Hegel had become in Germany at the time (Marx 2010: 19)? Are they images or comparisons, whose conceptual importance should not be exaggerated, however illuminating they may be? Or are we dealing with genuine 'operative concepts' (to use Eugen Fink's phrase) without which Marx would not have been able to theorize the deep reality of the capitalist mode of production? Thus, any translation of Marx must take a stand on the question of the place and status of Hegelianism in *Capital*.

Roy-Marx's choice was to erase almost all traces of Hegelian concepts – which is undoubtedly due to Marx not having a high opinion of the philosophical capacities of the French, but also to the fact that Hegel's philosophy was at the time largely unknown in France,[17] and there was no French lexicon of translation of Hegelian concepts. In addition, it's likely that Marx's main goal was to make his theory known in its broad outline, independently of its Hegelian roots. That decision may have had a great impact on the French reception of Marx. One may wonder how much the major theoretical debates around *Capital* (on its philosophical character, on its Hegelianism, on its relationship with the early works, etc.) are rooted in Roy-Marx's choice not to try to render the Hegelian conceptuality.

In the translation by Jean-Pierre Lefebvre and his team, on the other hand, the Hegelian distinctions are much more visible – despite the translators partly belonging to the Althusserian school for whom *Capital*, as a scientific work of Marx's mature period, is emancipated from Hegelianism, whose presence is deemed only residual and anecdotal. The corrected 2016 version further accentuates the visibility of the Hegelian legacy in Marx's work. The Lefebvre translation thus seeks to bring out the Hegelian lexicon mobilized by Marx to describe the relationship between different categories or types of phenomena. This can be seen first with the lexicon of mediation (*Vermittlung*, *vermitteln*, *vermittelst*, etc.). Thus, for example, at the end of chapter 2, Marx seeks to explain the relationship between the constitution of a commodity as money (*Geld*) and all other commodities' ability to express their value. The question is which phenomenon mediates the other. Marx shows that it is not because money exists that all commodities can express their value in it: on the contrary, it is because all commodities express their value in one commodity that it becomes money. However, it seems as if it were the other way around and that money was the real mediation. To explain this illusion, Marx writes: '*Die vermittelnde Bewegung verschwindet in ihrem eignen Resultat and läßt keine Spur zurück*' (Marx 1991: 89). The Roy-Marx translation, '*Le mouvement qui a servi d'intermédiaire s'évanouit dans son propre résultat et ne laisse aucune trace* [The movement that served as intermediary vanishes into its own result and leaves no trace]' (Marx 1948–50: 103), is correct in terms of meaning, but completely eliminates the Hegelian conceptual operator and thus the fact that Marx is implicitly drawing on the Hegelian analysis of mediation. As for the Lefebvre translation, it proposes: '*Le mouvement qui opère la médiation disparaît dans son propre résultat et ne laisse aucune trace* [The movement that performs mediation disappears in its own result and leaves no trace]' (Marx 2016: 92).

The same question arises in relation to the Hegelian concept of presupposition (*Voraussetzung, voraussetzen*), which refers to that which, of a thing not yet fully posited, must necessarily be posited first in order for that thing to come about – and is distinguished from a purely external condition (*Bedingung*). This concept is mobilized at the beginning of chapter 4:[18] '*Die Waarencirkulation ist der Ausgangspunkt des Kapitals. Waarenproduktion und entwickelte Waarencirkulation, Handel, bilden die historischen Voraussetzungen, unter denen es entsteht*'[19] (Marx 1991: 134). Roy-Marx renders *historischen Voraussetzungen* [historical presuppositions] by the formula '*n'apparaît que là où* [only appears where]' (Marx 1948–1950: 151)[20] – which makes all conceptual traces disappear. The Lefebvre translation opts in 1983 for the '*préalables historiques* [historical preconditions]' (Marx 1983: 165), and in 2016 for '*présupposés historiques* [what is historically presupposed]' (Marx 2016: 145) – which makes the Hegelian reference more visible, although he does not go so far as to translate the term with '*présupposition* [presupposition]'.

In the first chapter of *Capital*, Marx also uses the Hegelian triad of the Singular (*Einzelne*), the Particular (*Besondere*), and the Universal (*Allgemeine*) in his analysis of the development of the *Wertform*. The first moment corresponds to the *einzelne Wertform* (two commodities stand opposite each other and express their value in each other), the second moment to the appearance of the *besondere Äquivalentform* (a series of commodities express their value in one commodity), and the third moment to the *allgemeine Wertform* (all commodities express their value in one). While the translation of *besondere* by 'particulier [particular]' is not a problem and has been adopted by Roy-Marx as well as by Lefebvre, the other two terms are less easy to translate. Indeed, *einzelne* can be translated by '*singulier* [singular]', which allows the Hegelian conceptuality to be heard but has the defect of pointing in French to the idea of a unique or defining quality of a thing (which is not what Marx has in mind); but *einzelne* can also be translated as '*isolé* [isolated]', which conveys the idea of a relation between two commodities that have been cut off or isolated from any link with the other commodities (Marx also says that they are *vereinzelte*), but occludes the reference to Hegel. Roy-Marx abandons the reference to Hegel and generally translates *einzelne* as 'simple' (without making the difference with *einfache*) and *vereinzelte* as '*isolée* [isolated]'; whereas Lefebvre preserves the reference to Hegel and translates as '*singulier* [singular]' and '*singularisée* [singularized]'.

Finally, the term *allgemeine* can be translated by '*général* [general]' or by '*universel* [universal]'. However, while Roy-Marx opts for the translation of *allgemeine Wertform* by '*forme valeur générale* [general value form]', Lefebvre is considerably more hesitant and oscillates between the two possible translations of *allgemeine* (he even feels obliged to explain this in a footnote. Cf. Marx 1983: 76; Marx 2016: 68). Thus, although the title of point C is '*La forme-valeur générale* [The General Value-Form]', in the course of the analyses he frequently uses '*forme-valeur universelle* [universal value-form]'. Throughout the book, Lefebvre mostly favours the translation by '*général*', which is not without its problems, since in order to maintain the distinction with the term *überhaupt* [in general], he is led to translate the latter by '*tout court* [simply]'. The rigorous and philosophical meaning of the latter term as well as its philosophical filiation (through the Kant's 'object in general', for example) disappears, which is not the case in the Roy-Marx's translation (which opts for '*en général* [in general]'). Thus, a crucial concept such as *menschliche Arbeit überhaupt* remains unclear when it is rendered by Lefebvre as '*travail humain tout court* [simply human labor]'. The expression actually means undifferentiated human labour – labour that has been stripped of all its particularities.

Thus, the Lefebvre translation is overall much more attentive to Marx's Hegelian intertextuality and has genuinely seeks to allow the Francophone reader to identify the Hegelian conceptuality that Marx draws on – and it does so while largely avoiding the pitfall of over-conceptualization.

Conclusion

At the end of this comparison between the two main French translations of *Capital, Volume I*, it appears undeniable that the 1983 translation of the team led by Jean-Pierre Lefebvre is superior in its concern to render in the most faithful, rigorous, and systematic way possible, the complex semantic and conceptual architecture of Marx's text, the manifold distinctions made by Marx to differentiate types of reality and appearance, as well as the Hegelian philosophical heritage which Marx continues to mobilize in his theoretical masterpiece. However, the Lefebvre translation is at the same time more technical and philosophical than the Roy-Marx translation, and hence somewhat more difficult to read for a non-specialized audience. In the 1872–1875 Roy translation revised by Marx, the major concern was, on the contrary, not so much the perfect rendering of Marx's text with all its philosophical subtilities, but the widest possible dissemination of Marx's ideas in France, especially among the working class. And in order to attain such an objective, Marx was ready to give up on some of his conceptual and analytical distinctions. For more than a hundred years, the French audience therefore massively read and studied a slightly simplified version of *Capital, Volume I*. But, with the diffusion of political and philosophical Marxism in France during the 20th century, the French readership became better acquainted with Marx's ideas and was more eager to have access to a more rigorous rendering of *Capital, Volume I*. Louis Althusser's teachings insisted upon this point among the new generations of post-war France and it is therefore no surprise that Lefebvre's team was largely based at the Ecole Normale supérieure.

Hence, the quality of a translation cannot be measured in an absolute way: it must always be referred to the translation's target audience – an audience that is necessarily historically, socially, and politically situated. Moreover, as the translator and translation theorist Jean-René Ladmiral (2000) reminds us, we have to distinguish between a *first translation*, which aims first and foremost to make a work exist in a particular linguistic space (which necessarily implies certain compromises and adaptations to the habits and expectations of an audience unfamiliar with the work, and thus a possible simplification of the original text), and a *retranslation*, which takes place in a linguistic space where the work already exists, where the author's thought is already known, and has been the subject of debate and discussion. The translation can then accept to lose readability in order to gain precision – and thus address a more specialized and demanding audience.

This is what fundamentally opposes the two principles of the French translation of *Capital, Volume I*. Whereas the Roy-Marx translation in 1872–75 was primarily intended to *make Marxism exist in France*, Lefebvre's translation in 1983 and 2016 can draw on more than a hundred years of Marxist reception in France, in order to offer a translation capable of responding to the various questions and difficulties that have arisen from interpretative debates, as well as from the evolution of the historical and political situation. This is why a translation is always historically situated, and why no translation can ever claim to be definitive.

Notes

1 The twenty translators in the team were: Étienne Balibar, Gérard Cornillet, Geneviève Espagne, Michel Espagne, Luc Favre, François-Marie Gathelier, Vincent Jezewski, Françoise Joly, Jean-Baptiste Joly, Elisabeth Kaufmann, Marie-Odile Lauxerois, Jean-Louis Lebrave, Jean-Pierre Lefebvre, François Mathieu, Jean-Philippe Mathieu, Jacques Poumet, Philippe Préaux, Régine Roques, Michaël Werner, and Françoise Willmann.

2 See, in particular, the letter to Sorge on 23 May 1872 (Marx and Engels 2010: 377) or the letter to Danielson on 28 May 1872 (Marx and Engels 2010: 385).

3 In order to determine what is a difference in edition and a difference in translation, we have systematically compared the two French translations with the second and fourth German editions (published in MEGA²/6 [Marx 1987] and II/10 [Marx 1991]) and made extensive use of the Apparat of MEGA Volume II/7 (cf. in particular 'Verzeichnis von Abweichungen', Marx 1989: 757–933).

4 The spelling used by Marx (and reproduced as such in the MEGA) is no longer in use today. Thus, he writes *Werth*, *Waare*, or *Process*, rather than *Wert*, *Ware*, or *Prozeβ*. When we refer to German terms, we adopt the modernized spelling, except when quoting Marx's text.

5 But not systematically. It is sometimes translated by '*forme valeur*'.

6 In the 1983 edition, the hyphen is not used systematically. This was corrected in the 2016 edition.

7 '*Dieses Inkrement oder den Ueberschuβ über den ursprüngliche Werth nenne ich – Mehrwerth (surplus-value)*' (Marx 1991: 137). English translation: 'This increment or excess over the original value I call "surplus value"' (Marx 2010: 161).

8 Cf. also Lefebvre's introduction to the 1983 edition (Marx 2016: LII–LIV).

9 For a bibliographic overview of these debates, see for example Bouffard, Feron, Fondu (2017: 116).

10 The Grande édition de Marx et d'Engels (GEME), founded in 2009, has adopted the translation of *Mehrwert* by '*survaleur*'.

11 In Roy-Marx, the term is not always translated, and when it is, we find: '*corps de la marchandise*', '*matière marchande*', and so on. In Lefebvre, we find '*corps de la marchandise*', '*marchandise concrète*', '*marchandise comme corps*', '*denrée matérielle*', '*nature corporelle*', and so on.

12 This endnote is not included in the Lefebvre translations of 1983 and 2016, nor in the English translation of *Capital*. The passage of the footnote quoted above could be translated as follows:

> The exact translation of the German words '*Geld, Geldform*' presents a difficulty. The expression '*forme argent*' can be applied indiscriminately to all goods except precious metals. One could not say, for example, without causing some confusion in the mind of the reader: '*forme argent [money] de l'argent [silver]*', or '*l'or [gold] devient argent [silver-money]*'. Now the expression '*forme monnaie*' has another disadvantage, which comes from the fact that in French the word '*monnaie*' is often used in the sense of coins.

13 The footnote does not figure in the English translation. It could be translated as follows: 'In German *Arbeits-Process* [Labor Process]. The word "*procès* [process]", which expresses a development considered in all its real conditions, has long belonged to the scientific language of all Europe. In France, it was first introduced in a timid way in its Latin form – "*processus* [process]". Then, stripped of this pedantic disguise, it was slipped into books on chemistry, physiology, etc., and into some works of metaphysics. Eventually it will obtain its letters of grand naturalization. Let us note in passing that the Germans, like the French, in ordinary language, use the word "*procès* [trial]" in its legal sense'.

14 The chapter numbers in the 1872–75 French edition is not identical to the chapter numbers in the German editions (and hence in Lefebvre's translation of the fourth German edition). Chapter 7 here corresponds to chapter 5.

15 'Labour is, in the first place, a process in which both man and Nature participate, and in which man of his own accord starts, regulates, and controls the material reactions between himself and Nature' (Marx 2010: 187).

16 'Here and there, in the chapter on the theory of value, [I] coquetted with the modes of expression peculiar to him [Hegel]' (Marx 2010: 19).

17 Vera's translations (*Logic, Philosophy of Nature, Philosophy of Spirit*) were published from 1859 onward and were consulted by Joseph Roy, but he deemed them 'unreadable' (Marx 2016: XXXVI).

18 This example is given in Post (2009).

19 The English translation of this passage is: 'The circulation of commodities is the starting-point of capital. The production of commodities, their circulation, and that

more developed form of their circulation called commerce, these form the historical ground-work [*historischen Voraussetzungen*] from which it rises' (Marx 2010: 157).

20 'La circulation des marchandises est le point de départ du capital. Il *n'apparaît que là où* la production marchande et le commerce ont attient un certain degré de développement' (Marx 1948–50: 151. Our emphasis).

References

Balibar, Étienne and Lefebvre, Jean-Pierre (1978) 'Plus-value ou survaleur?', *La Pensée*, n. 178 (February): 32–42.

Bouffard, Alix (2019) 'De la langue au discours: réflexions sur la traduction de Marx', in *Les Logiques du discours philosophiques en Allemagne de Kant à Nietzsche,* edited by Céline Denat, Alexandre Fillon and Patrick Wotling, Reims: Éditions et Presses universitaires de Reims, pp. 227–47.

Bouffard, Alix, Feron, Alexandre and Fondu, Guillaume (2017) 'Les éditions françaises du Capital', in *Ce qu'est Le Capital de Marx*, edited by Guillaume Fondu, Michael Heinrich and Alexandre Feron Paris: Les éditions sociales, pp. 91–145.

Engels, Friedrich (2010 [1885]) 'How Not to Translate Marx', in *Marx Engels Collected Works*, vol. 26: *Engels 1882-89*, London: Lawrence & Wishart Ltd, pp. 335–40.

Hetzel, Ludovic (2021) 'Appendix on Translation', in *Commenter Le Capital. Livre 1*, Paris: Les éditions sociales, pp. 1065–131.

Ladmiral, Jean-René (2000) 'Traduire des philosophes', in *Traduire les philosophes*, edited by Jacques Moutaux and Olivier Bloch, Paris: Publications de la Sorbonne, pp. 49–73.

Marx, Karl (1948–1950 [1872–1875]) *Le Capital. Critique de l'économie politique. Livre premier. Le développement de la production capitaliste*, 3 volumes, Paris: Éditions sociales.

Marx, Karl (1983) *Le Capital*, Paris: Éditions Sociales.

Marx, Karl (1987 [1872]) *Das Kapital*, in *Marx Engels Gesamtausgabe* (MEGA²), vol. II/6, Berlin: Dietz Verlag.

Marx, Karl (1989 [1872–1875]) *Le Capital*, in *Marx Engels Gesamtausgabe* (MEGA²), vol. II/7, Berlin: Dietz Verlag.

Marx, Karl (1991 [1890]) *Das Kapital*, in *Marx Engels Gesamtausgabe* (MEGA²), vol. II/10, Berlin: Dietz Verlag.

Marx, Karl (2010) '*Capital, vol. I*', in *Marx Engels Collected Works*, vol. 35: *Capital, Vol. I*, London: Lawrence & Wishart Ltd.

Marx, Karl (2016) *Le Capital*, Paris: Les éditions sociales.

Marx, Karl and Engels, Friedrich (2010) *Marx Engels Collected Works*, vol. 44: *Letters 1870-1873*, London: Lawrence & Wishart Ltd.

Post, Laurent (2009) 'L'objet de la traduction', *La Pensée*, n. 360 (October–December): 141–8.

12 The French Edition of *Capital* in Germany, France, Anglophone Countries, and Japan

Babak Amini

An overview of the influence of the French edition in the dissemination of *Capital*

The full picture of the influence of the French edition in the history of the dissemination and reception of *Capital* would need to take a global perspective.[1] This chapter limits the scope of the examination to German – the original language of *Capital*, English – the language of international communication, Japanese – the most translated editions of *Capital* after Russian, and of course, French. To critically examine the novelties and limitations of contemporary debates on the 1872–75 French edition of *Capital* among German, Japanese, Anglophone, and French scholars, it is essential to have a broad understanding of the longer history of the dissemination and reception of *Le Capital* in these countries. Far from a purely scholarly exercise in dissemination studies, such a history illuminates the larger political and intellectual landscape within which various editions of *Capital* and the debates around the French edition emerged. Therefore, the chapter begins with a brief overview of the history of *Capital* in German, Japanese, English, and French, in an effort to trace the influence of the French edition on various editions of *Capital* in these languages.

The dissociation between the German and French editions had already begun when the publication of the third German edition of *Capital* edited by Friedrich Engels and published a few months after Karl Marx's death in 1883.[2] Engels prepared the fourth German edition for publication shortly after the formation of the Second International in 1890, with a few changes based on the French edition. This edition came to be viewed as the authoritative version and was reprinted several times until 1922. Engels' scepticism towards the French edition of *Capital* in general and his editorial choices in preparing his editions in particular are well known and subject to scholarly debates to this day.

In 1913, Karl Kautsky, the leading theoretician of the Second International, was commissioned by the executive committee of the German Social Democratic Party to prepare a 'popular edition [*Volksausgabe*]' of *Capital*. This edition was based on the second German edition (1872) and took a far greater account of the French edition, while also incorporating most of Engels' editorial changes and insertions. This edition was published in 1914, the year when

DOI: 10.4324/9781003336365-15

the Second International collapsed at the outbreak of World War I. As Kautsky's ostracization from the Third International accelerated after the War, his edition of *Capital* was marginalized. Two new German editions of *Capital* appeared in 1932 on the 50th anniversary of Marx's death. One was prepared by the Marx-Engels-Lenin Institute (MELI) in Moscow, and another was edited by the dissident heterodox theoretician, Karl Korsch.[3] The MELI edition essentially produced a 'popular edition' of the fourth German edition, thereby reasserting what was conceived as the correct foundation of scientific socialism. Conversely, Korsch's 'popular edition' was based more strictly on the second German edition, distancing itself from both Engels' editions and the French edition. Given the stature of the MELI in the Third International, its edition was widely viewed as the most authoritative German edition of *Capital* and continued to be reprinted until after World War II.

Thereafter, the fault lines within the political landscape of the divided Germany reflected themselves in the new editions of *Capital,* not along the significance of the French edition per se but the Engelsian and non-Engelsian German editions of *Capital*. In East Germany, a new edition of *Capital* appeared in 1962 as part of the *Marx-Engels-Werke* (MEW), commissioned by the Socialist Unity Party of Germany (SED). In line with the Soviet ideological line, this edition was even more strictly oriented towards Engels editions. In West Germany, two new editions of *Capital* appeared. One was published by Cotta-Verlag in 1962, under the editorial work of Hans-Joachim Lieber and Benedikt Kautsky, and another by Ullstein-Verlag in 1969. Cotta's edition essentially followed Kautsky's edition. The Ullstein edition was modelled after Korsch's edition while also citing the changes made by Engels in the third and fourth editions in footnotes. It was the Ullstein edition that became quite popular in the late 1960s student movement in West Germany, with more than 100,000 copies printed by 1987. Nevertheless, this number pales when compared to the scale of publication of the MEW edition which continues to circulate widely among German-speaking readers to this day. The scholarly edition of Marx's and Engels' works (MEGA[2]) that began in the 1970s published all the preparatory manuscripts of *Capital, Volumes I–III,* and the published editions during the lives of Marx and Engels in 15 volumes from 1976 to 2012. A detailed 50-page appendix was published in 1991 as part of MEGA[2] Volume II/10 which provided a list of textual differences between the third and fourth German and the French editions.

Therefore, the influence of *Le Capital* on the German editions of *Capital* was rather limited and never went beyond the editorial considerations of Engels and Kautsky, both with their own shortcomings and limitations. But this changed in 2017, with the publication of a new edition of *Capital*. Under the editorial work of Thomas Kuczynski, this edition presents the most sustained and daring attempt to reconstruct a version of the book according to all of the editions, personal copies, and editorial instructions prepared by Marx.

The dissemination of *Le Capital* in its native country, France, has a contentious history.[4] Marx's direct intervention in the complete revision of the first French translation of Volume I, translated by Joseph Roy and published by Maurice Lachâtre, naturally gave this edition an authoritative character in France. This edition has been reprinted 10 times since its first publication, totalling approximately 140,000 copies. In 1920, a divide within the French Section of the Workers' International led to the formation of the French Communist Party (PCF) and a rivalry between the communists and socialists over the Marxist legacy. The French socialists embarked on an extensive project of publishing the collected works of Marx and Engels in French. As part of this larger project, the publisher, Alfred Costes, commissioned a new translation of *Capital* by Jules Molitor in 1924 based on the fourth German edition. Due to the inaccuracy of Molitor's translation, it did not become authoritative, leading the publisher to reissue Roy's translation in 1949–50. It was indeed this edition that was used by some of the most influential Marxist intellectuals in France and became a standard edition of Volume I until the 1960s. Even Bureau d'éditions, the publishing house associated with the PCF, published its edition of Volume I in 1938 based on Roy's translation, though after a prolonged contention with the MELI on the issue.

The resistance of communists against the German occupation during the war made the PCF enormously popular after the war, whereby they occupied various influential positions within the political and intellectual landscape in France. At least until the 1960s, the party followed Soviet ideology quite closely but continued to reprint *Capital* through its associated publishing house, *Éditions Sociales*, which printed Roy's translation eight times between 1948 and 1978, totalling tens of thousands of copies.[5] Conversely, the socialist party's interest in publishing Marx's works rapidly declined, especially after the 1950s. Even Moscow's Progress Publishers reprinted Roy's translation in 1965, 1982, and 1986, totalling approximately 30,000 copies. Although these did find their way into militant bookstores, they did not gain as much popularity as the other editions already in circulation among French readers.

The emergence of the New Left in France in the mid-1960s, critical of the PCF, laid the groundwork for the proliferation of dissident Marxist approaches in France. In this context, Maximilien Rubel, one of the most renowned Marxologists in France, who was very critical of the PCF and Soviet Marxism-Leninism, began preparing his edition of Marx's *oeuvre* for the prestigious Éditions Gallimard. Rubel radically distanced himself from Engels' editorial work on Marx's texts because he viewed Engels as the pioneer of 'Marxism', which became the foundation of a rigid ideological stance that was fundamentally at odds with Marx's own open-ended approach. With respect to *Capital* the solution was simply to reproduce Roy's translation. However, even in this case and under the auspices of stylistic improvements, Rubel eliminated and changed the text and inverted the order of the last two chapters. This edition was printed seven times from 1963 to 2008, totalling approximately 40,000 copies.

On the centennial of Marx's death in 1983, Éditions Sociales commissioned a new translation of *Capital* by the Germanist Jean-Pierre Lefebvre based on the fourth German edition. However, the collapse of the Soviet Union impeded the influence of this edition of *Capital* as Marxism in France rapidly declined after 1989, with Éditions Sociales declaring bankruptcy in 1991. Nevertheless, this edition was reissued first in 1993 and then four times from 2006 to 2016, for a total of 12,000 copies.

The first full English translation of *Capital* in 1887 by Samuel Moore and Edward B. Aveling was done under the supervision of Engels. Ernest Untermann, the German American translator of *Capital, Volumes II* and *III*, also revised Volume I based on the fourth German edition. Volume I was translated by Eden Paul and Cedar Paul, both members of the Communist Party of Great Britain, and active members of the Plebs' League, which was instrumental in the popular dissemination of Marx and Marxism in Britain. Their translation, which was based on the fourth German edition, was accompanied by an introduction by G.D.H. Cole, one of the most prominent English Fabian theorists and historians. But even when Allen & Unwin published the second translation, it also published a revised version of Moore and Aveling's translation with supplements that were translated and edited by the British Marxist historian, Dona Torr, who used the fourth German edition. But, at the end of this edition, Torr notably included a list of changes that Marx had made to the last part of the book, 'The Accumulation of Capital', in the French edition.

The most extensive production of the English edition of *Capital* was completed in the Soviet Union. In the 1950s, Moscow became increasingly interested in the systematic publication of Marxist texts in English as a means to bolster the reception of these ideas in the world. The Foreign Languages Publishing House was the first attempt towards this goal, issuing *Capital, Volumes I–III*, from 1954 to 1959. Another Moscow-based publisher was Progress Publishers, founded in 1931, which engaged in printing the English edition of *Capital, Volumes I–III,* from 1956 to 1978 using Aveling and Moore's translation of Volume I. Progress and Foreign Languages Publishing Houses together published Volume I eleven times, for a total of more than 230,000 copies. To this day, it remains the most widely distributed English edition of *Capital*.

After the student uprising and anti-war movement during the second half of the 1960s, which was greatly influenced by the intellectual orientation of the *New Left Review*, and some of the Trotskyist groups, and other outlets rather than the official communist party, interest in *Capital* increased. A few years after the publication of the first English translation of *Grundrisse* in 1973, the *New Left Review* commissioned Ben Fowkes to prepare a new translation of *Capital*. This translation was essentially based on the MEW edition of *Capital*, though it followed the content structure of the French edition, as did the 1887 English edition. The edition of *Capital,* which appeared as Volume 35 of the *Marx and Engels Collected Works* in 1996, was basically the same as the edition previously prepared by Progress Publishers. It included significant textual divergence between the English translation and the German editions, as well as some of the addenda found in the fourth German edition. Therefore, an English edition of *Capital* based on the French edition has yet to be produced. We will have to wait to see the extent to which the French edition will be incorporated into the forthcoming translation of *Capital* by Paul Reitter commissioned by Princeton University Press.

It might be surprising to point out that Japan ranks highest among one of the countries with the greatest number of translations and highest number of printed copies of *Capital* in the world. To date, there have been 11 full editions of *Capital* in Japanese, many of which have been reprinted numerous times in hundreds of thousands of copies with each publication. Prior to World War II, there were numerous attempts to translate *Capital* resulting in two full editions of Volume I. The first, translated by Motoyuki Takabatake based on the fourth German edition, appeared in 1920–21 amidst the impetus created by the Russian Revolution. The second, translated by Fumio Hasebe based on the 1932 MELI edition, came out in 1937, one year before the total ban on the publication or possession of any Marxist literature.

The situation changed dramatically after World War II as Marxism came to be viewed as a symbol of intellectual freedom, thanks to the heroic resistance of communists during the country's fascist period, and became hegemonic within academia in Japan.[6] This situation led to a substantial increase in the dissemination of *Capital* in Japan, with seven full translations of *Capital* being published until 1989 and reprints of all the existing editions together in millions of copies.[7] Itsuro Sakisaka, one of the leading intellectuals of the Social Democratic Party of Japan, published his translation of *Capital* in 1947–49 based on the MELI edition. His revised translation based on the 1962 MEW edition was published in 1967 and soon exceeded one million copies, making it one of the most widely available editions in Japan to this day. The fact that the editorial direction of Sakisaka followed the Soviet Union should not be surprising. The Social Democratic Party of Japan remained ideologically close to Soviet Marxism-Leninism, to an even greater extent than the Japanese Communist Party which in fact distanced itself from the Soviet Union, especially after the Soviet Union's reaction to the 1969 Prague Spring. Jiro Okazaki, who had previously been involved in the translation of *Capital* with Sakisaka, but was controversially sidelined, published his translation of *Capital* in 1961, based on the MEW edition. The two student editions of *Capital* that came out in 1979 (translated by Minoru Miyakawa) and 1982–83 (translated by Minoru Miyakawa) were based on the MEW edition.

Despite the strong influence of the Soviet and East German editions of *Capital* in Japan, Michiho Enatsu broadened the philological field in Japan by translating *Le Capital* (with Masahiko Uesugi) in 1979,[8] the first German edition of *Capital* in 1983, and the second German edition in 1985. This marked the completion of all of the Japanese translations of all the editions of *Capital* that had been published during Marx's life. However, despite the availability of new resources, the rapid decline of Marxism in Japanese academia after 1989 hindered a substantial scholarly debate. Nevertheless, there have been two new translations of *Capital* in 2005 (by Hitoshi Imamura, Kenichi Mishima, and

Tadashi Suzuki) and in 2011 (by Gen Nakamura), each printed in thousands of copies, but both were reverted to the MEW edition.

As this historical overview of the dissemination of *Capital* demonstrates, the influence of the French edition on various translations of *Capital* in Germany, the Anglophone countries, and Japan has been at best marginal. In Germany, at least until Kuczynski's 2017 edition, the editorial politics manifested itself overwhelmingly around the Engelsian editions and the second German edition, with the influence of the French edition playing a proxy role insofar as it was partially incorporated into the former. The English editions of *Capital* all followed more or less the Engelsian editions and failed to pay sustained attention to the French edition. Of all the numerous Japanese translations of *Capital,* only the Enatsu's 1979 edition was centred on the French edition. However, even that edition was a direct translation of *Le Capital*, leaving the complex work of systematic comparison and integrations between different editions to future translations. Even in France, while *Le Capital* continued to enjoy its status as an edition approved by Marx, other translations based on the third and fourth German editions asserted themselves significantly at different points in time.

On the significance of *Le Capital* in the 20th century

Critical reflections on the merits of the French edition of *Capital* had begun prior to its publication, starting with Marx and Engels themselves. But amidst the emerging 'Marxism', the publication of the third German edition and then the fourth edition prepared by Engels, particularly given the way Engels expressed his consideration of the French edition and other relevant material in his possession, quelled the debate. Engels' preface to the first English edition of Volume I provided further assurance to readers of his meticulousness. These certainly contributed to a sense of finality of Engels' editions of Volume I.

Kautsky's edition, which revisited the French edition although rather modestly and without directly challenging Engels' editorial work, did not lead to any debates relating to the significance of the French edition. Furthermore, the appearance of this edition just before the outbreak of World War I, Lenin's polemics against Kautsky in the subsequent years, and the establishment of the MELI in 1919 which became hegemonic within the Communist Movement, made Kautsky's edition far less impactful than those produced by the MELI based on Engels' editions.

The image of the finality of Volume I in France was based not on the Engelsian editions but on the French edition, the last revised and approved edition by Marx that was published during his lifetime. As previously discussed, while this edition was not unchallenged, the first French edition continued to assert itself remarkably in France. While Molitor's translation challenged the status of the first French edition and was indeed the edition used by influential intellectuals such as Maurice Merleau-Ponty and Jean-Paul Sartre, its poor translation quality and lack of systematic comparison between the earlier editions of *Capital* did not lead to substantial debates on the first French edition (see Ducange 2023).

After World War II, one of the leading Marxist-Humanist and feminist philosophers, Raya Dunayevskaya, drew attention to the significance of the French edition of *Capital* in her book, *Marxism and Freedom* (1958), which became influential, especially within the New Left. Her remarks on the French edition did not stem from a philological interest per se. They were rather a part of the much larger thesis of the book to apply Marx's method of analyzing historical developments as a dialectical process from practice to theory onto Marx's own intellectual development and the history of Marxism thereafter. She challenged the false dichotomy between the young Hegelian Marx and the mature scientific Marx by offering a humanist reading of the evolution of Marx's ideas throughout his life. It is in this context that she examined the impact of the Paris Commune on Marx's understanding of commodity fetishism under capitalist social relations. She argued that even though Marx had already expanded on the fetishism of commodity in the first German edition of *Capital* 'it is only *after* the eruption of the Paris Commune that his French edition shifts the emphasis from the fantastic form of appearance to the *necessity* of that form of appearance' (italics in the original; Dunayevskaya 1958: 100). She also underscored the importance of the conceptual distinction between concentration and centralization of capital that Marx made in the French edition for the first time (Dunayevskaya 1958: 100). What is particularly significant in Dunayevskaya's detailed engagement with *Capital* in general is her consideration of the book as an open-ended project that continued to evolve until the last day of Marx's life. Dunayevskaya noted, though largely in passing, the significance of the French edition in various writings afterwards.[9]

She dedicated a section of her 1982 book, *Rosa Luxemburg, Women's Liberation, and Marx's Philosophy of Revolution*, to the topic. Again, this was not a philological but a directly political intervention that was integral to her larger critical project. In this text, she examined aspects of Luxemburg's critique of *Capital, Volume II,* and how they had already been addressed in Volume I, especially if one followed the French edition. She also provided a translation of relevant sections from the French edition that were left out of the first English translation. Therefore, she highlighted the importance of *Le Capital* with respect to the question of colonialism and imperialism.

In the early 1970s, there were some debates among Japanese scholars focusing on the significance of the French edition of *Capital*. These, however, paled in scale and intensity when compared to the larger academia debates on *Capital* in Japan. Kiyoaki Hirata, a professor of economics and a prominent member of the Civil Society School [*Shimin Shakaiha*], paid some attention to the French edition in an effort to distinguish between different forms of private and social properties.[10] His focus on specific passages in the French edition (and their translations in the German and English editions) was rooted in his interest in a theory of property in Marx's writings, socialism as the reestablishment of individual property, and the development of civil society under different social relations.[11] In 1971, Sato Kinzaburo, a professor of economics, published an article that sought to capture the extent of the debate on *Capital* beyond the French edition by discussing Marx's instructions for the 'American' edition. He listed 119 references to textual changes, compared to the second German edition, listed by Marx in 1877 in preparation for an 'American' edition.[12] There were other Japanese scholars,[13] including Enatsu (1976) – the translator of the French edition into Japanese, who published the French edition in this decade. Most of this edition focused on specific aspects of the French edition, often concerning the political-economic categories found in *Capital*.

A notable article in English on the French edition was published in 1983 by the Marxist-Humanist sociologist, Kevin B. Anderson.[14] Strongly critical of Fowkes' English translation of Volume I, Anderson argued that the translation essentially followed the MEW edition and failed to incorporate important changes made in the French edition despite the translator's claim to the contrary. Anderson extended his criticism to Engels' editorial work on Volume I, providing examples of textual changes in different parts in which the French edition contained crucial modifications when compared to other editions. The article concluded its discussion by arguing that 'we should avoid the pitfalls of treating Marx and Engels as the same person, or a single entity as is so common in the literature' (Anderson 1983: 79). His rather polemical style to draw attention in the English language literature to the continued relevance of the French edition was certainly a commendable intervention. However, this short article conflated different aspects of the question: an analysis of the textual changes between the French and other editions of Volume I and their significance in relation to Marx's broader arguments in *Capital*; a philological examination of these changes within the context of Marx's intellectual development in the first half of the 1870s; and a critical study of Engels' editorial work on the subsequent editions of Volume I vis-à-vis the French edition. Indeed, the above conflation remained a recurring characteristic of Anderson's writings in the French edition.

Despite their differences in conceiving the open-ended character of *Capital*, there is an affinity between Anderson and Rubel regarding *Capital* in their attempt to recover a Marx unscathed by later Marxism. As Anderson put it in another article on the topic in an issue of the *Beiträge zur Marx-Engels-Forschung*, for him 'getting a full text of volume one of *Capital* is part of a far larger problem: separating Marx's work from that of the post-Marx Marxists, beginning with Engels' (Anderson 1997: 136). He also criticized the editors of MEGA² for not including all the key textual differences between the French edition and the Engelsian editions of *Capital* and provided a few examples to support his claim. In the quest to purify Marx, the French edition continued to present itself in Anderson's work as a source that can reveal an unknown Marx, hidden since the time of Engels and not fully revealed even after MEGA² editions.

Towards the end of the 1980s and early 1990s, Japanese scholars made a number of contributions to the debate surrounding the later editions of *Capital*.

While a few were published in Japanese university journals (e.g., Nakazima 1987),[15] the most significant ones were published in *Beiträge zur Marx-Engels-Forschung*, a journal linked to MEGA². Due to the nature of that publication, these contributions were quite philological and narrowly focused.[16] For example, Izumi Omura published a number of articles in which he criticized scholars, including the editors of MEGA² at the time, for considering either third or the fourth German editions as the last edition of Volume I. Instead, he argued that Marx's attempts to revise Volume I in 1877 for an 'American' edition should actually be considered the last edition.

In 1989, there were also a few contributions by German Marxlogists on the significance of the French edition. In an article that outlined the history of the development of *Capital* from 1867 to 1890, Rolf Hecker, Jürgen Jungnickel, and Carl-Erich Vollgraf identified three stages in the revisions of Volume I from the point of view of its content, namely, the revision of the second German edition, the completion of the French edition, Marx's preparatory work for the third German edition, and the 'American' edition. They pointed out a number of new formulations in the French edition, including the enrichment of the concept of 'collective worker' and 'expanded reproduction', the distinction between centralization and concentration, the elaboration on alternative historical development, and the role of state power and systems of public debt and taxes in the historical transition to capitalism (Hecker, Jungnickel, Vollgraf 1989: 28–30). In a more focused comparison between the French and second German editions, Bernhard Henschel argued that while Marx made significant changes in the French edition both to enhance the accessibility of the material to French readers and other substantial modifications, he was not completely satisfied with the final result as is evident in his letters to Nikolai Danielson, the translator of the Russian edition of *Capital*.

Overall, the reception of the French edition of *Capital* was largely absent in the first half of the 20th century and appeared only in a scattered manner among the German, Anglophone, Japanese, and French scholars in the second half of the 20th century. In the period after World War II, the debate surrounding the French edition generally focused on two, though not necessarily mutually exclusive, purposes. Some scholars, such as Dunayevskaya and Anderson, used the French edition politically as a way to challenge two fronts simultaneously: the cooptation of the 'scientific Marx' as seen per excellence in *Capital* by the Soviet Union and the East German state and the relative dismissal of *Capital* by significant segments of the New Left in the 1960s and 1970s. In Japan, although the nature of the debates on Marx and *Capital* were generally highly academic, the implications of some of the interventions did have a broader political dimension. This was the case insofar as scholars such as Hirata used the French edition to substantiate their argument towards a vision of socialist property relations as subversively different from what existed under much of the actually existing socialist states at the time.

The French edition was also used in Marxlogical debates. There were some attempts in Japan to use specific aspects of *Capital* as highlighted in the French edition to gain support for comparatively heterodox approaches to the political economy within Japanese academia. However, the most sustained research and scholarly output in this period on the French edition took place around the publication of historical-critical editions of *Capital* in MEGA². Yet, given the political and intellectual context of the time, even this generated very little debate on the French edition.

Recent debates on *Le Capital*

Freed from the inevitable entanglement with the ideological calculus of the actually existing socialism of the 20th century, *Capital* has presented its readers, now equipped with the historical-critical edition in MEGA², with new interpretive horizons. As part of the general revival of debates on Marx, particularly after the 2008 economic crisis, there has been a renewed interest in the French edition of *Capital*.

In a contribution to new readings of Marx, Michael Heinrich, a German Marxist political economist whose books have gained some popularity outside Germany in recent years, argued that the critical edition of *Capital* in MEGA² has made it clear that 'the search for the editorial form which "the author himself wanted" is like chasing a phantom' (Heinrich 2009: 77). Invoking post-structuralist methodological concepts, he proposed that the interpretive work on *Capital* should not be seen as contestation over an unambiguous reading that the text withholds but '*an active process of construction* depending on changing political and discursive conditions' (italics in the original; Heinrich 2009: 77). This was made clearer in a more recent piece in which Heinrich denied that 'in *Capital* there is such a core that can simply "reconstruct" as there are deep ambivalences even in the basic categories of *Capital*' (Heinrich 2018: 18).

Heinrich's interpretive approach conceives of *Capital* as a radically open-ended process. This extends beyond the well-known incompleteness of Volumes II and III and includes Volume I as well. In this view, Volume I on the one hand continued to evolve during Marx's life as Marx made headway in his work on the other volumes of *Capital* and configured Volume I according to new theoretical and empirical reflections, all within changing political contexts. On the other hand, the conceptual inconsistencies that Heinrich has pointed out within the highly complex theoretical arguments of Volume I create a further source of interpretive dynamism that cannot simply be resolved by referring to particular editions of *Capital*. This open-ended process did not end when Marx died or when Engels completed his edition but continued at different wages as the dissemination and reception of *Capital* unfolded within different historical contexts. In such an approach, the French edition stands as one moment in a larger process whose significance can only be examined by locating it in the discursive totality within which it emerged and periodically re-emerged.

Anderson's approach to the French edition stands in sharp contrast to the above insofar as it considers *Le Capital* as the most advanced and accurate articulation of Marx's arguments in Volume I. In *Marx at the Margins*, Anderson repeatedly referred to the French edition in ways that give it a sense of authoritative finality compared to the other editions (see, e.g., Anderson 2010: 172, 173, 175, 180). The French edition, therefore, played a central role in substantiating Anderson's main claim that 'Marx's continually evolving stance towards non-western societies helped to shape the overall argument of *Capital, Volume I*' (Anderson 2010: 172). While this was already present in the previous editions of *Capital*, it was in the French edition that this essential characteristic has been, for Anderson, most clearly pronounced.

While maintaining his previous antagonism towards the Engelsian editions,[17] Anderson underestimated the significance of Marx's subsequent attempts and desire to revise Volume I after the French edition. He delimited Marx's subsequent editorial instructions to the first six chapters of *Capital* that were to be revised by comparing the second German and the French edition. However, Marx ultimately did not make such a clear demarcation between the portions that should be taken from the existing editions. And even if he did, such an indication would not trivially overcome all the translational and conceptual complications arising from basing the later editions and translations of Volume I on two different editions of *Capital* in two very different languages.

Anderson nevertheless made creative use of the French edition to substantiate his main claim. For instance, contrary to prominent scholars such as Jean-Pierre Lefebvre (1983: LV–LVIII), he interpreted the removal of dialectical language from the French edition, not in terms of popularization of the content or rejection of Hegelian dialectics per se, but as a way, at least in some cases, 'to avoid merging India and the Americas – and China as well – into a single totality in which all societies could be seen as necessarily following the same pathway' (2010: 188). Similarly, Anderson interpreted important qualifications added to the French edition as Marx's attempt to restrict the theoretical exposition of Volume I to Western Europe (2010: 179) and to separate the analysis of non-western societies 'since their history did not fit into the stages of development that he had worked out earlier on the basis of European history' (2010:180).

Some scholars have built on Anderson's discussions constructively to delve into lesser-explored aspects of Marx's ideas while engaging with the question of the French edition quite differently from Anderson's approach. Lucia Pradella, for example, elaborated on Anderson's arguments to tie Marx's deepening analysis of colonialism to his conception of the capitalist mode of production and international relations (Pradella 2010: 82). As Pradella explored the relevant passages in the French edition in support of her argument and its implications, she presented a new formulation of the question of the French edition. She highlighted the fact that the majority of conceptual, linguistic, and structural changes made by Marx in the French edition indeed belong to the second half of Volume I, compared to the second German edition. Also, even though the structural changes that Marx made in *Le Capital* were not reflected by Engels in the third German edition, but the latter is structurally almost identical to the second German edition. Therefore, instead of basing her comparison on the French and Engelsian editions, she focused largely on the former and the second German edition which had been prepared consecutively. This allowed her to avoid the controversy around the Engelsian editions in relation to the French edition.[18]

Pradella notably contended that just as Marx's intellectual development in the early 1870s presented new horizons that grounded his revisions in the French edition, it also made new theoretical limitations more evident to Marx (see, e.g., 2010: 94–6). This approach effectively renounces the temptation to consider the French edition the last word of Marx on the subject of Volume I. Indeed, she argued that as the second half of Volume I already contained references to Volumes II and III, a closer examination of the development of Marx's thinking with respect to Volumes II and III would be needed to make sense of the specific developments in the French edition (2010: 84). In other words, her approach connects the past, present, and future of the making of *Capital*, at least during Marx's life – and here lies one of the limitations of this approach – while also highlighting the unique significance of the French edition in that process which continued for another 8 years before his death in 1883.

Paul Zarembka has taken Anderson's approach to the French edition in a different direction. His book published in 2020 engages extensively with the French edition. Aside from substantive references to the French edition throughout the book,[19] Zarembka also examined the question of the French edition extensively. Underscoring the importance of the editorial instructions that Marx wrote in anticipation of future editions and translations of *Capital*, Zarembka carefully catalogued the structural and textual changes indicated in the instructions and systematically compared their corresponding appearances in the French, third German, and English editions of Volume I. He also explored the broader implications of some of these changes. Accordingly, Zarembka's claimed that these instructions can be used to reconstruct what he called the '1882 edition' of *Capital* (2020: 48). One of the distinct characteristics of his approach is the level of emphasis he put on the difference in the structural divisions that appeared in later editions of *Capital* and their broader implications. The formidable significance that is given to such seemingly innocuous structural differences, which indeed can be interpreted in other ways (see, e.g., Kemple 2022), gives one a sense of unduly exaggeration.

Even though Zarembka's contribution is a useful resource, especially for those who cannot access the MEGA[2] editions, there are a number of issues with his approach to the question. His seemingly straightforward use of Marx's instructions, although more nuanced than Anderson's over-simplification of the issue, still trivializes the path from the French edition to a new third German edition. Contrary to what Zarembka implied, these primary sources, some of which he did not consider in his analysis, form a 'rather confusing network of relationships between entries and instructions' (Kuczynski 2010: 106). Lastly, even though Zarembka made passing references to the intellectual biography and political history in relation to the early editions of *Capital*, his commendable accounting of the structural and textual changes nonetheless lacked adequate contextualization to illuminate the factors shaping these transformations. This shortcoming is most visible with regard to Zarembka's treatment of Engels. His harshly critical assessment of Engels in his failure to account for the instructions in his editorial work on *Volume I* does not adequately contextualize when and which of these instructions reached Engels, let alone accounting for the political and intellectual factors influencing Engels' editorial process.[20]

Regina Roth (2018; 2009) has taken a more balanced view of Engels' editorial work on *Capital* in light of its critical editions in MEGA². She argued that Engels was in fact very careful in his editorial work on *Volume I* and generally 'tried to take up Marx's hints or phrases whenever possible' (Roth 2009: 42), even though he remained sceptical of the French edition and considered it as a simplification. Roth provided a useful characterization of Engels' editorial interventions and offered some explanations for why he might have made certain editorial decisions. Building on Vollgraf and Jürgen Jungnickel's systematic classification (2002), Roth grouped Engels' editorial work on *Capital* in general into: 'structuring the text and ordering Marx's terms and ideas; mitigating inconsistencies; shifting emphasis; discarding variations' (2018:35). After examining each, Roth speculated on Engels' motives behind his editorial decision that Engels

> appears to have been more focused on presenting the results of the process of reasoning, such as a clearer prospect of a possible breakdown of capitalist production, or a more universal development of capitalist production – passing over Marx's considerations about possible qualifications or restrictions of the argument.
>
> (2018: 46–7)

However, Roth fell short of substantiating these hypotheses, as reasonable as they might appear, by delving deeper into Engels' own intellectual and political preoccupations to examine their influence on his editorial work on *Capital*. Nevertheless, Roth's more detailed and sympathetic approach to the question of Engels' influence on *Capital* allowed her to go beyond what is now a rather tired argument that Marx and Engels should be treated as two distinct theorists with 'some theoretical differences between [them]' (Anderson 2010: 173).

In a recent publication that has sought to qualify the significance of the French edition of *Capital* in relation to the third and fourth German editions, as well as the 1887 English edition, William Outhwaite and Kenneth Smith made the claim that 'both Marx and Anderson are too generous (and Engels too negative) in their respective assessment of the translation' (2019: 208). They criticized Anderson's presentation of the French edition as the final or superior version of *Capital*, rather than 'simply one among other versions' (Outhwaite and Smith 2019: 209). Despite their pluralistic approach to the different editions of *Capital*, Outhwaite and Smith singled out the new edition of *Volume I* edited by the German Marxlogist, Thomas Kuczynski (2017), as 'most likely to have been what Marx intended' (2019: 209) – a claim that even Kuczynski himself has effectively rejected, claiming that 'all speculation about what this reworking [by Marx] might have looked like is misleading' (e.g., see Kuczynski 2018: 35).

Outhwaite and Smith further contended that, in some notable respects, the French edition is inferior to the Engelsian and English editions by arguing that it 'simplifies much of what is more fully explained in the current English and the fourth German editions' (Outhwaite and Smith 2019: 215). They critically examined the sections of the French edition pointed out by Anderson as demonstrating its superiority but concluded that the textual differences mentioned by Anderson are either insignificant, inferior to the other editions, or sufficiently incorporated into the existing editions. Regarding Anderson's criticism of Engels' editorial work, they called for a more careful analysis of Engels' correspondence, claiming that even though Engels continued to believe that the French edition was not a suitable basis for the English translation, 'it was not Marx's translation that Engels had read but Roy's and that [...] Engels was in fact fairly happy with Marx's (but not with Roy's) French version' (2019: 215).

Kuzynski has done the most in German literature in recent years to engage with the question of the French edition in detail, with several publications on various philological and editorial aspects of the topic. Given his underlying project to bring together a new German edition of *Capital* in light of the current state of scholarship on Marx and *Capital* as well as the wealth of resources provided in the MEGA^2,[21] Kuzynski's approach to the French edition has been distinctly practical. Kuzynski entered into a careful investigative work to compare various editions of *Capital* and Marx's own interventions into the text both through direct involvement in the revision process, as in the case of the French edition, or through Marx's insertions in his handwritten copies and the editorial instructions that he prepared in the leadup to new editions and translations of Volume I.[22] This examination extended itself to the question of Engels' editorial process partly as a baseline for Kuzynski himself to make editorial decisions with respect to various textual differences between different editions and partly as a way to justify the need for a new German edition.

To reconstruct the editorial transformations of *Capital* between the publication of the first edition in 1867 and the fourth German edition in 1890, Kuzynski carefully mapped out the chronology of various editorial interventions both by Marx and Engels.[23] He provided compelling reasons for why it was necessary to consider all these sources and to examine the textual differences between them to create a new 'third German edition' of *Capital*. While clearly emphasizing the undeniable significance of the French edition (Kuzynski 2010: 145), he denied the notion that the French edition somehow presented the ultimate edition of Volume I. He supported this claim by highlighting the subsequent instructions prepared by Marx (Kuzynski 2014: 207) but also by underscoring Marx's own reservations about the French edition (Kuzynski 2010: 147; 2014: 199, 204–5). Similarly, he criticized Omuri for considering the 'American' edition for limiting the process to the 1877 'American' edition since 'already one year later, Marx saw things substantially differently' (Kuzynski 2010: 149; see also Krätke 2005).

Such a practical approach as an editor also allowed him to espouse a more balanced view of Engels in light of the complexity of the task in front of Engels at the time, the pieces of the puzzle that at least for a time, he did not have access to, and the crucial requirement to produce an edition that is readable by non-specialists (see Kuzynski 2010: 106–8). While sympathizing with some of Engels' editorial decisions including aspects of his reservation towards the French edition, Kuzynski nevertheless criticized Engels – sometimes quite harshly – in a number of cases (e.g., Kuzynski 2010: 146; 2014: 199; 2017: 769). Aside from the merits of this practical and scholarly approach which has resulted in one of the most promising new editions of *Capital*, its hyper-attention to textual aspects leads to an underestimation or underappreciation of broader political and theoretical reasons shaping the editorial process of the early editions.

There have been a number of French publications in recent years that have delved into the political history of the making, dissemination, and reception of the French edition largely within France. As part of the reprint of the first French edition, the editors, Alix Bouffard, Alexandre Feron, and Guillaume Fondu (2017), published a supplemental volume that contained three contributions to the history of the French translation, including an essay by François Gaudin on the publisher Lachâtre, letters concerning the preparation and publication of the French edition, and the French translation of all the prefaces written by Marx and Engels for different editions of *Capital*. Having surveyed the political history of the French translations of *Capital*, in one of the chapters, the editors pointed out several issues related to the translation of various terms and concepts found in the first French translation. They, therefore, challenged the authority of the first French edition not simply in favour of the Engelsian editions but on philological accounts concerning translational accuracy and linguistic fluidity. Gaudin, the author of a biography of Maurice Lachâtre (2014), published a book in 2019 that brought together previously unpublished correspondence between Maurice Lachâtre, Marx, Engels, and their collaborators between 1872 and 1879. Aspects of the research by these scholars have been published in German and English (counting the present book). For example, Fondu and Quétier (2015) published an article in the *Marx-Engels-Jahrbuch* providing an overview of the reception of Marx and *Capital* in France since the 1970s. They recounted certain perspectives left behind from the heyday of Marxism in France between 1970 and 1983 and highlighted the missed opportunity to provide a careful retranslation of *Capital*.

Aside from these publications, which have in different ways engaged with the question of the French edition and its place among other editions of *Capital*, there have been a growing number of contributions in recent years that have engaged with the French edition to address specific conceptual questions without entering into the larger debate about the French edition. These contributions often refer to selection passages or theoretical developments that were uniquely articulated in the French edition to support a specific aspect of their argument.[24] These have shown that it is now readily possible to invoke the

French edition without the ideological, political, or philological connotations that such references might have had in previous periods, which would often require having to engage with the broader question of the French edition.

Futures of *Le Capital*

In the 20th century, references to the French edition, aside from (or sometimes underneath) purely scholarly interests, directly or indirectly pointed towards unsettling certain ideological aspects of actually existing socialism. Now they largely contribute to pluralizing the perspectives on *Capital* and Marx beyond the past orthodoxies and traditional readings to expand the interpretive possibility within which we might hope to revive Marx and his critique of capitalism for the conditions of the 21st century. There is a growing consensus in the literature on at least two crucial points concerning the French edition. The first is that the French edition contains at least some novel ideas – though the place and extent of these original articulations remain an open question. And second that the French edition was not the last time Marx attempted to revise *Capital* – although what and how the later indications should be taken into account continue to generate discussion.

The two poles in the spectrum of approaches to the French edition that appears in the literature consist of what can be called 'French edition essentialism' – the views that consider the French edition as the most definite version of *Capital* and superior to other versions – and what can be called '*Capital* deconstructionism' – the views that consider *Capital* as a radically open-ended project that cannot be simply reconstructed but perpetually deconstructed. Most perspectives fall somewhere between these two poles.

On the question of Engels and Engelsian editions, there are interpretations that still try to purify Marx from post-Marx Marxists. Of course, the stature of *Capital* in Marx's writings and the direct role of Engels in preparing the third and fourth German editions and supervising the English translation put him in the crosshair. While it can be argued that such interventions played an important subversive role in the past, they now seem to respond to a political reality that is long gone. Although this position is becoming less palatable in the literature, there is still a lack of scholarly care in considering Engels' role in the making of *Capital* in its dynamic practical, intellectual, and political context. It also implies that being systematic rather than selective about the accounting of the differences between the Engelsian and the French edition and appreciating the non-trivial path from the French edition to the 'third German edition' by whoever this may have been done.

The growing research on the political history of the French edition has substantiated the question of the making and the dissemination of the French edition. These are part of broader research on the global dissemination and reception of Marx's ideas and writings. They follow the evolution of *Capital* within changing political contexts, not just at the level of diverse theoretical receptions of it but specifically at the material, institutional, and political levels.

By shedding light on the diverse contributions of the French edition in different contexts that shape and, to some extent, were shaped by its dissemination and reception, this research can bridge scholarly debates concerning various theoretical aspects of *Capital* and the present possibilities of reappropriating (aspects) of the French edition to illuminate the contemporary conditions.

Overall, the research paths with regard to the French edition point towards the following directions: deploying the French edition as an indispensable resource in the study of Marx's intellectual development in the last decade of his life; using the French edition to clarify certain aspects of Marx's arguments in *Capital*; analyzing the editorial transformations that *Capital* underwent after Marx's death; reconstructing a new edition of *Capital*, out of a complex relationship between different editions and Marx's editorial instructions. These are not necessarily mutually exclusive endeavours, but they also need not be conflated. The research field on *Capital*, freed from the hegemonic pressures of past orthodoxies and informed by the existing scholarship, is now wide open to help us critically examine and envision alternatives to capitalism.

Notes

1 Throughout the chapter, 'the French edition' refers to the first French edition of *Capital* (1872–75) translated by Joseph Roy and revised by Karl Marx. This work was supported by the Social Science and Humanities Research Council of Canada (SSHRC), Partnership Development Grant (Project n. 890-2020-0091).

2 This section on the dissemination of *Capital* in Germany draws on Kuczynski and Rauhala (2023).

3 Korsch's edition was published by both Kiepenheuer Verlag and the publishing house of the General German Trade Union Federation [*Verlagsgesellschaft des ADGB*].

4 This section on the dissemination of *Capital* in France draws on Ducange (2023).

5 The PCF began a process of ideological reorientation in the 1960s amidst changing sociopolitical context. One of its associated research institute, *Institut Maurice Thorez*, established in the mid-1960s, published a special issue on the French edition in 1972 on the 100th anniversary of the publication of the *Le Capital*. The majority of the contributions in that special issue focused on the historical context within which *Capital*, Marx's ideas, and Marxism more generally were received in France. Émile Bottigelli's article (1972) in particular provided a detailed historical account on the making of the French edition.

6 This section on the dissemination of *Capital* in Japan draws on Saito and Sasaki (2023).

7 The Hasebe's 1937 edition also was reprinted five times between 1947 and 1964, in a total of 1,886,000 copies.

8 The reprint of the French Edition (in the French language) had been published by the Tokyo-based Far Eastern Book Sellers/Kyokuto Shoten Ltd. in 1967.

9 Among a number of articles such as 'Marx's Humanism Today' (1965), such passing references also appeared in her popular pamphlet 'Outline of Marx's Capital Volume I' (1979). At least on one occasion, she even called it 'the definitive French edition, 1875' (Dunayevskaya 2002).

10 For more on Hirata's ideas, see Yamada (2018).

11 As Hirata puts it, 'only by the re-establishment of individual property, the de facto social property [which has been formed in the capitalist era] becomes a real social property' (Hirata 1971: 475; as quoted in Yamada 2014: 13).

12 The Japanese economist, Naomichi Hayashi, published a monograph in 1975 on his study of these changes in previous years (e.g., Hayashi 1973, 1974) in which he reported that 64 instances aimed at replacing the text of the second German with that in the French edition, and that Engels followed 19 of the 64 in their entirety and took other 54 changes either partially or not at all.

13 For example, see Kyuzo (1978, 1971); Umino (1976); Tatebe (1976). Special thanks to Ryuji Sasaki for pointing out these publications in Japanese.

14 This came after a letter exchange with Dunayevskaya in which Anderson sought advice on a number of potential topics to write on for the *News & Letters*, a Marxist-Humanist newspaper founded by Dunayevskaya in 1955. Among the proposed topics was an article to outline some of the differences between the French and the English editions. In her response, Dunayevskaya enthusiastically underscored the importance of the topic (see Dunayevskaya 1981).

15 Special thanks to Ryuji Sasaki for pointing out these publication in Japanese.

16 For example, Akira (1989) argues that the link between chapter 21 of *Capital, Volume I,* and the other chapters in Part VII, which had been questioned by scholars such as Ryozo Tomizuka, can be found more clearly in the French edition.

17 In this book, Anderson dramatized this even more by claiming that 'Marx never won the argument with Engels about the French edition' (2010: 75). This is a rather misleading characterization not only because Marx did not engage in any substantive argument with Engels on the French edition but also because Marx himself showed reservations towards the French edition in the subsequent years. Anderson even went as far as interpreting Engels' objection to Roy's translation as stemming from a sense of German linguistic and cultural superiority (2010: 174).

18 It should be noted that despite this shift in the comparative framework, Pradella consistently indicated when referring to a specific passage from *Capital* whether it has been carried forward to the third German edition. This is an excellent scholarly method to keep track of the wider textual differences in different editions of *Capital* while containing the scope of the comparison.

19 For example, Zarembka used the French edition, in addition to the second German edition, to support his claim that Marx's use of Hegelian language diminished significantly after 1868 which he took to be the sign of the decline of the influence of Hegel on Marx's dialectical approach.

20 See Kuczynski (2014, 2017) for a careful study of which instructions were consulted by Engels at different periods in his editorial work on *Capital*.

21 See Outhwaite (2019) for a review of Kuzynski's edition of *Capital, Volume I.*

22 Indeed, Kuzynski focused considerably on the 1877 instructions made by Marx and their role in Engel's editorial process after Marx's death (see esp. Kuzynski 2017, 2010).

23 These were the four German editions, the translations that took place under their direct supervision (hence, both the French edition and the 1887 English translation), indications in Marx's hand copies of second German edition and those in his copy of the French edition, and the instructions (in its various drafts and the final form) that Marx prepared in anticipation of an 'American edition'.

24 Just to mention an example, Tomonaga Tairako (2021, 2019) has also used the French edition in his examination of Marx's theory of pre-capitalist societies.

References

Anderson, Kevin (1997) 'On the MEGA and the French Edition of Capital, Volume 1: An Appreciation and Critique', in *Beiträge zur Marx-Engels-Forschung*, Berlin: Argument Verlag, pp. 131–6.

Anderson, Kevin (1983) 'The "Unknown" Marx's Capital, Volume I: The French Edition of 1872-75, 100 Years Later', *The Review of Radical Political Economics*, vol. 15, n. 4: 71–80.

Anderson, Kevin. (2010) *Marx at the Margins: On Nationalism, Ethnicity, and Non-Western Societies*, Chicago: University of Chicago Press.

Bottigelli, Émile (1972) 'La première édition française du *Capital*', *Cahiers de l'institut Maurice Thorez*, vol. 6, n. 28: 12–31.

Bouffard, Alix, Alexandre Feron, and Fondu, Guillaume (2017) *Ce Qu'est Le Capital de Marx*, Paris: Les éditions sociales.

Dunayevskaya, Raya (1958) *Marxism and Freedom: From 1776 Until Today*, New York: Bookman Associates.

Dunayevskaya, Raya (1965) 'Marx's Humanism Today', in *Socialist Humanism: An International Symposium*, edited by Erich Fromm, Garden City: Doubleday, pp. 68–83.

Dunayevskaya, Raya (1979) *Outline of Marx's Capital Volume I*, Detroit: News and Letters Committee.

Dunayevskaya, Raya (1981) Archival Document no. 15258, available at www.marxists. org/archive/dunayevskaya/archives

Dunayevskaya, Raya (1982) *Rosa Luxemburg, Women's Liberation, and Marx's Philosophy of Revolution*, Atlantic Highlands: Humanities Press Inc.

Dunayevskaya, Raya (2002 [1983]) 'Marxist-Humanism: The Summation That Is a New Beginning, Subjectively and Objectively', in *The Power of Negativity: Selected Writings on the Dialectic in Hegel and Marx*, edited by Peter Hudis and Anderson B. Kevin B., Lanham, Boulder, New York, Oxford: Lexington Books, pp. 257–66.

Enatsu, Michiho (1976) 'furansugoban "shihonron" no honyaku to kenkyū ni tsuiteno zyakkan no oboegaki', *tōkyō keizai hōka daigaku kiyō*, vol. 95: 1–30.

Fondu, Guillaume and Quétier, Jean (2015) 'Ist das französische Publikum "stets ungeduldig nach dem Ergebnis" – Zur gegenwärtigen Marx-Rezeption in Frankreich', in *Marx-Engels-Jahrbuch 2014*, edited by Gerald Hubmann, Claudia Reichel, and Timm Graßmann, Berlin: Akademie Verlag GmbH, pp. 172–92.

Gaudin, François (2014) *Maurice Lachâtre, éditeur socialiste – 1814-1900*, Limoges: Éditions Lambert-Lucas.

Hayashi, Naomichi (1973) 'furansugoban "shihonron" to rekishi kagaku: azia teki seisan yōshiki wo chūshin ni', *rekishi hyōron*, vol. 273: 51–66.

Hayashi, Naomichi (1974) 'shihonshugi teki chikuseki no rekishiteki keikō to "kojin teki shoyū" no saiken no mondai', *keizaigaku zasshi*, vol. 71 n. 2: 1–30 [Part 1] and n. 4: 24–51 [Part 2].

Hecker, Rolf, Jungnickel, Jürgen and Vollgraf, Carl-Erich (1989) 'Zur Entwicklungsgeschichte des ersten Bandes des "Kapitals" (1867 bis 1890)', *Beiträge zur Marx-Engels-Forschung*, vol. 27: 16–32.

Heinrich, Michael (2009) 'Reconstruction or Deconstruction? Methodological Controversies about Value and Capital, and New Insights from the Critical Edition', in *Re-Reading Marx: New Perspectives after the Critical Edition*, edited by Riccardo Bellofiore and Roberto Fineschi, London: Palgrave Macmillan, pp. 71–98.

Heinrich, Michael (2018) 'New Readings and New Texts: Marx's Capital after MEGA2', in *150 Years Karl Marx's "Capital" Reflections for the 21st Century*, edited by John Milios, Athens: Rosa Luxemburg Stiftung, pp. 15–26.

Hirata, Kiyoaki (1969) *Shiminshakai to Shakaisyugi*, Tokyo: Iwanami Shoten.

Hirata, Kiyoaki (1971) *keizaigaku to rekishi ninshiki*, Tokyo: Iwanami Shoten Publishers.

Jean-Numa Ducange (2023 forthcoming) 'France', in *The Routledge Handbook of Marx's 'Capital': A Global History of Translation, Dissemination and Reception*, edited by Marcello Musto and Babak Amini, London and New York: Routledge.

Kemple, Thomas (2022) *Marx's Wager: Das Kapital and Classical Sociology*, London: Palgrave Macmillan.

Krätke, Michael R. (2005) 'Le dernier Marx et le "Capital"', *Actuel Marx*, vol. 37, n. 1: 145–60.

Kuczynski, Thomas (2010) 'Welche Einträge in Marx' Handexemplaren von Kapital Bd. I dienten der Vorbereitung einer dritten deutschen Auflage?' in *Marx-Engels-Jahrbuch 2010*, Berlin: Akademie Verlag GmbH, pp. 101–58.

Kuczynski, Thomas (2014) 'Die historisch-kritischen Editionen von Kapital Band I in der MEGA – unabdingbarer Ausgangspunkt einer neuen Textausgabe', *Zeitschrift Marxistische Erneuerung*, vol. 100: 197–214.

Kuczynski, Thomas (2017) 'Nachwort zur neuen Textausgabe', in Karl Marx, *Das Kapital Kritik der politischen Ökonomie | Erster Band Buch I: Der Produktionsprozess des Kapitals*, Hamburg: VSA Verlag, pp. 761–89.

Kuczynski, Thomas (2018) 'Die Erstausgabe von "Kapital" Band I und ihre weitere Bearbeitung durch Marx', in *Marx' "Kapital" im 21. Jahrhundert*, edited by Dieter Janke, Jürgen Leibiger and Manfred Neuhaus, Leipzig: Rosa-Luxemburg-Stiftung Sachsen, pp. 35–50.

Kuczynski, Thomas and Rauhala, Paula (2023 forthcoming) 'Germany and Austria', in *The Routledge Handbook of Marx's 'Capital': A Global History of Translation, Dissemination and Reception*, edited by Marcello Musto and Babak Amini, London and New York: Routledge.

Kyuzo, Asobe (1971) 'furansugoban "shihonron" dai ichi kan dai ichi shō "shōhin" no kenkyū: doitsugo honbun tono hikaku taishō', *mita gakkai zasshi*, vol. 64, no. 2/3: 106(54)–117(65).

Kyuzo, Asobe (1978) 'furansugoban "shihonron" dai ichi kan dai san shō dai ni setsu "ryūtsū shudan" no kenkyū: doitsugo honbun tono hikaku taishō: ikō', *mita gakkai zasshi*, vol. 71, n. 5: 629(1)–647(19).

Lefebvre, Jean-Pierre (1983) 'Introduction de l'édition de 1983', in Karl Marx, *Le Capital*, Paris: Les éditions sociales.

Miykawa, Akira (1989) 'Umschlag der Aneignungsgesetze in der einfachen Reproduktion. Zu den Verbesserungen in der französischen Ausgabe', *Beiträge zur Marx-Engels-Forschung*, vol. 27: 201–9.

Nakazima, Yoko (1987) 'furansugoban "shihonron" ni okeru "shūseki"', *keizaigaku ronso*, vol. 39, n. 1: 313–35.

Naomichi, Hayashi (1975) *furansugoban shihonron no kenkyū*, Tokyo: Otsuki-Shoten Publishing House.

Outhwaite, William (2019) 'Book Review: Das Kapital', *Journal of Classical Sociology*, vol. 19, n. 1: 105–7.

Outhwaite, William and Smith Kenneth (2019), 'Karl Marx, Le Capital', *Review of Radical Political Economics*, vol. 52, n. 2: 1–19.

Pradella, Lucia (2010) 'Kolonialfrage und vorkapitalistische Gesellschaften: Zusätze und Änderungen in der französischen Ausgabe des ersten Bandes des Kapital (1872–75)', in *Marx-Engels-Jahrbuch 2010*, Berlin: Akademie Verlag GmbH, pp. 82–100.

Roth, Regina (2009) 'Karl Marx's Original Manuscripts in the Marx-Engels Gesamtausgabe (MEGA): Another View on Capital," in *Re-Reading Marx: New Perspectives after the Critical Edition*, edited by Riccardo Bellofiore and Roberto Fineschi, London: Palgrave Macmillan, pp. 27–49.

Roth, Regina (2018), 'Editing the Legacy: Friedrich Engels and Marx's Capital', in *Marx's Capital: An Unfinishable Project?*, edited by Marcel M. van der Linden and Gerald Hubmann, Leiden and Boston: Brill, pp. 31–47.

Saito, Kohei and Sasaki, Ryuji (2023 forthcoming) 'Japan', in *The Routledge Handbook of Marx's 'Capital': A Global History of Translation, Dissemination and Reception*, edited by Marcello Musto and Babak Amini, London-New York: Routledge.

Sato, Kenzaburo (1971) '"shihonron" dai 1 kan ame rikaban no tame no henshū sashizusho (marukusu)', *keizaigaku nenpō*, vol. 31: 1–11.

Tairako, Tomonaga (2016) 'A Turning Point in Marx's Theory on Pre-Capitalist Societies: Marx's Excerpt Notebooks on Maurer in MEGA IV/18', *Hitotsubashi Journal of Social Studies*, vol. 47: 1–10.

Tairako, Tomonaga (2019) 'Marx on Peasants and Small-Scale Industry: The Changes of Marx's Insight into the Pre-Capitalist Societies', *Hitotsubashi Journal of Social Studies*, vol. 50: 15–56.

Tatebe, Masayoshi (1976) 'furansugoban "shihonron" no kagaku teki kachi: Hayashi Naomichi "furansugoban shihonron no kenkyū"', *kikan kagaku to shisō*, vol. 20: 703–16.

Umino, Hiroshi (1976) 'furansugoban "shihonron" dai ichi kan dai ni hen dai roku shō ni okeru "rōdōryoku no kachi kitei" no kenkyū', *keiei ronshū*, vol. 24, n. 1: 131–56.

Vollgraf, Carl Erich and Jürgen Jungnickel (2002) '"Marx in Marx's Words"?: On Engels's Edition of the Main Manuscript of Book 3 of Capital', *International Journal of Political Economy*, vol. 32, n. 1: 35–78.

Yamada, Toshio (2014) 'Hirata Kiyoaki and His Thoughts on Civil Society', *The History of Economic Thought*, vol. 56, n. 1: 1–20.

Yamada, Toshio (2018) *Contemporary Capitalism and Civil Society: The Japanese Experience*, Singapore: Springer.

Zarembka, Paul (2020) *Key Elements of Social Theory Revolutionized by Marx*, Leiden and Boston: Brill.

Part IV

Letters on *Le Capital*

13 'Selected Correspondence on the French Translation of *Capital*'

Karl Marx, Maurice Lachâtre, Just Vernouillet, and Friedrich Engels

(Introduced, edited, and translated by Patrick Camiller)

Introduction: *Le Capital* in the shadow of the Paris Commune

Patrick Camiller

The project for a French translation of *Capital* dates from October 1871, five months after the Versailles troops fought their way into the French capital and drowned in blood – the first serious experience of a democratic workers' government. Over the following months, the ongoing repression drove most prominent Communards into exile. One centre, the Spanish Basque city of San Sebastian, became the residence of the left-wing publisher Maurice Lachâtre, who had narrowly escaped death in France and lost a close friend to assassins charged with hunting him down. Nor was this the first time he had found himself seeking refuge in Spain: his publication in the 1840s and 1850s of the novels of Eugène Sue (*Les Mystères de Paris*) and of a universal dictionary, as well as his own ten-volume *History of the Popes*, had earned him the reputation of a lively socialist and anti-clerical publisher and attracted the ire of the Second Empire of Louis Bonaparte. This time, however, San Sebastian proved to be a rather unsafe haven, as a civil war raged in the surrounding countryside and threatened to become a real danger in the event of a victory for the autocratic royalist forces. Marx keenly followed the course of this Third Carlist War and more than once asked Lachâtre for the latest news.

Among the fellow refugees with whom Lachâtre mixed in San Sebastian were the couple Paul Lafargue and Marx's second daughter Laura, who would both play a major role in the development of the socialist movement in France. Together they persuaded him of the need for a French translation of *Capital* – a work of which he had undoubtedly heard, but which he had not, and probably could not have, read in the original. It cannot be said that Lachâtre was ever a Marxist in any meaningful sense; and Marx, for his part, would scarcely have been impressed by Lachâtre's 'spiritualist' tendencies, which he shared with much of the French socialist tradition and occasionally aired in letters to Marx. Nevertheless, the two men felt a bond that went well beyond mere politeness or business relations. It is clear from the tone of Lachâtre's correspondence that

DOI: 10.4324/9781003336365-17

he had enormous esteem and affection for Marx, whose famous address on *The Civil War in France* had been circulating as a pamphlet since 13 June 1871.

On Lachâtre's suggestion, he agreed with Marx on a strategy for *Capital* that he had used before with Sue's novels and the history of the Popes: to bring out periodic instalments and to market them as brochures in sets of five. As their signed contract stated in February 1872, the main priority was that the translation should be 'in a form and at a price that place the work within reach of the smallest pockets'.[1]

At first everything seemed to be going well. Lafargue and others proposed Joseph Roy, a highly praised translator of Feuerbach among others, to take on the project, and Marx accepted with enthusiasm. Roy began work at once and was already delivering sizeable batches by December 1871. As Marx pored over this material, however, he became convinced that Roy was not up to the task and expressed this view confidentially to Lachâtre in the first letter of January 1872. It was the beginning of a fraught relationship over several years, in which Marx continually wavered in his judgement. Beset with serious health problems, which forced him to undertake lengthy cures, he repeatedly complained of the days he had to spend revising and sometimes rewriting whole passages of the translation. Some of the difficulties were perhaps inevitable, especially in the opening sections, where the need to render Marx's complex theoretical prose had to be reconciled with the wish to make the text as accessible as possible to a working-class readership. At least Marx, more fluent in French than he ever was in English, closely followed each stage of the translation, took the opportunity to make extensive changes and additions that were incorporated into the second German edition, and gave his personal approval to the final outcome. Yet as late as February 1875 Lachâtre was still pleading with Marx to make his 'admirable theories' more intelligible to the 'common people',[2] in which he included himself.

The first letter in this selection also contains the first and most extensive in a stream of Marx's complaints to Lachâtre about failings at the printers. Some of these concern delayed or missing postal deliveries, but the despatch of instalments out of sequence is another grievance that Marx lays more squarely at the door of Louis Lahure, a conservative Parisian printer for whom *Le Capital* and the servicing of exiled Communards were anything but a key priority. A further complication was that Lachâtre too received the proofs of each instalment, and he was finally compelled to flee San Sebastian in late 1873 and, still on a French hit list, to lead the itinerant life of an insecure refugee in Belgium, Switzerland, and Italy.

Meanwhile, Lachâtre's publishing house in Paris was in the hands of Just Vernouillet (1840-1892), an early member of the First International who had

---

1 'Le contrat d'auteur entre Karl Marx et Maurice Lachâtre et C.ie', in François Gaudin (Ed.), *Traduire Le Capital. Une correspondence inédite entre Karl Marx, Friedrich Engels et l'éditeur Maurice Lachâtre*, Mont-Saint-Aignan: Presses Universitaires de Rouen et du Havre, p. 178.
2 See the letter n. 23.

initiated a low-cost 'Bibliothèque démocratique' of his own in 1869. Managing to survive in the climate of repression – the *loi Dufaure* of 14 March 1872 outlawed any socialist propaganda aiming to change the nature of society – Vernouillet did his best to reassure Marx and to proceed with the publication project. But in December 1873, when Lachâtre was officially sentenced in absentia to deportation, the property of his publishing house was impounded, and the following year a 'provisional receiver', Adolphe Quest, was appointed to replace Vernouillet in the management of the house. Whether through incompetence or design, or a mixture of the two, this bourgeois conservative hostile to the business in his charge proceeded to turn a healthy balance into a sizeable debt and to block further progress in publication. Vernouillet wrote discreetly to Marx advising him to take legal action to force Quest's hand.[3]

Given all the obstacles in its path, it seems a little short of miraculous that the informal group of Communards and sympathisers finally succeeded in their venture to publish *Le Capital. Critique de l'économie politique* at the Maurice Lachâtre & Co. publishing house in November 1875. The climate had still not changed enough to permit widespread publicity and free circulation of the book in the French public space. The publisher himself was living in exile in Switzerland, soon to move on to Italy, and would return to France only four years later under a partial presidential amnesty, resuming his long and productive career in the writing and publishing of democratic and socialist literature. The cull of the Communards and the subsequent repression cast its long shadow over the whole decade, with a full amnesty legislated only at the very end, on 14 July 1880. The 'republic without republicans', as French socialists dubbed the post-Commune regime, gave way to most of the trappings of a bourgeois democratic state. When Lachâtre inspected the stocks of *Le Capital* at his publishing house in Paris, he drily noted that of the thousand copies in the concluding print run of 1875 a mere six or seven hundred had actually been sold. A paltry total indeed. For French socialism, however, the first volume of Marx's great work represented a milestone in the development of a class-conscious labour movement, now informed by a theoretical understanding of its role in the capitalist mode of production and of its capacity to move beyond it.

★★★★★

This selection of 31 letters from correspondence relating to *Le Capital* has been made from the more extensive selection of 53 letters in the invaluable work by François Gaudin (see footnote n. 1), which also includes a few items to or from other figures active in producing the French edition of Volume 1 of Marx's *magnum opus*. All the materials have been freshly translated for the present volume, and with the exception of letters 1, 4, 13, and 16, none of it has, to the best of my knowledge, previously appeared in English.[4]

---

3 Cf. the letter n. 26.

4 I am also particularly grateful to François Gaudin for much of the biographical information relating to Maurice Lachâtre and other actors in the publishing project. The interested reader may well care to consult Gaudin's full-scale biography *Maurice Lachâtre, éditeur socialiste – 1814-1900*, Limoges: Éditions Lambert-Lucas, 2014.

Karl Marx, Maurice Lachâtre, Just Vernouillet, and Friedrich Engels

'Selected correspondence on the French translation of *Capital*'

1. Karl Marx to Maurice Lachâtre

9 January 1872

Dear citizen,

From your letters it would seem that I, not you, am responsible for what is done at the Lahure printers. Here are the successive delays that originate with it alone:

1   The delay caused by the M. Lahure's unclear and contradictory letters regarding the so-called lost manuscript.
2   The delay caused by the non-despatch of those proofs of the manuscript, which had already been run off when I was busy making a new translation of it.
3   The delay caused by M. Lahure's sending me proofs 11–16, while holding back the proofs of instalment 10 (the last of the first section) and instalment 15.
4   New delay caused by sending only one copy (instead of the agreed two) of the proofs and sending the second copies only after *repeated* requests on my part. I was even forced to write to M. Vernouillet to obtain the second copies.
5   Delay caused by the sending of insts. 8, 9, 10 and 16, but not of inst. 11, which is necessary for the plating of the second section to go ahead.
6   In general, I do not receive the instalments in the right sequence, but haphazardly; and not separately after they have been printed, but in one mass after long interruptions, as if all I had to do was execute M. Lahure's capricious and unforeseen orders. All these causes of delay are incontestable, because I have in my hands the letters from M. Lahure and Vernouillet in answer to my complaints where I even speak of *bad faith*.

On 30 Dec., I sent insts. 8, 9 and 10 (with the final page proofs) and 16; on 31 Dec. insts. 13 and 14, but the final proof of inst. 11 could not be sent because it only arrived later from Paris.

So, the delay in publishing section 2 was entirely M. Lahure's fault.

I come now to another point. In a letter he sent to you, M. Lahure already complained that he kept receiving new proofs with little changes marked on them. But is it my fault if the same printing errors are reproduced with remarkable persistence, or that two new errors are made in the correction of one?

I informed M. Lahure – after agreeing it with you – that in order to deliver the final page proofs and the text ready for plating I would need all five instalments of a section and the following instalment. I have been forced to do the opposite for the second section, (1) because I never received the whole set of instalments 6–11; and (2) because I reached the end of my patience. I therefore gave M. Lahure my permission to go-ahead with the plating, while I held him responsible for making the ever-new corrections and pointed out to him that it was his duty, not mine, to check for setting errors.

Finally, I come to the final reason for the delays. M. Roy's translation perhaps causes me more work than if I did the whole task myself. It is true that you did not choose him, but, in leading me to believe that the first instalment would be printed at the beginning of 1872, you encouraged me to accept him on the recommendations of Longuet and Vaillant.[5] Keller would not have had time until May and Mme. Jaclard's whereabouts were not then known to me.

Nearly all my work keeps being interrupted by the reworking of this translation. Either I have to redo whole pages, or I have to correct details on the manuscript, although in the latter case, after consulting Lafarge and Longuet, I often find the most adequate form only when I have the proofs in front of me.

Longuet wrote a letter to M. Roy in which he openly reproved him, and I tell you this *on the express condition* that you say nothing about it to M. R. After all it would serve no purpose; I am now convinced that he is not the translator I needed.

Chs. XIII and XIV are not yet in Paris because I have not yet finished reworking the manuscript. Besides, how can that prevent publication of the second instalment?

As for my biography, you would do well to approach M. Engels in person – you have his address.

I am, dear citizen,
Loyally yours,

Karl Marx

P.S.: I had to pay 10 shillings and two pence for the last batch of proofs. As M. Lahure only paid part of the postage, the French post office sent the packet by letter post. I have written to Mss. Lahure and Vernouillet that if this occurs again, I shall refuse to accept such despatches.

---

5 Charles Longuet (1839–1903), married to Marx's daughter Eleanor, was a prominent Proudhonist figure in the Paris Commune and the later French socialist movement. Marie-Édouard Vaillant (1840–1915), also a prominent figure in the Commune, went on to become a founding member of the French Socialist Party (SFIO) in 1905.

2. Maurice Lachâtre to Karl Marx

17 February 1872

Dear Monsieur and renowned philosopher,

So now we are committed to each other for the publication of your book *Le Capital*, which I am told is the cornerstone of the modern edifice you are constructing where future liberated generations will find a home.

A peculiar destiny presides over the creation of this book, for its translation into French is a true act of creation.

The author is an exile living amid the fogs of the Thames; the publisher is also an outlaw, who as if by a miracle escaped three gangs of killers sent to shoot him on the infernal day of 24 May! The man who put us in touch with each other, your son-in-law, is also an outlaw, driven into exile by the winds of persecution and followed by your beloved daughter and the poor dear child, whose frail health causes you so many worries.

Born in the midst of suffering, your book will perhaps earn me much persecution; I willingly accept it.

Life is short, and each of us must use it as best we can for the happiness of our fellow creatures. You have not failed in this task; I will do as you, my dear maître, to the extent of my powers.

Permit me now to send you some remarks on how we should proceed with the publication:

Please instruct M. Lafargue[6] to get in touch with the translator so that the work can begin at once.

A framed portrait of the author will be sent to you by the publishing house in Paris.

Your autograph, if you wish, will be in slightly larger characters so that it is easier to read.

M. Lafargue will kindly tackle your biography forthwith.

I would ask you not to have any communication with the press about the French translation of your book; let us be prudent. Everything will come in its time. The book should proceed on its way quietly, out of the spotlight. We should wait for it to appear in full before announcing it in the newspapers and generating reviews.

Kindly let me know if your opinion is the same as mine. If it is not, I shall sacrifice my own feelings about the wisdom of such wranglings with the newspapers.

As I am living abroad, under an assumed name, you should address any letters you care to write me either to your son-in-law or to: Señor Leconte, correo, San Sebastian (España).

Respectfully yours,

Maurice Lachâtre

---

6 Paul Lafargue (1842–1911), Marx's son-in-law by marriage to his daughter Laura, also spent a period in 1871–72 in Spain, as a refugee from the post-Commune repression in France. While staying in San Sebastian, he played a major role in winning Lachâtre to the idea of a French edition of *Capital*.

3. Karl Marx to Maurice Lachâtre

7 March 1872
1, Maitland Park Road,
Haverstock Hill – London

Dear Monsieur,

After I received your overly complimentary letter, I immediately wrote to M. Roy, the translator, asking him to send the first manuscript dispatches to Paris.

As to the biography, I shall be obliged if you do not insist on its immediate publication. My friend F. Engels, who will provide M. Lafargue with the details, is currently too overloaded with work to deal with it. In my view we should not waste time and there is nothing to stop you publishing the biography later.

I am completely of your opinion that there should be no communication with the press about the French translation. The same precautions are being taken with the Russian edition, and unfortunately France is today subject to a 'Russian' regime.

It will be useful to say (for your part) in the first instalment that the translation has followed *the manuscript of the second German edition*, the publication of which will begin only a few weeks from now.

Between ourselves. My German publisher will copy you in publishing the second edition in instalments.

I hope the book will not earn you fresh persecutions. The method is quite different from the one applied by French and other socialists. I do not take as my starting point such general ideas as equality, etc., but rather begin by objectively analysing economic relations as they are – which is why the revolutionary spirit of the book only gradually reveals itself. What I fear, instead, is that the dryness of the initial analyses will put off the French reader.

Still, the first chapters contain some anti-religious jokes that might hurt devout members of the rural republic.

I have the honour to be loyally yours,

Karl Marx

P.S.: I inserted in our agreement that the 2,000 francs should be paid on request within fifteen days. If that is not a problem for you, I would prefer that you pay the money on 1 July, because otherwise I would have to sell a good investment.

4. Karl Marx to Maurice Lachâtre

London, 18 March 1872

Dear citizen,

I applaud your idea of publishing the translation of *Das Kapital* in periodic instalments. In this form, the work will be more accessible to the working class and for me that consideration outweighs any other. That is the bright side of your medal, but here is the other. The method of analysis I used, one not previously applied to economic subjects, makes for somewhat arduous reading in the early chapters, and it is to be feared that the French public, ever impatient for conclusions and eager to know how the general principles relate to the immediate questions that excite them, may be put off if they have been unable to press straight on in the first place.

I can do nothing about that disadvantage, other than alert and forewarn readers concerned with the truth. There is no royal road to learning and the only ones with any chance of reaching its sunlit peaks are those who do not fear exhaustion as they climb the steep upward paths.

I remain, dear citizen,
Yours very sincerely,

Karl Marx

5. Karl Marx to Maurice Lachâtre

London, 20 March 1872

Dear citizen,

Our letters crossed. Enclosed is the autograph.

In the final corrected paragraph are the words: 'will not let their reading be stopped by *the exposition of our analytic methods*'. There is a misunderstanding here. I *do not expound* my method; I *apply it* from the beginning, but its application, in the first chapters, to the analysis of the *'commodity'*, *'value'*, *'money'* is by the nature of the thing itself a little difficult to follow.

But it is easy to change: 'will not let their reading be stopped by the application of our analytic method to the first concepts of political economy, which by their very nature are very abstract' – or something like that – we would have thereby finished with the preliminaries.

My photograph will be done tomorrow.

Loyally yours,

Karl Marx

6. Maurice Lachâtre to Karl Marx

27 April 1872
Saturday morning
Señor Leconte
Postal box, San Sebastian (Spain)

Dear Sir and illustrious Maître,

I have received a letter from M. Lafargue with a useful warning for my family and myself, about the danger of living in a town that may be invaded at any moment by the Carlist bands present in all the mountains — a letter in which your son-in-law encourages me to give you news about the publication of *Capital* in Paris.

Since your photograph reached us, not a day has been wasted in preparation for the printing of your important work. The portrait was reproduced on wood; then the design sent to the engraver, who has devoted all his moments to the task and should finish it in a few days, according to what M. Dervaux[7] has written to me. The autograph has also been entrusted to a skilful artist.

I have been constantly told to expect the proofs, and they will first be sent to the author, as is natural. [...] As for the resolve to change my residence, because of the danger my family may face in San Sebastian, I keep hesitating because I don't know where to go; if the Spanish government is the weakest, we won't be in safety in any part of Spain. As for returning to France, I still don't dare to dream of it; the tigers are not sated! I had the good luck to get beyond reach of their claws, and it would be most imprudent of me to get near their den again.

I shall wait a few days to see how the events turn out, then I shall decide with my little family which is the wisest course to take.

Be assured, dear maître, of all my warmest feelings.

Maurice Lachâtre

P.S.: The Spanish troops who left San Sebastian a few days ago in pursuit of the Carlist bands[8] returned yesterday, having proved unable, I am told, to stand up to the Insurrection. This morning, rumours have been circulating that the Carlists are in control of Pamplona and Tolosa, and that they are continuing their march on San Sebastian. But you know that one has to be wary of the alarming rumours that the fear or ardour of both sides always exaggerates.

---

7 The portrait artist Adolphe Dervaux (1825–after 1883).

8 Forces seeking to restore the autocratic Bourbon rulers of Spain (called Carlists after the pretender Don Carlos) launched a series of three uprisings against the constitutional monarchy and the First Spanish Republic in the course of the nineteenth century. The Third Carlist War (1872–76) had its main theatre in the Basque Country and Navarre.

7. Karl Marx to Maurice Lachâtre

London, 1 May 1872

Dear citizen,

You are mistaken! Monsieur Roy is French. He was for a few years (but when he was already an adult) in Germany. He translates too literally in the easy passages, but he shows his strength where things are difficult. Nevertheless, your corrections would always be useful for the final correction.

The first instalment of the second German edition (the German publisher imitated you by accepting the form of instalments for the second edition) will probably appear next week.

I have received the Russian translation from St. Petersburg (based on the first edition). It is excellent. The book had to pass the censorship, but the censor deleted nothing except my portrait. Still, as there are attacks on Russia in the book, the Russian publisher is not yet out of all danger.

For the final correction I have accepted the help of Longuet, Vaillant, Lissagaray and other competent Communards.

Your political news interests me and you will do me a great favour by continuing it.

By the way, a French publisher (in Paris) – while asking me not to name it – has offered to reprint my French book against Proudhon: *Poverty of Philosophy. Reply to M. Proudhon's Philosophy of Poverty*, Brussels and Paris 1847.[9] It is completely out of print.

I have bad news from Madrid about the state of health of the little Lafargue.

Loyally yours,

Karl Marx

---

9 The new French edition would finally appear nearly 25 years later, long after Marx's death: *Misère de la philosophie*, Paris: V. Giard & E. Brière, 1896.

8. Maurice Lachâtre to Karl Marx

Señor Leconte
Postal box, San Sebastian (Spain)
5 May 1872
Sunday morning

Dear Maître,

I received your letter of 2 May yesterday afternoon, and this morning I wrote to Paris and Bordeaux to meet the two points that you raised. I even added your communication to my letter for M. Roy.

You are quite right to ask for the quotations from dead or foreign languages to be translated; our edition is intended for people who know absolutely nothing but French, so that alongside the quotations a translation must be given in italics and between brackets. If you think it in place to keep the quotations in dead or foreign languages, please say so to M. Roy, but he should take care to place alongside, in italics and between brackets, the translation into French of all the quotations without exception.

I have recommended that M. Dervaux send you two sets of proofs instead of one, but that he should print the proofs on thinner paper to keep down the cost of the corrected proofs that you put in the post and pay for as letters.

The proofs of my history of the Popes are printed on thin paper and each batch of eight pages weighs no more than ordinary postage, whereas each batch of *Capital* costs double, and for two batches three stamps – which is what happened when I sent you back my corrected proofs.

I think you will approve these recommendations to keep down the expense of returning the proofs.

I am drinking milk – as the wicked Villemessant[10] would say – when reading the batches of *Capital*; beginnings are hard work, as you warned your readers, but I look forward to the conclusion, and I rejoice in advance at the stupefaction of the bourgeois when you lay out before their eyes the truths that are embryonic in your thesis on the value of their commodity, of the labour product.

Allow me, dear Maître, to suggest an idea regarding *Capital*. Everything, absolutely everything, may be considered as capital, and the privileged classes do not fail to appropriate all they can, even water and air, and to ensure ownership of them forever for their descendants, thanks to the inheritance principle that consolidates theft and squandering, which – akin to fire – purifies all the original impurities.

So if a new Rothschild, surrounded by five children with high aspirations for the vanities of life, lay hold of all the rivers and sources of water throughout Europe and amassed all these waters in a gigantic reservoir, an inland sea; if this deadly higher genius managed to convince other men of his property rights

10 Jean Hippolyte de Villemessant (1810–79) was a prominent French journalist, instrumental in reviving *Le Figaro* in 1854.

over all the waters and – thanks to inheritance law – to pass on ownership of the liquid element to his progeny; all the inhabitants of Europe would find themselves at the mercy of that family, and no one would be able to drink or live except at the pleasure of the owner of the river waters.

My comparison may seem extravagant at first sight, although the thing itself exists in a degree through the concession of watercourses, the formation of companies for the distribution of water in the big cities, for the building and operation of canals, etc.

But if we pass from one element to another, from water to land, we end up with the same result; no one can live in Europe except at the pleasure of the land-owners. And if, in my first hypothesis, people faced the threat of death from lack of water, in my second hypothesis – which, alas, is no longer a hypothesis but a major reality – they are already threatened with death from starvation. And it is all too lamentable a truth that people are dying from a lack of land, a lack of break. No more than water, then, should the land ne appropriated by a few individuals.

And, with a quite natural extension of the hypothesis, absolutely nothing should be appropriated for the profit of a few.

As everything, absolutely everything is Capital, all men have a certain incon-testable right to enjoy and possess the share that falls to them in the total wealth of society.

No one can be deprived of this, so long as they remain on this earth. Afterwards, their share returns to the General Reserve; each is the inheritor of all, all are the inheritors of each.

Please tell me in a few words, dear Maître, whether the principles I set out here are in conformity with your doctrine, and whether the conclusion from the principles developed in your book are in conformity with the com-munist maxim.

The political situation in Spain still does not seem about to change; the manhunt continues on a vast scale in many provinces. Here, nothing new. San Sebastian is calm; the track has been repaired and trains are running from Madrid to Zumarraga – and from there to Irun – but I assume there is still a point of intersection at Zumarraga.

The small town of Irun, which was emptied of troops, has again been filled with soldiers withdrawn from Navarre; these soldiers say that they spotted Carlist bands in the distance, without managing to engage with them.

It is said that Don Carlos has managed to advance into Navarre, and that he has been joined by Rada at the head of a large force of men.

Your son-in-law may send you news from Madrid about the Carlist movement as a whole, which is spreading just about everywhere. San Sebastian is almost a frontier town, and I can see only a small corner of the picture.

If it becomes dangerous to stay here, I shall arrange for my family to return to France and try to travel by sea to Italy, not daring yet to re-enter my country where the tigers are still in a feeding frenzy.

Loyally yours,

M. L.

9. Just Vernouillet to Karl Marx

Paris, 18 September 1872
38, Boulevard Sébastopol

Dear outstanding citizen,

You are right to be dissatisfied with the delay in selling of the first batch of *Capital*. I was as upset as you about it, because I felt that the Hague Congress [of the First International] would be particularly interested in your book and that it was the right moment to put it on sale. But the printer did not work as we would have wished; the Manager had taken his holidays and the running of things was left up to young people who do not know what it is to be serious in business. In the end I was able to put the edition on sale this morning, and at the present hour (4 p.m.) I have 234 sold. You will receive one by post.

Rest assured, Dear citizen, of all my best wishes for the *work of regeneration* to which you have devoted your great intelligence, and count on me to help its spread.

With cordial greetings,

J. Vernouillet

Manager of the Maurice Lachâtre & Co. Library

10. Karl Marx to Maurice Lachâtre

London, 19 October 1872

Dear citizen,

From the enclosed letter from the director of *La Liberté* in Brussels, you will see that it is not even known where the first part of *Le Capital* is on sale. I have received letters saying the same from Bordeaux, Toulouse and other towns in France. For example, a friend of mine in Bordeaux writes: 'In Bordeaux nothing is known about the existence of this translation of *Capital* [...]. It seems to me that the ways of letting everyone know of its publication have been neglected'.

On 8 October I sent some *registered* manuscript to Paris. On 15 October Lahure informed me that the manuscript did not arrive. I immediately addressed myself to the English Post Office. It is very rare for *registered* letters to be lost. I do not believe it. In a few days I shall have a reply from the Post Office. It would be very disagreeable for me to have to redo the whole of Chapter VII (3rd section). I have already corrected all of M. Roy's manuscript that I have in my hands – Chs. VIII, IX and a large part of Ch. X – but what is the use of sending it to Paris before I know what has become of Ch. VII?

Another thing. When I asked why the second series has been delayed so much, M. Lahure replied, in his letter of 17 October, that proofs 8 and 9 have been sent to Bordeaux, to M. Roy, and that they will be sent to me after their return from B. Considering that I received proofs 8 and 9 on the *third* of October and that I sent them off almost at once, it seems to me that a lot of time is being lost for no reason. According to M. Lahure's letter they have enough composition material for Batch 2. That proves that the delay is not at all my doing.

I will be obliged if you give me some more of Batch 1. I could not refuse to satisfy the numerous demands from impoverished French refugees, and so I am not left with enough of the first hundred for the newspapers. Of course, I am not dealing with the newspapers published in France.

I have the honour, dear citizen, to be your loyal,

Karl Marx

11. Just Vernouillet to Karl Marx

Paris, 2 November 1872
38, Boulevard Sébastopol

Dear outstanding citizen,

Today I safely received your letter and the manuscript contained in it. On sending the manuscript to M. Lahure, I recommended that he return it to you together with the proofs.

Please believe me, dear citizen, I feel as annoyed as you at the sloppiness with which the post delivers the correspondence entrusted to it. The French authority assumes the right to hold back many things that are sent to it by the English Post Office. Thus, the *Courrier de l'Europe* is regularly sent to me every Saturday and I have not received a single number for more than four months. These doings are the result of the government of the *Republic without Republicans*.

On 26 October I sent M. Roy the advance of 400 francs for his work – the remainder will be paid at the rate of 300 francs a month, payable at the end of each month, up to the sum of 1,500 francs for his work on the translation of *Capital*.

Warm regards, once again, dear citizen,

J. Vernouillet

P.S.: On this occasion, kindly remember me to Citizen Longuet, who I know is near you.

12. Karl Marx to Maurice Lachâtre

11 February 1873
1, Maitland Park Road,
N.W.

Dear citizen,

I have received your introduction to Volume VIII of Eugène Sue, which was of great interest to me. For two reasons I would not know how to add anything to it. First, I am so overloaded with work at the moment that I do not even find time to take the daily walks that my doctor has prescribed and that my very weakened health would need. But the decisive obstacle is this: I have always had a great liking for Eugène Sue, both for the original novels of his early period and for his socialist novels. As for the 'foundlings',[11] it has always seemed to me that it better served the class struggle, the real basis of socialism, than did the titular socialists of his times. As for his last work, I cannot judge it because I have only seen the first instalment. But it is infected with sentimentality, as is the French socialism of his age. He mixes in the spiritualism that I detest. Like all novelists and artists, he draws his heroes and portraits not from the working class proper but from the last layer of bourgeois society, what are called 'the dangerous classes'. On the occasion of his *The Mysteries of Paris*, I criticised his mode of social criticism and his plans for social improvement, doing so even quite vigorously in a German book that I published in 1845 during my stay in Paris.[12]

Engels's address you already have, since you always write to me through his intermediary – Mrs Burns, etc.

In reply to your letter of 13 January, I will limit myself to pointing out:

1   You skate over the causes of the delay (during the time in question) without saying a word – causes I have enumerated that originated exclusively in Paris. There can be no disputing these, since M. Vernouillet's explanatory letters and M. Lahure's apologetic letters are in my hands, all justifying what I wrote to you. M. Vernouillet – whose perfect precision I gladly recognise – lays the blame on M. Lahure. As all that belongs to the past, there would be no point in going back over it. But I will tell you quite frankly that all my French friends in London thought there were hidden political or other reasons delaying publication. Besides, for my part, I was always convinced that your forced absence from Paris would give rise to some irregularities.

---

11 Marx is referring to a new French edition, published by the Lachâtre library, of Sue's *Martin, the Foundling: Or, The Memoirs of a Valet-de-Chambre* (English translation: New York: W.K. Colyer, 1847).

12 See Karl Marx and Friedrich Engels, *The Holy Family, or Critique of Critical Criticism*, in *Marx Engels Collected Works*, vol. 4: *The Holy Family, The Condition of the Working Class in England*, Moscow: Progress Publishers, 1975.

2   I have always argued to my French friends that you were the first to judge correctly the value of the translation. I was misled first by the praise I heard of the translation of Feuerbach (which is anyway explicable given that Feuerbach had already been translated by Everbeck before Roy: it is much easier to work on such a base); secondly, by the fact that the beginning of the first chapter (pp. 14, 15) was well translated. Lastly, I took into account the real difficulties that the first chapter presents.

What is certain, however, is that if I had foreseen the early delays in publication, I would have taken my precautions. Now it is too late to change – it must be seen through to the end. Only, I am correcting the manuscript more radically and that is why fewer corrections are necessary on the proofs.

As for the purely typographical corrections, they are not being done carefully enough at the printers.

Things in Spain are becoming more and more confused, and you would greatly oblige me by giving me some details.

Loyally yours,

Karl Marx

P.S.: At Versailles there are storms in a teacup. The antics, stratagems and parliamentary jousting of those mannequins are all the weirder in that everyone knows – and the English, German and Russian press has fun pointing it out every day – that they pull on the chain held by M. Bismarck. He supports Thiers because he does not want the clericals (whom he hounds in Germany mainly for police reasons and because of his relations with Italy) to win out in Paris. On the other hand, the Prussian ambassador in Paris, on direct orders from the king, supports the rural forces that have all the sympathy of his master. Unfortunately, all this reminds one of the Polish Diet at a time when the Russians were giving the final blow to Polish independence, or of Byzantium when the Turks were at its gates.

13. Friedrich Engels to Maurice Lachâtre

122 Regent's Park Road N.W.
London, 11 March 1873

Citizen,

I accept your proposal that I write the life story of Karl Marx, which will at the same time be a history of the German communist party before 1850 and of the socialist party after 1852. Seen in this way, the biography of a man will become the history of the party of which Marx is indisputably the highest personification − a history of the greatest interest for French democracy. It is this consideration that will commit me to lay aside my work so as to devote myself to a task that will take time and research if it is to be worthy of its subject. But I cannot agree to set to work until you send me a further letter with your terms and conditions, which, no doubt by an oversight, you failed to mention in your letter of 14 February.

Yours faithfully,

Friedrich Engels

14. Karl Marx to Louis Lahure

17 March 1873

Monsieur,

I no longer have any copy. On 16 February I wrote to M. Vernouillet that he had been letting me down for weeks. He then wrote at once to M. Roy, and after a new wait I finally received some copy but not enough. In this way, continual interruptions are resulting, the more so as it seems you do not run off proofs before you have the plate, and that, for example, you must also have instalments 18–24 in order to publish instalments 15–20.

M. Roy is obliged under his contract with M. Lachâtre to send me sixty pages every ten days. As the revision of the copy already gives me too much work, I surely have the right to ask that the clauses of the agreement are rigorously and regularly executed.

Be so kind as to get M. Vernouillet to write to M. Roy so that he sends copy, and to communicate *this letter* to M. Lachâtre.

Yours truly,

Karl Marx

15. Maurice Lachâtre to Karl Marx

22 March 1873
Saturday
Señor Leconte
Postal box, San Sebastian (Spain)

Dear Maître,

I have just received a letter from the printer with a communication from your-self, dated the 17th of this month.

I know of no way to oblige a translator to do work against his wishes. It seems to me that the simplest would be to give him formal notice to comply, through a letter directly from you informing him that, if he fails to meet your perfectly reasonable demand, you will decide to approach another translator.

A sum of 700 francs has been paid to M. Roy, corresponding to five series of five instalments, that is, to 25 instalments; I think 21 or even 22 instalments have been composed, hence almost the equivalent of the money paid. The rest of the established price is available to pay the new translator of your choice, in case M. Roy should refuse to continue his work or be prevented from carrying it out.

In the event that M. Engels refuses to do your biography, I should like Citizen Longuet to agree to take it on. It would be a crowning touch worthy of the book.

It is well established, dear maître, that our printer is not to blame for the interruptions in publication. Similarly, I cannot be charged with any negligence in this regard. Our agreement stated that the author reserves for himself the choice of translator, so my only obligation is to pay the price of the translation and I have not failed to do this. I am even a little in advance with the payment. M. Roy told me in a letter that he would supply pages for a series of 5 instalments per fortnight; he has not kept his promise. I do not know his current address and cannot write to him, and anyway he has to send copy not to me but to you; I shall continue to pay for copy only when you confirm receipt and authorise it.

Neither M. Just Vernouillet nor myself has any influence over M. Roy; we do not know him and it was you who chose him.

Here we are still in the midst of the Carlist uprising; the *gentle* priest Santa Cruz operates around San Sebastian with the greatest solicitude, murdering people here and there, administering new sacraments in the shape of beatings with sticks or whips that result in the death of victims, raiding cash desks, and forcibly recruiting partisans for Jesus, Mary and Joseph, the holy Trimurti[13] of devout Catholics.

---

13 Trimurti ('three forms'): the Hindu trinity of Brahman, Vishnu, and Shiva.

The northern train service, which has not been operating for the past fortnight, does not seem likely to reopen soon. The connection from Irun is provided by coaches on the ordinary road.

But apart from this blackspot things in Spain are good; the federal democratic republic presses on, while awaiting the social republic, which would be the best of all. Commune and Federation with the red flag.

Adieu, dear maître, with my best regards and all my good wishes,

Maurice Lachâtre

16. Friedrich Engels to Maurice Lachâtre

122 Regent's Park Road N.W.
London, 31 March 1873

Citizen,

In your letter of 16 March, you appear to believe that I am 'offering you a book on the communist party', whereas it was you who, in asking me to write a serious biography of Karl Marx, asked for the history of that party. As Marx has led an essentially active life, an account of it involves writing a history of the philosophical & revolutionary movement, both German & international, since 1842, in order to chart his personal participation in it and the influence of his writings.

If all you want is a reporter's biography, that has already been done. *L'Illustration* has published one, and if you send me a copy I am prepared to make the necessary corrections.

Since the study I had in mind would be a serious work, I thought it would be insulting of me to suppose that you, who play the role of capitalist in this business matter, would wish to evade the first social rule, operative even in our bourgeois society: that the capitalist pays the workman in proportion to his labour. However, since you say that you enlarge your capital solely to place it at the service of the community, I agree to donate my labour on condition that you allocate a sum of money for the foundation of a weekly international organ, for which the party has an urgent need, and of which Marx would be the editor.

With cordial greetings,

F. Engels

17. Karl Marx to Maurice Lachâtre

London, 4 August 1873

Dear citizen,

Enclosed is the biography you asked me for. Longuet did it, but his name should not be mentioned. I have added one of my photographs, which has been reproduced very badly in *Capital*.

The state of my health still does not allow me to work for more than a few hours a day. Hence the lack of manuscript for M. Lahure. Nevertheless, he will get today the proofs that already comprise part of the thirty-second sheet. So, after they are sent off, there will be no reason not to publish instalments V and VI.

I hope I will be able to provide him with new manuscript by the end of the week.

Yours truly,

Karl Marx

18. Karl Marx to Just Vernouillet

28 October 1873

Dear citizen,

Yesterday I received the end of the translation from M. Roy. He should be paid the rest of the 1,500 francs that I advanced (to M. Lachâtre) for his remuneration. My health is more or less restored and M. Lahure will soon receive a good part of the manuscript.

Yours,

Karl Marx

19. Maurice Lachâtre to Karl Marx

Brussels, 24 December 1873
42, Boulevard de Waterloo

Dear philosopher,

Your little letter has given me great joy, for your long silence made me fear that you were indisposed; now I feel reassured. You are quite right to decide to finish your work as promptly as possible. French officialdom is tetchy; they have already refused authorisation for instalments of my history of the nineteenth century, and publication has come to a halt. Happily, the history of the popes was completed with the 230th instalment; the Consulate and the Empire were still able to pass, up to the 240th instalment. [...] I shall therefore continue publication in Brussels with one of the correspondents of my publishing house in Paris.

I have been compelled to remove *dubious* French and foreign brochures from the shopfront on Boulevard Sébastopol in Paris. This covers *The Popes*, *Mysteries of the People*[14] and *Capital*. Fortunately, I have completed 8 volumes of *Mysteries of the People*, out of the ten it was supposed to comprise; I'll leave it at that.

I hope we shall be able to finish off *Capital*, since we have very carefully avoided any fuss about the book and publicity around your name. We shall be prudent until the end of publication. Then we shall see.

Sales are nil for your book; that is understandable, given the long breaks between the instalments. The print run is eleven hundred, nearly all in stock.

I would ask you to please inform Citizen Longuet that I am planning to prepare the history of the siege of Paris, the Prussian invasion of France, as soon as I have finished the reign of Napoleon III. If he wished to provide me with some material on the Second Empire, I would be charmed to receive it. [...] When the moment comes to tackle this period of our history, I shall approach your son-in-law, Citizen Longuet, if he tells me that he can cooperate on this work.

Adieu, dear citizen, I squeeze your hand most affectionately,

Maurice Lachâtre

P.S.: Please accept, and pass on, my wishes for happiness and good health – on the occasion of the new year – to you, dear philosopher, and your family.

May God and the Good Spirits – I am a spiritualist – preserve you in the tenderness of your family, and to help in the progress of society.

Commune and Federation with the red flag.

---

14 *Les Mystères du Peuple,* a socialist novel by Eugène Sue, was first published in 1848.

20. Maurice Lachâtre to Karl Marx

Brussels, 14 May 1874
128, rue du Trône

Dear Maître,

I shall be very happy when you tell me that your health is fully restored; your existence is precious for humanity and for your dear family.

The book *Le Capital* is a monument; it should be finished in the interests of the underprivileged classes for which you wrote it. Let us make haste: who knows what will become of press freedom in France when the Rurals of Versailles have passed a law against book publishing? Perhaps I will not be granted a licence and my publishing house will risk being closed down.

Even here in Brussels, where you thought I could reside in complete safety, I am the object of severe measures. The public security official sent me a notice *asking* me to leave Belgium within eight days. True, they have since postponed my expulsion, once for 15 days and a second time for fifteen days; the date has now been set for the 26th of this month, with no further respite. I am told the measure will not be upheld.

I am ready to leave and go to Geneva, if they are willing to put up with me there.

Adieu, dear maître, I squeeze your hand with affection,

Maurice Lachâtre

21. Maurice Lachâtre to Karl Marx

Brussels, 21 July 1874
128, rue du Trône

Dear Maître,

I had the pleasure to write a month ago asking you to charge Citizen Longuet with seeing Henri Rochefort; I don't know if my letter reached you, because I have not received an answer.

I also asked you to update me about the translation of your work *Le Capital*. The few subscribers who withstood the long breaks in publication are finally becoming demoralised – and the publisher, I must tell you, is no less unhappy than the subscribers. If the work is not to continue, please be so kind as to fore-warn me; I will have the plates of the instalments pulped and grieve over the 8,000 francs they cost me.

I shall still remain your admirer and most loyal servant,

Maurice Lachâtre

22. Karl Marx to Maurice Lachâtre

Karlsbad, 18 September 1974

Dear citizen,

I took the waters at Karlsbad[15] for 5 weeks and am leaving Germany in a few days to return to London. I think that my health is restored and that I shall now be capable of finishing once and for all with the French edition. If I pass through Belgium – I haven't yet fixed my route of travel – I shall take the pleasure of looking you up.

Yours,

Karl Marx

P.S.: I read in *La Patrie* a critique of *Capital* by a certain Goussen. This gentleman has never had the book in his hand. He dares to quote whole passages, between quotation marks, that are his own invention, and which he has the impudence to attribute to me.

---

15 Today's Karlovy Vary, in Czech Bohemia.

23. Maurice Lachâtre to Karl Marx

Brussels, 15 February 1875
128, rue du Trône

Dear Maître,

I received instalments 33, 34 and 35 this morning to look over your corrections; I noticed quite a few more mistakes, so please examine the new corrections and, if you approve of them, be kind enough to send the proofs back to the printer in Paris.

Allow me to repeat the recommendation that I have sent you already – to charge one of your sons-in-law or French literary friends to read the proofs, so as to remove a number of Germanisms that the translator left in the text.

Your book continues to carry the reader into spheres above the understanding of the common man. I note this with real sadness: French workers, being less educated than German workers, will be unable to absorb anything from your work. I correct the proofs, I read your dissertations with respect, but without understanding them. And, considering my intelligence to be at a very ordinary level, I conclude that the mass of readers will understand no better than I your admirable theories, if you do not finally translate them into a language in reach of the common people of which I am part.

Yours most truly,

Maurice Lachâtre

24. Maurice Lachâtre to Karl Marx

4 May 1875
Chalet Lambert
Vevey (Switzerland)

My publishing house in Paris is still in the hands of the Philistines. M. Just Vernouillet has been dismissed by the agent of the Versailles government. Therefore, do not write to me at the address of my publishing house.

Dear and honoured maître,

I have finished correcting the proofs of instalments 36–44.

On instalment 40 – page 319 – a whole line has been omitted in the left column and the meaning of the sentence is lost. I have indicated what is missing on the proofs.

There are so many corrections that I think it wise for you to read new proofs before giving the go-ahead. Kindly write to the printer for him to send you more proofs after correction and before setting the pages.

These last instalments gave me the keenest satisfaction; workers will understand what is in them; the text is within reach of all levels of intelligence.

Please send the manuscript for the table of contents. It should not be longer than 5 pages, which are spare and complete the 44th instalment.

The printing will cover two instalments at once; instalments 43 and 44 will be printed together.

Adieu, dear maître. I send you my fondest regards,

Maurice Lachâtre

25. Maurice Lachâtre to Karl Marx

11 June 1875
Chalet Lambert
Vevey (Switzerland)

Dear and honoured maître,

I am returning the proofs, to which added a few more corrections; there are also two lacunae, at the beginning of the table of contents; you forgot to indicate the pagination. As I do not have the pages before me, I was unable to fill in the numbers. This falls to you. [...] The afterword could be removed or at least greatly shortened. I did not want to carry out this pruning; it is your responsibility and dictated by requirements at the printer. The text must be brought back within 44 instalments. Be so kind as to undertake this revision without delay, so that we finally go to press and finish the work of publication.

In my view, it is regrettable that you drew the readers' attention to *the defects in M. Roy's translation*, and that you picked up the faults in the *errata* while indicating that there were many others. You thereby *do in advance the work* of the critics and denigrate your own book. In my view, you should also remove this reference and the note concerning the *errata*. Anyway, it serves no purpose, since readers never take the trouble to consult them. This elimination would save you a page; you would then have no more than three pages to remove, which is easy to do: one to remove in the afterword, and at least two in the table of contents, or two in the afterword and one in the table.

With fond regards,

Maurice Lachâtre

26. Just Vernouillet to Karl Marx

Paris, 13 July 1875
3, rue de la Vieille Estrapade

Dear citizen,

I most readily give you the address of the receiver who has ordered M. Lahure not to proceed with the printing of your book. Here it is:

Monsieur Quest, adminstrateur judiciaire
91, Boulevard Beaumarchais
Paris

It is necessary that you write to him at once to oblige him to give the go-ahead for the printing; if he does not comply he should be sent a bailiff's order. Do not fear to act, you are fully within your rights. Monsieur Quest has been appointed to administer the publishing house and to continue the business; the house is required to publish your work; nothing should be done to oppose it. I have read a letter from this administrator, who forbids M. Lahure to proceed with the printing. You could demand damages and interest from today. M. Quest is a supporter of the Government of All-Out Combat, highly disposed to crack down on anyone expressing liberal and republican ideas.

If you need a lawyer you could speak to Monsieur Henri Cellier, avocat, 14, rue du Pré-aux-clercs, Paris. He is a man qualified to handle publishing matters, who enjoys a good reputation at the bar and a certain notoriety at the Palais. As I have a share in the publishing house, I am interested in the business side. It matters to me that it should fulfil its obligation to publish your book *Le Capital*. M. Quest is responsible for his actions; you should therefore not fail to attack him if he does not obey your first letter. I count on you to keep me up to date with the matter.

With affectionate regards,

J. Vernouillet

27. Maurice Lachâtre to Karl Marx

20 July 1875
Chalet Lambert
Vevey (Switzerland)

Dear Maître,

When the *provisional* receiver was placed in charge of my publishing house, there was a sum of 20,000 francs in the portfolio, to be received at different dates. There were no debts other than the usual current accounts rising to 12,000 francs: approx. 2,000 francs due to the Lahure printers, 10,000 due to the Didot house for supplies of paper. These figures appear in the accounts report that M. Just Vernouillet sent me precisely every week.

The house takings came to an average of two thousand francs a month. There was a respectable sum in the till, nearly 5,000 francs.

Production took place very regularly, as and when sales required it. In the space of 42 months M. Just Vernouillet had a very respectable number of five million instalments printed, that is, an average of 120,000 a month.

When M. Just Vernouillet was laid off by the *provisional* receiver, for the single reason that last February 'I had made a donation of two-twelfths of the publishing house to my faithful and loyal employee', there was *not one sou of debts*: the current account due to M. Lahure totalled just 1,700 francs. There was absolutely nothing due to anyone, absolutely nothing.

Since M. Quest, in the letter he wrote to you, thinks he should introduce my testimony – 'For reasons that M. Lachâtre himself could explain to you, we have been obliged to delay the printing of your work' – I regret that I am unable to support with my testimony the assertions of the Provisional Receiver; indeed, I declare that good management demands the printing without delay of the fourteen instalments that remain to be published, which, with eleven hundred copies, will involve an expense of approx. 540 francs all told, for paper, printing, binding, etc. This low expenditure will restore the value of the existing stock of 100,000 instalments of the same work, which will be worth only the value of the old paper if the work is not continued. [...]

No reason can be given for delaying the printing of the 14 instalments. The harm that M. Quest's refusal causes to the publishing house and the author could certainly give rise to legitimate claims at a court of law. But I have the firm hope that the Receiver, when enlightened by the explanations in this letter – and I authorise you to convey it to him *in extenso* – will hasten to comply with your demand for publication. [...]

My role in this sad business is very delicate; I do not wish to cause any trouble to the receiver, who is supposed to be my guardian; I think that the current management is compromising the interests of my associate and the donors, but

I am forbidden to pronounce on the matter. I foresee serious problems for all parties in the future, if the *provisional* regime does not end soon.

M. Quest has taken on a heavy responsibility, by accepting the management of a publishing house for which my experience of a third of century was necessary, and which he was not capable of directing. This is not said to disparage a person I do not know, but simply to emphasise that what was needed was a man broken into the publisher's trade, not someone alien to the profession.

I do not know if the donors will want to approach the courts for the righting of a wrong done to them by M. Quest's administration: this is the question for the future. For the present, I shall always try to bring about a reconciliation of the interested parties. It's better to have peace than war. You can make any use you think pertinent of the present letter.

Kindest regards,

Maurice Lachâtre

28. Maurice Lachâtre to Karl Marx

16 October 1876
26 Via Vittorio Emanuele
San Remo – Liguria – Italy

Dear citizen and honoured maître,

Your letter of the 12th addressed to Switzerland has been forwarded to me in San Remo, where I have had my residence since the 18th of June, and where I plan to remain until new tribulations occur and compel me to leave Italy.

The publishing house is in the hands of the Philistines; M. Quest declares without beating about the bush 'that he detests the orientation of the works whose selling has been entrusted to him'. The result is easy to see. The lady commissioned to sell my books is very devout; M. Quest is reactionary and clerical; and their bosses, the heads of Public Administration, are conservatives!

All the people who on 24 May sent three gangs of assassins, on three separate occasions, to shoot me down, and who – finding their victim absent – turned their rage against my unfortunate cashier, my dear lamented friend, E. Profilet, and slaughtered him; all the people who committed this crime against an inoffensive, non-political old man, for the simple reason that he was attached to my publishing house: will they be more indulgent towards my books? Yet, in spite of them, all my books continue to sell, in sufficient number to allow the product to meet the huge costs of the house: we have to pay 15,000 francs (I repeat, fifteen thousand francs) just to rent the stores.

No announcements are made of the books; the publicity is done through the instalment covers on which our publications are announced. That is enough.

A publisher is never obliged to spend money on publicity for a book, or to print leaflets or posters. If you start a lawsuit for these purposes with M. Quest, you will most certainly lose it.

'You have to suffer what you cannot prevent', says the proverb.

I am the victim in a greater degree than you, dear citizen, and I have to resign myself. Louis Blanc is no more content than you or I with this state of things. But what remedy can be brought to bear?

If M. Quest agreed to let me run de facto the publishing house, doing no more than receive and preserve the takings, things would go much better. He is no expert in publishing, as he knows perfectly well. Some external pressure should force him to take a different path and to leave me with the reins: it would be run better than by his kind of inexperienced hand.

Perhaps a firm request from yourself might stand some chance of being heard. Try it out, if you think it appropriate.

There are several ways of spreading the word about your book, apart from announcements, but only I, not M. Quest, can make use of them.

Alfred Naquet[16] has just approached our house to have *Mystères du Peuple* serialised in his journal *La Révolution*, which will be an essentially socialist journal. It would be an idea to contact Naquet to offer subscribers *Le Capital* as a bonus. In this way, we could manage to offload 10,000 or perhaps 20,000 copies of your work.

You could write to M. Quest and ask him to let me negotiate over this with the deputy A. Naquet, or with other journals, in order to get *Le Capital* out of the torpor into which it has been plunged.

Adieu, dear citizen and honoured maître, I cordially shake your hand,

Maurice Lachâtre

P.S.: Citizen Arthur Arnould[17] is also in San Remo: I fixed him up with lodgings in the house where I live. In winter the foreign colony mostly consists of German compatriots of yours.

My affectionate regards to your two sons-in-law, and my respectful regards to Madame Laura.

When you write to me, give me news of your health; I profoundly wish that your illness has been overcome thanks to your strong constitution and the care given you by your nearest and dearest.

As M. Quest gets 5 per cent of the house's takings, he might listen to your advice – not out of duty but out of self-interest, to increase his share of the takings. In your letter to him you could highlight that his interest is the same as yours, to sell the largest possible number, and that my assistance might be precious for everyone concerned.

---

16 Alfred Naquet (1834–1916): French chemist and radical socialist politician, later a supporter of the Boulangist movement.
17 Arthur Arnould (1833–95): French writer and journalist, occultist and theosophist.

29. Just Vernouillet to Karl Marx

Paris, 21 November 1876
3, rue de la Vieille Estrapade

Dear citizen,

You know better than anyone that we live in an age where political life needs to be, and is apparently being, reborn. No doubt you have been following the creation of new journals that defend various political doctrines and really respond to certain aspirations. Like me, you will certainly have noted that the thinking or theory that it is most important to propagate, the *international socialist* doctrine – the only one that will allow us to achieve general progress and that you uphold in your fine book *Capital* – is without a press organ here. We believe that such an organ would have great chances of success, especially if you attach your name to it. If such is your thinking too, I should be happy – together with a friend, a former editor of *Le Reveil* – to give you my support. Paris has remained, for the time being, the centre of intellectual life, and I am convinced that a socialist paper bearing the name Karl Marx would soon radiate around the whole world, or at least the whole of Europe.

I submit my idea for your reliable judgment, dear citizen, and would be grateful if you sent me your considered opinion on the matter. We can produce something great, and greatly useful; I would ask you to think carefully about it.

Fond regards,

J. Vernouillet

30. Maurice Lachâtre to Karl Marx

25 January 1877
26 Via Vittorio Emanuele
San Remo (Italy)

Dear citizen and honoured maître,

Your letter of 26 December last did not reach me, and I think your small and sometimes illegible handwriting caused it to be mislaid or sent to the wrong address.

I thank you for your new year's greetings and send back my wishes of health and happiness for you and your nearest and dearest.

You know that I am one of the living dead, that I have no legal existence in France, and that my opinion therefore has no value for an abridgement of your book. Only the official receiver can give the authorisation for the book you wrote to me about, and I think we would expose ourselves to legal proceedings on his part if we published the abridgement without his permission.

Everything that can help the spread of enlightenment and the propagation of your ideas will have my approval; but I do not have the right to 'take legal action', in the time-honoured expression used for those convicted in absentia.

Your loyal and affectionate,

Maurice Lachâtre

31. Maurice Lachâtre to Karl Marx

21 June 1879
Librairie du Progrès
11, rue Bertin Poirée
Paris

Dear and honoured maître,

Here I am back in France, pardoned/amnestied, but not repentant or bowed.[18]

> I was and still am
> the enemy of princes, priests and abuses,
> friend of the poor, and nothing more.

I have again taken up my place in the combat and shall continue to publish democratic and socialist books. Nothing has changed for me; I am ready for the new struggles.

The gates of France must be thrown open for the outcasts; it must be a full amnesty, without a single exclusion or exception.

One of my first concerns on returning to my publishing house was to enquire about the stocks of *Capital*. There still remain three hundred copies of the last instalments, which were printed in a thousand copies. So, only 600 or 700 copies were sold in a period of six years! It is a very sad result.

We are setting the works of Lassalle,[19] to be published at the cost of a German socialist, which B. Malon is translating with the help of a German friend of his. I am told that this book might get the sales of *Capital* moving.

In France we have neither a socialist newspaper nor a socialist review. Publication efforts of this kind have ended in failure.

Kindly remember me to Mme. Laura, and to your sons-in law M. Lafargue and Citizen Longuet.

All my best wishes,

Maurice Lachâtre

---

18 Lachâtre benefited from a partial presidential amnesty on 3 March 1879, but a full amnesty for former Communards came only on 14 July 1880.

19 Ferdinand Lassalle (1825–64): founding member and leader of the first German socialist workers' party, the *Allgemeiner Deutscher Arbeiter-Verein*.

Index